Duke Ellington's Music for the Theatre

Duke Ellington's Music for the Theatre

by

JOHN FRANCESCHINA

McFarland & Company, Inc., Publishers
Jefferson, North Carolina, and London

For
my parents,
John and Ruth Franceschina,
who gave me an appreciation of music
and
Annie Kuebler
who gave me the music to appreciate.

***Frontispiece:* One of Al Hirschfeld's caricatures of Duke Ellington (Courtesy of the Duke Ellington Collection, National Museum of American History Archives Center, Smithsonian Institution).**

Library of Congress Cataloguing-in-Publication Data

Franceschina, John Charles, 1947–
Duke Ellington's music for the theatre / by John Franceschina.
p. cm.
Includes bibliographical references and index.
ISBN 0-7864-0856-1 (soft cover : 50# alkaline paper) ∞
1. Ellington, Duke, 1899–1974.—Criticism and interpretation.
2. Ellington, Duke, 1899–1974. Musicals. 3. Musicals—History and criticism. I. Title.
ML410.E44 F7 2001
782.1'4'092—dc21 00-46456

British Library cataloguing data are available

Manufactured in the United States of America

McFarland & Company, Inc., Publishers
Box 611, Jefferson, North Carolina 28640
www.mcfarlandpub.com

Contents

Acknowledgments

To the College of Visual and Performing Arts at Syracuse University for a generous faculty development grant that enabled me to begin the research on this book.

To the Duke Ellington Estate for generously permitting me to quote from the unpublished music manuscripts in the Archives Center at the National Museum of American History of the Smithsonian Institution.

To Helen Tuttle Votichenko, Frank Tuttle's daughter, for allowing me access to her father's papers and permitting me to quote from his lyrics.

To Dana Sergent Nemeth, Curator of Popular Culture at the American Museum of the Moving Image, for continued support and assistance in examining the Frank Tuttle Collection.

To James Huffman, Photographs and Prints Division of the Schomburg Center for Research in Black Culture, for his invaluable assistance.

To Wayne Furman, Special Collections, the New York Public Library, for permitting me to publish photographs from the special collections.

To the staff of the Library of Congress Music Division for their amenable assistance in finding music manuscripts.

To the Archives Center at the National Museum of American History of the Smithsonian Institution for allowing me to reproduce photographs from the Ellington Collection.

To Annie Kuebler of the Archives Center at the National Museum of American History of the Smithsonian Institution whose continued support, boundless enthusiasm, healthy skepticism, and monumental knowledge of the manuscripts in both the Ellington Collection and Billy Strayhorn Estate have helped create this book. This book is as much hers as it is mine, and I hope it is worthy of her generosity.

Finally, to all the Ellington scholars around the world whose identification of manuscripts and scholarly research has paved the way for a study such as this.

My deepest admiration and gratitude.

Introduction

Dramatis Felidae

The year is 1999 and the Pulitzer Prize Committee awards a posthumous citation to Duke Ellington, commemorating the 100th anniversary of his birth, 34 years after he was denied the award in 1965 because his "jazz" compositions were considered outside the parameters of "serious" music. The musical world resounds with celebratory accolades ranging from calling him "the most important American composer of the 20th Century" to "the most important composer of any music anywhere." *Jazz at Lincoln Center* is devoting the final six months of the 1998–99 season to 19 separate programs including concerts, lectures, film screenings, panel discussions, even performances by the New York City Ballet, beginning on 14 January 1999 with *Happy Reunion—Memories of Duke* at Alice Tully Hall, when Ellington alumni Louis Bellson, John Lamb, and Aaron Bell reminisce and jam.

Although Duke would certainly appreciate all the attention—especially from the ladies present—he would note the significant under-representation of a major portion of his creative work: his compositions for the theatre. Though individual songs written for revues or musicals might be included in one or another concert program, no single complete work composed for stage production was performed. His son Mercer Ellington was clearly correct in his observation that the only area of music in which his father was frustrated was in "his desire to do his own Broadway show" (165), for a quarter century has passed since Ellington died and jazz historians, musicologists, and music theatre historians have to acknowledge his creative contribution to the stage.

The lack of critical interest in Ellington's theatre compositions is not difficult to understand. Because he never had a financially successful show during his lifetime, the innovations that were introduced in many of his musicals went unnoticed and failed to spawn any imitators. In addition, Ellington's monumental success as a bandleader, jazz composer, and recording artist tended to obscure his lesser-known work, rendering it peripheral to his popular hits. With the exception of the revue *My People*, none of Ellington's

Duke Ellington at the piano, in an early publicity photograph (from the author's collection).

musical theatre works was commercially recorded. What's more, Ellington was fickle; he tired of projects quickly and always wanted to try something new before the old job was done. As a result, he tended to leave his musicials incomplete, creating the persona of a dilettante dabbling in the theatre but not a serious craftsman.

While critics are quick to point to Ellington's 50-year career with his orchestra, none have noted his 50-year romance with the theatre beginning in 1925 with *Chocolate Kiddies* and ending in 1974 with *Queenie Pie* (a show that was in Duke's mind for 30 of those 50 years), with each decade exhibiting a representative gem or two. Ellington acknowledged that he was a man of the theatre. That was clear from the way he behaved and the way he approached composition. In *Beyond Category: The Life and Genius of Duke Ellington*, John Edward Hasse notes that Duke demonstrated a theatrical flair at a very young age, "telling jokes, dancing, and playing the Jew's harp"(26). Don George, Ellington's lyricist, biographer, and friend, adds:

> He adored pomp and ceremony and phoniness and affectations and costumes; the whole fanfare. He liked to parade like a peacock. Everything about him was for show and appearance and theatrics; always theatrics. Life was one great big stage and living was a big fairy story and he was Prince Charming throughout the whole thing [147].

Even in Ellington's own autobiography is there evidence of his theatricality when he uses the term "dramatis felidae," a play on the theatrical term "dramatis personae," to introduce the cast of characters in his life. Perhaps even more significantly, Ellington divides the book into acts rather than chapters, again reaffirming his reliance on a theatrical context.

As a composer, Ellington described himself as one who writes "supporting music for guys to play solos. I'm really an accompanist." Don George adds that Ellington was "the first orchestra leader and composer ever to write music especially for an individual instrumentalist, like a Puccini might fashion an aria for an opera" (102–03), utilizing the soloists as characters in a play with carefully calculated entrances and exits. In "And What Might a Jazz Composer Do?" written for the *Music Educators Journal* (January 1975), Martin Williams makes an important point regarding the symbiosis between music and drama in Ellington's work:

> It was not until he encountered night club "show" work, with its call for overtures, choruses, and specialty dance accompaniments, and the other demands of the miniature musical "review" these establishments featured, that his genius began to show itself. He made his dance band into a show band, and his show band a vehicle for a collaborative yet personal musical expression.
>
> Ellington worked with the individual talents of his musicians in the same way that the great dramatists of the past have worked with their actors or the great ballet masters have worked with their dancers [28].

Reminding us that Ellington had briefly considered a career as a painter, Whitney Balliett adds that Duke was a "colorist who painted with sound"

("Celebrating the Duke" 139), reaffirming his instinctive ability to create atmosphere and emotional expression—two highly significant dramatic textures—in sound.

Of course what we have been discussing has found its way into Ellington's "programme" suites (*Black, Brown and Beige*, and *A Drum Is a Woman* are among the most familiar examples) but it would be wrong to believe that Ellington's theatrical instincts were used merely as a springboard to non-dramatic work. From the very beginning, it did not escape Ellington's notice that most of the successful African American composers of the first quarter of the twentieth century were writing for the theatre. As Eileen Southern notes in *The Music of Black Americans*, "in the early twentieth century the black theater served as a secular temple for black communities. One went to the theater not only to see the latest musical comedies and the most recent vaudeville acts but also to listen to presentations of local and touring concert companies, choral organizations, orchestral groups, vocal and instrumental recitalists, and dramatic troupes. These programs were produced by black, white, and integrated groups"(291). The theatre, for Ellington, was a place of endless variety where culture is defined, refined, and exchanged through entertainment—a factor Duke will emphasize throughout his career. Moreover, two of Duke's major influences, Will Marion Cook and James P. Johnson, were deeply imbedded in the fabric of the New York stage.

At the turn of the century, Will Marion Cook (1869–1944) and Bob Cole (1868–1911) had engaged in a philosophical debate about an aesthetic of African American culture that still resonates. Though Cook had been trained as a serious musician at Oberlin College, and in Europe, studied violin under the great master Josef Joachim and composition with Anton Dvorak[1] and John White, his compositions remained firmly rooted in African American culture. As Allen Woll points out in *Black Musical Theatre*, Cook believed that "Negroes should look to themselves for the wellsprings of creativity, developing artistic endeavors that reflected the soul of black people"(6). To that end, Will Marion Cook prepared an opera, *Scenes from the Opera of Uncle Tom's Cabin*, for the Colored American Day at the Chicago World's Fair, 25 August 1893. The work was not performed and, for five years, Cook pursued a career in popular music, as a member of Bob Cole's All-Star Stock Company in New York City, and, for a short time, directing a band in Chicago.

Bob Cole, believing that African Americans were in constant competition artistically with whites, felt that it was his responsibility to demonstrate "that the Negro was capable of matching whites in all realms of cultural production" (Woll 6). The son of former slaves, Cole received an elementary music education in his hometown of Athens, Georgia. It was in Chicago, however, that, as an apprentice to various vaudeville acts Cole began his serious study of the music theatre. In 1891, he signed on with Sam T. Jack's Creole Burlesque Company, serving as comedian and stage manager of the troop, until he met and formed a vaudeville act with Stella Wiley, a beautiful young singer, whom he later married. Around 1894 Cole formed the All-Star Stock Company that supplied the African American performers for John Isham's innovative productions in 1895–97.[2] Bob Cole and Will Marion Cook could not come to any kind of compromise regarding the position of African American artists in a dominant white culture, and parted ways in 1896; Cole joined the Black Patti Troubadours and Will Marion Cook set about interesting Bert Williams and George Walker in the story of how the cakewalk came about in Louisiana in the 1880s.

In 1898, both Cole and Cook produced landmark musical shows that would demonstrate their artistic philosophies. First to appear was Cole's *A Trip to Coontown*, opening 4 April 1898 at the Third Avenue Theatre in New York City, and considered the first full-length musical written, directed, produced, and performed by African Americans. Reminding the audience of the extraordinarily popular white musical farce, *A Trip to Chinatown* (the show that introduced "The Bowery," "Reuben Reuben," and "After the Ball," and set the long-run record in 1891 and held it for 25 years), *A Trip to Coontown* was loosely structured around the efforts of confidence-man Jim Flimflammer to bilk Old Man Silas Green out of his $5,000 pension. Three months later, on 5 July, Cook's musical about the cakewalk in Louisiana, *Clorindy, The Origin of the Cakewalk* was produced at the Casino Roof Garden as the afterpiece to a revue called *Rice's Summer Nights*. Both shows featured "coon" songs, and it is in their treatment that the differences between Cook and Cole can best be demonstrated.

Cole's song, "No Coons Allowed!" with lyrics by Billy Johnson, emphasizes a cultural dichotomy based on color, and demonstrates the aspirations of the African American to cross the color boundaries:

> There's a dead swell gentleman of color
> Saved up all the money he could find
> He call'd one night and said to his baby
> "My Lulu gal we'll go and cut a shine"
> He put her in a cab and told the driver
> "To drive to the swellest place in town
> I'm gwine to buy my gal a fine supper
> So I want the finest place that can be found"
> To a swell restaurant the driver took them
> With his Lulu gal he started in so proud
> But that coon almost went blind
> When he saw a great big sign up o'er the door which read
> "No coons allowed."

The second chorus tells of the hero's wounded pride, his going to a lawyer to sue the restaurant, and his subsequent discovery of a sign over the courthouse door reading, "No coons allowed!" An anthem to racial prejudice, Cole's piece found approbation from an audience used to experiencing prejudice in a white society, but viewing acceptance in that society as the ultimate success. By comparison, Cook's song, "The Hottest Coon in Dixie," with words by African American poet Paul Laurence Dunbar, makes no allusion to a dichotomous culture; to be successful within an African American context is the goal, not to compete with white Americans.

> When I go out to stroll away,
> I wear my Regent suit,
> Put on my silk plug hat so gay,
> My necktie is a beaut',
> Put on my gloves and cane in hand,
> I wander down the way,
> Whene'er I meet some merry beaux,
> Here's what the darkies say.
> Behold the hottest coon,
> Your eyes e'er lit on,
> Velvet ain't good enough,
> For him to sit on,
> When he goes down the street,
> Folks yell like sixty,
> Behold the hottest coon in Dixie.

Where the first chorus details the hero's position among African American men, the second chorus proceeds to describe his success with the ladies. In either case, no allusion is made to white culture as an evaluative force since the character described evokes the "Old Zip Coon" archetype that emerged in the late nineteenth century. The philosophical differences between the two writers were heavily pronounced, so much so that it was difficult for them to be together in the same room without coming to blows. Even the music written for the songs betrayed the composers' prejudices.

Cole's music in the verse of his song recalls the patter songs of the late nineteenth century with a duple *parlando* repetition of a single melody note over a repetitive, and fairly static, harmony. The chorus recalls a Sousa, or Offenbach, galop with no jarring syncopation until the eleventh bar with the words, "move on darky." The use of syncopation is less a musical device than a simple emphasis on the scansion of the words. Cook's verse is in triple rhythm, recalling the *barcarole,* or folk song, of Venetian gondoliers. The chorus is ragtime, with a piano accompaniment that invokes Joplin, and a melody filled with syncopated entrances that not only emphasize the rhythm of the text, but propel the melody forward with great energy. Both composers use

European forms for the verse but Cook is the more indigenously African American in the chorus. Cole in collaboration with the brothers Johnson would go on to create the all-black Broadway musicals *The Shoo-Fly Regiment* (1906) and *The Red Moon* (1908)—the first African American treatment of Indians on Broadway, as well as several white-cast shows, the most popular of which was *Humpty Dumpty* (1904). Cook would continue telling the story of the African American experience in *The Southerners* (1904)—perhaps the first Broadway musical to use an integrated cast, *The Cannibal King* (1914), and *Swing Along* (composed with Will Vodery in 1929).

The polar aesthetics of these two rivals would not be lost on Ellington, who looked to Will Marion Cook, "His Majesty the King of Consonance," as his musical mentor.[3] Virtually a self-taught musician, Ellington drew upon what he heard, adapting the forms and formulas of European harmony, the 12-bar blues, the 32-bar popular song, and the improvisation and syncopation of "jazz" into music that was his own individual sound.[4] Like Cook, Ellington would be dedicated to expressing the African American experience. As he has said repeatedly, "I don't write jazz. I write Negro folk music." But trained only in the rudiments of music like Cole, Duke was not adverse to attempting success in a specifically white context (with shows like *Pousse-Café* or *H.M.S. Times Square*) though he never really achieved Cole's success.[5]

James P. Johnson (1894–1955) pioneered the Harlem "stride" style of piano playing and worked as the accompanist to Bessie Smith and Ethel Waters in addition to composing musical theatre works. Perhaps his most famous composition, "Charleston" from the African American musical *Runnin' Wild* (1923)[6] would have a significant impact on early jazz composers, especially George Gershwin, who will make heavy use of the syncopated "Charleston" rhythm in his *Rhapsody in Blue* (1924), and Duke Ellington, who will integrate it into much of his early "Jungle Music." Ellington not only admired Johnson's pianistic style (which he tried to emulate), but the fact that even after the great success of "Charleston," Johnson never lost contact with his African American roots.[7] As Duke notes in *Music Is My Mistress*, "he never lost contact with his foundations, with the real, wonderful people in Harlem. Harlem had its own rich, special folklore, totally unrelated to the South or anywhere else" (94). This special feeling of racial pride, coupled with a dynamic burst of creative activity in and around Harlem and an increased interest by white audiences in the African American experience, gave rise to what is usually known as the "Harlem Renaissance" in the 1920s and provided further impetus for Ellington to gravitate toward the African American theatre.

Another pianist that would inspire Ellington was Eubie Blake (1883–1983) who, along with Noble Sissle (1889–1975) composed the monumentally successful *Shuffle Along* (1921), the show that established a vogue for African American revues on Broadway, challenged many of the taboos associated with early African American musicals, and set the standard for black musicals for the next 20 years until Ellington's own *Jump for Joy* (1941) revitalized the form.[8] In these early shows, the plot would typically center around a plantation scene, a jungle scene, a camp meeting or church service, and a Harlem rent party. Ellington's earliest efforts in the musical theatre will make ample use of these conventions established by Cook, Cole, Blake, and Johnson, as well as those employed by Maceo Pinkard in *Liza* (1922), Ford Dabney in *Rang Tang* (1927),[9] "Fats" Waller in *Keep Shufflin'* (1928) and *Hot Chocolates* (1929), and Porter Grainger in *Hot Rhythm* (1930).

Even though Ellington's affinity for the theatre might be an established fact, his compositions for the stage remain a grey area for historians and musicologists because of the very nature of theatre composition. When Duke composed a piece for his band, there was a fairly direct route from inspiration to performance. Granted that Ellington appropriated musical ideas from his band members and, after 1939 when Billy Strayhorn joined the Ellington organization, it would become more difficult to determine the authorship of particular numbers. Still, the route from composition to performance was relatively clear. In a musical show, however, a composer only necessarily provides the songs—sometimes with written accompaniment, often only in lead sheets (melody lines with chords). Often the composer does the musical underscore, but that can also be provided by the musical director, or rehearsal pianist, or "continuity" person, or dance arranger (who is often the rehearsal pianist for the choreographer). Although the composer might provide vocal arrangements, those are usually the work of a separate arranger who is independent of the orchestrator. Add to this a cast who may need songs transposed, a director who may require constant rewrites, and a producer who hires ghostwriters to perform the actual rewrites, what actually appears on stage may only vaguely resemble the composer's original intention. It is no surprise that critics of Ellington's compositions are much more interested in the work over which he had a fair amount of performance control, rather than that which he permitted to be realized by others.

It is, however, that very situation that makes Ellington's compositions for the stage so important because it allows the critic to examine the music on its own merits—on its appropriateness dramatically, on its musical interest—rather than on a performance or arrangement supervised by the composer. Critics have been quick to suggest the importance of Ellington's film score *Paris Blues* as an example of Ellington (and Strayhorn) writing for an orchestra other than their own (in this case, a group of French jazz musicians). Stanley Dance is enthusiastic about *My People* for the same reason: It is one of the few recorded examples of Duke Ellington and Billy Strayhorn writing for a different band. Such an endeavor requires a fair amount of patience, though, since the success or failure of a musical theatre work is attributable to as many people as were involved with realizing the score.

Attribution is an especially problematic issue, even at the point of creativity. Few holograph manuscripts exist for musical theatre works, and when there are alterations between the composer's manuscript and that of the copyist, or the copyist's manuscript alone exists, identification was made from extra-musical documents, such as contracts, scripts, letters, playbills, and personal interviews with individuals involved with the project. In addition, the musical symbiosis between Ellington and Strayhorn was so profound that each might contribute to the other's music without being properly credited in copyright registration or in program copy. Because Duke Ellington was the celebrity, his name was sometimes appended to work that was only marginally his, much in the same way that Irving Mills put his name to many early Ellington compositions, because he was the white publisher with clout. However, every attempt has been made to give proper credit to the originator of a musical idea even when the work is attributed solely to Ellington.

Duke Ellington with his early collaborators, Irving Mills and Henry Nemo (courtesy of the Duke Ellington Collection, National Museum of American History Archives Center, Smithsonian Institution).

What follows is a survey of every theatre piece Duke Ellington is known to have worked on during his lifetime, beginning with *Chocolate Kiddies*, a revue, and ending with *Queenie Pie*, a "street opera." [10] In between, there are full-length book musicals with a more-or-less developed consecutive plot and songs in varying degrees of integration, African American revues, plays with "incidental music" descriptive of and contributing to the action, and ballets of various length, atmosphere, and continuity. The plot of each work is described and the score analyzed according to its dramatic function in the piece. Where associations can be made with other well known Ellington compositions, they are so noted.

Taken as a body of work, the music theatre of Duke Ellington offers an interesting perspective on the recurring themes present throughout all of his music. There are shows with an emphasis on night club performance (*Harlem Is Heaven, H.M.S. Times Square, Beggar's Holiday, Be My Guest, The Man with Four Sides*, and *Pousse-Café*); those that are based on legend (*Swing, Helene, Swing; Shout Up a Morning*); those based on African American history (*Cinque, Boola, Cock o' the World, Saturday Laughter*); those based on fantasy (*Free as a Bird, Satin Doll, Queenie Pie*); and those based on religious motifs (*The Crystal Tree, My People, The Jaywalker, Murder in the Cathedral*).

Clearly the music that will be discussed in the following pages will not be to everyone's taste. Those who will find Ellington's music theatre compositions inferior to Duke's band work can now have firm evidence of the importance of his maintaining control over his material. Those who will find the new work provocative can continue to celebrate Ellington's genius in every genre of American music. As Jim McNeely stated in *Jazz Times* (March 1999), "Ellington isn't a mere chapter of jazz history, but his own history, relevant as much to the non-jazz world of '20th century music' as he is to jazz" (35). What matters, I hope, is that a significant body of work written by, perhaps, the greatest American composer of any century is finally, to quote Duke himself, "beginning to see the light."

One

Jungle Music

Duke Ellington's first compositions for the theatre were written for revues. The first, *Chocolate Kiddies*, would presage Ellington's unidiomatic methods of writing a musical. The European impresario Leonidow was looking for a revue similar to *From Dover Street to Dixie*, an American import which he had seen at the Pavilion Theatre in London. While the "Dover" part of the piece was performed by white English actors, the "Dixie" half featured the *Plantation Revue* company of African American actors. The latter half was clearly the more successful, for when the show returned to the United States for a Broadway run, the white half was jettisoned and the name of the revue changed to *Dixie to Broadway*. Leonidow, hoping to cash in on the African American phenomenon, approached Arthur S. Lyons, the producer of *From Dover Street to Dixie*, and publisher Jack Robbins, to suggest songwriters for the new project. Because Leonidow wanted to produce the revue cheaply, Robbins kept his distance from established composers the likes of Maceo Pinkard, and James P. Johnson, and hired Duke Ellington and Jo Trent, pawning his wife's engagement ring to give them a $500 advance. While the Duke manages to exaggerate the amount of work actually required by the duo to create the show, his version of the story goes as follows:

> One day Joe Trent came running up to me on Broadway. He had a big proposition and there was urgency in his voice.
>
> "Tonight we've got to write a show," he said. "*Tonight!*"
>
> Being dumb, and not knowing any better, I sat down that evening and wrote a show. How was I to know that composers had to go up in the mountains, or to the seashore, to commune with the muses for six months in order to write a show. The next day we played and demonstrated our show for Jack Robbins, who liked it and said he would take it [*Music Is My Mistress* 71].

In *Ellington: The Early Years*, Mark Tucker explains that the actual work performed was probably the creation of four new numbers, "With You," "Love Is a Wish for You," "Jim Dandy," and "Jig Walk," all written in late March

Mercury Theatre Inc.

ORSON WELLES | JOHN HOUSEMAN

Mercury Text Records
Mercury Shakespeare (Harper & Bros.)
Mercury Theatre on The Air
The Campbell Playhouse
Orson Welles—Mercury Productions (RKO Radio Pictures)

1430 BROADWAY
Pennsylvania 6-2530

June 10, 1941

Mr. Duke Ellington
William Morris
Hollywood, Cal.

Dear Sir:

May I thank you for your cooperation in making the Canada Lee broadcast last Monday night a successful one. If there is anything we can do for you, please don't hesitate to call upon us.

Thanks again for your assistance.

Sincerely yours,

Leo Rose

LR:ss

Leo Rose

Julius Caesar ◆ *Heartbreak House* ◆ *The Cradle Will Rock* ◆ *The Five Kings* ◆ *Shoemaker's Holiday* ◆ *Danton's Death*

Letter from Leo Rose of the Mercury Theatre, sent to Ellington the day after the Canada Lee broadcast. Orson Welles, one of the founders of the Mercury Theatre, considered Ellington the only true genius he knew (himself excepted), and tried to develop collaborative projects between them at various points in their careers (Courtesy of the Duke Ellington Collection, National Museum of American History Archives Center, Smithsonian Institution).

or early April 1925 since rehearsals for the show began in New York at the end of April (120–21). Sam Wooding's 11-member orchestra was chosen to accompany the nearly three dozen chorus girls, comics, and dancers who left in May 1925 aboard the SS *Arabic* for a Berlin premiere on 25 May 1925. Not untypically, Ellington had little involvement with the actual production of the show, though Garvin Bushell, one of Sam Wooding's alto sax players, noted his presence at one or two early rehearsals at Bryant Hall, something that will be an even greater rarity in the years to come.

The revue was a potpourri of songs, sketches, and dance routines taking place in either a plantation or Harlem cabaret setting. Typically the evening was divided into three acts, with the first and third acts alternating the two locales and the second act devoted to a concert presentation of the latest jazz tunes.[1] According to the program for the Stockholm leg of the tour (August 1925), three of Ellington's four tunes appeared in the third act of the revue. Set in the South, Act 3 began with spirituals and Stephen Foster songs, followed by Adelaide Hall's rendition of "Jungle Nights in Dixie," a comedy routine, and Jessie Crawford singing "Jim Dandy," Trent and Ellington's paean to the strutting dandy archetype, already seen in Will Marion Cook's "The Hottest Coon in Dixie." Unlike Cook's aggressive use of syncopation and ragtime accompaniment, Ellington's music is more subtle, "using mild syncopation and a jaunty accompaniment to evoke an earlier era of cakewalk and ragtime songs" (Tucker 123). [2] After act three changes locale to Harlem, the second of Ellington and Trent's songs, "With You," is introduced within a dramatic sketch involving children, a mother, a postman, and two lovers. Tucker asserts that "Popular songs produced by blacks in the early twenties tended to be either blues numbers or jazz-related.... 'With You,' by contrast, is a sweet Tin Pan Alley ballad that avoids identification with stylized black-American speech or music" (124). While his point is well taken, especially in terms of the lyric being a straightforward expression of love—something highly unusual for African Americans to sing in the mid-twenties—it is important to note the repeated, though subtle, syncopation of the chorus with its constant emphasis on beats 2 and 4, insinuating ever so skillfully the offbeat accents of ragtime. Even when Ellington was attempting assimilation into a more traditional Tin Pan Alley formula, he refused to abandon his jazz roots.[3]

"The Jig Walk" came near the end of Act 3. It was the Charleston dance trading on the popularity of "Charleston," written by James P. Johnson and Cecil Mack for the 1923 revue *Runnin' Wild*. Whether or not the song was written specifically for the *Chocolate Kiddies*,[4] the lyric to the release directs the cast to "Show these kind folk New York's dancing craze / It has got that big Broadway ablaze" something appropriate for an American company touring in Europe. More importantly, as Tucker notes, the phrase "jigwawk" was used in black minstrelsy to refer to African Americans, so that in Trent and

Ellington's song, the Charleston dance step becomes directly associated with the identity of African Americans. The number was staged with great success by Charlie Davis, a principal dancer in the *Shuffle Along* company and choreographer for the Lafayette and Apollo Theatres in New York City.

Two other compositions by Ellington and Trent, "Love Is a Wish for You," and "Skeedely-Um-Bum," were inserted into *Chocolate Kiddies* in various productions. Unfortunately all that is known about their music and lyrics exists from the promotional excerpts shown on the back cover of the published copy of "Jim Dandy." "Love Is a Wish for You," possibly the European version of Trent's "Love Is a Dream of You," copyrighted 22 June 1925, is a waltz with a simple, singable, scale-like melody, with no leaps greater than a third. The harmony is of much greater interest because of its use of altered chords. Of the seven bars provided in the excerpt, four have chromatically altered tones. The jaunty "Skeedely-Um-Bum" seems more typical of Ellington's early compositions with blues suggested by the first four bars, and the "jungle music" of Ellington's Cotton Club period anticipated in the minor harmonization, emphatic beat, and use of flattened, or "blue" notes.[5]

While only "Jim Dandy," "With You," and "Jig Walk Charleston" were published by Robbins Engel, Inc.,[6] "Love Is a Wish for You" was advertised as having been recorded. *Variety* 17 June 1925 noted:

> All the principal numbers in the "Chocolate Kiddies" colored show at the Admiral Palast, Berlin, have been recorded on the "mechanicals" by the German branch of the Victor Company. Jo Trent and Duke Ellington wrote all special numbers, which have been acquired by Jack Robbins… . Among the leaders is a fox trot-ballad, "With You," which Lottie Gee sings in German. A waltz number, "Love Is Just a Wish," also in German, is rendered by Thaddeus Drayton (Greenlee and Drayton) and Margaret Sims. A fast number, a Charleston, "The Jig Walk," is introduced by Greenlee and Drayton and chorus [40].

While the mention of a recording of "Love Is a Wish for You" seems to verify its use in *Chocolate Kiddies*, nothing has been located to associate "Skeedely-Um-Bum" with the show beyond the promotional excerpt on the back cover of "Jim Dandy."

While the reception of *Chocolate Kiddies* on tour was highly enthusiastic, its premiere in Berlin was met with an initial hostility because the German audience thought that the actors had come from French Colonial Africa. The year before, France had sent a black regiment into Bavaria hoping to intimidate the Germans into paying their war debt, and German audiences were not amused at the sight of a skin color they had associated with mercenary tax collectors. However when it was explained that the actors were African American, not French, tensions cooled and audiences began to warm up to the jazz sound that would have a provocative effect on German music later in the twenties. Although audiences may have started to appreciate the show, all Germans were not especially tolerant of the skin color of the cast. Sam Wooding, orchestra leader for the production, recalled to his friend Josephine Baker, the situation of two performers accosted by Germans in hiking suits at the hotel where they were staying—a hotel run by an old Jewish couple:

> They walked over to where this Jewish lady was standing behind the bar and started a conversation. All of a sudden, one of the Germans slapped the woman's face several times, and the other man broke some glasses. Then they walked out.
>
> My men and I jumped up and ran to her as she was crying. She said, "They asked what right had we to have this hotel, why didn't we get out of Germany."
>
> We felt sorry for her; most of the men only wished they had understood enough German so they could have caught the bastards before they slapped this old lady.
>
> We didn't have long to wait. A couple of days later, in walks six of these same guys. They were drunk. The hotel had small rooms for private parties, and two of our people, Chick Horsey (one of The Three Eddies) and Bobby Martin from my band, were in one of these rooms eating with a couple of chorus girls, and these Germans came into the room. Chick told the girls to get lost, and after they left, one of the Germans locked the door and walked over and said something in German, and his friends laughed.
>
> But Chick Horsey was a master at gang fighting. He smashed this German and the German went down like a bull in a slaughterhouse, blood flying everywhere. Bobby picked him up and threw him out the window—it was on the ground floor—and from then on, as Chick would smash these bastards, Bobby would throw them out the window.
>
> Chick said every time he socked one of those guys, he saw the German that slapped that poor Jewish woman and he thought of how some of the white Southerners had treated black men and women in America, and this gave him strength.
>
> It seemed like a miracle, we didn't know Chick and Bobby was that good. Well, the Germans never came back [Baker and Chase 125–126].

While Chick Horsey and Bobby Martin were able to overcome bigotry in their own way, many members of the cast were not, and by the time the *Chocolate Kiddies* returned to Berlin at the end of the tour, Lottie Gee, Adelaide Hall, and Charlie Davis, significant members of the original cast, had left.[7]

Back in the United States, aware that downtown whites wanted to "observe" African Americans in Harlem, not "mix with them," the Cotton Club, at 644 Lenox Avenue, on the corner of 142nd Street, under the aegis of Owney Madden, developed a policy of providing black entertainment for a whites-only audience. The practice came to a grinding halt in June 1925 when Judge Francis A. Winslow of the Federal Court padlocked the door to the Cotton Club because of its 44 violations of the Volstead Act. When the club was reopened in the fall of 1925, Herman Stark became stage manager of the all-black revues, and Dan Healy was hired to produce and stage the

Cotton Club Shows.[8] Two years later, when King Oliver refused the position of house band for the establishment, Jimmy McHugh, who had been writing Cotton Club material since 1923, suggested Duke Ellington and his band, the Washingtonians. Because of a time-honored tradition of hiring only Chicagonians in musical positions at the Cotton Club, McHugh's suggestion went unheaded, until the manager, having run out of alternatives, agreed to audition the group.[9] As Ellington recalls:

> The next big step was when we went into the Cotton Club on December 4, 1927. We had to audition for this job, but it called for a band of at least eleven pieces, and we had been using only six at the Kentucky Club. At the time, I was playing a vaudeville show for Clarence Robinson at Gibson's Standard Theatre on South Street in Philadelphia. The audition was set for noon, but by the time I had scraped up eleven men it was two or three o'clock. We played for them and got the job. The reason for that was that the boss, Harry Block, didn't get there till late either, and didn't hear the others! That's a classic example of being at the right place at the right time with the right thing before the right people [*Music Is My Mistress* 75–76].

Ellington's debut at the Cotton Club was not as serendipitous as Ellington suggests. In fact, the band was already engaged by a theatre in Philadelphia when the management at the Cotton Club required his services. The Philadelphia engagement ran a week beyond when Ellington was needed in New York and the manager in the City of Brotherly Love proclaimed heatedly that nothing could persuade him to release Ellington a week early. The Cotton Club responded by enlisting the services of Boo Boo Hoff, an underworld figure in Philadelphia who, in turn, sent Yankee Schwarz to the theatre manager with the message, "Be big, or you'll be dead." Faced with such an alternative, the theatre man released Ellington and the band, who arrived at the Cotton Club excited though exhausted, only minutes before the performance was to begin.

Beginning with the Cotton Club show on 4 December 1927, Ellington began to develop and experiment with the "jungle style" he had introduced in miniature in "Skeedely-Um-Dum."[10] Although the principal songs were written by composer McHugh and lyricist Dorothy Fields, Ellington contributed the "Creole Love Call" (from Rudy Jackson's adaptation of King Oliver's "Camp Meeting Blues"), "The Blues I Love to Sing," and "Black and Tan Fantasy," all co-composed with Bubber Miley, the trumpeter in the band.[11] None of the songs were composed specifically for the revue since "Black and Tan Fantasy" had been recorded on 7 April 1927, 26 October 1927, and 3 November 1927, while "Creole Love Call" and "Blues I Love to Sing" had been recorded on 26 October 1927.[12]

Most evocative of the "jungle style," with its growling harmon-muted brass, and heavy use of tom-toms in the percussion, was "Black and Tan Fantasy." Beginning with a 12-bar statement, firmly establishing the key of B♭

minor, the piece suddenly shifts to B♭ major in a B section filled with syncopation, chromatic harmonies, and improvisatory-like motifs. A third section follows in the traditional 12-bar blues vein, anticipating the "Train" motif that will appear in *Man with Four Sides*, much later in Ellington's career; and a fourth section, again repeating the blues pattern, and suggesting a kind of improvisatory variant of section three, concludes the composition.

The singularity of Ellington's "jungle" sound was so marked, that in a short time, the Washingtonians became known as Duke Ellington's Jungle Band, and many of the titles associated with him during this period were designed to capitalize on the notoriety of the "jungle" rubric, whether or not the music actually evoked the style. Ellington and his band substantially increased the drawing power of the Cotton Club, so much so that, within a year, the management agreed to Ellington's request to relax the "whites only" policy so that his friends and family, and those of his band members, might be able to enter the club and hear the band perform. Jim Haskins notes that the club's acquiescence was not indicative of a new policy of integration: "black customers were still carefully examined before being admitted. The complexion of the Cotton Club audience did not change radically; after all, there were not that many Harlemites who cared to patronize the new *semi*-Jim Crow establishment" (57). Regardless of the racial policies, the Cotton Club was good to the Ellington band, with side musicians making better than $40 a week, not including tips.

In 1929 the band appeared simultaneously at the Cotton Club and at the Ziegfeld Theatre where, between 2 July and 5 October, they were members of the cast of Gershwin and Youmans's *Show Girl,* staring Ruby Keeler, Ed Wynn, and Eddie Foy, Jr.[13] According to the playbill, the band's appearance was limited to the final scene of act one, a "Club Caprice" sequence, in which the band performed "Black and White," "Jimmie, The Well Dressed Man," and "Harlem Serenade," all written by George and Ira Gershwin, and a number entitled "African Daisies," which Gershwin scholar, Ed Jablonski suggests may have been composed by Ellington.[14] At the Cotton Club, Ellington performed "The Mooche" (written with Irving Mills), one of his most characteristic "jungle" compositions, the "Cotton Club Stomp" (composed with Johnny Hodges and Harry Carney), "Misty Mornin'" (in collaboration with Arthur Whetsol), and "The Duke Steps Out" (with Johnny Hodges and Cootie Williams). Even the stock market crash of 23 October 1929 had little effect on the soaring fortunes of the band, for in March it appeared simultaneously in the *Blackberries of 1930* at the Cotton Club and the *Maurice Chevalier Show* at the Fulton Theatre. For the *Blackberries of 1930*, opening on 2 March 1930, Ellington provided "Bumpty-Bump" (with lyrics by Irving Mills), "Doin' the Crazy Walk" (lyrics by Irving Mills), "Swanee River Rhapsody" (with lyrics by Irving Mills and Clarence Gaskill), and the "Cotton Club Stomp"(from the 1929 edition of the Cotton Club revues). "Bumpty-

Bump" recalls the Charleston flavor of "Jig Walk," and the lyric directive to teach the audience the newest African American dance craze—this time, in slightly more racy and provocative movements. Likewise, "Doin' the Crazy Walk" associates African American society with musical innovation: "I got a tune and rhythm / nobody ever did them" (3). With a schitzophrenically syncopated melodic line, juxtaposing stepwise motion with awkward leaps, and an easy-to-assimilate chromatic harmonization, "Doin' the Crazy Walk" is all that its title suggests. It is interesting to note that, while neither dance piece makes use of the jungle style in the chorus, both utilize its minor tonality in the verse. While it is not unusual for a piece to begin in minor and resolve to its relative major, Ellington's consistent use of the device both capitalizes on and deflects the popularity of the jungle idiom, fulfilling an audience's expectations, while leading them into yet another variation of the form.

The *Maurice Chevalier Show* opening 30 March, starred Maurice Chevalier and Eleanor Powell in a vaudeville produced by Charles Dillingham at the Fulton Theatre. However, the entire first act was devoted to Ellington and his band playing a variety of popular hits as well as Ellington's own "Black Beauty," "The Mooche," and "East St. Louis Toodle-Oo" (composed with Bubber Miley).[15] "East St. Louis Toodle-Oo" was later interpolated into the mildly successful revue, *Sweet and Low* (17 November 1930), featuring Fanny Brice, George Jessel, and Arthur Treacher.[16]

Published in 1927, "East St. Louis Toodle-Oo"[17] is again representative of the "jungle" style so popular in the Duke's early compositions. Firmly rooted in D minor, the 14-bar opening statement full of melodic syncopation gives way to a chromatically harmonized release, now beginning to be typical of Ellington, that vacillates between major and minor tonalities and finally returns to a six-bar recapitulation of the D minor motif. An 18-bar second section (comprised of two eight-bar statements and a two-bar extended coda), in the relative major key, recalls the ragtime genre in its syncopation and demonstrates a marked development since "Jig Walk" for Ellington in that style of writing. Particularly noteworthy is the suspension at the cadence in bar eight, where the Duke resolves to an accented dominant chord only on the fourth (a weak) beat, giving the phrase an abrupt, syncopated resolution. The third section is a recapitulation of the first, ending somewhat abruptly in the primary key of D minor. Full of growls in the orchestration and syncopation in the composition, "East St. Louis Toddle-Oo" is jungle music at its best.

From 3 May through 9 May 1930, Ellington and his orchestra appeared in the *Pepper Pot Revue* at the Lafayette Theatre in Harlem, produced by choreographer, Clarence Robinson, who had recently choreographed the Cotton Club's *Blackberries of 1930*. As John Edward Hasse notes in *Beyond Category*, this performance gave the African American residents of Harlem "a rare opportunity to hear Ellington in person" (126). On 28 September,

Ellington opened his seventh Cotton Club revue, *Brown Sugar: Sweet But Unrefined*, and in October, during a radio broadcast from the Cotton Club, Ellington performed "Dreamy Blues," his first composition written "specially for microphone transmission." Public approval of the new work was such that Irving Mills fit a lyric to the tune, now retitled "Mood Indigo," and a masterpiece was born.

In 1931, the Cotton Club Show was known as *Rhythmania*, with Harold Arlen and Ted Koehler replacing Jimmy McHugh and Dorothy Fields as principal composer and lyricist, and Cab Calloway's band replacing the Duke's band. As Jim Haskins explains it:

> By the end of 1930 the Cotton Club life had begun to pall for Duke Ellington. He felt cramped in his style. He was tired of playing show tunes. He had to admit that the people at the Cotton Club were good about letting the band off to play outside gigs, but he needed a real change. He needed to get back in touch with his music [68–69].

On 6 February 1931, Duke Ellington left the Cotton Club to begin a concert tour with his band in the northeast and midwest sections of the United States, to cities including Boston, Chicago, Cleveland, St. Louis, Philadelphia, Pittsburgh, Washington, D.C., Buffalo, and Toronto. Though the band's presence might have been missing in *Rhythmania*, the Duke's was not, for interpolated into Arlen's score was an Ellington composition recorded on 14 November 1929, called "The Breakfast Dance."[18] It is not unusual in the early African American revues that choreographers (and white composers, for that matter) turned to Ellington for music that would sound indigenously African American. The following year, while Ellington continued to tour American cities from Los Angeles, California, to Old Orchard Beach, Maine, *Earl Carroll's Vanities of 1932*, a spectacular revue opening 27 September at the Broadway Theatre, featured Ellington's recently recorded "Rockin' in Rhythm" (composed in collaboration with Irving Mills and Harry Carney).[19] In March 1933, Ellington and his band returned to the Cotton Club to replace Cab Calloway, who was preparing for a Southern tour in the final performances of the 21st *Cotton Club Parade*, and the Ellington Band remained in residence to perform in the 22nd *Cotton Club Parade* opening 16 April 1933. Although this revue contained no Ellington original compositions, it featured Ethel Waters and a Harold Arlen–Ted Koehler song that *Variety* called the "biggest song hit of the last ten years": "Stormy Weather." On 2 June, Ellington and his orchestra left for a 55-day tour of England, the Netherlands, and France, sponsored by the English bandleader Jack Hylton.

By 1937, after a rather extensive regimen of touring and making films,[20] Ellington was ready to return to the Cotton Club, but by then, a lot of things had changed. Prohibition had been repealed and the club had moved to a new home, in the heart of the theatre district, on the rooftop of a building on the corner of Broadway and Forty-eighth Street. For the Duke, it was a hero's welcome. In the decade since he and the band first played at the Cotton Club, they had become international celebrities because of the string of commercial hits that seemed to flow out of him: "It Don't Mean a Thing If It Ain't Got That Swing," "Sophisticated Lady," "Solitude," "In a Sentimental Mood," "Caravan" (with Juan Tizol), to name just a few. Herman Stark, the producer, chose not to rely solely on Ellington's celebrity to promote the new Cotton Club revue, but hired Ethel Waters, George Dewey Washington, and the Nicholas Brothers, a move he felt sure would draw crowds.

Opening on 15 March 1937, the new revue, the *Cotton Club Express*,[21] the fastest show of the series, and guaranteed to monopolize what Ed Sullivan called "the hi-de-ho and ho-de-ho market" (Haskins 121) was hailed by critics and public alike as "easily the most elegant colored show Broadway has ever applauded" (Haskins 124). Ellington's contributions to the evening were recycled hits: "Black and Tan Fantasy" (written with Bubber Miley), "Rockin' in Rhythm," and "Peckin'," a newly composed rhythm number, destined to replace a dance craze called the "Suzy Q." While the reviewers had little to say about Ellington's contributions, the fact that classical musicians the likes of Leopold Stokowski came to listen to Ellington's band suggests the impact that his style of music was having on the world of music at large. When asked by the great conductor what he was striving to accomplish in his music, the Duke is said to have answered, "I am endeavoring to establish unadulterated Negro melody portraying the American Negro." And, after Ellington illustrated his point, leading the band through several of his compositions, Stokowski is reported to have concluded, "Now I truly understand the Negro soul" (Ulanov 188–189).

Although Ellington's work for *Cotton Club Express* won him the adulation of serious musicians, his most important contribution to the Cotton Club series came the following year with the *Cotton Club Parade of 1938*.[22] For the first time he would be composing an entire score and the prospect thrilled him. His journeyman period had clearly come to an end. He had been named one of the twenty most prominent African Americans by *Life* magazine; he was a hit among the Broadway crowd and a success—if only a polite one—among the aristocracy. The Duke was on a roll and ready for the challenge of creating an entirely new score, with a brand new lyricist, Henry Nemo, a singer, dancer, and songwriter in his own right, although all of the published songs cite Irving Mills *and* Henry Nemo as lyricists. It is not known whether the Duke wanted a familiar face as part of the collaborative team, or if Mills's owning the publishing company had anything to do with his taking primary credit for the words.[23] The principal ballad in the show, "I Let a Song Go Out of My Heart," offers an interesting case in point. The lyric is credited to Henry Nemo by Haskins (130), to Irving Mills and John Redmond by Ellington (*Music Is My Mistress* 497), and to all three lyricists in the published edition. Citing lyrics by both Nemo and Mills, the program for the *Cotton Club Parade*, opening on 9 March 1938 offers the following list of compositions: "A Lesson in C," "Braggin' in Brass," "Carnival in Caroline," "I'm Slappin' Seventh Avenue," "If You Were in My Place," "Swingtime in Honolulu," and "Doing the Skrontch." [24] The New York City *Sun* of 19 March 1939 adds the titles "Oh, Miss So and So," and "I Bear a Torch for You," and David Hummel in *The Collector's Guide to the American Musical Theatre* lists "A Gal from Joe's," "Dinah's in a Jam," "Posin'," "Hip Chick," and the one standard hit from the show, "I Let a Song Go Out of My Heart," cut prior to the New York opening (128–29).[25]

The show featured the Peters Sisters in their New York nightclub debut singing the evocatively atmospheric "Swingtime in Honolulu" and "Posin'," the one-legged dancer Peg-Leg Bates performing the highly syncopated "I'm Slappin' Seventh Avenue," and Mae Johnson sang and danced "A Lesson in C," a rhythmic evocation of a "New Deal" for music. The cast also included the "adagio dancers" Anisy and Aland, the Four Step Brothers, Aida Ward, Bill Maples, Cracker Jacks, Flash and Dash, and the Chocolateers. "Braggin' in Brass" was a featured bravura number for the band, and Will Vodery's Jubileers performed "A Carnival in Caroline" that also featured the famous Cotton Club chorus line. The "Cotton Club Girls," as they were known, had to be beautiful, personable, not older than 21, at least 5 feet 11 inches tall, and able to carry a tune. Because their costumes were usually quite revealing, they had to be exceptionally shapely as well. Among the more well-known Cotton Club Girls are Lena Horne, Dorothy Dandridge, Isabel Washington (who married Adam Clayton Powell, Jr., Harlem's first African American congressman), and Lucille Wilson (Mrs. Louis Armstrong).[26] Two of the girls would play an important part in Ellington's private life: Mildred Dixon, who lived as Ellington's "wife" at 381 Edgecombe Avenue in Harlem's Sugar Hill district in the early 1930s, and Beatrice (Evie) Ellis, a member of the *Cotton Club Parade* cast who replaced her in the Duke's affections in 1939.

Ellington's score was markedly different from his earlier Cotton Club pastiches. Certainly the audience was treated to the growling brass and blues harmonies for which the Duke was famous, but the "jungle music" of the previous revues had been tamed into the prevailing jazz style of the late 1930s, *Swing*. Although Ellington had experimented with swing as early as 1932 in his popular "It Don't Mean a Thing If It Ain't Got That Swing," he resisted being categorized as a swing composer because swing was "like the monotonous rhythmical bouncing of a ball. After you hear just so much, you get sick of it because it hasn't enough harmony and there isn't enough to it." Instead, Ellington preferred to turn to the color, harmony, melody, and rhythm of African American music which, he predicted, would far outlive the swing phenomenon (*The Cleveland News* 8 October 1938). In spite of his feelings, however, Ellington did take advantage of the swing craze because, as

Gunther Schuller notes, "the depressing and uneasy years of the mid-1930s gave way to a new sense of prestige for Duke. Not only was he considered a leader in the vanguard of swing and jazz, but as a veteran bandleader of a dozen years or more, Duke now found himself garnering a level of respect from audiences as well as colleagues that was new in jazz history" ("Ellington vs. the Swing Era"). The success Ellington found in this genre in the late 1930s and early 1940s led him to change his views, if only publically, about swing. In an article titled "Swing Is My Beat" in the *New Advance* of October 1944, Duke writes:

> Swing is my beat. Not jazz in the popular sense of the word, which usually means a chatty combination of instruments knocking out a tune. Swing, as I like to make it and play it, is an expression of sentiment and ideas—modern ideas. It's the kind of music that catches the rhythm of the way people feel and live today. It's American music because it grew out of our folk music, picking up a little from every section of the country as it traveled from New Orleans to Chicago to Kansas City to New York....
>
> What swings? Rhythm. A few notes, a chord combination, a simple musical phrase is developed into a series of rhythm patterns which creates form that is listened to as seriously as a concert hall piece. Part of the reason is that this rhythm hits home to the people who hear it. It speaks their language and tells their story. It's the musician and his audience talking things over [1].

In the *Cotton Club Parade*, the big swing finale was "Doing the Skrontch" a number designed to replace earlier dance crazes such as "Truckin'," "Peckin'," and the "Suzy Q." Sung by Ivie Anderson, the song exhorted the audience to go up on their toes, do a quick turn, and "Skrontch on the fourth beat" in swingtime syncopation. The chorus made good use of a heavy emphasis on the fourth beat that anticipated the downbeat of the next measure, giving the tune a great forward momentum as well as sustaining rhythmic interest by the constant displacement of accents. The harmonic simplicity of the song does not imply a lack of creativity but rather an attempt to make the piece more easily assimilated by the listener. Typically, musical theatre songs trading on rhythmic variety are predictable harmonically, and "Skrontch" is no exception. The number was recorded on 24 March 1938, in a performance at the Cotton Club that included old favorites, "Mood Indigo," and "East St. Louis Toodle-Oo," and again at the Cotton Club on 24 April 1938, but never attained the status of a popular hit.

On 28 November 1936, before Ellington returned to the Cotton Club, the Chicago African American newspaper *Defender* published this teaser about Duke's ambitions in writing a musical:

> The dream of Duke Ellington is a musical with an entire Negro cast. He has been working on the synopsis and score for several months. It is this which is taking him to the West Coast. Several movie producers are

> interested in the book Duke and Richard Mack wrote and which is copyrighted in their names. Duke has the book and the entire score with him on this trip.
>
> The synopsis revolves around an unknown orchestra playing in a Georgia "gut-bucket" with the typical hoi polloi. Then it moves with a complete simplicity of progression until this same orchestra ends in a Harlem hot spot surrounded by Broadway glamour. It has a wide scope and should be splendid working material [*Ellington Scrapbooks*].

Although there is no surviving evidence of a collaboration between Ellington and Mack (a gag writer for W.C. Fields) in either U.S. Copyright Records or the Ellington Collection at the Smithsonian, the idea for the show appears to have surfaced in an incomplete and undated scenario by Will Strickland entitled *Harlem Is Heaven*. The typed manuscript begins at the Savoy Ballroom where a bandleader named Dude is providing music for a group of dancers in their eccentric "rug cutting." Smiley and his friend Skeeter enter and find themselves both attracted to a girl, obviously unattached, pushing her way through the crowd to get Dude's autograph. Smiley gets the autograph and wins the right to take the girl home to Sugar Hill, although he has to borrow cab fare from Dude who turns out to be Skeeter's friend. The next day, Smiley runs into Skeeter and Dude in front of a barbecue stand and confesses to being a singer and needing a job. Dude takes them inside to dinner and explains the hazards of a music career, arguing that "he never gets a chance to write the sort of music he wants to." Always ready with advice, Skeeter suggests that Smiley investigate the possibility of a job from Madame Croqinole, a wealthy Harlem beautician, who is throwing a party that very evening.

That night at the Sugar Hill home of Mr. and Mrs. Croqinole, Smiley is discovered performing the duties of a waiter. When Honey, the girl from the Savoy Ballroom, enters to sing for the guests, he removes his waiter's apron and behaves like one of the guests to impress her, not knowing that the girl is Madame Croqinole's protégé. When the lady of the house discovers them together, she fires Smiley on the spot, although her action only serves to create an even closer attachment between the two young people. A few days later, Dude asks Smiley to introduce one of his recent songs at the club. A music critic in the company of Madame Croqinole raves about Dude's music, and Madame invites the bandleader to her home on Sugar Hill in an attempt to take advantage of his celebrity status. There, Dude listens to his hostess complain about her thwarted desires to be a great singer and tells her about his serious music and "the opera that he is composing." She advises him to go to Africa to study primitive rhythms in order to make his opera all the more authentic and offers to finance the trip if she, her husband, and her protégé can tag along.

A few weeks later en route to Africa, Mr. Croqinole asks Honey why she appears so sad and sullen. When she replies that it is because of the boy she left behind, Smiley and Skeeter suddenly climb out of a lifeboat, having stowed away. On their arrival in Africa, however, the boys are thrown into jail where they are visited by Dude and Mr. Croqinole who promise to intercede with the American consul on their behalf. A few days later, we find Smiley and Skeeter hired as porters for the Croqinole safari (their release from jail being contingent upon employment) into the interior of Africa in search of primitive rhythm. On the following day, in a native village, the chief regales the group with stories about "weird melodies" that his hunters bring back to him. He suggests that the safari go even farther into the jungle, but refuses to go along with them for fear of the witches and evil spirits that supposedly live there. Later, at a native celebration given in honor of the safari, the chief's favorite, Boola, dances seductively, and becomes the unwilling object of Skeeter's flirtation.

The next day, the expedition presses on into the jungle only to hear the sound of "jungle music" coming from a large hut in the middle of a clearing. Dude rushes into the hut to discover a fat native chief wearing a G-string and top hat, playing phonograph records from Harlem. When Dude attempts to communicate using sign language and grunts, the chief replies in perfect English that he is a graduate from Oxford University. Dude is clearly disappointed with this discovery so the chief, attempting to cheer him up, offers to show him his "new English house" under construction. When Dude hears the sounds of the native artisans with tools, the call of the birds, and the natural sounds surrounding them, he is filled with inspiration and begins creating music. In contrast, Skeeter begins singing a low blues ballad "of levee variety," Honey sings a "scat song," that reminds Dude of Harlem, and Madame Croqinole sings a spiritual that recalls the cotton fields. Suddenly Dude is teeming with ideas.

At this point, the typed scenario ends. A handwritten page follows that suggests a prologue to the action. The scene is a southern cotton field at evening when the cotton-pickers return home from the fields after a long day's work. The spiritual-like melody sung by the workers suddenly becomes swingtime when a group of boys, acting as a kind of "Tramp Band" playing guitars and kazoos, enter under the leadership of Smiley. Zeb, Smiley's father, bawls him out for making music while the rest of the men are working, and Smiley replies that he wants to leave the plantation to seek his fortune in New York City. Skeeter, Smiley's best friend, decides that he wants to tag along as well. After tearful farewells at the boat dock, the scene changes to Beale Street in St. Louis, where Smiley and Skeeter wander into a cabaret. There Skeeter gets involved with Stream-lined Lou, and the boys barely escape with their lives and begin hitchhiking toward Harlem. The scene changes to Palisades overlooking New York City at dawn. Hearing a group of stevedores singing the spiritual "City Called Heaven," Smiley responds by singing his own version of the hymn. The last scene of this prologue finds Smiley and Skeeter in a "small hall bedroom" dressing to go to the Savoy Ballroom. The boys talk about their ambitions and the difficulties in achieving them in song, "Gimme a Break."

Not only are there parallels between *Harlem Is Heaven* and the Ellington-Mack project, but hints of future Ellington projects such as *Boola, Queenie-Pie, Air-Conditioned Jungle, Cock o' the World, Black Brown and Beige,* and *Drum Is a Woman*. On 14 February 1937, Ellington is quoted in the Portland, Oregon, *Oregonian*:

> My most serious attempt is to try to establish an unadulterated Negro music. I am attempting a musical play to outline the history of the American Negro, going back to Africa. We are a new people, a strange people; we have our own language and our own music, cruder perhaps than other languages and music, but it is our own, and I want to get it written.
>
> I have this play outlined, but I'll not write it until I'm about ready to present it. I'm learning all the time, and something I'd write this year wouldn't be as good as it would if I waited a year. But I hope to do the play pretty soon. I think the time is ripe for it [*Ellington Scrapbooks*].

It is unknown if Ellington wrote any music specifically for this project.[27] A version of the lyric to "Azure," a ballad published in 1937, is written in manuscript in the middle of the typewritten scenario on the same kind of paper, so it can be assumed that the project dates from at least 1937.[28] In the same year, "I've Got to Be a Rug Cutter" was published and may be referential to the term "rug cutting" in the text, although there is no specific reference to that number in the scenario. More important are two piano parts marked "Opening" written in an unidentified copyist's hand. The first, titled "Harlem Is Heaven" and "Inside Harlem," is a single page fragment in E♭ that utilizes a lazy blues progression, a "Charleston" rhythm, and a syncopated downbeat, not unlike "Skrontch." (See example 1.1.) The relaxed feel of the motif is in counterpoint with the upwardly chromatic dominant seventh chords that follow, supplying a more frenetic ambiance to the music. When the part begins to "swing" with a walking bass, the fragment ends.

The second piano part, found among the manuscripts entitled "Echoes of Harlem," but clearly a different composition entirely, is also marked "Open-

Example 1.1.

ing," and in the key of E♭. It begins with an eight-bar introductory fanfare that is much less syncopated than the other fragment, but quickly moves into Charleston-like motifs in a second section that appears to be a more musical development of the chromatic dominant sevenths of the previous example. A third section relies on stepwise melodic movement and syncopation to create a tune that is highly evocative of the flashy Hollywood musicals of the thirties. The piano part quickly dissolves into chord changes pounding out the second and fourth beats in common time and would have little interest but for a line of dialogue appearing before a key change into D♭ major, "Well wait." So generic a line could fit almost any circumstance, so it would be foolish to make too much of it here. However, it is appropriate to the business described in Strickland's scenario and provides yet another possible clue to one of Ellington's earliest musical theatre works.[29]

In November 1937, *Tempo* ran the headline, "Duke at Work on Ballet for Von Grona Dancers," and nine months later, the New York City *Amsterdam News* announced that "Duke Ellington has completed the score for a musical show which will be produced and directed by Eugene von Grona and presented this autumn on Broadway in association with Continental Productions 30 Rockefeller Plaza. Most of the book is based upon episodes in colored life, both in the south and in Harlem, but it includes an elaborate and fanciful production, a satire in swing time, with the story of Helen of Troy as its foundation. The cast will include the American Negro Ballet and a large colored singing chorus" (13 August 1938).

This was to be *Swing, Helene, Swing*, a musical comedy about the "Golden Apple" myth in which Paris chooses Venus as the fairest of the goddesses, runs away with Helen of Troy, and starts the Trojan War. The gimmick here was that the myth was to be presented from an African American perspective, using jive discourse, swing rhythms, and popular dances. The musical opens with the poet Pelleus recounting the background to the myth in "Frankie-and-Johnny" style. When Paris awards the prize to Venus, the spectators perform the "Venus Hop," in celebration and the goddess contacts Helene by telephone (compliments of Cupid) in order to introduce her to Paris. The second act begins at the airport in Troy where the paparazzi, bored with waiting for the two lovers to appear, perform the "Lindy," "jiving" the time away; and once the war has begun, Helene is shown in an operating room, getting her face lifted, to denote a passage of time. The clever, though dated, scenario anticipated such modernizations of the myth as *Helen Goes to Troy* (1944) and *The Golden Apple* (1954) in its attempt to make the audience connect in an immediate and visceral way to the old tale, and led the way for African American productions of classic shows such as *The Hot Mikado, The Swing Mikado*, and *Swingin' the Dream* (the jazz version of Shakespeare's *A Midsummer Night's Dream*), all in 1939.

Swing, Helene, Swing was never produced. The work appears never to have developed beyond a scenario, and there is no evidence that Ellington ever composed a note of music for the project. However, the Pittsburgh *Courier* of 5 November 1938 lamented that "Ellington could have had a backer and been well fixed on Broadway now, but he refused because he felt that this was something of the Negro and by the Negro and should be produced by the Negro. Production has been held up because of that" (*Ellington Scrapbooks*). If, indeed, Duke was attempting to emulate the practice of African American *production* in the musical theatre denoted by artists like Bob Cole and shows like *Shuffle Along*, it was a brief attempt, for his next musical theatre statement about the African American experience would be produced by white, left-wing, Hollywood stars.

Two

The Sun-Tanned Revu-sical

Kaj Gynt was a childhood friend of Greta Garbo. She had immigrated to New York City early in the 1920s only to find herself in the service of her famous friend when the actress came to New York in 1925 to sign a contract with MGM Pictures. Working as translator for the actress, Gynt found herself escorting Garbo not only in and out of movie moguls' offices, but to Broadway theatre, where the pair of Swedish women developed a love for American jazz. While Garbo's career would extricate her from so popular an idiom, Gynt's love for jazz developed into an interest in African American culture, an interest that led to the creation of a successful musical revue entitled *Rang Tang*, produced at the Royale Theatre on 12 July 1927.[1] With a book by Kaj Gynt, lyrics by former Ellington collaborator Jo Trent, and music by Ford Dabney, *Rang Tang* capitalized on the popularity of the African American vaudeville team of Flournoy E. Miller and Aubrey Lyles.

Designed as a sequel to the duo's roles in *Shuffle Along* (Sam Peck and Steve Jenkins), and inspired by Lindberg's flight across the Atlantic, Miller and Lyles portray two debt-ridden barbers escaping from their creditors in Jimtown by stealing a plane and flying to Africa to find buried treasure. Forced to land near the Island of Madagascar, the pair endure a series of boisterously entertaining misadventures among the inhabitants of the island. Fierce animals, jungles, and deserts notwithstanding, they find the lost treasure and return to the United States and celebrate their nouveau riche status at a Harlem cabaret.

The success of the revue propelled Gynt into the creation of a full-length musical play about the African American experience. Conceived as a piece for Paul Robeson, the African American bass baritone who had won acclaim in Eugene O'Neill's *Emperor Jones* and Kern and Hammerstein II's *Show Boat*, *Cock o' the Walk* was three years in the making before Gynt approached Langston Hughes, African American poet and dramatist, to join the project in 1931 and revise her libretto. At first Hughes was highly enthusiastic about the musical that would chronicle the adventures of "Mammy Bless'em's" son,

Cocko, who "went out in rags to conquer the world—and came back in rags; found love, found beauty, adventure, gold—and lost them all each time" (Rampersad 1:220). Kaj had suggested that George Gershwin was interested in providing the music, and that Robeson was on the verge of committing to the project, though as time wore on, however, it became clear to Hughes that Gynt's hopes were unrealistic.

Having given up any thoughts of a production of *Cock o' the World*, the musical's new working title, Hughes found himself drawn again to the property in 1936 when Gynt informed him of Robeson's renewed interest in appearing in the play (this time in London), and the fact that she had interested Duke Ellington in writing the music. Because he considered Ellington "his musical counterpart in black America" (Rampersad 1:328), Hughes renewed his contract with Gynt and began writing lyrics for the work. A series of undated lyrics in the Ellington Archive at the Smithsonian (301.4B.11.7) are possible representations of his efforts, evoking the moods and situations depicted in Gynt's libretto.

The first lyric, "After the Ship Is Gone," details the plight of courtesans who fall in love with a sailor, left lonely with the "memory of strong arms that held me until the dawn." "I'll Drop My Anchor with You" is written as a duet between a sailor and his lover. He vows that his "sailin' days are over," and seeks the security of his lover's eyes; she claims to have heard it all before and tells him to go away unless his intentions can be proved to her satisfaction. "A Land of Sun" is a glorification of weather in the tropics. Associating the sun with gold and rivers with emeralds, the lyric concludes, "Everybody's happy livin' in the sun." "Moon Magic" trades on the old concept of "lunacy," madness related to the various phases of the moon. Hughes's lyric affirms that moonlight makes humans long for love, and concludes with the desire to be taken by the lover, before the speaker goes "crazy with the magic of the moon." The last lyric in the collection, "Be a Little Savage with Me," recalls Ellington's jungle idiom in its raw depiction of eroticism. The speaker may resemble a dove, but feels like a tiger, who desires a "great big jungle man" to "be a little savage with me." The rest of the lyrics delineates what being "savage" means, usings words like "scratch," "bite," "squeeze," "break," and "grab."

It is unknown if Ellington completed the setting of Hughes's lyrics at this point in his career. In his biography of Langston Hughes, Arnold Rampersad notes that, in 1936, when Ellington and Hughes were both in Cleveland, the Duke played the poet "some charming music he had written for 'Cock o' the World'"(1.329). Faith Berry questions that assumption in her own biography of the poet, arguing instead that Hughes was despondent over "hearing nothing definite about his script or its musical score by Duke Ellington" (253). In an undated letter to Arna Bontemps, Hughes complains that Kaj Gynt's agent "prevented us from having a Duke Ellington score for *Cock o' the World*," and that the author, having given up her agent, would not give up on getting Ellington (Nichols 70). Since the letter refers to the Los Angeles production of *Run Little Chillun* (1938–39) in the past tense, it is likely that the report dates from the early 1940s, a significant period in the collaboration between Ellington and Langston Hughes. Bontemps had accepted the post of cultural director for the American Negro Exposition in Chicago to run from 4 July to Labor Day 1940, to commemorate the 75th anniversary of the Emancipation Proclamation, and he invited Hughes to write the book for *Jubilee: A Cavalcade of the Negro Theatre*, a review of African American musical theatre, and the libretto for *The Tropics After Dark*, an intimate revue. Rampersad notes that Hughes wrote two songs for the shows: "Jubilee, Sweet Jubilee" was set by Thomas A. Dorsey, a gospel composer, and the other entitled "Diamond Jubilee," by Duke Ellington.[2] Unfortunately, because of production problems and the lack of money, when the American Negro Exposition opened at the Coliseum in Chicago, neither revue was performed as intended. A quarter of a century later, Ellington will have a much better experience at the Exposition with *My People*.

Langston Hughes will move on to an African American musical revue sponsored by the New Negro Theatre in association with the leftest white Hollywood Theatre Alliance. The collaboration between the organizations was a difficult one, causing much internal conflict over the writing and editing of material. As Faith Berry recalls:

> Some of the skits, written by eight to ten people of varying temperaments, had produced chaos. Except for Donald Ogden Stewart, who was editing a few of the comedy scripts, and Charles Leonard, the producer, who had staged the Wallace Thurman play, *Harlem*, on Broadway, Hughes couldn't see eye to eye with several of the white writers. They seemed familiar with writing sophisticated Chaplinesque humor but unfamiliar with creating black characters beyond Amos 'n' Andy. He was unable to convince them that presenting material in Negro dialect did not always make it humorous. They could not make up their minds whether the production should be "half-Negro," "half-white," very Negro," have a social message, or none at all. Hughes thought the material had no feeling for black characters, even if it was to be performed by black actors [293].

Despite the rumors that Paul Robeson was interested in joining the show, and that Duke Ellington had signed on to compose music and provide the orchestra for the event, Hughes resigned from the creative team of the *Negro Revue*, giving a free hand to Charles Leonard, a member of the Columbia Pictures family, and his main collaborator on the revue, to sell off any material they had written to anyone who wanted to buy.[3] Ellington expressed interest in "Mad Scene from Woolworth's" and included the number in *Jump for Joy*, the "Sun-Taned Revu-sical" that emerged from the ashes of the *Negro Revue*.

Duke Ellington and his band were contracted to appear at Casa Mañana, a popular ballroom in Culver City, California, from 2 January through 20 February 1941. Sid Kuller, a contract writer for MGM currently involved in pumping out *The Big Store* for the Marx Brothers, was in the habit of dropping in at the ballroom on his way home from the studio. One Saturday night, late in January, after the last set, he invited the band to his house for a jam session that would last until Monday morning and continue the following weekend. Until the end of the engagement, Duke Ellington and his band had a standing invitation to spend their weekends jamming at Sid Kuller's house. At one of those sessions, the concept of *Jump for Joy* emerged from the reputed exchange between Kuller and Ellington concerning the electricity of the music, "Hey, this joint sure is jumping! Jumping for Joy!" (Emory Homes 9). One of the guests present, Paul Francis Webster, had been unsuccessfully struggling for nearly a year to convince his show-business friends to support his concept of the *Negro Revue*, which he called *Rhapsody in Black*. Supportive of the idea but not the title, Kuller proceeded to interest other Hollywood guests[4] in the project, and by sunup, a producing organization had been formed called the American Revue Theatre, and nearly $20,000 had been raised—almost half of the $42,000 it cost to produce the show. The rest of the money did not materialize as easily but, eventually, principally through the efforts of actor John Garfield and director Joseph Pasternak who contributed $15,000 on his own, the production of *Jump for Joy* was financed.

Duke Ellington was excited about the project, calling it "a show that would take Uncle Tom out of the theatre, eliminate the stereotyped image that had been exploited by Hollywood and Broadway, and say things that would make the audience think." He also bragged about the interracial mixture in the audience ranging from the Hollywood aristocracy (including Marlene Dietrich, Deanna Durbin, and Martha Raye) to the "sweet-and-low, scuffling-type Negroes" who "always left proudly with their chests sticking out" (*Music Is My Mistress* 175). According to Ellington, 15 writers took part in the production, and since the Duke and his orchestra were on the road during much of the early creative period, his actual contact with the other 14 collaborators was minimal. Typically, Ellington would play a tune over the phone, or mail a lead-sheet to the lyricists and they would create the words independent of his imput. While this is an unusual way of working for most Broadway teams, it established Ellington's pattern of collaboration for the rest of his theatrical career.

Since the band was a central focus of the revue, they were in California for the entire rehearsal period, residing at the 115-room Dunbar Hotel, an all-black establishment on 42nd Place and Central Avenue. Unfortunately, presence does not insure creation, and two weeks into rehearsals, Ellington had completed only about half of the music he had agreed to compose for the show. Henry Blankfort, the production supervisor, in a state of panic, went to Ellington's hotel to hurry things along. He recalls:

> Duke was in the bathtub. Beside him was a stack of manuscript paper, a huge container of chocolate ice cream, a glass of scotch and milk, and Jonesy. Jonesy was his valet, and his job was to keep adding warm water and let out cooling water to maintain a constant temperature in the tub for the Maestro. And Duke was serenely scribbling notes on the paper and then calling to Billy Strayhorn. Billy would take the notes and play them on the beat-up old upright piano in Duke's room. Duke would listen and then write more notes, which he would give to Strayhorn. The band seemed to be all on the same floor of the hotel—like a very long railroad flat—and the sound of Strays at the keyboard was like some kind of signal. Pretty soon you'd hear Ben Webster playing a line, then Ray Nance would start tooting from somewhere down that hall, Sonny Greer would come in with his sticks, and the music would start to form ... Duke writing more and more notes for Sweetpea ... Duke keeping the water just right ... and about four or five hours later, two more songs for the show were finished [Quoted Willard 9].

"Sweetpea," Billy Strayhorn, had joined the Duke's organization in 1939 when he was 24 years old, and quickly became Ellington's musical alter-ego.[5] A talented pianist, composer and arranger, Strayhorn had a major voice in Ellington's creative work, especially the theatrical scores, until his death in 1967. David Hajdu notes that Strayhorn had a hand in at least five songs for *Jump for Joy* including "Rocks in My Bed," "Cindy with the Two Left Feet," "Uncle Tom's Cabin Is a Drive-In Now," and "Bugle Breaks," the only composition in which Strayhorn is cited in the copyright (92). Only "Rocks" and "Bugle Breaks" were composed by Ellington; "Cindy" and "Uncle Tom" were written by white songwriter Hal Borne, and for those tunes, Strayhorn's contribution may have been that of an arranger rather than co-composer. At any rate, Billy Strayhorn received no creative credit on the front page of the program (even Mickey Rooney was credited as one of the show's composers, having contributed a single tune[6]) but was relegated to the list of musical arrangers at the end. Blankfort and Kuller noted that, although Duke Ellington had the drawing power, Strayhorn should have been listed as part of the creative team—so important were his contributions to the score. According to Sid Kuller, "Billy really did write a whole lot for the show. They [he and Ellington] were writing together all the time. They were collaborators in fact, in spirit, in mind, and in talent. When we were writing the thing, sometimes I'd work with Duke, sometimes I'd work with Billy. It didn't matter—we were all writing it, as far as we were concerned" (Hajdu 92).[7]

Although Charlie Chaplin and Orson Welles expressed interest in directing the show, the honor went to Nick Castle, who would later gain celebrity as the choreographer for 20th Century–Fox. Castle assembled a huge 60-member cast that included African American tap dancers and comics as well as Ellington singers Ivie Anderson and Herb Jeffreys, Marie Bryant, a versatile singer-dancer, and a former parking lot attendant named Wonderful Smith. Eighteen-year-old Dorothy Dandridge, soon to become a movie celebrity, was the featured ingénue.

The show the opening night audience saw on 10 July 1941 at the Mayan Theatre in Los Angeles had the following structure:

ACT ONE

1. "Sun-tanned Tenth of the Nation." Lyrics, Paul Webster; Music, Hal Borne, Otis Rene.[8]
2. Tap specialty—Al Guster: "Stomp Caprice." Music, Mercer Ellington.
3. "Brown-Skinned Gal in the Calico Gown." Lyrics, Paul Webster; Music, Duke Ellington. Performed by Herb Jeffreys and Dorothy Dandridge.[9]
4. Sketch: Human Interest. Author, Hal Fimberg. Featuring Pans Ware, Potts Jackson, and Skillet Mayhand.
5. "Bli-Blip." Lyrics, Sid Kuller; Music, Duke Ellington. Performed by Marie Bryant and Paul White.
6. "I Got It Bad and That Ain't Good." Lyrics, Paul Webster; Music, Duke Ellington. Performed by Ivy Anderson and Alice Key.
7. Comic monologue: "A Call to the President." Written and performed by Wonderful Smith.[10]
8. Dance specialty: "Cindy with the Two Left Feet." Lyrics, Paul Webster; Music, Hal Borne.[11]
9. Comic specialty: "Bugle Break," "Subtle Slough." Music, Duke Ellington. Featuring Pans Ware, Potts Jackson, and Skillet Mayhand.
10. "Flame Indigo." Lyrics, Paul Webster; Music, Duke Ellington. Performed by "Garbo."
11. "Mad Scene from Woolworth's." Authors, Langston Hughes, Charles Leonard. Performed by Ivy Anderson, Avanelle Harris, Suzette Johnson, Alice Key, Al Guster, Wonderful Smith.
12. "Shhhh! He's on the Beat!" Lyrics, Sid Kuller, Hal Fimberg; Music, Duke Ellington.
13. "I've Got a Passport from Georgia." Lyrics, Paul Webster, Ray Golden; Music, Hal Borne. Performed by Paul White.
14. Sketch: "Garbo and Hepburn." Author, Sid Kuller. Performed by "Garbo," and Marie Bryant.
15. "The Emperor's Bones." Lyrics, Paul Webster; Music, Otis Rene.
16. "Cymbal Sockin' Sam." Lyrics, Sidney Miller; Music, Mickey Rooney. Performed by Dorothy Dandridge, Sonny Greer.
17. Finale: "Uncle Tom's Cabin Is a Drive-In Now." Lyrics, Paul Francis Webster; Music, Hal Borne.[12]

ACT TWO

1. "Jump for Joy." Lyrics, Sid Kuller, Paul Webster; Music, Duke Ellington.

2. Sketch: "Vignettes." Author, Sid Kuller. Performed by Dorothy Dandridge, Herb Jeffries, Marie Bryant, and Udell Johnson.
3. "Old-Fashioned Waltz." Lyrics, Sid Kuller; Music, Duke Ellington. Performed by Herb Jeffries and dancers.
4. Sketch: "We Aim to Please." Authors, Hal Fimberg, Sid Kuller. Performed by Roy Glenn, Paul White, Skillet Mayhand, and Al Guster.
5. "If Life Were All Peaches and Cream." Lyrics, Paul Webster; Music, Hal Borne. Performed by Dorothy Dandridge, Herb Jeffries, Marie Bryant, and Paul White.
6. Sketch: "Rent Party." Author, Sid Kuller. Performed by members of the band playing "Concerto for Clinkers," with music by Duke Ellington.
7. Sketch: "The Finished Symphony." Author, Richard Weil. Performed by Roy Glenn, and Pans.
8. "Chocolate Shake." Lyrics, Paul Webster; Music, Duke Ellington. Performed by Paul White, Al Guster, Ivy Anderson, and Marie Bryant, plus the ensemble.
9. "Hickory Stick." Lyrics, Paul Webster; Music, Hal Borne. Performed by Dorothy Dandridge, and Pete Nugent.
10. Sketch: "Resigned to Living." Author, Hal Fimberg. Performed by Suzette Johnson, Al Guster, Henry Roberts, Wonderful Smith.
11. "Nothin'." Lyrics, Sid Kuller, Ray Golden; Music, Hal Borne. Performed by Paul White, Ivy Anderson, and the ensemble.
12. Sketch: "Made to Order." Author, Sid Kuller. Featuring Pans Ware, Potts Jackson, and Skillet Mayhand.[13]
13. "Sharp Easter." Lyrics, Sid Kuller; Music, Duke Ellington. Performed by Herb Jeffreys, Marie Bryant, Andrew Jackson, Henry Roberts, "Garbo," Pans Ware, Potts Jackson, and Skillet Mayhand.[14]
14. Finale. Entire cast.

Although the original running order had received good notices from many of the Los Angeles critics,[15] the *Variety* review, 25 July 1941, was not as positive: "Main trouble with 'Jump with Joy' is that it doesn't jump. Rather, and more to the point, it lags." Even worse, the critic was not impressed with the writing: "Original score by Ellington, Hal Borne and a few others hasn't a number worthy a reprise; skits and blackouts are, for the most part, pointless and not too funny." After taking the cast to task, finding only Dorothy Dandridge and the dance specialists, "Pot, Pan, and Skillet," worthy of note, the reviewer concluded: "A Negro revue always whips up an appetite in this town since 'Run Li'l' Chillun' had a long run in the same house. This one looked like a winner and was heavily ballyhooed, but the verdict was negative… Mebbe the piece can be tightened and whipped into acceptable form, but the chances are against it. Material and cast are off the big time beam and 'the dook' can't carry the show by himself."

It is not known whether the memo to Duke Ellington,[16] Jack Boyd, production stage-manager, Joe Stevens, assistant stage-manager, Hal Fimberg, and Sid Kuller suggesting changes in the running order and major alterations to the production came in reaction to the *Variety* notice, or was simply the result of the nightly meetings among the creative team "to discuss, debate, and make decisions as to what should come out of the show the next night" (*Music Is My Mistress* 175).[17] Ellington himself had been uneasy about the lack of blues in the show and was nagging the creative team to fly Big Joe Turner out from New York to appear in the show. In any event, the memo, from producer Henry Blankfort, urged members of the production to lick the problems by the end of the week—a mandate of some urgency in the theatre.

Perhaps unconsciously demonstrating the success of "Bli-Blip" in the original show, the new running order suggested that Wonderful Smith replace Paul White in the opening pantomime, followed by "Bli-Blip" (with three choruses only), "Calico Gown," a reprise of "Bli-Blip" (with a reference to "Calico Gown"), and a sketch involving men in overalls (led by Joe Turner) working in a garden, paying no attention to Judy Carol, but following "Fortune" because of the "fine chops" she's carrying from the market! A running gag with a baton, performed by an actor whistling "Bli-Blip," precedes a sketch entitled, "How to Be Beautiful," which is followed by a specialty dance for Pot, Pan, and Skillet, to the tunes of "Calico Gown" and "Bli-Blip." Wonderful Smith follows with his telephone call to the president, then Joe Turner, dressed in a soldier's uniform, performs "Rocks in My Bed," a new Ellington composition. Three sketches follow: "Noel Coward," "Running Gag"—this time involving an umbrella—and "Rent Party," in which Skillet comes to the party with the umbrella of the previous routine. Al Guster's tap specialty follows, and the act concludes as usual, with a restaged "Uncle Tom's Cabin."

Although the second act opens with the title song, Blankfort's memo demands that something be done to "heat up" the number. A sketch, "You're in the Army Now," precedes a number for Joe Turner, Judy Carol, and the girls, "You and Me," and the hit ballad of the evening, "I Got It Bad," follows another running gag sketch, this time with a coffee pot. "Bli-Blip reappears after the ballad as a specialty dance for Marie Bryant and Paul White," and precedes a literary sketch, "Saroyan," "Hickory Stick," and "Concerto for Clinkers," both from the original show. A new Ellington composition, "Mardi Gras" is expected next, followed by "Nothin'," and "Shhh! He's on the Beat." The end of the running gag routine precedes the original ending of "Made to Order," "Sharp Easter," and "Finale."

Notably absent from the new running order are Mickey Rooney's "Cymbal Sockin' Sam," "Garbo and Hepburn," "Flame Indigo," and "Mad Scene from Woolworth's." While Langston Hughes, who attended the premiere of the revue, suggested that the song was cut because he had asked Duke Ellington for his share of the royalties, he had to admit that the audience response to the piece was poor, even though it was expertly sung by Ivy Anderson (Ampersad 2:26). Dorothy Dandridge had quit early in the run of the show and the new running order makes note of the actress who replaced her, Judy Carol. Joe Turner recalls that when he joined the show, there were no songs written for him, so he performed numbers from his New York Act. A copy of the program in Sampson lists a "Joe Turner" segment with no indication of musical numbers, though "Rocks in My Bed" was clearly part of his repertoire by the end of the run on 27 September 1941. As Turner recalls:

> Duke didn't have no songs for me to sing when I got there, so I just sang some of my songs for awhile until he could write me some. We all lived in the Dunbar, so we would get together and play the piano in Duke's room, and we put together "Rocks in My Bed." He wrote that for me, and I helped him on that. Billy Strayhorn was writing all the arrangements. we did a bunch of songs for me to sing in my spot, and they went over so good that they put me all through the show, had me running back and forth on the stage all the time. Sometimes I sang "Jump for Joy" [Willard 20].

The chorus of the song the producer wanted to feature, "Bli-Blip," is a catchy, blues, rhythm number, divided into easily assimilated eight-bar phrases. The highly syncopated melody line, filled with skips, and scat-like riffs, is accompanied by a steady, repetitive, passacaglia-like bass line that outlines a simple harmonic progression based on seventh chords, with just enough chromaticism for interest. The melody basically outlines an E♭ major triad until bar 7 when the listener is surprised by what sounds like a jazz improvisation that resolves, in bar 8, to a repetition of sixteenth notes a half-step apart. A return to the E♭ major triad in the next six bars is a welcome relief, but even an ear expecting the scat riff is surprised when it returns in bar 15 because of the syncopation of the phrase. The release offers some relief since it is constructed in scale tones with easily discernible leaps. Its simplicity provides an excellent contrast to, and preparation for, the recapitulation of bars 1–8 that follows. Also noteworthy is the arhythmical quality of the melody in which no two bars are exactly alike, and the introduction of the "Charleston" rhythm in bars 6, 14, and 30.

Of like interest is "Sharp Easter," Kuller and Ellington's hip African American version of Irving Berlin's 1933 favorite, "Easter Parade." The lyrics of both numbers revolve around showing off the latest fashions on Easter Sunday but, while Berlin finds sartorial spendour on Fifth Avenue, Kuller sets the promenade in Harlem from Sugar Hill to Central Avenue. Easter bonnets are replaced by wide-brimmed hats and the sophisticated fashions depicted by the *Rotogravure* are replaced by spats, plaids, and suedes. Berlin's lazy, step-wise melody is much more sedate than Ellington's energetic swing tune, with the words "Sharp Easter" emphasized by melodic leaps of a fifth and the syncopated displacement of beats in bars 3 and 4 (See example 2.1).

Example 2.1.

The voicings in the short score suggest a very brassy, full-band arrangement that creates an atmosphere quite different than the typical string and woodwind arrangement of the Berlin classic. Here, and throughout the show, Ellington was demonstrating the similarities as well as the differences between white and black environments, thus attempting a realistic portrait of the African American presented in terms accessible to a mixed audience.

Jump for Joy had always been intended for a New York run. The Los Angeles *Times* 8 July 1941 advertised the show as "Broadway-bound" (1:14), and Paul Francis Webster recalled that even Orson Welles had offered to produce the show at the Mercury Theatre, though his terms were ultimately found to be unacceptable.[18] After *Jump for Joy* closed on 29 September 1941, Derek Jewell recalls Ellington's claim that the show couldn't move on from Los Angeles because of the United States' involvement in World War II, but concludes that, from a more realistic view, "*Jump for Joy* was too far ahead of its time to get commercial backing" (79). Because of the lack of racial stereotyping in the piece, the show was considered by many to be dangerous to both blacks and whites. Ellington's refusal to allow comics to "black up" with cork was initially met with great resistance by many cast members, and the blatant honesty of some of the show's musical numbers and sketches resulted in bomb threats and the beating of various cast members outside the theatre.[19] Political correctness notwithstanding, *Jump for Joy* did serve its purpose. As Ellington recalled in *Music Is My Mistress*, "The show was done on a highly intellectual level—no crying, no moaning, but entertaining, and with social demands as a potent spice. The Negroes always left proudly with their chests sticking out" (175).

The show was revived for a week beginning 19 November 1941 at the Orpheum Theatre in Los Angeles, with most of the original cast performing seven shows a day to SRO audiences. In August of the following year, while Ellington was performing at the Oriental Theatre in Chicago, rumors had begun to spread that *Jump for Joy* would be revived in the "Windy City," but such a production failed to materialize.

An early outline of the show exists in the Ellington Archive (301.4B.5.14) that is significant because it suggests plans for a production of the show in

New York City in the late 1940s. Though the manuscript is undated, references to the United Nations Organization, President Truman, and the novel *Forever Amber* limit the date to 1945–1953, at least four years after *Jump for Joy* opened in Los Angeles, and the continual references to New York critics, and the New York season suggest that this was a production scenario designed for Broadway. In any case, the Duke Ellington band was still central to the structure of the piece.[20] This incarnation of the revue begins with an overture entitled "Evolution of Rhythm," designed to introduce Ellington and his orchestra. After the house goes to black, the sound of a rhythmical pulse, beaten on a hollow log, rings through the theatre. Suddenly, from behind the scrim, we see a "primitive savage" beating the hollow log. Gradually other drum beats are added to the primitive sound, performed first by native Africans circa 1800, then by Afro-Cuban drummers, playing on gourds, maracas, and Cuban tom toms. Finally we hear a riff played on the high-hat and snare drums of a modern jazz percussionist. The drum platform rises on an elevator from the pit and reveals Sonny Greer, Ellington's drummer, dressed in tails, and "going to town" on his drum set. After his solo, a blare of trumpets rises from the pit, and the elevator reveals Duke Ellington conducting his entire orchestra, climaxing in a "hot" performance of one of the several rhythm numbers in the show.

An opening number entitled "Over Here" follows in which a chorus of soldiers sing about the joys of returning home after the war, and ask the question, "What's been going on over here, while we were busy over there." From this question evolves the rest of the show, covering stage, screen, radio, domestic and international politics, literature, and a most significant aspect of contemporary life, love. Following the opening chorus, the Duke turns and faces the audience, expressing his "Credo," that the African American has traditionally been portrayed through "Stephen Foster's glasses." Ellington's monologue is followed by a brief pantomime sketch, "The Ghost Dies," in which a young African American boy is being followed across the stage by a huge menacing ghost, accompanied by horror movie music. When the boy realizes that he is being followed, he turns and shouts "Boo! at the ghost, who collapses in fright. The boy turns to the audience and declares: "I told you, it was only propaganda," and the scene goes to black.

A production number, "Any Old Time in New York" follows, designed to provide the show with "sophistication and grace," because while lovers need "April in Paris," "Tulip Time in Holland," "Springtime in Brazil," to get them in the mood, lovemaking in New York City is possible any old time at all! Another of Duke's monologues follows, this time suggesting that, instead of portraying the stereotypical African American dialect and behavior to which audiences have become accustomed, the show will present African Americans behaving like Noel Coward. A sketch satirizing *Private Lives*, or *Pygmalion*, makes good Ellington's promise. A change of pace, in a blues number with the provocative title, "Give Me Some Good Whiskey and a Bad Woman," immediately follows.

Next comes "The Ballet Strays," a typically traditional ballet, showing dancers frolicking in a meadow, "beautifully costumed with soft lighting, and a pastoral decor." Suddenly from the shepherd's hut emerges a trumpeter who blows a 16-bar riff. The dancers respond with boogie-woogie steps, but when they realize that the jazz dance is out of character, they exit in "traditional ballet style." A short blackout sketch ensues inquiring into the creation of patriotic songs that seem to emerge with every major war. Suddenly we see a couple in the honeymoon suite of the Waldorf Astoria pop up from bed and sing, "We did it before and we will do it again." The ballad "Time Gets Lost" follows with lyrics subtly recalling Rodgers and Hart's "I Didn't Know What Time It Was."

Next comes a novelty piece for the band, "Concerto for Clinkers," in which Johnny Hodges, Lawrence Brown, Harry Carney, Taft Jordan, and Cat Anderson demonstrate "notes that are not supposed to be played on brass instruments" except by great performers.[21] The rousing climax of the number leads to a rhythm song called "Patty Cake for Sweetie Pie" that develops into a dance routine.[22] Next comes "Jungle Law Satire" in which girls, "grinding it out," explain that they are financing their education by exotic dancing. The number leads into a burlesque of the Broadway season called "Life with Mama, or I Remember Papa," in which the Father of *Life with Father*, and Mother of *I Remember Mama* have a few too many drinks after an Actors' Equity meeting and end up in each other's show. The finale of the act, "Rump-de-Dump," begins as a round-table discussion among a group of college professors, exploring the "inevitability of the inevitable." When the philosopher is asked to summarize the discussion, he reduces it to the philosophy of "Rump-de-Dump"—no matter how prepared you get, things will always happen beyond your control, and when they do, accept them with a "Rump-de-Dump."

The second act opens with an orchestral jam session in the aisles of the theatre, converging at the end in the pit for a rousing climax. This leads into the title song, "Jump for Joy," that develops into a rousing singing and dancing finale. A sketch, "The Lost Quart," satirizing the popular film *The Lost Weekend* and filled with physical comedy, follows and leads into a production number, "Love and Plenty of Grand Piano," in which a poor boy serenades a beautiful girl, dancing on a grand piano. A specialty number for the comic female follows in which she reveals her unfortunate relationships with members of the band: the drummer told her to "beat it," the trumpeter told her to "blow," and the alto player said he like "sax" better than "sex." The comic business leads to a blues ballad, "Who Brought You Up—To Bring Me Down," sung by a young man about his unfaithful sweetheart: "I brought you clothes—remodeled your nose / Made you the belle of the town / Don't act so big—or I'll snatch off that wig / Who brought you up—to bring me down."

An extended pantomime sketch entitled "Wish Fulfillment" follows in which a hobo's dream of behaving like a bon-vivant is played out in a café setting. The directions for the scene get quite racy, ending with the loveliest woman in the room throwing herself "into an embrace as long and sensual as the censors will permit," an invocation of the Production Code with which the authors, as Hollywood professionals, would indeed have been familiar. An intimate jam session, featuring a group of Ellington's star musicians follows, called "Fox-Trot for Fox Holes," recalling the fact that wherever the United States army went during World War II, they carried their music with them—even into the foxholes. The musical interlude leads into a comedy scene, "Where Is Harvey?" in which Duke Ellington convinces African American comic Dusty Fletcher that things that seem invisible *really are there* (including the famous rabbit from Mary Chase's play). It is significant to note that the outline has high hopes for this particular routine: "The scene is really a riot, and has never been done on Broadway."

An ensemble number, "Doghouse Blues," demonstrates how a rumor grows as it passes from one person to another, and discovers, in about a dozen choruses, the moral: "Don't believe everything you hear, and only half of what you see." This lengthy piece is followed by a ballad, designed to have commercial appeal, "My Heart's Desire," and a comedy sketch showing what might happen if one had to renew a marriage license every year (like a dog license, or a liquor license). Dante's Cocktail Lounge, a modern inferno, is the scene for the next production number, "The Devil Ain't No Gentleman," depicting the young ladies of today being led astray by the devil, portrayed as a "modern wolf." A sketch determining that the official language of the United Nations should be jive follows in which member nations "beat it out" in the interests of international security. An undetermined ballet production number is next on the list followed by a comedy monologue entitled, "A Call to the President," recalling Wonderful Smith, the radio comic, who made a personal call to President Roosevelt, and suggesting that the show's comic could make a personal call to President Truman.

The scenario ends with a series of notes listing possible songs and sketches for consideration. This included special material, "The Lost Chord," and "Saturday Night Is for Sex," ballads, "That Ain't for Me and That's for Sure," "Pardon My Heart," and the generic "songs," "What Have You Got When You Haven't Got Love," and "I'm Just a CPA Who's in Love with a Ph.D.," sketches, "Radio Satire," and "Forever Ambush" (a burlesque of the popular novel, *Forever Amber*), production numbers, "Harlem Airshaft," "Atomic Jive," and "Braggin' in Brass," a comedy trio, "Molotov, Bevin, and Byrnes," a rhythm number, "Suddenly It Jumped," and a blues number, "Go Away Blues." While there is no further documentation regarding the project and its New York incarnation, the existence of the outline suggests Ellington's tendency to stay with certain projects over the years, rethinking, revising, until they either emerge as a finished, produceable piece, or are fragmented into their constituent elements and reassembled as another work. *Jump for Joy* will have one more incarnation before Ellington will put it to rest, a production in Miami Beach, Florida, in January 1959. But, before he can conclude his creative efforts with the "sun-tanned revu-sical," another unfinished project will return to haunt him.

A letter dated 22 March 1951 from Kaj Gynt to Ellington reveals the truth of Langston Hughes's prediction, a decade earlier, in the letter to Arna Bontemps. Writing from the home of Warner Oland's widow in Carpinteria, California, to Ellington on tour at the Orpheum Theatre in Omaha, Nebraska, Ms. Gynt continues the saga of *Cock o' the World*, full of enthusiasm over a promised production:

> Dear Duke,
>
> Please forgive me for not having sent you this part of the manuscript sooner. I have just not been able to work because of the darned flu, and I hope you can read the script as it is, until I can send you a better one. The *first* scene of the *second* act I will mail you tomorrow. I just have not been able to work on it.
>
> The synopsis I sent you a year and a half ago to Chicago was simply a synopsis of the "old version" of the play. I sent it to you at that time to refreshen your memory.
>
> The second act as is now is a revised version, in spots rewritten, in others entirely new. And far better than originally. It is also far shorter, since we must confine the play to 2 and a half hours, or such.
>
> I am thrilled over that it finally will be produced. I know you are too.
>
> I am so sorry that I had to see you, when I was so ill and almost disfigured. I will be better next time.
>
> Please explain to the young beauty you brought along that I was certain she could sing, when she perhaps was a society girl, and had no desire whatsoever to be in a show. When I called her "Africa," I meant the girl Cocko calls "Africa" in the "Devil Bush" in the play. According to George Landy the line that *she is Africa*, is the finest line in the whole play.
>
> Landy has not as yet heard from Langston, but wants me to send the play immediately just the same, so that he can get it to Hammerstein.
>
> I know you will write mighty fine music for Cocko. It will be a joy to hear it. Take care of yourself, and drive carefully.
>
> With love faithfully yours,
> Kaj Gynt

At the Ellington Archive (301.4B.4.3), Gynt's letter accompanies a draft of the second act which offers a telling view of the scope of the musical.

The draft begins with a prologue to Act 2, in which bodies are at work and play in Africa on river and land. A voice chants about the beauties of Africa: animals, people, etc. Flute and drums suggest marching feet. This atmospheric scene leads directly into Act 2, Scene 1, subtitled, "Addis Ababa."

Enter a group of soldiers marching in celebration; everyone is happy. Hailie Selassie's army is leaving for the front. After the regular army come the volunteers and miscellaneous fighting forces, the last ones carrying spears, homemade weapons, etc. This march becomes syncopated jazz. The "strutting" characters, Buster and Frog, look for their friend, Cocko. They have walked from the palace all the way to town searching for him. Cocko enters with a Somali girl; this does not surprise Buster and Frog because they know their friend is a real ladies' man. Cocko pays a shop keeper to translate what the girl is saying, and he learns that she wants to be a camp-wife. The friends are stopped by some soldiers, and arrested as Italian spies. Cocko, Buster, and Frog show their passports to get out of trouble, but the soldiers warn them to beware of spies hovering in the vicinity. Cocko sings "Cock o' the World" to the Somali girl, but his attention soon wanders to the Arabian cafe, across the street, where there are musicians, posters, and Fatima, among the girls who dance for money. Having promised to bring Fatima back to New Orleans with him, Cocko goes over to her and proceeds to impress her with his large wad of bills. Meanwhile, since Frog and Buster are loaded down with luggage, like a new group of slaves who have just entered, they are drafted into the army—in other words, hijacked. After Fatima manages to divest Cocko of his money, he too is enlisted into military service.

The scene changes to the desert at night, subtitled, "Chain Gang." Frog, Buster, and Cocko are chained with the other slaves, and while they sleep, they are sold for 1,000 gold pieces. When they awake, they are astonished and angry when they realize that they have been sold to the Bakarab mines. They and the others sing "The Chant of the Slaves" as they walk perilously in the sun. A sand storm marks the change of scene to a diamond mine in Africa ("Diamonds"). Cocko tells the Foreman (15 years a slave himself) that he came from America to find his country, the *Real Africa*, and his ancestors. He wanted to learn more about the country, but he thought that his homeland would be a lazy place where one does not have to work, with fun, food and sun, but he has yet to see *that* Africa. The "Miner's Song" is sung by the slaves, then Buster sings "My Little Black Diamond," describing the dreams it might inspire if he had it, and the rest of the men join in. Cocko cheers himself up by the talk of stealing diamonds for some girls, but turmoil follows when he and the men begin to sing a freedom chant. The scene ends with the sound of guns and shouting mixed with a medley of dancing diamond girls, voices of barkers selling and wanting to buy diamonds, merchants with diamonds for sale—a frenzy of noise and voices.

Scene 4: "Jungle" ("Real Africa"). In the jungle of Cocko's dreams, lush and cool, he sings "I'm on ma journey now." He loves the jungle, feels safe, has a large diamond, and he could stay there forever, singing "To fling my arms wide." The scene changes to "The Puberty Bush" (or Devil's Bush) where young girls of the tribe are sent on the eve of puberty to live in seclusion away from men, and to learn the art of love from the older women. Young maidens enter and sing "Flowers in my hair." Lolidjeh, the young, beautiful maiden betrothed to the native Chief, is already onstage. A fat native named Mamba takes care of these girls; she was in New York and thinks she knows the American language, but she sounds comic. Cocko appears, not knowing any better, and kisses all the girls; but he is especially enchanted by Lolidjeh, and calls her *Africa* (the beauty of Africa he had expected in women of this country). Mamba runs to call the Chief. The scene changes to the village. A bound Cocko is brought before the Chief, still struggling to break free. The Chief has been to Oxford and speaks perfect English. He wants money in reparation for Cocko's having soiled Lolidjeh, and as a tribute for taking her as a wife, since he doesn't want her now. Unfortunately, all Cocko has is a large diamond, and diamonds are too plentiful in the jungle to be of any value. The Chief sentences him to go into the jungle, where no one can survive, but, suddenly, Cocko remembers the word, "kalulu" which his mother mentioned, and the utterance of it makes all the natives jump. Cocko sings "Kalulu," about being king over all of Africa, and orders the villagers to dance, which they do, to wild African music. However, in the dance, the witchdoctors advance and push Cocko into the jungle. Lolidjeh dissolves in tears.

Scene 6: "Veldt." Before the curtain, Cocko walks alone, unhurt from the jungle, on his way to the port town from which he will sail home with his friends. He sings "The Leavin' Song," and admires the diamond he carries with him, claiming that "Those glitterin' bright stars up there in heaven are nothin' to this lil' diamond o' mine!" The scene changes to "Chez Dinah-Belle." Guests arrive, including Cocko, now dressed in a business suit, strutting between Prince Achmed of Egypt and the wealthy Henri. They sing "Claire de Lune." His two friends constantly call him Pierrot (after the romantic character who sighed for the moon), and Cocko does not appear concerned. A frolicsome party ensues. The stunning Dinah-Belle stands in the doorway and sings "L'amour Diable." Cocko's rich friends had first heard him sing at a waterfront cafe and introduce him to Dinah-Belle, thinking that the two have something in common—song. At the insistence of his friends, Cocko sings "Water Boy," and, growing very homesick during the party, reprises "I'm on ma journey now!" The guests on the patio sway to the rhythm of a waltz, and dancers begin filling the stage. Frog and Buster are seated, like cats, with banjos on their knees. Cocko dreamily sings "The Snake Eye Blues" (or "Dream of Home" refrain, an alternative suggested in the script). Singing amidst phantom shadows, Cocko wants to go home, but Dinah-Belle waltzes into his arms, and they dance. Suddenly, Cocko "hears" a whistle blow on a boat to take him (and the audience) home, and hums the refrain to "Leavin' Time."

Scene 8: An alley beneath the wall of Dinah-Belle's. Cocko, Frog and Buster drop down from the party, only to be caught by sitting soldiers. Claiming to be friends of Dinah-Belle's, and the singers and dancers, they sing "Lilli Marlene" or "Madame from Armentiere" for the soldiers. The scene quickly changes to "Mardi Gras," New Orleans, the stage displaying the side view of Madame Mclaine's courtyard. On a balcony ladies drink and flirt, and Leota tends bar. A crowd of people are milling on this level, and the "Cake-walk" is heard being played by the piano and a jug-band coming from the Serenade Wagon. Cocko enters suddenly, returning to his mother, Mammy Bless 'Em. Madame Mclaine and the other girls crowd around them. They tease him about his promise to come home with riches and women, but Cocko quiets them down with a display of large denominations of cash and a reprise of "Cock o' the World." He announces that he has returned home to marry Leota. Everyone sings "Snake Eye Blues" in celebration and the curtain falls amid a great deal of festivity and cheering.

It is not surprising why Ellington, desiring to portray African American soul in his music, would be attracted to Ms. Gynt's modern morality musical. It has all the elements of the earliest African American musicals with the hero, a poor black American, returning to his native soil, some primitive environment, where he will discover wealth and or happiness, if only within himself. The parallels go back to J. Rosamond Johnson, Jesse Shipp, and Alex Rogers's *Mr. Load of Koal* (1909) and will continue on to Ellington's own *Queenie Pie* (produced 1986). The great misfortune is the lack of any music created by Ellington specifically labeled for this show.

Among the unidentified manuscripts in the Ellington collection there exists a two-page fragment in Ellington's hand entitled "Background Music." The first motif and its development (See Ex. 2.2) is labeled "Dock arrival" and the broken chord motif, beginning in quarter note triplets and becoming eight notes—to suggest an increase of movement or activity, such as an engine warming up or a crowd gathering—is labeled "suggestion when Whistle Blows." The augmented fourth, suggestive of the Lydian mode, draws the listener out of the diatonic major of the broken chord motif and is both bluesy and dramatic in the way that it provides tension in an otherwise simple harmonic fabric. A few bars later, a character named "Sporty" is announced in the manuscript and two bars later women are singing, "If you love me, pretty papa." The locale of the dock, the name Sporty and the presence of seductive women suggests the opening of Act Two, Scene 9 of *Cock o' the World*, set in New Orleans where Creole Belles flirt with passers-by and Sporty Joe appears with a bevy of girls surrounding him. While the evidence is circumstantial,

Example 2.2

the identification of a character by name in the manuscript and the presence of similar activity in both text and score make a good case, especially given the recent discovery of other fragments that correspond to the titles of Langston Hughes's lyrics. Unidentified manuscripts in the Strayhorn Estate reveal titles that are associated with *Cock o' the World* and identified as "Lyrics by Langston Hughes: 'I'll Drop My Anchor with You,' 'Dream City,' 'Kalulu,' 'Little Savage,' 'I Own the World,' 'After the Ship Is Gone,' 'Cock o' the World,' 'Land of Sun,' 'My Little Black Diamond,' and 'Somewhere in Someone.'" Because of Strayhorn's ability to realize Ellington's intentions musically, he may have set Hughes's lyrics when Duke was too busy to attend to the project. Once the collection is made available to researchers, we will perhaps learn more about who wrote what for this fascinating show.

Three

"I'm Afraid I'll Live"

On January 30, 1943, *Collier's Magazine* featured a human interest story by Harry Henderson and Sam Shaw entitled "This Strange Bright Land." It narrated the adventures of British sailors on leave in New York City while their ships were dry-docked for repairs. Teeming with winsome photographs of His Majesty's tars—"bungup and bilge-free" for the camera—the article reminded its readers of the natural wonders of the United States by examining them through the eyes of young, handsome, and naive British seamen.[1] With an emphasis on "wine, women, and slang,"[2] Henderson and Shaw apotheosized Yankee food ("America is a land where a man can order a steak and get it."), bars ("All America runs on a twenty-four-hour day and you can obtain anything you want at any time because none of the natives live on a fixed schedule."), standard of living ("If you visit a home, do not be surprised to find it has an electric refrigerator as well as such labor-saving devices as an electric vacuum cleaner, washing machine and ironer."), and cleanliness ("Their cities, compared to ours, are much cleaner, and in the summer the streets of cities like New York are washed."), but warned that, compared to British women, American girls "are more interested in careers in business, in which they regard themselves on as equal footing with men." With a subtle jibe at Yankee slang ("if a native says "Are you kidding?" in a most serious way after you have made some remark, merely smile and keep on with your story.") the feature concludes as innocuously as it began, cementing sturdy, sanguine Anglo-American relations.

Today, such a human interest feature might prompt a cynical smile or two but would hardly earn the popularity that Henderson and Shaw's two-page sketch engendered in the 40s. So beloved was *Collier's* piece that the authors began to search out ways to exploit their gold mine. Three months after the article first appeared, the international phenomenon called *Oklahoma!* opened in New York to rave reviews and changed the face of musical theatre. As Bordman notes in his *American Musical Theatre: A Chronicle*, *Oklahoma* "rejected the topical and even the contemporary and instead embraced a sentimental look at bygone Americana. For the most part it also rejected wit and patently polished sophistication for a certain earnestness and directness" (534). Rodgers and Hammerstein's first collaboration had become the motherlode of musicals, and every tunesmith and hack writer was ready to leap onto the bandwagon. Henderson and Shaw were no exception. After all, their "story" had already capitalized on the naive charm and sentimental jingoism so critically acclaimed in *Oklahoma!*, even if it turned on British sailors instead of American cowboys.[3] All they needed for a hit was to hire a composer, a lyricist, and a book writer!

It is not surprising that Duke Ellington was attracted to the project from the start. All of his musical theatre work until 1943 had been focused on African American themes and rhythms and, like Bob Cole who sought to rival the work of white composers and lyricists in order to demonstrate the ability of the African American composer to compete on an equal basis (Woll 6),[4] the Duke aspired to break through into Rodgers and Hammerstein territory. Always concerned about the injustices of racial discrimination, the Duke saw this project as an opportunity to explore prejudice and cultural difference in terms that would be accessible to a heterogeneous audience. As he noted when he was composing *Jump for Joy*, "I think a statement of social protest in the theatre should be made without saying it" (Mercer Ellington 94). In addition, Ellington loved the British. As he notes in *Music Is My Mistress*:

> To me, the people of London are the most civilized in the world. Their civilization is based on the recognition that all people are imperfect, and due allowances should be and are made for their imperfections. I have never experienced quite such a sense of *balance* elsewhere. What is cricket, and what is not, is very well understood by everybody. And hysteria is something you may sometimes hear about there, but you never are exposed to it except at a very great distance. Self-discipline, as a virtue or an acquired asset, can be invaluable to anyone [140].

In his chapter on Ellington's "Trip to England," Collier adds that the British "saw him not merely as a successful bandleader but as a major American composer whose music had a value beyond providing entertainment for big-spending tourists at the Cotton Club" (152), and Constant Lambert, music critic of the *London Referee,* called Ellington "a composer of uncommon merit, probably the first composer of real character to come out of America" (Nicholson 157). So, when the authors of a magazine piece of which he was especially fond approached him about collaborating on a musical adaptation, Ellington, invigorated by the possibility of a Broadway venture, jumped at the opportunity.

As lyricist, Ellington suggested Bob Russell, the wordsmith responsible for two of the Duke's greatest hits, "Don't Get Around Much Anymore," and

"I Didn't Know About You," as well as the popular "Do Nothin' Till You Hear From Me," "Ring Around the Moon," "Chicken Feed," and "Warm Valley." Though Russell was a Broadway neophyte, his earlier lyrics for Ellington subtly tapped into the colloquialisms so important to the original *Collier's* feature. Conversational, "hip," and sentimental, Bob Russell's words were an apt accompaniment to Ellington's jazzy melodies, and the authors hoped that they might soon rival the Broadway lyrics of the "Americana School" established by Oscar Hammerstein. The vernacular tone that Russell was to bring to Broadway wasn't new. It wouldn't be the "hip" urbanity of a Cole Porter lyric, filled with sexual innuendo and a shopping list of topical references; nor would it be the clever rhyming of Lorenz Hart or Ira Gershwin, each of whom were writers of their own indigenous brand of wit. Rather, Russell's lyrics look back to those of George M. Cohan and P.G. Wodehouse, whose songs demonstrated a commingling of up-to-date colloquialisms with middle-class sentiment, wrapped up endearingly in the American flag.

With the songwriting team in place, the next artist to join the creative team was not the librettist but the designer, Boris Aronson. Aronson was a Russian émigré and resident designer for the Yiddish Art Theatre until 1932 when he moved to Broadway with *Walk a Little Faster*, a musical revue by Vernon Duke, E.Y. Harburg, and S.J. Perlman. Following that project, he moved to the Group Theatre where he designed *Awake and Sing* and *Paradise Lost*, both by Clifford Odets, George Abbott's *Three Men on a Horse*, William Saroyan's *The Time of Your Life*, and Irwin Shaw's *The Gentle People*. Leaving the Group Theatre in 1939, he designed *Cabin in the Sky*, a musical by John Latouche and Vernon Duke in 1940, and *What's Up*, the first of the Alan Jay Lerner–Frederick Loewe collaborations, in 1943. Between these shows, Aronson created designs for two musicals that never were produced: *44 Simple Mistakes, or What's Wrong with This Picture*, written to feature the clowning of Ed Wynn, and *Miss Underground*, a circus musical set in Paris during the Occupation by Vernon Duke and Lorenz Hart (Hart's only non–Rodgers show). Although the 40s were considered "a lean period in Aronson's career" (Rich and Aronson 79), given all of the new faces to Broadway on the creative team, Boris Aronson's presence gave the project a dose of solid experience.

All of Aronson's professional credentials, however, could not counterbalance the inexperience of the neophyte librettist chosen to create the text for the show. Sandy Morrison was a journalist acquaintance of Harry Henderson and Sam Shaw who had written a number of plays produced successfully by amateur theatre groups. As a journalist-playwright he had received pleasant enough nods from second and third-string critics that were sufficient to inflate his résumé but not to teach him the craft of playwriting. So, late in 1943, in Duke's office at 1619 Broadway, the collaborators gathered: the two original authors armed with the confidence that their magazine essay would transfer into a sure-fire hit; the librettist armed with amateur theatre credits; Ellington and Russell armed with international recording hits; and Boris Aronson—the only member of the creative team who had ever done a Broadway show—craving another successful musical after a series of misses.

Almost immediately the project was in trouble. Not from incompatibility among the creators—everyone was almost too amenable. Problems arose instead from Ellington's commitments. As John Edward Hasse notes, the performance of *Black, Brown and Beige* at Carnegie Hall on 23 January 1943 "altered his reputation and patterns of composing and performing. In addition to his other mantles, from now on, he would wear that of concert artist" (264). This gave rise to a series of concert performances at that hallowed venue for each of which Ellington was expected to compose a new concert piece. At the December concert in 1943 Ellington premiered his piano concerto, *New World a-Comin'*, and the following year, the Duke added *Blue Cellophane*, *Frantic Fantasy*, *Air Conditioned Jungle*, and the Ellington-Strayhorn collaboration, *Perfume Suite*, to the list of concert pieces performed at Carnegie Hall. Add to that Ellington's supper club bookings which, inevitably, ran longer than projected (the band was booked for five weeks at The Hurricane at 51st and Broadway but ended up playing for six months)[5] and it became clear to all concerned that *This Strange Bright Land* would have to wait until Ellington's desk was clear.

When Ellington sat down in earnest to work on the show early in 1945, the face of Broadway was different than it had been two years earlier. *Oklahoma!* was still running strong but, with 882 performances, the outstanding success of *Follow the Girls* (1944), "more in the dying line of rowdy modern musicals" than the Rodgers and Hammerstein type of musical play (Bordman 541) demonstrated that "glorified burlesque" was far from dead. With a cast filled with spit-and-polished soldiers and bedizened chorines, and set in a servicemen's canteen, *Follow the Girls* was simply a show that the authors of *This Strange Bright Land* could not ignore. But just as the creative team began to shift toward a more old-fashioned type of soldier show, another significant phenomenon occurred on Broadway to alter the format of the musical: the revival of Gilbert and Sullivan's *H.M.S. Pinafore*. Ever since *Pinafore* burst on to American soil in 1878 it was a huge success, giving rise to imitations, adaptations, and burlesques.[6] The recent revivals in New York by the Boston Comic Opera (1942) and R.H. Burnside (1944) gave rise to two Pinafore-based extravaganzas: *Memphis Bound*, which scrambled Gilbert and Sullivan with a heavy dose of Americana, and *Hollywood Pinafore*, a satire of the film industry to Sullivan's music. Both shows arrived in 1945 and achieved decent reviews if not long runs.[7] Chapman in the *Daily News*, for example, found *Memphis Bound* "as good-natured as a puppy, and frequently very smart," the adjective he also applies to George S. Kaufman's lyrics in *Hollywood Pinafore*. Wilella Waldorf, reviewing *Memphis Bound* for the *Post*, noted that "the modernized *Pinafore* is interesting musically and often very funny as presented by the showboaters" and concludes that in *Hollywood Pinafore*, "Mr. Kaufman is the only modern playwright we can think of at the moment who would dare to tamper with Gilbert without getting shot for it." Though neither show lasted longer than a month, the *H.M.S. Pinafore* phenomena left a lasting impression on *This Strange Bright Land*, newly christened *H.M.S. Times Square*.

Finally, late in 1945, a draft of the musical amalgam of *Oklahoma!*, *Follow the Girls*, and *H.M.S. Pinafore* was complete. The first Broadway show to feature Fiorello LaGuardia, the mayor of New York from 1933 to 1945, as a song and dance man, *H.M.S. Times Square* presented the following cast of characters:[8]

Hughie Short, a British Sailor on leave in New York,[9]
Sandra, a torch singer at the Club Flamingo,[10]
Cameo Sherman, the proprietor of the Club Flamingo,[11]
Joan Quinn, the nightclub photographer,
Mayor LaGuardia, the "*Hat* himself in song and dance,"
Eagle Joe, an Iroquois Shill on Times Square,
Louie, the waiter,
Pitchmen, City Auditors, Councilmen, the "Underground" of LaGuardia's government in exile,
Walter Winchell.[12]

The first scene of Act One begins in Times Square with a "Runyonland" kind of choreographed sequence in which characters and their environment are introduced. It is noteworthy that Ellington's show anticipates the device used by Loesser and his librettists five years later in *Guys and Dolls.* A song ("We're in There Pitchin'") follows, defining the objective of the various shills at work in Times Square. Into this den of thieves enters Hughie Short who, having been accosted by the pitchmen, ends up buying the deed to Manhattan Island for $24.11 (all the money he has) and an I.O.U. for a pair of nylon stockings. The scene changes to the Club Flamingo where Sandra is sultrily crooning the first of Ellington's "nightclub performance" songs ("A Woman and a Man"). During the song, we learn in dialogue that Cameo Sherman, the proprietor, is trying to cover his tracks, having defrauded the city of New York, and that the mayor, Fiorello LaGuardia, is trying to clean things up. At the end of Sandra's number, Short enters and asks directions to the Stork Club. He and Sandra are attracted to one another only long enough to sing a novelty duet (no title or lyrics are supplied in the typewritten manuscript). Spotting an easy mark, Cameo decides to pad Hughie's nightclub bill. Vaudeville-like comic business follows with the overcharging of add-on items such lettuce, crackers, butter, etc. where everything extra costs $5. Eventually the sailor spills the pepper (for which he is charged $5), sneezes (another $5), and Sandra blurts out "Gesundheit" (which costs him an additional $5).

Without the cash to pay his overly inflated bar bill, Hughie begs for credit. Realizing his only possession is the deed to Manhattan, he brandishes it, hoping it will buy him time and or credit. Unwilling to accept the deed in lieu of cash, Cameo threatens to bury Short in a vat of lime. Suddenly, the sailor who had been viewing New York from the perspective of a glamorous tour book (filled with all of the positive stereotypes about Manhattan), becomes truly frightened. Arguing the possibility of good publicity for the club, Hughie convinces the proprietor to present the deed on his behalf in court. In addition, Cameo hires the innocent tar as a waiter to insure that he works off his bar bill.

Scene Three is a radio broadcast taking place "in one" (in front of the traveler curtain). In his own inimitable, gossipy style, Walter Winchell reports the details of the court battle, hyperbolizing the historical significance and precedence of the event. Cut to the Supreme Court, where the case is now being tried only to find the Supreme Court judges singing in patter like the judges in *Of Thee I Sing*, the 1931 Pulitzer Prize musical by Kaufman, Ryskind and the brothers Gershwin. Not content with simply relying on the current popularity of the Gilbert and Sullivan idiom, the authors of *H.M.S. Times Square* hedge their bets by borrowing one of the signature devices from possibly the most celebrated political musical to date.

Scene Four brings us back to Club Flamingo where we find Hughie mopping the floors and commenting on the American way of life. This is actually the only point in the text where lines from the original *Collier's* feature are used. But life for the British sailor is not all bilgewater and heartache: he has dreams ("I Wanna Stop and Go") and a girl, the club photographer Joan, who enters just in time to sing a love song (unspecified in the typed manuscript). Jealous of Joan's hold on the sailor and sent to steal the deed to Manhattan away from him, Sandra interrupts the lovers' reverie of a better life once Hughie can quit the nightclub (a situation parallel to that of most wartime romances when life is expected to improve considerably upon discharge from the service). Joan leaves and Sandra goes in for the kill. To put Hughie at ease, she offers to get Cameo to forget his bar bill, then playfully seduces him, undressing him just enough to get possession of the deed. Realizing he's been duped, Hughie engages in a fair amount of clever physical maneuvering to reclaim the document and succeeds, just moments before we learn that his deed to Manhattan is in fact valid (the Gilbertian judges of the Supreme Court have ruled in its favor). In an obvious parody of Gilbert's "I've Got a Little List" from *The Mikado*, the sailor sings of his plans for New York, now that he owns it.[13]

Scene Five follows as a crossover scene during which Cameo continues his attempts to rob Hughie of the deed, by sending out either a myriad of leggy B-girls to seduce him, or a gang of B-movie henchmen to mug him.

Scene Six takes place in Mayor LaGuardia's office where the city council is blaming the mayor for allowing the city to be sold right under his nose ("Where Is the Mayor, What's He Waiting For?"). After the choral diatribe, a Gilbert and Sullivan hallmark, Hughie enters and the following vaudeville turn is exchanged:

> LAGUARDIA: I like you, Short.
> HUGHIE: Thank you, Mr. Mayor. I like you short, too.

Following the laugh at the expense of Fiorello's size, Cameo rushes in to announce that Hughie is taking over the mayor's office. When Short protests, the proprietor reminds him of his outstanding debt and forces him to acquiesce. From dialogue between Cameo's cronies who have followed him on-stage, we learn that Cameo intends to move a gambling casino into the city hall and the mayor's office into the Club Flamingo. All of this has occurred just as Mayor LaGuardia and Hughie were about to make a radio broadcast. With Fiorello caught short and Hughie speechless, Sandra takes the microphone and announces in song that the city has a new mayor who will make Manhattan one big Times Square! In typical musical comedy fashion, the ensemble echoes her sentiments and the curtain falls on Act One.

Act Two opens outside the Club Flamingo. Sandra and Cameo are discovered discussing the scam. She is reluctant to pursue it but he is adamant.[14] He even suggests that she marry Hughie if that is what it will take to get her hands on the deed to Manhattan Island. A brief reprise of "A Woman and a Man" leads us into Scene Two, the Mayor's Office at the Club Flamingo. While "Lord Mayor" Short is getting a haircut, a radio technician enters with a microphone and Cameo Sherman follows. Before Cameo can get a word in, the barber starts complaining that Short's mayorship has not been the boon that the proprietor had promised. Hughie chimes in with the fact that he's beginning to enjoy the office but complains about the traffic in New York City and the inconvenience of driving on the wrong side of the street. Before Sherman can utter a complete sentence in defense of the American way of life, six wizened septuagenarians enter. Catching sight of the ubiquitous chorus girls, they suddenly revive and dance around like hyper-active children, singing an unspecified comic novelty song.

After the song, Cameo cons the Lord Mayor into making him *Commissioner of Marriage*, and Hughie, exhausted from the morning's activities, goes on the air to announce a recipe for boiled rice.[15] Another gaggle of chorus girls enters (this time from a raided Broadway show), followed by Sandra who makes yet another play for the sailor. Cameo begins to assume more and more power under the aegis of *Commissioner of Marriage*. For example, he rationalizes that if love and romance flourish on the highways, he should administer the highways. Midway through his delusions of grandeur which include a mass marriage scheme in Times Square, the finance commissioner enters to complain about the Lord Mayor's inability to balance the city budget. Cameo suggests that to do that job properly, Hughie should be married since "married people know how to balance budgets." Completely rattled, Short proposes to Sandra and kisses her just as Joan makes an entrance, perfectly timed for her to witness the whole thing. Noticing her, Hughie abruptly drops Sandra and rushes to Joan in an attempt to explain, but a troop of Boy Scouts enters suddenly and separates them.[16] Disgusted by the whole affair, Joan sings "It Couldn't Have Happened to a Sweeter Guy" and the scene changes to Sandra's bedroom, above the Club Flamingo.

Alone, Sandra reveals a sympathetic side to her personality, singing "What Is a Woman to Do?" but returns to the hard-as-nails persona when Cameo enters to announce that he is going into the blackmail business. She opposes his scheme to marry her off to the Lord Mayor even though he guarantees that the marriage will be performed by a bogus minister. Because she views even a counterfeit marriage as an "extreme measure," Sandra continues to plead for alternatives. But Cameo is deaf to her reasoning and beefs up his arguments with simulated sentiment ("Love Is Everything"). Sufficiently affected by the song to imagine that she might really be in love with Hughie, Sandra sends for the Lord Mayor. Sherman leaves and the Indian flimflammer, who sold Short the deed to Manhattan Island in the first scene, appears in the dark. Mistaking him for Hughie, Sandra tells him that they've got to be married immediately. Unexpectedly, Cameo knocks at the door. Sandra tells Hughie (the Indian) to hide. He rummages through a pile of Sandra's clothes until he finds a pair of silk stockings, after which he dives under her bed. Cameo enters to report that the Lord Mayor has disappeared and asks Sandra if she has any idea where he is. After a long comic routine exploring the most ridiculous ways of looking for Hughie in Sandra's bedroom, Cameo leaves. As soon as he is out the door, the phone rings. It's the Lord Mayor. Sandra realizes that the man beneath her bed is not the British sailor but an Indian and screams.

Scene Four, at the Penny Arcade, opens with a ballet of soldiers, sailors and girls.[17] Joan runs into Hughie who explains that, though he still loves her deeply, he feels he must marry Sandra for the good of the city. At the moment, however, he is enjoying the shooting gallery so much that he doesn't want to be mayor or marry Sandra. Joan advises him to do the "right" thing; after all he "represents America and the political machine and white knights everywhere!" Hughie leaves to do his duty, and Joan sings the big blues "ballad" of the show, "I'm Afraid I'll Live," in which Joan likens love sickness to actual physical maladies—loss of appetite, weight loss, sleeplessness—highly reminiscent in tone and perspective to "I Wish I Were in Love Again," from Rodgers and Hart's 1937 hit, *Babes in Arms.*

Scene Five opens on the site of LaGuardia's "government in exile" on a deserted beach in Brooklyn to the strains of "Ode to Brooklyn," an alphabet song evocative of George M. Cohan's "H-A- Double R-I-G-A-N" from *Fifty Miles from Boston* (1908). The "government-in-exile" aspect of the libretto is indebted to the 1933 Kaufman, Ryskind, Gershwin musical, *Let 'Em Eat Cake* where the convoluted plot is resolved by a baseball game between the Supreme Court and the League of Nations.[18] Here LaGuardia's counter-revolutionary forces in Dodger baseball uniforms plan to attack the mass marriage day planned by Cameo in Times Square ("I'm Gonna Say No," a novelty song answering the question "do you take this woman for your lawful wedded wife?"). Joan has joined the resistance followed by Hughie, who has come to Brooklyn to beg LaGuardia to return to the mayor's office. Evidently the city has gone amuck with the BMT turning into the Pennsylvania Railroad and ending up in Punxatawney! Having refused phone offers of the mayoralty in other cities, LaGuardia turns down Short's request, saying that his interest now lies in developing his post-war program for the City of New York. A concerted musical fantasy (not unlike the "Somewhere" sequence in *West Side Story* a dozen years later) follows in which the following episodes occur:

1. A dozen men and women sing "I Got a Steady Job,"
2. Streamlined baby carriages cross the stage accompanied by a song about babies,
3. A stork flies in carrying a diaper to the tune of "Something Always Needs Changing,"
4. Children on their way home from school perform a leap-frog ballet singing:

   "No more teachers, no more books.
   No more teachers' dirty looks!"[19]
5. A song about playgrounds,
6. A song about romance in a safe, clean city environment,
7. A song about international diplomacy anticipating a world with nation-helping nations.

After the musical fantasy, Hughie replies: "Coo! what an idea! The world's like one big apartment house." Another Dodger-clad member of the resistance named Mr. Kelly further endorses the idea with an exuberant song about a "New World of Happy People" and the scene changes to Sandra in a phone booth calling to tell her mother about the wedding and singing an unspecified "specialty" number.

Scene Six opens on Times Square just before the *Marriage Day* ceremonies. After an ensemble novelty song characterizing Broadway's conception of love, the four principals enter in a dither: Short wants to call the wedding off, Sandra doesn't want to be left at the altar, Cameo continues to push for a wedding, and Joan raises a loud voice against the entire concept of *Marriage Day*. In response to the bickering which by now has reached deafening proportions, the officiating minister suddenly goes into a kind of fast jive patter encouraging the group to "let love win out." LaGuardia rushes in and proposes to officiate at the ceremonies but his offer is declined by the *Commissioner of Marriage*, saying that it would make the proceedings legal. Impulsively, Cameo professes his love for Sandra and Hughie finally proposes to Joan. Knowing a good thing when he sees it, LaGuardia sings a song about the various kinds of love: love that is talked about, love that is felt, larger-than-life love that is found only in the movies, and the unmeasurable kind of love that is "real."

LaGuardia marries the couples (as well as the entire coupled chorus) and receives the deed to Manhattan in payment. Like a bolt from the blue, the Indian appears only to quip: "You should have given that back to the Indians!" and runs off. The chorus steps forward for a reprise of "Now There's Love and *Love*" when the music stops abruptly for the entrance of a dignified gray-haired man who announces that the president of the United States has chosen LaGuardia as ambassador to Mesopotamia—which is exactly what Fiorello has been waiting for all along.[20] Curtain.

If the original intention was to produce a show that was sentimental, flag-waving, and gently satirical, in the spirit (if not imitation) of the new musical formula, the authors certainly succeeded, even if the result turned out more like *Follow the Girls* than *Oklahoma!* The songs were designed to advance the plot, not serve as mere diversions or tours de force for the performers. And if the topical references in the libretto were backsliding to the days of *I'd Rather Be Right* (1937), Ellington and Russell were on hand to inject the score with a sound that had never been heard on Broadway. Even the Gilbert and Sullivan parodies seemed right. After all, they were giants of the musical theatre. For years audiences had enjoyed the musical jokes as well as the harmonic complexities of Sullivan's music and delighted in the convoluted plots and puns of his collaborator Gilbert. They had served as models for Rodgers and Hart and the Gershwins, so why not Ellington and Russell? *Black, Brown, and Beige* had demonstrated that a composer rooted in the jazz idiom could cross over into the territory of "serious" musical form. Drawing upon the masters of English musical theatre was another step in Ellington's development of the mastery of European form. Even though *H.M.S. Times Square* was never produced, Duke never lost the desire to imitate the British masters of comic opera (as noted in a later chapter, even his last work, *Queenie Pie*, demonstrates the Gilbert and Sullivan influence with its patter songs, musical jokes, and interlocutory chorus).

The only song completed for *H.M.S. Times Square* was a bluesy rhythm ballad called "A Woman and a Man," sung by Sandra in Act One, Scene Two. Although there is no copyright registration for the piece, it was recorded on 30 December 1947 in New York City, but never released by Columbia Records. Written in a traditional AABA structure, without a verse, the melody recalls Ellington's 1945 hit, "I'm Just a Lucky So and So," with its lazy syncopations and *parlando* rhythms. The idiom of the "torch-song" is also invoked through the downward, "sighing," contour of the melodic phrases and the "blue notes" anticipating the cadences at bars 3, 7, 11, 15, 27, and 31, with flatted sixths and sevenths. Most interesting is the release where the melody acquires a kind of recitative structure, with repeated notes and leaps, and a harmony displaying a constantly changing tonal center through the continued use of the flatted seventh of the original key. The four bars immediately preceding the recapitulation are perhaps the most interesting harmonically because of the use of chromatically altered chords and the progression of minor seventh chords rising by half steps in a desperate search for the home key, echoing the passion of the lyric, "You're all mine, You're all mine / To love and call mine." (See Example 3.1)

The recapitulation restates the first eight parts with only slight rhythmic changes for lyrical emphasis. Unusually, the final cadence does not take the melody home to the tonic note but back down to the fifth of the key, implying the kind of irresolution that exists dramatically in the scene. The "Coda" added on the recording reinforces this uncertainty by resolving the melody on the ninth degree of the scale. The recording of "A Woman and a Man" was finally released by the Meritt Record Society in 1981 on a vinyl disc entitled *The Studio Records, Volume Two: 1947–1949*, with Dolores Parker as vocalist, Ellington on piano, Harold Baker and Al Killian on trumpet, Lawrence Brown on trombone, Jimmy Hamilton on clarinet, Al Sears on tenor sax, Johnny Hodges on alto sax, Harry Carney on baritone sax and bass clarinet, Junior Raglin on bass, and Sonny Greer on drums.

The reason why such an interesting and commercial theatre-song should never have been published is suggested in a letter written to Ruth Ellington on 19 November 1960, in which Bob Russell, the lyricist, implies that the Duke failed to honor a verbal agreement:

> Dear Ruth,
>
> I am in receipt of your letter of 25th October last regarding the song that Duke and I wrote entitled "A Woman and a Man."
>
> True that 'Edward Kennedy' and I agreed on a contract with Tempo Music, but I do believe that E.K. neglected to inform you fully of our agreement. It is my understanding that the above entitled song is to be published

Example 3.1.

> by Tempo, provided that Duke and I write a song that will be published by my firm and also that Tempo will issue an S.P.A. contract to me as a writer, which is the character of contract, that my firm, Harrison Music Corp. will issue to Duke. A contract of this type grants benefits to song writers that has taken hard fought years to acquire.
>
> I explained the above to your office manager on August 25 '59 prior to my departure for London and points Continental; indicated my reasons for not signing your firm form contract; gave her my London address and also spoke to Duke on the telephone, explaining my position. I felt that she and he concurred and that I would receive the necessary document and provision forthwith. It is now fifthwith.

Evidently, the matter was settled because on 16 December 1960, Russell sent Ellington a letter enclosing the lyric to "A Woman and a Man," reconstructed from memory, and two other lyrics "written in today's vernacular" which he nervously hoped might interest the Duke who writes in "tomorrow's idiom." He ends by trying to interest Ellington in composing music for two "highly marketable" album ideas that could be completed "via mail and periodic meetings," and offered to go to Paris, where Ellington was working on the film *Paris Blues*, to spend time with him "sketching out the ideas." Nothing ever materialized from these projects, and although Bob Russell did provide the lyrics for "Like Love," based on a theme from *Anatomy of a Murder*, "A Woman and a Man" remained unpublished.

While Ellington and his collaborators were attempting to reach Broadway with *H.M.S. Times Square*, in Spring 1944, Duke was approached by Richard W. Krakeur to compose a score for *Frankie and Johnny*, a musicalization of the legendary love-triangle (in which Frankie kills Johnny because of his attentions to Nelly Bly), with a libretto by John Huston and Paul Milton. John Huston had written a short play on the subject during his stay in Mexico in 1928 that utilized portions of the ballad narrative to connect the various scenes. It was performed by puppets in 1929 and published in 1930 with caricature-like illustrations by the celebrated Mexican artist, Covarrubias. According to the New York *Times* (26 May 1944), Krakeur was reported to have engaged Vinton Freedley as co-producer and was supposed to have cast the show in Los Angeles in early June.[21] Although the Ellington collection has several different scripts for *Frankie and Johnny*, there is no evidence that Ellington seriously considered the project.[22]

However, some of Ellington's music did find its way into a short-lived "musical pageant," called *Blue Holiday*, at the Belasco Theatre on 21 May 1945. For eight performances only, audiences were treated to a retrospective look at African American entertainment by an all-black cast that included Ethel Waters, Josh White, Bill "Bojangles" Robinson, the Katherine Dunham Dancers, the Three Poms, the Chocolateers, and the Hall Johnson Choir. The music and lyrics for the evening were provided by Al Moritz, with assistance from Morey Amsterdam, E. Y. Harburg, Earl Robinson, and Duke

Ellington, whose contribution lay in a medley of "hits" consisting of "Mood Indigo," "Sophisticated Lady," and "Solitude."

The reviews for the evening were devastating, with headlines like, "'Blue Holiday' Has Ethel Waters, Josh White and Too Little Speed," "Vaudeville at Its Dullest," "Not Very Much Holiday Spirit," "Blue, but No Holiday," and "One Meat Ball" (*Theatre Critics' Reviews* 6.8 [7 May 1945]; 216–218). Because the critics found too many targets for their captious reproaches, Ellington's classics happily went unnoticed in the press. However, the magic of Ellington's music on Broadway *was* noticed and appreciated by the designer for the production, a young African American set designer who had been acclaimed for his work with Orson Welles and John Houseman at the Federal Theatre, as well as for his work with the WPA Negro Theatre in Harlem, and his designs for *Mamba's Daughters* on Broadway. He had dreams of becoming a producer, and his name was Perry Watkins.[23]

Four

"Here's a Strange Mess"

It had long been the aspiration of Perry Watkins, the only working African American designer in the New York theatre in the 1940s, to convert John Gay's political satire, *The Beggar's Opera*, the runaway hit of the 1728 London theatre season, into a contemporary, politically conscious, bi-racial Broadway musical that would not only involve bi-racial producers, bi-racial authors, and bi-racial cast, but an on-stage bi-racial romance as well.[1] As Watkins explained to the *Chicago Sun*:

> In making it bi-racial, it expressed the integrated cross-sectional spirit of the true American scene.... The collaboration is a proof of the universal character of the arts and artists of the theater. It also shows that democracy works. The harmonious relationships among all concerned and the success of the venture indicates that intelligent Americans regard color as no barrier to artistic co-operation and points the way to collaboration along more general lines for the common good of all Americans [6 April 1947: 29].

Though Kurt Weill and Bertolt Brecht had already adapted Gay's anti-heroic fable into *The Threepenny Opera* little more than a decade earlier, the Brecht-Weill musical played only a week and a half on Broadway in 1933, so the idea was still fresh to American audiences. In the fall of 1945, Watkins enlisted the help of lyricist John Latouche, the *wunderkind* who had penned the highly successful African American musical *Cabin in the Sky* (1940), known for his trenchant satire and sensitive lyrics. Though hard at work on *Polonaise*, a costume operetta, set during the American revolution, based on the music of Frederick Chopin, Latouche jumped at the opportunity of adapting one of the classics of the English-speaking stage, and began work transforming the 18th century highwaymen into contemporary gangsters. Watkins had had a long appreciation of Ellington's work as a songwriter, so after *Blue Holiday* had closed, seeing Ellington come out of a midtown Manhattan restaurant, Watkins walked up to him and spontaneously commissioned Duke to compose the score. This began a practice that would continue through Ellington's career as a musical theatre composer: he would always be paid in advance.[2] Ellington surprised Watkins by accepting his offer immediately, without knowing the slightest detail about *The Beggar's Opera.*

Ellington's impulsive acceptance alarmed Watkins, who was certain that Duke had no idea of what he was getting himself into as the composer of a "book" musical. This was not, however, Ellington's first time dealing with scripts. The problems surrounding *Cock o' the World* and *H.M.S. Times Square* had educated the Duke in the exigencies of writing for the theatre, and whether or not he wanted the *recognition* of being a Broadway composer rather than the actualities of the job as Luther Henderson has suggested, it is clear that he took on *The Beggar's Opera* project with the best intentions, seeing it as another step in his ever-blossoming career. [3] It, unfortunately, never occurred to him that writing a Broadway show would require his being in some proximity to the librettist, and almost immediately upon his accepting the job, he went out of town with his band. Latouche, prone to fits of alcoholism and long periods of indolence, used Ellington's tours as an excuse for not getting work done, or for moving on to other projects,[4] and threatened to quit unless Ellington would accommodate his working schedule.

While the collaboration was by no means smooth, it did bear fruit, and in January 1946, Perry Watkins approached John Houseman, a white fellow-worker at the WPA Negro Theatre, to direct the project. Watkins described it as "a wholly integrated black and white production—beginning with the authors and producers and right down through the cast and chorus" (Houseman 188), a novelty in the history of the Broadway stage.[5] Highly interested in so appealing a concept, Houseman met with Watkins and then-co-producer Dale Wasserman, a white playwright,[6] but both appeared disorganized and vague in their plans for production and refused to allow the director to read the script or listen to more than two or three numbers from the score. Though this meeting put Houseman off, his subsequent meetings with Ellington ("one of the world's great spellbinders"), and Latouche (whom he had known since the Depression) assured him that everything was on track for the production. Houseman left for California in February 1946, still interested, but as yet unsigned. For the next several months, Houseman reports that Perry Watkins would call him once a week to give a progress report: "'full steam ahead' was his phrase; money was pouring in and Latouche and Ellington were 'cooking with gas'" (Houseman 189). By mid–July, Perry Watkins began to press Houseman to sign a contract; the director had yet to see a script, so he continued to stall until several film projects on the West Coast fell through. Seeing this as his golden opportunity, in September, Perry Watkins flew John Houseman and his assistant, Nicholas Ray,[7] back to the East Coast to discuss the musical. Houseman recalls:

> Within a few days of my arrival several things became apparent about *Beggar's Holiday*[8]—none of them good. Latouche was not only lazy, but he had

> been working on several other projects during the summer; he had written a number of lyrics but only the roughest draft of our first act and almost nothing of the second. Ellington, teeming with tunes and mood pieces, still had not faced the necessity of composing a complete musical score. Added to these unpleasant discoveries was another of which I only gradually became aware: our producers were desperately short of money. Finally—owing to the Duke's enormous list of future commitments—we had no leeway at all but must start rehearsals within four weeks or not at all [191].

The script that Latouche had provided was structured very much like Gay's text, broken up with short, ballad-like lyrics, recalling the prosody, and often the content, of Gay's original. For these quasi recitatives, Ellington provided a jazz patter formula that evoked both the style of eighteenth-century ballad opera and 1940s jazz riffs. Unfortunately, the Duke's music was insufficient to drive the show. Gay's original satire of static opera conventions in the 18th century, became dramatically static in Latouche's revision, and Houseman and Ray, now under contract, found themselves in the fall of 1946 struggling to hammer out a playable script in spite of what appeared to be the reticence and outright opposition from the librettist.

Not all was troubled, however. The concept of total integration gave the director the opportunities for "adventurous and exhilarating casting" (Houseman 191). Alfred Drake, the original Curley of *Oklahoma!*, was selected as the gangster Macheath; Libby Holman, an alumna of *The Garrick Gaieties, The Greenwich Village Follies, The Little Show*, and *Three's a Crowd*—all classic Broadway revues—was cast as Jenny Driver, the prostitute/moll who turns Macheath into the police; police chief Lockit and his daughter Lucy were both African Americans, played by Rollin and Mildred Smith; the Peachums, dealers in stolen goods, were white, with Zero Mostel as Hamilton Peachum, Dorothy Johnson as his wife, and Jet MacDonald as Polly Peachum, Macheath's bride. Avon Long, the original Sportin' Life in *Porgy and Bess*, was hired as Careless Love, a pimp, and Marie Bryant, featured in *Jump for Joy*, was cast as the Cocoa Girl. Valerie Bettis joined the creative team as choreographer, hiring highly disciplined, attractive, lithe dancers, among whom were the young Herbert Ross, who would rise to fame as a film director, and Marjorie Belle, who would soon become the dance partner and wife of Gower Champion. Set designer Oliver Smith also joined the team shortly before the start of rehearsals when Perry Watkins, who had intended to produce and design the production, was convinced by the director of the impracticality of trying to accomplish too much.[9] Smith's sets were so well-received by the press that he recreated them a decade later in his designs for *West Side Story*. The costumes, called "extravagant and scandalous and exactly right" by the director were created by Walter Florell, a "wild male *modiste* with gold-lacquered hair" (Houseman 192).

Among the most important members of the creative team, and certainly the least heralded, was Billy Strayhorn, who left the Ellington tour in September 1946 to nurse *Street Music / Twilight Alley / Beggar's Holiday* into production. Strayhorn was not only the Duke's representative on the project, he acted as the show's arranger and orchestrator, and when occasion demanded, he functioned as the show's composer. Hajdu notes that Strayhorn was deeply committed to the endeavor,[10] producing a "collection of sophisticated yet swinging, harmonically uncommon theatre songs" that included "Maybe I Should Change My Ways," "The Wrong Side of the Railroad Tracks," "Girls Want a Hero," "Women, Women, Women," "Brown Penny," and the deleted "I'm Afraid" (102). It is unimportant to quibble about how much of these songs was actually *written* by Ellington and or Strayhorn; the simple fact that Strayhorn attended production meetings and rehearsals, and shaped the music to fit the actors' vocal ranges and the choreographer's needs, argues that he had a hand in everything that was heard in the show. Houseman remembers Strayhorn as an invaluable asset: "When we needed additional music, Ellington's arranger Billy Strayhorn ... would run up to the Duke's apartment and

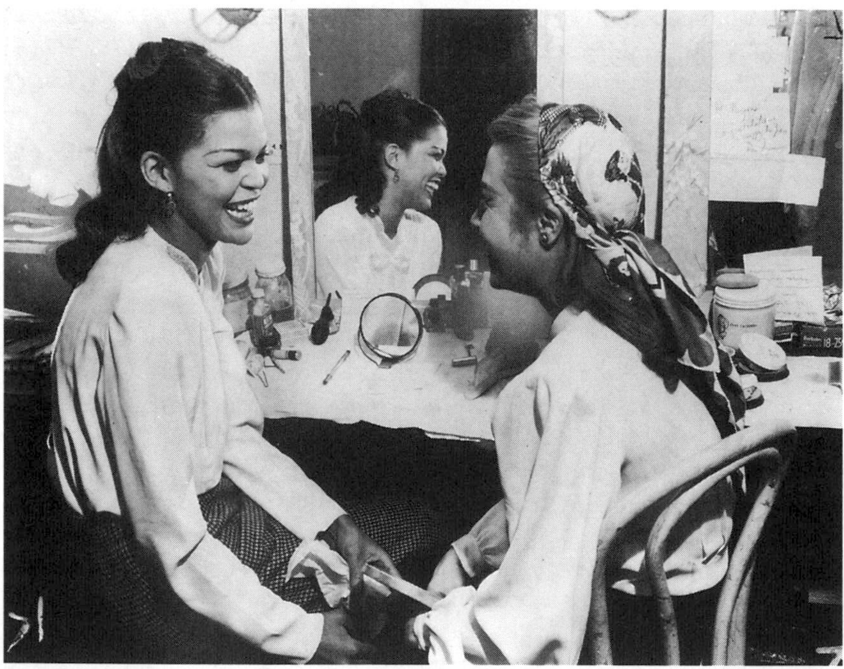

Mildred Smith as Lucy Lockit and Marjorie Belle as the Girl in a publicity still from *Beggar's Holiday*. Photo by W. Smith—Rapid News Photo, courtesy of the Photographs and Prints Division, Schomburg Center for Research in Black Culture, The New York Public Library, Astor, Lenox and Tilden Foundations.

Photograph of the chorus dressing room for *Beggar's Holiday*. Photo by W. Smith—Rapid News Photo, courtesy of the Photographs and Prints Division, Schomburg Center for Research in Black Culture, The New York Public Library, Astor, Lenox and Tilden Foundations.

fish out of a drawer, crammed with unperformed music, whatever tune seemed to fit the scene" (192). When Houseman handed the reigns to veteran Broadway director George Abbott during the pre–Broadway tryout in Boston, it was Strayhorn who provided for the new director's musical needs, not Ellington. Abbott recalls: "I never saw Duke Ellington, never worked with him. Billy took care of whatever I asked for. He sat down and wrote it right there, whatever was needed" (Quoted in Hajdu 102).

Due to the presence of Billy Strayhorn, a favorite of both the management and the cast, rehearsals got off to a good start. The songs were extraordinary in the mouths of the performers, and even the text seemed to soar in the hands of the talent at hand.[11] But by the middle of the second week, the second failed to come alive, and the producers' checks began to bounce. The shops building scenery and costumes refused to continue working until the debts had been paid, and production virtually came to a halt until a new investor, John R. Sheppard, Jr., described by Houseman as "a small, ill-favored, timid alcoholic" (193) poured much of his inheritance into the show. While the money did eventually appear to quell every crisis, the producers' credit was ruined, and the rehearsal rhythm irrevocably damaged. Opening night in New Haven was a nightmare since the cast had never completed a runthrough of the show with costumes and scenery until the first public performance. The script was said to have been in such bad shape that Alfred Drake virtually improvised the last twenty minutes of the evening—his dream of death in the electric chair and his subsequent reprieve—in front of a paying audience. After the performance, the creative team consisting of John Houseman, John Latouche, Duke Ellington, Nicholas Ray, and the "alcoholoc angel" assembled in a suite at the Taft Hotel. Their reactions to the show were divided on everything except the fact that *Twilight Alley*, the pre–Broadway title, had no book and no score. John Latouche responded by passing out drunk; Nicholas Ray decided to elope to Cuba with Valerie Bettis, the choreographer (from which they were ultimately intercepted), and Evie Ellis, known to the company as "Mrs. Ellington," took the Duke to bed. Houseman recalls:

> At the time I worked with him the Duke had abandoned all attempts to organize his own life. Between late-night engagements with his band, concerts, recordings, interviews, composing and other activities he had turned over the scheduling of his days and nights to his wife, his manager and other associates. They woke him up when it was time, fed him, laid out the right clothes for him, transported and delivered him on time for whatever engagement he was committed to, picked him up, changed his clothes, delivered him once more, fed him again and finally put him to bed. In this way, he explained, by ceasing to concern himself with time and space, he was able to preserve his energy and his sanity [194].

When *Twilight Alley* arrived in Boston, after a run in Hartford Connecticut, everything seemed to be under control.[12] Weeks of a back-breaking schedule—rehearsal during the day, performance at night—seemed to have paid off. The actors were more secure in their business, giving the show a kind of polish, a "semblance of cohesion," to use Houseman's phrase, that would cover, if not solve, the show's inherent weaknesses. In *Music Is My Mistress*, Ellington describes his experience after watching a preview in Boston:

> At a meeting after the show, the director was still asking for more music, as he had been up to and through over fifty songs.
>
> "What we need here is a song," he began right away.
>
> "Well, listen now, I love to write music," I answered. "Let's put ten new songs in the show. I'll sit here and write 'em tonight. But here is a man (Latouche) who has written the lyrics for over fifty songs. I just saw the matinee, and I couldn't hear the words."
>
> I was immediately challenged on that.
>
> "Why couldn't you?"
>
> "Well, the actors are not projecting, and the orchestra is too loud."
>
> "Now, Mr. Ellington," the musical director protested, "you ordered these orchestrations made by your man, Billy Strayhorn, who ... "
>
> "Yes, but they're only notes on paper," I replied. "They can be played loudly or softly, and the orchestra is playing what is supposed to be an accompaniment, or under dialogue."
>
> I got into a big thing about it, and they let that go by.
>
> There was a section two hours into the show where they had a ten-minute soliloquy by Alfred Drake—just he and his pistol walking around—followed by a ten-minute, slow-moving ballet over the original set of fire escapes.... "A high school play wouldn't put two slow-moving, ten-minute sequences back to back," I said. "Why can't they be separated?" [185–186]

Structural notes in Ellington's hand, taken presumably during a Boston run-through, also provide an interesting view of his dramatic instincts, which were certainly acute. Written on stationary embossed with the crest of the Copley Plaza, Boston's premier hotel, the notes address the opening of the show.

With the words, "Those Who Do and Those Who Say They Do" scrawled at the top of the page, Ellington suggests that the Beggar begin as usual into the expostulation of two kinds of people: "those everyday people who work today and dream of tomorrow" and "those who just wait for the opportunity to prey upon them." Ellington then gives the Beggar a speech: "I"ll show you a character who really dreams of tomorrow but who likes to be thought of as tough and cold-blooded; inside, beautiful but selfish outside. The meanest, dirtiest, lowest, lousiest rat—May I present—" and Macheath discards the Beggar's costume, walks to center stage where he meets Marjorie Belle. Ellington indicates "Brush off routine" here—and the Duke, once again, adds dialogue to the script, this time for Marjorie Belle: "But Mac, what about our place for the future, that place we were going to build?" Macheath replies, "Live for today" to which Ellington appends the direction "Song" followed by "Ballet."

On a note labeled "B" with the words, "Mac Commentary about nice people," on the top, Ellington continues. At the end of the ballet, he notes that Majorie exits, and suggests that Macheath is down "in one" silhouetted with gangsters crouched about the set on the fire escapes, etc. The corrugated iron curtain—a design element in the show behind which scenes can be changed while action continues in front—comes down. He gives Macheath a speech: "There's only 2 kinds of people, those who do and those who admit it." Ellington then calls for a phrase of "Tooth and Claw" as underscore for Pimp and Chick business, which pulls Macheath up to the stage right corner. An optimistic version of "Let's Go Down to Miss Jenny's," the opening number of the show, leads to hissing, warning of Lockit's entrance stage left forcing Macheath and the girls to retreat to the stage right wing. Lockit continues to walk slowly onstage, singing the old version of "Miss Jenny" as a kind of warning, completing the chorus as he exits stage right. After he leaves, someone shouts, "Is the Police Department telling us where to enjoy ourselves?" On the verso of page 3, Ellington suggests the addition of four bars from "Let's Go Down to Miss Jenny's," that segues into "Here's to Loose Living." The corrugated iron curtain flies out and the pimps and girls turn and go into the interior of Jenny's, half-singing, half-humming "Here's to Loose Living" (301.5.5.9).

It is unknown whether these ideas were original to the Duke, or the result of discussions among the creative team. In any case, Ellington's notes have more than curiosity value as they demonstrate his interest in, and understanding of, dramatic rhythm and in the ability of music to complement, and control, that rhythm. The notes also demonstrate that Ellington was more than casually interested in musical theatre. He was no dilettante, not simply a songwriter hoping to impersonate a theatre composer. He knew how to tell a story through the use of music. But a Broadway show demands an artist's complete attention, and as Luther Henderson so eloquently stated, "Duke Ellington would never leave his band—never, ever, not for anything" (Hajdu 101).

As if he had read Ellington's notes, Cyrus Durgin, critic for the *Boston Globe*, announced that the show needed "cutting and tightening, clarification of the story, faster pacing in certain spots, further rehearsal and better projection of John Latouche's lyrics and Duke Ellington's works" (4 December 1946: 2.26), and the dean of Boston critics, Elliot Norton, found the show despicable on all counts. When the Boston critics were unimpressed by what they saw, the producers realized that something drastic had to be done, and they called in George Abbott, the dean of Broadway directors and play-doctors, to come to Boston to watch the next performance, a decision that would have several repercussions: John Houseman resigned from the project and Libby Holdman was fired. When she became aware of Abbott's association with *Twilight Alley*, Holman knew her days with the show were numbered because she and Abbott had fought eight years earlier on a production of *You Never Know*. The day after Mr. Abbott arrived, he scrapped two of Jenny Driver's songs, leaving Libby Holman with virtually nothing to do in the show. When she refused to quit, he instructed Nicholas Ray to fire her. Nicholas and Libby had been having an affair throughout the rehearsal period, so that evening, after they had made love, Libby found out she was being replaced. Nicholas Ray was kept on as assistant director, although his function was significantly reduced. Alfred Drake noted that "once Mr. Abbott came in, we hardly heard a peep out of Nick any longer, because he was put in such a subordinate position. He made a joke about it at some rehearsal when Mr. Abbott wasn't there and he had been asked to give some notes or something. He said he seemed to have lost his voice for quite a long time during the out-of-town" (Eisenschitz 87).

Between Boston and New York City, *Twilight Alley* became *Beggar's Holiday* with new scenes and songs, a facelift so remarkable that a newspaper report on 23 December, three days before the opening, noted that "even members of the cast don't recognize it as the same show." Although Mr. Abbott claimed to have been able to fix the show had he been able to make sufficient cast changes, he complained that the producers refused to give him the money to get the job done. As a result, he refused to have his name listed as director for the production. Houseman, who had left the show, but still maintained directorial credit, decided before opening night in New York City to have his name removed. In an odd turn of events, Nicholas Ray, whose name had not even been associated with the show during the pre–Broadway run, was now given sole director credit for the dialogue scenes in New York City: "Book directed by Nicholas Ray."

The musical that opened on 26 December at the Broadway Theatre was far removed from Gay's original.[13] Gone were most of the recitatives and patter refrains. Gone were the ten-minute monologues and dreary ballets. What the audience saw in New York City was slick and colorful owing to the brilliant designs of Oliver Smith, Valerie Bettis's choreography, and the pacing of veteran director George Abbott. Act One now had six scenes, the first of which, "Exterior of Miss Jenny's," introduced the Beggar, his transformation into Macheath, and Macheath's love of women, much in the way Ellington suggested in his Boston notes, but with an extended dialogue between Macheath and the girls, and an added number for Macheath to proclaim his solipsistic point of view, "I've Got Me." Scene Two, "Interior of Miss Jenny's," a brothel, introduced the club environment, a staple of Ellington's musicals, offering a raison d'etre for performance numbers by "entertainers" such as the Cocoa Girl and Miss Jenny herself. The club atmosphere was important since it allowed Ellington to evoke the jungle music of the Cotton Club days, and the swinging dance band arrangement of his club-date tours without the necessity of creating musical characterizations demanded by the plot. That the club songs in *Beggar's Holiday* did propel the action—since they essentially dealt with the sexual attraction between gangster and moll, not unlike the club songs in Frank Loesser's *Guys and Dolls*, though without the satiric point of view—attests to the craftsmanship of the lyrics, and the inherent dramatic sensibilities of both Ellington and his "representative," Billy Strayhorn.

Alfred Drake as Macheath and Avon Long as Careless Love in a publicity still from *Beggar's Holiday*. Photo by W. Smith—Rapid News Photo, courtesy of the Photographs and Prints Division, Schomburg Center for Research in Black Culture, The New York Public Library, Astor, Lenox and Tilden Foundations.

In the second scene, Jenny is complaining about Macheath's gang monopolizing her girls, and Macheath's men are complaining about their recent inactivity. Macheath assures them that soon "Mister Big," Hamilton Peachum, will be eating out of his hand, but since Peachum has an impressionable daughter, Jenny expresses concern. Macheath's attempts to assuage her jealousy are interrupted by the arrival of Careless Love, a young spy Macheath placed in the Peachum organization, who announces the presence of Polly, Peachum's daughter outside the brothel. Jenny suddenly realizes that Macheath plans to marry Polly and turns on him, only to have Careless Love tell her to "Take Love Easy," in a reprise of the song Jenny sang to a drunken customer earlier in the scene. Scene Three, "Exterior of Miss Jenny's," depicts the courtship, proposal, and wedding of Polly Peachum and Macheath, all done to the accompaniment of "When I Walk with You," Ellington's attempt at composing a "square" Broadway ballad.

Scene Four changes to Hamilton Peachum's residence, where Peachum and chief of police Lockit are discussing the necessity of finding a scapegoat to prosecute to get the crime commission off their backs. When Mrs. Peachum enters with the news that Polly has married Macheath, they decide that he's their man and suggest that Polly "insure him, then turn him in!" As the police are on their way to capture him, Macheath crawls through Peachum's window to spend the night with his bride. Polly reveals her father's intention of trumping up a charge against him, and Careless Love enters to report the presence of police. Macheath escapes, and, as the police follow after him, Peachum inquires if his daughter remembered to ask if Macheath was insured! Scene Five is "in one" in front of the corrugated iron curtain and depicts the police chasing after Macheath.

Scene Six, "A Hobo Jungle—two days later," opens with the sound of a trumpet playing "Take Love Easy." Macheath's gang, nervous and disorganized, complain that their persecution at the hands of the local authorities is unfair, since they are simply observing the universal law of "Tooth and Claw." Macheath enters and displays his weaker side; running from the law has made him question his values momentarily, but, after considering the alternatives in song, "Maybe I Should Change My Ways," he vows to remain the way he is. The girls from Miss Jenny's enter to boost the morale of the men, and the Cocoa Girl and Careless Love entertain the troops with "On the Wrong Side of the Railroad Tracks," a number anticipating the roof scene in *West Side Story* where the Sharks' girls sing "America." [14] Jenny enters, surprising Macheath, who responds by telling her and the gang of his plans to take them "across Tomorrow Mountain," where they can all live in perpetual crime. After the production number that ensues, Jenny kisses Macheath and removes his gun, giving it to the Cocoa Girl. Held close in Jenny's arms, Macheath is a sitting duck for the police, who enter and arrest him. Lockit appears and gives Jenny money, which she at first refuses, but, on reconsideration, puts inside her stocking, as the curtain falls.

The second act begins in front of the corrugated iron curtain with newsboys announcing, "Macheath in court today!" Lockit's daughter Lucy appears and philosophizes about women's attraction to men who are criminals, noting that "Girls want a hero / Who's a cross between a Dillinger and Nero." Scene Two takes place in Lockit's office, where Macheath is tried and convicted according to the law of "Tooth and Claw." Scene three finds Macheath in jail where he continues to attempt to persuade Jenny to help him escape to the country where they could have a "charming little vine-covered roadhouse." Jenny rejects Macheath's proposal in song, describing sarcastically, the fate of their offspring, born out of wedlock, weaned on alcohol, with a submachine gun for a rattle. After Jenny exits, Lucy Lockit enters, bringing Macheath a Spam sandwich. He sweet talks her into releasing him from his cell, and when she exhibits the slightest doubt, he tells her to flip a coin, "Heads we go—tails we stay." The penny he provides comes up tails twice, but Lucy is so smitten with the gangster that she runs off to get the keys to the cell. Polly enters, all hearts and flowers, and Macheath finds himself between two women suddenly fighting over him. He manages to acquire the keys to the cell and escapes in a flash, followed by Polly. Lucy, suddenly aware of her foolishness, sees the penny on the floor and reflects on the pain of loving, "Brown Penny."

Scene Four, in front of the corrugated iron curtain, depicts another pursuit, this time Careless Love in search of Macheath. Careless Love has enough time, however, to stop and sing a small group number about the chicanery of women, recalling "The Trouble with Women," in *One Touch of Venus*, and anticipating the "Standing on the Corner" routine from *The Most Happy Fella'*. Scene Five takes place in Miss Jenny's bedroom, where Polly has entered looking for her husband, followed by Lucy. The three compare notes on their respective treatment by Macheath and discover that they have all been conned. The fellon suddenly appears, and the three women crowd around him to hear a reprise of "When I Walk with You" sung to the three of them collectively. Peachum and Lockit enter in search of Macheath, the gangster escapes through the window, and Polly, Lucy, and Jenny unite to save him. In spite of their efforts, Macheath is recaptured in a ballet sequence in the following scene, "Under the Bridge." After performing a soliloquy, "The Hunted," reminiscent of "Soliloquy" from *Carousel*, and anticipating "This Is the Life," from *Love Life*, in which Macheath decides to shoot it out with the police, he is taken into custody and strapped into the electric chair. The final scene begins with the announcement of the newsboys, "Macheath to die today," and opens on the facade of the jail. Just as the criminal is to be executed, Macheath becomes the Beggar sitting in the electric chair and calls off the electrocution because such things are inappropriate for musical comedy! Macheath's women, Polly, Lucy, and Jenny, crowd around him and the ensemble joins in a reprise of "Tomorrow Mountain" as the curtain falls.[15]

To support such a melange of unsavory characters and situations, Ellington, Strayhorn, and Latouche created an unusually varied, but highly coherent score.[16] The opening "Chase" ballet recalled Ellington's jungle style with its insistent accompaniment and syncopated melody, rich in blue notes and whole tone scales. Suggesting a feeling of three against four, the melody and harmonic accents in the number emphasized the energy and frantic movement of the scene. Macheath's first song, "I've Got Me," begins with a parlando 12-bar verse, followed by a traditional AABA structure, in which the chromatic harmony and melodic line emphasize the "seedy" side of the gangster's personality. The melodic simplicity of the release implies a more vulnerable side to Macheath's personality that is reinforced by the lyrics.

Jenny's "Take Love Easy," comes straight out of Ellington's jazz style, with a rich, but easily assimilated harmony (based on falling fifth seventh chords) and a melody filled with movement, suggesting a spontaneous improvisation. The cool blues quality of the number certainly reflects Jenny's occupation as madam of the brothel, and also evokes the atmosphere of the "club" where the inhabitants are "performers" (musically/sexually) who are adept at improvising responses to squelch the unwanted advances of alcoholic patrons. Careless Love's introductory number, "I Wanna Be Bad," recalls Ellington's jungle style in its minor mode, but is very unusual in its ten-bar melodic structure, with an orchestral interlude appearing in bars 7–8, 17–18, and 35–36 to allow choreography or stage business. This is certainly not the work of a songwriter intent on writing only commercial hits. Emphasizing the lyrics, the melody of this song is full of unexpected leaps and dissonances, suggesting that the character is not what he appears, but much more volatile.

After a 20-bar verse, written like a recitative in an opera, "When I Walk with You" follows in an AB structure, with melodic syncopation emphasized in the B section. In the A section, the melody (and Macheath the singer) attempts to exist within restrictive boundaries, relying on quarter notes and half notes in mostly stepwise phrases. With the B section, however, the melody breaks into the syncopation of quarter note triplets that not only suggest the passion of the dramatic moment, but provide the ear with a series of three-against-two patterns destroying the clarity of rhythmic pulse. The B section is a clear indication that the melodic experiment in the A section—what Macheath wants Polly to believe—is not entirely true to his nature. The fact that Polly replies using the same melodic formula infers that perhaps she, too, is of a divided or dissimulating nature. The Gilbert-and-Sullivan style of "A Maiden Who Is Smart," paints the Peachums as a comic, patter couple, evoking both the style of English light opera, and providing a recitative-like framework for the lyrics to be understood.

"Tooth and Claw" is a return to the old "Bowery Waltz" formula, popularized in the turn-of-the-century hit, *A Trip to Chinatown*, and anticipates such modern gangster waltzes as "Brush Up Your Shakespeare" in *Kiss Me, Kate* and "Politics and Poker" in *Fiorello!* Using primitive harmony and a melody based on scales or leaps of a fifth, "Tooth and Claw" provides a neat, accessible counterpoint to the trenchant, almost Brechtian lyrics.

Macheath's "Maybe I Should Change My Ways" has an especially intriguing verse that changes metre five times within its last nine bars. Since the song appears at Macheath's most vulnerable moment psychologically in the first act, it is appropriate that the music should evoke the character's vacillation mentally. When the chorus finally appears, the exceptionally rangey melody meanders up and down, sometimes lighting on a consonance, more often on a dissonant harmony, until a clear-cut tonality is identified with the tonic at the very end of the piece.[17] Like the lyric, the music of this number wanders, looking for a solution that comes only in the last two bars. As musical characterization of an alternative subculture, dangerously attractive and typified by Careless and the Cocoa Girl, "The Wrong Side of the Railroad Tracks" evokes "I Wanna Be Bad" in style with the improvisitory nature of the highly syncopated melody that attacks "square" music's rigid structure in the same spirit that the characters flaunt the law.

The fact that the libretto underneath so interesting a score was a hollow shell did not go unnoticed, but for many, the riches of the production far outweighed its deficits. Ellington and Latouche were singled out by *New York World-Telegram* critic Robert Bagar as the stars of the production, a sentiment echoed by John Chapman of the *Daily News*, who called the work "the most interesting musical since 'Porgy and Bess.'" "What is important about 'Beggar's Holiday,'" he continued, "is the Ellington score and its accompanying words by Mr. Latouche." Brooks Atkinson of the *New York Times* was lavish in his praise for the score as a work of drama:

> Let appropriate salutes be fired in honor of Duke Ellington and John Latouche. Using John Gay's "Beggar's Opera" as a ground plan, they have composed a flaring musical play in modern style, "Beggar's Holiday" .... The word "composed" is used here advisedly. For Mr. Ellington, the hot drum-major, and Mr. Latouche, the metronomic word man, have constructed a musical play from the ground up with an eloquent score, brisk ballets and a cast of dancers and singers who are up to snuff....
>
> Mr. Ellington has been dashing off songs with remarkable virtuosity. Without altering the basic, he has written them in several moods—wry romances, a sardonic lullaby, a good hurdy-gurdy number, a rollicking melody that lets go expansively. An angular ballet comes off his music rack as neatly as a waterfront ballad. No conventional composer, he has not written a pattern of song hits to be lifted out of their context, but rather an integral musical composition that carries the old Gay picaresque yarn through its dark modern setting... . Mr. Ellington and Mr. Latouche have given Broadway a score and lyrics we can be proud of [27 December 1947: 13].

In a follow-up article, noting that "Mr. Latouche's lyrics are brilliant," Atkinson continued in his commendation of Ellington and Strayhorn:

> The distinction of "Beggar's Holiday" is a swift, withering score by Duke Ellington, who is the Broadway counterpart of the old New Orleans and St. Louis jive musicians. Although Mr. Ellington has written intelligible scores for the singers, his orchestrations are full of the abracadabra that hot instrumentalists manage to pick out of the midnight air without benefit of notes; and the music is wry, dissonant, contemptuous, and biting. Given a literary theme steeped in evil, Mr. Ellington has expressed it in febrile music that is more dramatic than anything John Gay wrote and that gives "Beggar's Holiday" the rhythm of a wild and sinister carnival for a thieve's market [26 January 1947: 2.1].[18]

Herrick Brown of the *Sun* concurred suggesting that "Duke Ellington has composed ... a delightful score that includes some of the best song numbers that Broadway has heard in a long time," but complained about the weaknesses in the script, concluding his review with, "It's a shame that Messrs. Watkins and Sheppard didn't have a better book to spend all that money on." Complaints about the text were rampant throughout the reviews, and the old theatre adage that a good score cannot rescue a poor libretto seemed especially true in the case of *Beggar's Holiday*, which closed on 29 March 1947, after giving 111 performances in New York City. A subsequent production in Chicago, from 5 to 19 April, to lukewarm notices, failed to ignite any further interest in the work, and not a penny of the original investment in the property, said to be in excess of $300,000 (*Billboard* suggests $350,000) was recouped.[19]

Was the show ahead of its time, as George Abbott has suggested? Was the possibility of an interracial relationship between a white Macheath and an African American Lucy too much for a New York audience to accept in 1946? In New York perhaps, but not Chicago. The African American newspaper, the *Chicago Defender*, lauded the production for being different, unlike the traditional musical theatre fare, even though it found the score to be unmemorable (12 April 1946: 20). Perhaps the view of Perry Bruskin, the actor who played Mooch in the original production, is the most accurate:

> Houseman felt he had the coming together of his own feelings about theatre, the kind of theatre he enjoyed doing because it was a unique original statement. I think it reflected Houseman's attitude towards the theatre of the 1930s, because those were his most exciting days, and Nick and I came from that same background. He and Latouche represented that same period. There was a dynamic reason for the grouping of those people. The only thing they did not anticipate was that the play wasn't that good [Eisenschitz 88].

In 1964, Mercer Ellington, Richard Carney, and Perry Watkins approached Tom Shepard, acclaimed for his production of original cast recordings for Columbia Records, about recreating a cast album of *Beggar's Holiday*, since no recording had been made of the original production nearly twenty years before. Shepard was promised the participation of Duke Ellington conducting the Ellington Orchestra, with an additional complement of strings; Alfred Drake, Libby Holman, and Zero Mostel had agreed to recreate their original roles on record; and Ellington, Carney, and Watkins expressed willingness to supply the front money for the project. Negotiations with Columbia Records did not continue and *Beggar's Holiday* would have no original cast recording until Blue Pear Records in Longwood, Florida, released a number of demo recordings, made by members of the original cast, over a decade after Duke Ellington's death.

In 1972 there was talk of a New York revival to be produced by Perry Watkins and Vincent Miniscalco, but nothing would be heard of *Beggar's Holiday* until a condensed version of the show was performed at the Museum of American History in Washington, D.C., at the beginning of February 1992, as part of the "American Song Series" at the Carmichael Auditorium. Under the direction of Ron O'Leary, the two-act musical was reduced to 70

Zero Mostel as Peachum, Dorothy Johnson as Mrs. Peachum, and Rollin Smith as Police Chief Lockit in a publicity still from *Beggar's Holiday*. Photo by Van Damm Studio, courtesy of the Photographs and Prints Division, Schomburg Center for Research in Black Culture, The New York Public Library, Astor, Lenox and Tilden Foundations.

minutes, keeping most of the songs and reducing much of the dialogue to narrative. Thomas Henry McKenzie was cast as Macheath; Harry Winter as Peachum; Julia Nixon played Miss Jenny; Michelle Rios-Acosta, Polly; and Gabrielle Dunmayer, Lucy.

Although the *Washington Post* critic found the cast highly attractive and adept at their roles, the star of the production again was Ellington:

> While some of the songs betray their age—mostly the comedy numbers—it's more often the fault of the lyrics than the music. Latouche is clever in his writing, but Ellington is masterly. The slighter numbers are those incidental the first time around, mostly ensemble tunes such as "When You Get Down by Miss Jenny's," "Loose Living," and "Women, Women, Women." ... The standout numbers in the show, however, tended to be the ballads: the easy come–easy go ramble of "Take Love Easy," the classically corny duet "When I Walk with You," the momentary reflection of "Maybe I Should Change My Ways," and "Brown Penny," a haunting little number that there's

> just not enough of.... This fascinating revival is more worthy, even in its unfinished state, than some of the historical musicals that have found second wind in a breathless Broadway climate [4 February 1992: D8].

If the Washington production is any indication, perhaps there is a future for *Beggar's Holiday*.[20]

Undaunted by the difficulties surrounding *Beggar's Holiday*, Perry Watkins took an option on a musical based on an article in *Time* magazine on 26 August 1940 about the rice harvest of the Chippewa Indians in Minnesota, entitled "Moon of Mahnomen." The libretto, created by a Broadway neophyte named Charles Matthew Underhill, was submitted to Watkins without the music for the songs, for the author had been unable to find a collaborator on the project. Watkins immediately turned to Ellington who accepted the project with great enthusiasm, and began sketching a score in the autumn of 1947.[21] This would not be the first time an African American composer has shown interest in the plight of the American Indian, another oppressed racial minority. As early as 1908, J. Rosamond Johnson had contributed the score for *The Red Moon*, a musical written by Bob Cole about the government school for Indians and blacks in the pioneering days of the West. Cole and Johnson found the opportunity to take a stand against bigotry and racial prejudice in their work, and Ellington was similarly attuned to the possibilities in Underhill's treatment of the story.

The magazine article detailed the history of wild rice, called "Mah-nomen" among the Chippewa Indians, and the gradual usurpation of the Indian rice fields by greedy whites who, using motorboats to collect the crops, destroyed many of the plants and altered the harvest cycle. To assist the Indians and preserve a valuable state resource, the Minnesota Legislature enacted, in 1939, a rice conservation law, restoring to the Chippewas their exclusive rights to 200,000 acres of Minnesota rice fields, and outlawed any method of harvest at variance with the traditional practice of the Indians. Chosen to police the new legislation, was a highly respected Chippewa half-breed by the name of Frank Broker. Such is the historical background of Ellington and Underhill's musical that begins at the harvest moon, the "Moon of Mahnomen."

The audience sees the silhouetted figures of Indian men and women celebrating the ritual of the rice harvest, and singing a chant-like anthem to the moon. At the end of the ritual, children announce the arrival of tourists, and the primitive, natural environment is transformed into a series of souvenir displays and shack-like shops, under the supervision of Wrinkle Meat, an old Indian entrepreneur. Mike Big Bear argues against the practice, claiming that Indians should not behave "like freaks in a side show," but the woman he loves, Little Fawn, the chief's daughter, quiets his objections as the tourists arrive. In the scene that follows, the Chippewas exchange the nobility of their traditions for Hollywood stereotypes and behave like the Indians in western films. After the tourists leave, Mike is goaded into revealing his desire to be treated like any other American citizen: "I'm sick of being a ward of the United States Government . . I want to buy a glass of beer like any other citizen. It's our right to bear arms but we can't buy a drink" (16). Fawn tries to soothe him with a reminder of their wedding after the rice harvest, and sings the "big" ballad of the show, "Live and Love," inaugurating one of the major motifs of the play, "find new life in love" (19).

Thunder Face, the medicine man, dressed traditionally, with bear teeth hanging around his neck, complains, in a patter song, about the hazards of being a medicine man in a modern world, haunted by the A.M.A. At the end of the number, Otto Fox enters to confer with the medicine man. Thunder Face is frightened at the possibility of being seen with Fox, a violator of the harvest laws because he uses a machine harvester, who bribes him with liquor to convince the other Indians that the white man's way is a good way. The meeting ends abruptly with the entrance of several Indians preparing for the next ritual, the jessakawing, a kind of hypnotic séance, during which members of the tribe commune with spirits, through the medium of the medicine man. In the midst of giving several weather predictions for the harvest, Thunder Face manages to convince the Indians of Fox's good intentions, and with a reprise of the opening chant, the scene comes to an end.

Scene Two opens on Wrinkle Meat's country store, displaying products evoking a modern world—dungarees and a Coca Cola dispenser—in the middle of a thunderstorm. Abruptly, the rain stops, and Mike and Fawn discuss Fox's harvesting machine, and the Indian council's decision to keep it off the rice fields. Sam Sloan enters, buying cigarettes and chewing gum and postcards, and checking out the place. Sam tells Chickadee, the girl behind the counter, that he works for the Buna Rubber company, but would rather be running a country store, and demonstrates his salesmanship in a song anticipating "Bargaining" in Richard Rodgers, Stephen Sondheim, and Arthur Laurents's *Do I Hear a Waltz?*, 20 years later. Following the number, establishing Sam and Chickadee as the secondary love interest in the musical, Otto Fox enters asking for stamps. Sam has been supplying Fox with the rubber for his harvester, and the two men converse about the obstacles "progress" has to surmount to succeed. Otto leaves abruptly looking for someone and Fawn and Mike reappear discussing political change, with Mike insisting on the necessity of violence—even if it means going to jail—to alter public opinion. Unable to change his mind, Fawn turns to Sam who inquires about native Chippewa traditions in a musical number evocative of "The French Lesson" in the film version of *Good News*. As Sam and Fawn begin to enjoy themselves, much to the dismay of Mike and Chickadee, Wrinkle Meat enters, followed by Irving Itchy, an assemblyman from Maribou, and Horace Handout, a food processor from Aitkin. Believing Mike to be the medicine man,

Itchy and Handout reveal Fox's underhanded plan to bilk the Indians of their rice, and the scene ends with the mistaken identity revealed.

Scene Three opens on the village meeting place with Sam attempting to convince Chickadee of his innocence in the plot. As Fox and Thunder Face enter furtively, the young couple hide behind a tree. Thunder Face confesses an uneasiness in proceeding with the plan in a rhythm number, "Someone's Upsetting My Apple Cart," during which they perform a pantomime dance, reacting in fear to every noise they hear in the forest. Suddenly Chief White Cloud appears with Mike and Fawn and other members of the tribe, to emphasize the fact that Fox's harvester will not be permitted in the rice fields, and that the tribe is not bound by Fox's negotiations with Thunder Face. Fox leaves in a huff and Mike banishes Sam from the reservation. Chickadee defends Sam who offers to help the Indians by contacting Mr. Foster, a member of the conservation department, where he once worked, who might be able to enact legislation to control the use of machinery in the rice fields. White Cloud supports the idea and Wrinkle Meat suggests that the Indians approach the government in "full dress, feathers and all" (82), a view that infuriates Mike, who is determined to maintain an identity in the modern world. Fawn tries to persuade him that "Modern is only an adjective for motor cars and clothes. Things of the mind and of the heart are old and new in one" (84) and convinces him that old, or new, their love will be forever.

Suddenly, the voice of the chief is heard announcing to the villagers his decision to go to the state legislature to lobby on behalf of Indian rights. Mike suggests that the Indians should stage a demonstration, causing just enough trouble to get their pictures in the newspaper, "a photograph of the Chippewas in war paint" (87), an appeal to public sympathy that would *make* the legislators act in their behalf. Clutching her "medicine doll" Fawn attempts to persuade Mike to rely on the traditional beliefs to solve their problems, but, claiming that the old beliefs mean nothing to him, Mike breaks the doll, and runs off to the lake to lead a demonstration against the machine harvester. Left alone on stage, Fawn fights back the tears to reprise "Live and Love," and the curtain falls on Act One.

Act Two, only a third the length of the first act, begins in the chambers of the Joint Committee on Game and Fish of the Minnesota Legislature. A chorus of civil servants self-consciously identify themselves in a Gilbert and Sullivan fashion, with reporters commenting on the banality of the day's legislation dealing with Indian rice crops. The entire sequence is highly evocative of the supreme court scenes in *Of Thee I Sing*. Various witnesses, including Itchy, White Cloud, and Mike give testimony before the Joint Committee, and after some deliberation, HR1100, the Conservation of Wild Rice Bill is passed and sent to the legislature. Scene Two returns to the Indian village square where Fawn sits, singing, "In a Misty Mood," playing with her broken medicine doll and dreaming of life with Mike as the perfect husband.

The dream ballet that appears behind her evokes the dream ballet in *Oklahoma!* and the "Venus in Ozone Heights" sequence of *One Touch of Venus*. Thunder Face enters and commiserates with Fawn about the death of the old traditions in song, "Everything's Against Us." They are interrupted by Mike, White Cloud, and Sam, returning from the legislature. Wrinkle Meat, entering with Chickadee, warns Fawn not to hope for too much in case the news is bad, but to expect the worst. The "worst" occurs when Fox, refusing to give up his harvester, gets into a fight with Mike; but a news report over the radio suddenly announces that the Indian bill had been passed by the legislature and Otto Fox finally concedes defeat. As the orchestra reprises the final bars of the opening chant, Mike gives Fawn her medicine doll, now fully repaired, as a token of his willingness to compromise at last, and the curtain falls.

Ellington has left a number of sketches for songs in *Moon of Mahnomen*, the most complete being the title chant which appears at several key points throughout the musical. The song has an opening statement in F-natural minor, with the melody clearly outlining an F-minor triad. As it progresses, through the use of chromatic alteration, the melody makes use of the melodic minor with the raised 6th and 7th scale degrees. The release makes extensive use of melodic chromaticism, raising the 5th, the 2nd, and even the tonic note, never coming to rest until the recapitulation reaffirms the F-minor triad. Melodically and harmonically the work is a splendid example of word-painting and mood-setting. The melody and harmony are both highly atmospheric and display the inherent conflict of the play: the old traditions (the F-minor mode) versus the modern world (the chromatic, jazz chords). (See Example 4.1)

The song "Plenty of Rice," sung as part of the opening rice ritual of the musical, exists in lead sheet with only the barest suggestion of accompaniment. In E♭ major, the melody is playful and folk-like, making extensive use of leaps of a third. An interlude to be sung by the children is indicated solely by chord changes on the first beat of the first measure and the fourth beat of the second bar. More interesting, perhaps, is the sketch of the lyric in 1.1.31 beginning "High above an eagle wheels." Again in F-melodic minor (since it is part of the traditional ritual formula), the melody begins on the fifth of the scale, then descends in half steps to the minor third, suggesting the undulating flight of a bird.

Thunder Face's number, "Someone's Upsetting My Apple Cart," evokes Careless Love's music in *Beggar's Holiday*, filled with syncopation and blue tones. Since Thunder Face is in league with "progress," it is appropriate that

Example 4.1.

his music be evocative of the modern world, and much "jazzier" than that of the more traditional characters. Once again, Ellington demonstrates his adeptness at musical characterization and melodic invention. The melody of this song appears spontaneous, a series of improvised riffs, absolutely appropriate for the dramatic situation of men frightened of being caught. (See Example 4.2)

Fawn's highly appealing "In a Misty Mood" evokes the best of Ellington's jazz compositions. Though the chorus is in the key of F major (F being the tonality that grounds the primitive traditions), the harmony wanders through a variety of chromatic changes that suggest a conflict in the character and the possibility of compromise between the old and new. The melody varies between repeated notes and wide leaps, again depicting a character in the process of decision making, a process that does not resolve in the song, since Ellington ends the melody on the third not the tonic. This is appropriate since the first statement of the song is followed by a dream ballet, and the second statement is interrupted by the abrupt entrance of Thunder Face. (See Example 4.3)

What exists of "Live and Love" comprises a short score for band, clearly indicative that Ellington wanted to use the song commercially. A close inspection of the number, however, indicates that the melody does not correspond to the lyric in the show, and is, in actuality, "Live and Love Tonight," one of Ellington's standards from the thirties.

Although these are the only extant sketches of the score for *Moon of Mahnomen*, a copy of a production budget for the musical suggests that Perry Watkins was serious about producing the show on Broadway. Ellington was to be paid $2,500 as an advance against royalties, the same amount as Underhill.[22] The artistic services (direction, design, orchestration, etc.) were budgeted at $23,000; the physical production costs (of scenery, costumes, electrics, etc.) amounted to $103,000; rehearsal expenses up to the out-of-town opening were budgeted at $38,475; bonds to the unions amounted to $32,300; and office expenses amounted to $10,000. Adding in a contingency fund of $38,225, the production budget of *Moon of Mahnomen* was $250,000, more than $50,000 less than *Beggar's Holiday*. That is where the story ends; no more was heard of the project. Perhaps, because of the total loss of the more

Top: **Example 4.2.** *Bottom:* **Example 4.3.**

than $300,000 invested in *Beggar's Holiday*, Perry Watkins was unable to raise money for the project, even on the strength of Ellington's name, and the topicality of the subject. Maybe Ellington was unable, or unwilling, to complete the score, given his hectic touring schedule in the late 1940s, and the 1947 commission from the Liberian government to compose a suite to commemorate the country's centennial as a free republic.[23] As early as 31 July 1947, Underhill noted his disappointment at not being able to talk to Duke or work closely with him in the development of the project. Evidently matters did not improve once Ellington had a script in hand. Whatever the cause, *Moon of Mahnomen* was never produced, and the next production to occupy Ellington's attention will not come from Watkins, but from the woman who shared his address and stationary, Doris Julian.

Five

"Night Time"

In 1953, Duke Ellington was approached by Doris Julian, a promising young playwright, sharing an office with Perry Watkins, to collaborate on a musical that would take the concept of interracial casting to an extreme by having the African American and white leading ladies actually switch roles in the course of the plot. [1] The musical, entitled *Be My Guest*, was an investigation into what life might be like for a white career woman if she somehow metamorphosed into an African American club singer. [2] Borrowing from *The Prince and the Pauper, The Front Page, The Woman of the Year*, and Mike Hammer, Julian created a lively two-act farce that realized many a woman's dream to be her opposite.

Act One begins in the office of the *Clarion*, a New York City newspaper, where the staff sing, "What's New, What's New?" introducing the audience to the highly charged atmosphere of the newsroom. The locale changes to the office of editor Maggie Martin, driven to make the paper number one in the city. Because of her heavy responsibility as editor, Maggie is torn between the need to be tough and the desire to be feminine. In the song "Be a Girl," she expresses a desire to be something other than she is: she wants to make the headlines, not write them. Her self-revelatory reflection is interrupted by the entrance of her boyfriend, Jeff Davis, a "Customer's Man," who brings her purple flowers and invites her to lunch. Maggie accepts the luncheon invitation, but refuses the flowers, saying that she never wears "purple flowers," referring, of course, to the "purple press." The scene changes abruptly to the street in front of the Clarion Building where a copyboy and Bill Prentiss, an assistant editor, complain about the "new" woman in a song anticipating "Standing on the Corner" from *The Most Happy Fella'* entitled, "Women, Women, I'd Rather Have a Fluff!" Following the song, the comic Hackie grumbles about waiting for Jeff and Maggie to come down to lunch in a very long soliloquy.

The scene changes to the Sweatbeat Club, a lush nightclub on the east side where Bill Prentiss and the copyboy are arguing with a girl (Dottie Ann) about their inability to remember her name. Jeff and Maggie are seated at another table close to the stage where Candy Lee Howard, an African American club singer, is talking to club owner Steve Hagen. The band's musical introduction interrupts their conversation, and Candy walks to center stage, and sings a beguine entitled, "Night Time."[3] After the number, Maggie and Candy discover that they share a desire to trade places with one another and, during a number in which Candy tries to teach Maggie to loosen up ("Live a Little"), the women exchange clothes, and Maggie completes the song in the persona of the African American clubsinger. Candy leaves the club with Jeff, who enjoys this somewhat "looser" behavior, and Maggie exits with Steve. The act continues in Lewben's Restaurant with Jeff and Candy, followed by Steve and Maggie, stopping for something to eat. The "Night into Day Ballet" marks a passage of time during which members of all classes wander home from night clubs, bars, restaurants, and dance halls.

The following morning, we discover that Candy is running the *Clarion*, making changes in the office decor, and in the contents of the newspaper as well. As she completes her plans to add a "Lovelorn" column and "Cooking" page to the paper, a woman looking for employment as a maid enters asking for Maggie. She is sent to Maggie's apartment, located in a brownstone in the fifties near Central Park, where we discover Maggie Martin still asleep at 11:30 in the morning. Awakened by a phone call, Maggie finds herself bombarded by manicurists, interior designers, florists and prospective maids, who either wish to do no work, or refuse to work on the west side. Steve arrives in time to save Maggie from having to deal with all of them, and takes her to lunch at the Café D'Or, a Central Park South street café with easy access to the park proper. Maggie expresses a delight in Steve's company, singing, "It's a Sunny Day, Honey" after which the scene changes to Central Park for the "Poodle Ballet" with business for a bag lady and the comic over feeding the pigeons, and a crossover for a drunk and a shoeshine boy. The act ends at the *Clarion* office where the changes instituted by Candy seem to be paying off ("The Clarion Rag"). Maggie enters, posing for pictures, her new persona having become quite fashionable, and reiterates her new philosophy, "Live a Little." However, because of her hatred of "purple" press tactics, she does not approve of the changes made to the newspaper, and warns her former employees that they are heading for trouble unless they "wake up before it's too late." The staff, high on their newfound success, remind Maggie of her own philosophy, and reprise "Live a Little" until the curtain falls.

Act Two opens on Madame Bellette's, a fashionable ladies dress shop, where a fashion show is in progress, during which the models do a satirical strip routine, burlesquing the "I dreamed I was a—in my Maidenform bra" commercial ads. The salesperson, Dottie Ann, is trying to interest Maggie Martin in the new line of dresses, but Maggie, recognizing Dottie as the girl from the Sweatbeat Club, is unimpressed with what she sees. Dottie, fearing that she may have upset Maggie at the club by saying, "What has she got I haven't got," reiterates the line and apologizes for it. Maggie, unconcerned, turns to her escort, Steve Hagen, to answer the question. Suddenly embarrassed by the situation, Steve suggests they turn their attention to the fashion show, when out steps a near-nude model wearing "Naked in Chiffon." Hagen enthusiastically urges Maggie to try on that particular item, and as she exits to the dressing rooms, he asks Dottie out for a date. Wondering why Steve is suddenly interested in her, Dottie replies that she has a previous commitment. Steve's surly response instantly makes her very interested in pursuing his invitation when Maggie enters, dressed "Naked in Chiffon" and singing "You like the way I look," in which she flirts with all the men in the store as a demonstration of her "sexy" persona. Jealous and embarrassed, Steve exits in a huff, and the scene changes to Candy's office at the *Clarion*, where Candy and Jeff are discovered arguing about a recent news story. In the midst of the discussion, Candy begins to seduce Jeff, who draws away horrified, afraid of being discovered *in flagrante* by members of the staff. Suggesting that Jeff does not know how to be a man, Candy sends him away, and sings, "Give Me a Man," in which she expresses her yearning for a man who is "rough," "tough," and sensual, in terms recalling "Find Me a Primitive Man" in *Nymph Errant*. Her private deliberations become a full-stage production number in which the entire office staff join in Candy's search for the "right man."

Abruptly, the number ends when the cooking editor, John Doe, begs for another assignment because dreaming up recipes in his sleep has become a series of murderous nightmares in which dead bodies emerge from stewpots, "Murder I Want." A "Mickey Spillaine Ballet" ensues satirizing the violence, sex, and suspense of the "Drop Dead My Lovely" school of crime fiction while cleverly mirroring the action of the musical:

> Steve as the gangster has killed another racketeer. When the racketeer's girlfriend discovers the body she accuses Steve. Steve tries to quiet her by seducing her. When she attempts to kill him, he shoots her. Some of his cronies try to get the bodies out of the way, when Maggie comes upon the scene. Maggie tries to run away, she doesn't want to be involved in this kind of sordid mess. Steve and his henchmen then gang up on Maggie. The sleuth who is woman-happy is suspicious of Steve, but Steve's friends and their women, in turn seduce the sleuth. Maggie is left on the spot. Into this picture comes Jeff who tries to carry Maggie off. She however is unwilling to go with him, and still feels the need to compete with the other women on their terms. She uses the same seductive tactics which they have employed, and the sleuth comes over to her side. Then Steve and Jeff are in combat. When Maggie refuses Jeff, he steps out of the picture, Steve manages to escape, Maggie and the sleuth go off in pursuit [II-26–II-27].

After the ballet, exhibiting many of the expressionistic devices of the dream ballet since *Oklahoma!* and reminiscent of the dream sequences in *Lady in the*

Dark as well, the scene changes to the stage door of the Sweatbeat Club where Jeff, longing for Maggie, reprises "Night Time," then walks into the club. Inside, the Lovelorn Editor, Copyboy and Second Reporter are seated at a table near the stage; close by are Dottie Ann and her date, and at another table, Candy and Steve who beckon to Jeff to join them. Maggie enters, dressed simply in a plaid skirt and navy blue cashmere sweater, a highly unusual costume for a night club performer, and sings "Another Woman's Man," about a woman's yearning for a man she cannot possess.[4] Following the number, Maggie gives Candy a Hollywood contract she won for her in a crap game, and each woman returns to her original partner to the tune of "Be My Guest." Candy and Steve argue over her leaving for Hollywood, and when he threatens to find himself "a broad who knows when she's well off" (II-40), Candy reveals that she knows all about his flirtation with Dottie Ann, concluding that, despite the exchange of personalities, everything is "Still the Same." Maggie and Jeff join in the sentiment as the curtain falls.[5]

Typically, work on *Be My Guest* was a long-distance affair, especially since biographers tend to look upon the period between 1951 and 1956 as the "night time" of his career. As John Edward Hasse has noted in *Beyond Category*: "From 1951 to 1956, Ellington made no theatrical motion pictures, enjoyed no renewing overseas trips. Rather, he was primarily struggling to hold the band together, and perhaps biding his time till he could stage a comback" (316).[6] Doris Julian's enthusiasm was unmistakable, yet the Duke's absence was clearly felt, a situation to which she alludes in an undated letter accompanying an early version of the text:

> Edward darling—
>
> This is *not* the way the *1st* Act closes—There is a bright fast number (Clarion Rag) with 4 principals involved—to be done—2nd Act is on the way—Everyone here *very* excited and enthusiastic about book and lyrics—"Fresh and fun"—Can't wait to really talk to you. B. Daniels investing—They seem to think we have a hit.—Strayhorn being a doll!—Keep your fingers crossed—They can't wait to hear the music—Opinion is we have tremendous moneymaker—Love *you* madly.

The tone of the letter seems designed to keep the Duke interested, with its emphasis on backers and the property's potential as a moneymaker. Given the fact that none of Ellington's musicals had been financial successes, it is a testament to his love of the idiom (and, as some will say, his desire to be known as a theatre composer) that Duke Ellington continued to write for the stage. "Can't wait to really talk to you" and "Strayhorn being a doll!" imply that Ellington has not made himself available for personal collaboration, but has once again asked Billy Strayhorn to *represent* him on the project. In the case of *Be My Guest*, Strayhorn's representation resulted in the composition of "Night Time," one of the few works in which Strayhorn gets top-billing over Ellington, when they share composer credit.

"Night Time," registered for copyright on 17 February 1954, is a beguine with a root-fifth ostenato pattern in the bass that continues unchanged for the first 30 measures of the song. Over the ostenato, the harmony changes every two bars in the first 16 measures, progressing from some embellishment of I to ii7 and back again until the B section at bar 17. Here, a "Charleston" rhythmic pattern is established in the harmony with three chords per measure, over the still-repeating ostenato. The recapitulation restates the original harmonic pattern until bar 31 where the bass line changes, and the "Charleston" rhythm returns for nine measures, forcing the harmony to change once, more often twice, per bar.[7] At bar 40, the "Charleston" rhythm gives way to two half-note chords that anticipate a return to the opening harmonic pattern at measure 41. At bar 44, the composer uses a real V7 (13,-9)–I progression for the first time in the entire piece, indicating a full and complete cadence. Melodically, "Night Time" is composed of a series of octave leaps, resolving in the outline of an F-major triad and ending on the second degree of the scale. The B section uses simple stepwise motion, creating melodic tones that outline the harmony. As a club "performance" number, the tune is designed to be immediately accessible to the ear, hence the significant absence of melodic or harmonic dissonance. Tension and resolution are provided by the changing harmonies over the stationary ostenato in the bass.[8]

By the end of 1954, when Ellington was still unable to free up the time necessary to score *Be My Guest* in earnest, Doris Julian turned to another composer, Clay Boland, an alumnus of the Mask and Wig Club at the University of Pennsylvania. Retitled *About Face*, the new show maintained the original structure and transformation plot of *Be My Guest*, but added a syndicate hoodlum named Lefty and his moll, appropriately monikered Dolly Doll, to capitalize on the popularity of *Guys and Dolls* (1950) and develop the Mike Hammer motifs into a full-blown subplot. Although *About Face* was registered for copyright on 9 December 1955, no music appears to have been composed for the show, and Doris Julian turned again to Ellington with a new idea.

Late in 1956, Julian, no longer sharing an address or letterhead with Perry Watkins,[9] presented Duke Ellington with a musical theatre project entitled *The Crystal Tree*, in an attempt to appeal to the Duke's religious interests. The play begins at a church bazaar, where booths for games and selling items have been set up in a few backyards in Harlem. In Della's yard is the tree that will be crystal, that is possessed by the spirit of a jealous woman. The parishioners sing "For the Lord," then Maxie, a "business" man, enters with his baby carriage full of hot loot. Jojo Johnson, who expresses a desire to become a preaching minister, but hasn't the money for the study it requires, enters, singing "Home Is the Entire World" to justify his inability to achieve his dreams, and accepts the fact that seminary school will have to wait a little longer so that he can buy a piano for his son, Lasson, who dreams of being a pianist. The scene changes to Jojo's apartment into which a piano is being moved. Adam, Jojo's blind father, bewails his physical infirmity, forcing him to always "take" from his son, rendering him unable to give anything in return.

In the next scene, a café, Della tells Lasson that she wants Jojo to love her, but Jojo never notices her; his mind is only focused on God. Lasson pretends this "old news" doesn't bother him, but since he is in love with Della, her attraction to his father causes him great pain. The following scene finds the boy dead, having fallen down the stairs in a drunken stupor. Jojo rushes to his son's side and is devastated by the tragedy. In the apartment after the funeral, Jojo is very angry and turns against God, arguing that if God really existed, such things would not happen. Adam wisely tells Jojo that he is angry at himself, not at God, because his pride led him to believe that God would allow him and his to live a kind of charmed existence. No man can expect that. Mary, a nurse who visits the Johnson family now and then, would like Jojo to love her, but now it looks more hopeless than ever. In the courtyard, a nightmare dance begins, and a crystal tree begins lighting up everything. Mary watches from the fire escape, as dancers writhe in and out of the shadows, and the curtain falls.

Act Two begins in the café where Jojo enters, gets drunk and flirts with Della. Jojo's father, Adam, is also present and tries to discourage his son's acceptance of Della's advances. But Jojo will not listen to reason: he wants to go home with Della, so he pushes his father away, causing him to slip and fall. The scene changes to the courtyard, now clear of the bazaar, where we discovered that Edna May and Maxie have married. Informed that Jojo is living with Della, Mary goes to Della's apartment and accuses her of murdering Lasson by giving him alcohol and drugs and trying to do the same thing to Jojo. Suddenly accepting the truth, Jojo slaps Della and begins to leave but Della grabs onto his heel, unwilling to let him go. While Mary sings "Oh, God" on the fire escape, lamenting the unfortunate turn of events, Jojo begins packing up his things, determined to run away. Adam tells him to go ahead, not to worry about his old father: he took care of himself and his wife before, he can do it again. Jojo goes across the courtyard, and everyone wants to know where he is going. All his neighbors stop him in song and dance, and give him presents of a big Bible, and big spectacles; and, in a tender moment, Mary gives him her heart. Jojo is moved and accepts everything, including Mary's love, and the curtain falls to the sound of joyous music.

With the headline, "New Ellington Musical Set," the Baltimore *Afro-American* announced on 8 December 1956 that Perry Watkins would produce and design the sets for the new Ellington musical, *The Crystal Tree*, scheduled to go into rehearsals in January 1957 with an "all-colored cast."[10] Helen Tamiris, responsible for the choreography of *Annie Get Your Gun* (1946), *By the Beautiful Sea* (1954), *Fanny* (1954), and *Plain and Fancy*, among many other Broadway shows, was signed to direct and choreograph, while costumes were assigned to Edith Lutyens. The New York City *Morning Telegraph* of 10 December 1956 added that the show, for which Ellington had composed 22 songs, would go on a seven-week tour before opening in Manhattan. However, on 22 December 1956, the New York *Herald Tribune* advised that "because of a heavy personal-appearance schedule," Ellington was forced to relinquish his claim to *The Crystal Tree,* and that the score would be composed by Luther Henderson, a Julliard classmate of Ellington's son, Mercer, and a longtime friend of the Ellington family.

Although the *Herald Tribune* article insisted that the musical "will be presented this spring by Perry Watkins," it was not performed until nearly 25 years later when the AMAS Repertory Theater in New York City would produce it for a 15-performance run, beginning 19 April 1981.[11] In the New York *Times* review, John S. Wilson notes that "Twenty years ago Duke Ellington was pushing for the production of 'The Crystal Tree,' a show with book and lyrics by Doris Julian and music by Luther Henderson, because he was so impressed by Mr. Henderson's music, according to Rosetta Lenoire, the artistic director of the AMAS Repertory Theater" (5 May 1981: C8). It is likely, then, that unable to work on the project because of other commitments, such as completing *Night Creature* for the Carnegie Hall Concert on 16 March 1955, Ellington passed the project on to a friend who, according to Wilson, produced "the kind of music that the Duke might have written himself." Similar to Ellington's experience with *Beggar's Holiday*, Luther Henderson found himself being praised by the critics for his work in a show that failed. As the New York *Times* concluded: "As happened in Mr. Ellington's efforts to write Broadway musicals, Mr. Henderson has composed music of Broadway quality but it is weighed down by a leaden book" (5 May 1981: C8).

Even before his lifelong struggle with deficient scripts, Ellington decided—as early as 1944—to write a play. Although Ellington claims to have written his musical *Man with Four Sides* in 1955 when the band was accompanying ice skaters at the Aquacades in Flushing Meadows, the germ of the work began in the 1940s in the notes for a script entitled *Mr. and Mrs. Lane.*[12]

Man with Four Sides begins in the living room of Martha Washington Penoctbottom Lane, and her husband Otho, a former bandleader, now white-collar worker. The curtain rises on Mrs. Lane and four women playing a word game called "Four Syllables," a version of Scrabble in which words under four syllables are not allowed. While they play, they hear the voice of Streamline Smith in the apartment next door singing a raucous song about marital infidelity, and the high-bred ladies begin to question Mrs. Lane about her overly genteel lifestyle (she calls her husband, "Mr. Lane," and insists that he address her as "Mrs. Lane"). Noticing the lateness of the hour, the ladies leave abruptly, and Mrs. Lane begins the usual preparations for greeting her husband after a hard day at work. On his way up to the apartment, Mr. Lane converses briefly with Streamline about the lottery, then enters his flat, greeting his wife with an unorthodox, "Hey ma" (1/1/6), for which he is immediately reprimanded. While he is getting ready for dinner, he hears Streamline singing "Like a Train" from next door and sneaks a nip from a bottle of whisky hidden from the eyes of Mrs. Lane, and sings "She" about the woman of his dreams.[13]

At the dinner table, Mrs. Lane sweetly inquires about overhearing Mr. Lane's conversation with someone on the stairs. When Lane replies that the person was "Smith," Mrs. Lane corrects his pronunciation, referring to J. Wallingford *Smythe*, whose wife acts as chair of the ladies cultural committee. When he corrects her, she complains about the next-door neighbor being a jazz musician, referring to the traditional stereotype: "carousing with all kinds of women—frequenting places of ill-repute—gambling—drinking—smoking those charged, those doped-up cigarettes" (1/1/13), such things as Mr. Smythe would never do! When she complains about Streamline's singing the blues (because his wife left him) at so loud a volume, Mr. Lane reminds her that when she plays classical music, the entire building shakes.[14] Disregarding his remark, Mrs. Lane forbids her husband to converse with their next-door neighbor and berates him out of smoking his pipe and cigar. Retreating to his alcoholic escape, Mr. Lane hears the voice of his imaginary woman singing a blues ballad, "Weatherman," in counterpoint with Streamline. He picks up the newspaper and, reading that Streamline Smith and the Atomic Five will be performing at the Bijou Café next week, decides to revisit the café—he had only been there once before—and behave like a "real hip character." He reads an article about Miss America, takes another nip from his bottle, and imagines his dreamgirl before him, wondering what life might have been had he married a girl like that. The erotic fantasy that ensues is rudely interrupted by Mrs. Lane calling him to bed, while the curtain falls on Act One.

Act Two takes place a week later, outside the Café Bijou and various other store fronts on the street where the "Cool One" stands motionless on the corner except for his twirling a long chain. After a jive routine between the Cool One, a chick, a crony, and a dictionary, Mr. Lane enters and asks, "What is a Square?" to which he receives a myriad of jive-rhymed replies. Finally, the Cool One expounds his philosophy in song, "Standing on the Corner, Watching the World Go By," lyrically anticipating the same number in *The Most Happy Fella*, the following year. When asked if a watch was on the other end of his chain, the Cool One replies: "I don't need a watch—I'm so hip I know what time it is all the time—what's happening everyplace—I got a million fingers—dipping into everything everywhere—just call me ubiquitous" (2/1/9).[15] A choral version of the number, followed by a frenzied dance, leads to the next scene, the interior of the café, where Moiselle is finishing a "shake and grind" strip poker number as the curtain rises. Streamline Smith is introduced and he follows with a bluesy tribute to the women he cannot attain, "The one I desire / Don't admire—me" (2/1/4), and reintroduces Moiselle, who proceeds to tell dirty jokes to the crowd. During her routine, Mr. Lane enters the café, orders a double, and strikes up a conversation with Bannaka, a man wearing a riding habit, standing next to him at the bar. Lane discovers that the man was wealthy and, at one time, Moiselle's husband—that is, until the money began to dwindle, and he called her a *sinful* woman and tried to beat the *sin* out of her. Lane appears to receive an almost erotic satisfaction at hearing about Bannaka's plight,[16] when the Cool One is discovered, standing at one end of the bar. Crony enters, complaining about having just struck out with the chick on the corner, but the Cool One turns a deaf ear to his lament, concluding simply that "You goofed—dad—you goofed" (2/1/12).

Bannaka and Lane toast and continue to drink, when Mr. Lane realizes that Moiselle is the exact replica of his imaginary woman, and begins to reprise "She." Bannaka invites the chanteuse to take a drink with them, but when Lane makes an awkward attempt to flirt with her, she humiliates him. Attempting to regain his composure, Lane asks her to dance, but soon discovers that everyone sees through his attempts to act "cool," and acknowledges him for what he really is: "a plain figure—with four equal sides and four right angles" (2/1/16). To save face, Lane orders drinks for the house, and begins to flirt with Snooky, a young woman stranded by her escort at the bar. After a passage of time,[17] Snooky and Lane, both very drunk, are discovered complaining about Moiselle's rude behavior. Lane collapses on the floor, dead drunk, and Bannaka carries him out, planning to take Lane home with him to the stables where the horses would enjoy his company. Snooky, abandoned again, pulls out an address book and sings "Woman Blues," wondering who she should go home to. Her exit is interrupted by the entrance of a wife looking for her wayward husband who is hiding with a young girl underneath a table. The wife and the girl get into a "real cat fight scratching and pulling hair" (2/1/23), until the police arrive and try to break up the fight. Snooky convinces them that the women are rehearsing an "apache" dance and the fracas continues until the curtain falls.[18]

Act Three begins with "Twilight Time" during which a choral group sings and two women mimic Mrs. Lane downstage.[19] After the number, Mrs. Lane is discovered on the telephone talking to the police, during which the mimics caricature her behavior and function as her backup singing group; and as the scene progresses, Mrs. Lane, truly concerned about her husband's truancy, even accepts the possibility of being dominated by her husband if he would only "come home and stay home" (3/1/6). When Streamline begins singing the blues, Mrs. Lane discovers that she is doing exactly the same thing, and, admitting that she has not been fair to the man next door, sings "The Blues" from *Black, Brown and Beige*. Mrs. Smith, Streamline's wife, appears at the door, asking Mrs. Lane to keep her bags until her husband returns home. In turn, Mrs. Lane asks Mrs. Smith why she bothered to leave her husband in the first place, to which Streamline's wife replies: fame and all his female fans. "Naturally I wanted to know where I stood, so I did my disappearing act—just to test my strength" (3/1/11). Over tea, the women discuss Lane's disappearance and Mrs. Smith concludes, in song, that in every woman's life, there comes a time when she realizes that a good man is hard to find, and races across the hall to reconcile with her husband. Lane reappears, fighting off a hangover, and complaining about Moiselle's behavior, whips her in his imagination, while he reconciles with his wife. A handwritten direction at the top of 3/1/15 indicates a four-part fugue that continues for five pages of text until the end of the play.

The end of the play is extremely complex, both musically and dramatically. It depicts the reconciliation of two couples in two separate locales, as well as Moiselle's appearance, in Lane's imagination, providing the incentive for Lane to carry on a independent action within his imagination while his wife is monopolizing his attention in real time. Musically, the finale reintroduces leitmotifs identified earlier throughout the play, such as "Weatherman" and "She," and redefines them in a new dramatic context. Ellington does not make use of simple reprises in *Man with Four Sides*, but weaves a complex fabric of musical motifs that, in their initial statements and various permutations, propel and complement the dramatic action. The original typewritten text calls for an inconclusive ending with the word "She" suspended on a high note, followed by a "suspensefil [sic] chord" (3/1/19). A handwritten addition to the text adds a happy ending: "Mrs. Lane comes out of kitchen—goes to Lane on couch—comforts him—she calls him by his first name—he relaxes in her arms—from upstairs, Streamline puts out light—Curtain" (3/1/19).

Two of the major leitmotifs of the musical, "Weatherman" and "Train," are variations on the traditional 12-bar blues pattern. Recalling the melody of a torch-song entitled "Black Coffee," "Weatherman" displays a recitative-like melody hovering around the root and fifth of E♭ Major. What makes the potentially monotonous melody interesting is the harmony in which chromatically altered chords enable the melody to wander easily from major to minor and back again to major. The tonal ambivalence of the number reflects the changes of mood in the lyrics and displays yet again Ellington's capacity for word-painting in his music theatre songs. "Train," harmonically following the blues pattern with few chromatic alterations, displays a melody alternating between long held notes and descending stepwise phrases, making ample use of the lowered seventh scale degree. The tune, suggesting the sound of a train in motion, was borrowed from Ellington's "Happy-Go-Lucky-Local" (1946), that was later released by Jimmy Forrest, a tenor saxophonist formerly with the Ellington band, as "Night Train" which became a substantial hit.

"She" evokes the highly atmospheric "In a Sentimental Mood," with long melody notes hanging as suspensions above harmonies anxious to resolve. Written in ABA[1]B[1] form, "She" invokes a dream-like mood with long held notes alternating with undulating eight-note figures that twist and turn in unexpected directions. It is significant that the melodic structure resembles that of "Train" because in such a way Ellington subtly associates the blues of Streamline Smith with the fantasies of Otho Lane, suggesting to the audience that the problems of a "hip" jazz singer and those of a "square" business are not dissimilar when it comes to women.

"Standing on the Corner" is interesting in its anticipation of Frank Loesser's much better-known hit of the same name. While Loesser's tune begins on the tonic chord and Ellington's begins with a II7 (chromatically adjusted to become a dominant seventh chord), both melodies begin on the third degree of the scale. Loesser takes his melodic line on an upwards extension whereas Ellington prefers to center around the original two notes (E, D#) and leap down. Both composers, however, provide a musical interlude after the lyrics, "watching the world go by," presumably to permit choreography. Loesser's interlude is filled with chromatic harmony and light, almost "cute" riffs, reflecting the 12/8 feel of the piece, but Ellington makes use of a kind of jazz improvisation, much more bluesy in character, indicative of a solid 4/4 rhythm. The differences are not surprising since the dramatic intention of the numbers is different in each show: in Loesser's piece, the number is sung by the comic characters in a attempt to pick up girls; in Ellington, the number is sung by the Cool One to demonstrate his "hip" philosophy. (See Example 5.1)

Though Derek Jewell claims that this period represented the "lowest point in Ellington's progress. His music *was* well below his best" (120), the extant score of *Man with Four Sides* demonstrates that the Duke had far from lost his touch, but was exploring new ground as a theatrical innovator.

A preliminary production budget for *Man with Four Sides* in the Ellington Archive verifies the author's interest in getting the show produced on Broadway. *Down Beat* (21 September 1955) announced that Loretta Val-Mery

Example 5.1.

had agreed to produce the show which was capitalized at $150,000 according to the preliminary budget, but in a letter from Ellington to a prospective investor, the figure was said to be $200,000. Of the total, $5,000 was earmarked for the author's advance, $33,000 for the building of sets, costumes, rental of lighting equipment, properties, etc., a very modest $6,250 to pay the director, choreographer, musical director, and designers, $12,500 for orchestrations and copyist fees, $30,750 in bonds to all of the unions involved, $21,600 for rehearsal salaries, $6,500 for preliminary advertising and publicity, $7,800 for office staff and supplies, and $3,000 for insurance and taxes. According to Ellington's letter to a prospective investor, a 1 percent interest in the show cost $4,000.[20] If 98 percent of the money was raised, the producer retained his option to produce the play on Broadway; if less than that amount was forthcoming, then all the investors' money (held, according to Ellington, in escrow until the target amount was reached) would be returned.

On one of his band tours in the fall of 1955, Ellington even found a prospective director who offered many good suggestions about dramatic construction and provided much needed encouragement regarding the overall quality of the property. Perhaps because he was waiting for a high-powered, Broadway director to take the reins, the Duke was reticent to sign his eager young director to a contract, as the following extract from an undated letter from "Phil" to Ellington indicates:

> You really must forgive me for trying to badger you every time we talk. I guess more than anything else, I can't stop thinking about the show. It's not easy for me not to since I've become so close to it in so short a time. Sure I would like to know that I will be directing it, you know that. I'm convinced that I can do it well, and that you will be pleased and excited about my work as I am about yours.... Naturally, I would like to continue working on the show, on a more than tenuous basis. When you can tell me that I know that the work can go ahead full steam, and we can get the show ready to go as we discussed it in Columbus. With what has yet to be done on the script, I know that it can be ready to go into the works by January first. As I said to you then, I think the basic structure is strong and the premise is good, what has to be changed, can be done if we can concert our effort along those lines. So that's it. I'll wait to hear from you [301.4.6.11].

Phil never received a reply and, by the autumn of 1956, *Man with Four Sides* was said to be in the hands of José Ferrer, the Academy Award–winning actor, and scheduled to open in Boston during the 1956–57 season.[21] Although Duke had broadcast much of the show on the NBC radio program "Monitor" in August 1955, *Man with Four Sides* was not produced in front of an audience until 20 February 1997, when the Duke Ellington Society funded a staged reading of the work, under the direction of Damon Kiely, at St. Peter's Church on 54th Street in New York City.[22]

With the production of *Man with Four Sides* at a standstill, Ellington looked for other creative opportunities, one of which he found on his own doorstep, in a project that had been announced as early as January 1946, during the run of *Beggar's Holiday*: *Cole Black and the Seven Dwarfs*, a "hip" revision of the Snow White story. On 25 August 1948, *Down Beat* announced that screenwriter William Cottrell and T. Hee, who worked for the Disney corporation, would produce the book and lyrics, and that William Hertz, Jr., was signed as producer. On 17 May 1949, a "Standard Uniform Popular Songwriters Contract" was signed by the lyricists with Ellington and Strayhorn for the show's big ballad, "Once Upon a Dream," and exactly two months later, on 18 July, another one of the principal songs from the show, "I Could Get a Man," was registered for copyright. Little developed of the project until August 1955, when a full script emerged, promising a production with sets and costumes by Mary Blair. Finally, inspired by the popularity of Strayhorn and Ellington's early 1950s hit, "Satin Doll," T. Hee, William Cottrell, and a new collaborator, Lowell Matson, transformed the African American equivalent of "Snow White and the Seven Dwarfs," *Cole Black and the Seven Dwarfs*, into *Satin Doll and the Seven Little Men*.[23]

Satin Doll begins with a prologue in which Queenie finds out, by way of her magic mirror, that there exists someone finer and fairer than she, by the

Storybook illustration from the musical *Cole Black and the Seven Dwarfs*. Courtesy of the Duke Ellington Collection, National Museum of American History Archives Center, Smithsonian Institution.

name of Satin. Suddenly the scene shifts to a nightclub called the Palace, where Queenie is both emcee and entertainer, and Satin is the hat check girl ("I Could Get a Man"). The Prince arrives, takes instant notice of Satin ("Once Upon a Dream"), and invites everyone to his house for a party, hoping that his interest in Satin will go unnoticed by Queenie. While Satin changes her clothes to go to the party, Queenie pays Hunter, her henchman and troubleshooter, to drive Satin far away from the city and cut her heart out. In the next scene, outside Queenie's Palace, a policeman comes by and spoils Queenie's plot by joining Hunter and Satin, who escapes into an alley and has a ballet dream about all that has happened. She is discovered the next morning by Cub Scouts who take her (conning Hunter into showing off his strength by carrying her) to the seventh floor of a boarding house, the "Cold Water Den of the Seven Little Men," where they think she will be safe, and the curtain falls on Act One.

In Act Two, Scene One, the "Cold Water Den," Satin has nowhere to turn, having telephoned the Prince but finding Queenie on the other end of the line (Hunter had informed her that Queenie was involved in the plot to kill her). However, she cheers up when she sings a "commercial" number about Wishy Washy Soap—a soap that can do anything! If a soap can do it, so can she! An extended jive ballet follows during which the seven little men (now shoe shine boys) do their work on various people including the Prince, who extemporizes in song about his emotional condition, "It's Love I'm In" with the help of the seven little men. Singing, "Hi De Hi," a marching song, the seven little men return home. Apparently, they were musicians at an earlier point in their career, but having been unable to get that kind of work for a long time, they now shine shoes. Initially surprised at finding Satin in the cold water den, they quickly get used to her presence and begin to enjoy singing with her ("Satin Doll"), even though at bedtime Satin appropriates all of their beds and the little men are forced to sleep on the fire escape. Back at the Palace, the mirror tells Queenie that Satin is still alive despite the fact that Hunter had brought her a heart ("all beef," says the mirror). The delivery boy, who delivered the heart, reappears and bungles Hunter's excuse. The mirror suggests that Queenie should do the "old poison apple" bit and suggests that Old Granny could take care of it. The hag appears when summoned and, during a Voodoo Ballet, creates the poisoned pippin. Queenie gets into her peddler-woman disguise, then telephones the seven little men as the curtain falls on Act Two.

At the beginning of Act Three, Queenie has sent the seven little men to the mortuary to "dig" a grave, a play on words they initially enjoy, until they realize its full significance. Suddenly remembering that they have left Satin all alone, they rush back to their cold water den, where Queenie, pretending to be a scent salesperson, convinced Satin to inhale a poisoned perfume. The seven little men arrive too late to prevent Satin's death and they take her to the cemetery where the Prince, who has been out of town on business, suddenly appears, and kisses the dead girl. As in all fairy tales, a Prince's kiss is magical, and Satin awakes.

The finale scene opens on "Satin Doll's Castle Club," a swinging place, where the seven little men return to their profession as musicians, and the Prince and Satin sing happily ever after "I Could Get a Man," and "It's Love I'm In" reprise.

Four songs exist for *Satin Doll*, either written specifically for the project, or borrowed from Ellington/Strayhorn's vast catalog of tunes. In "I Could Get a Man," Satin identifies her bad luck with men. Beginning in F-minor, the melody makes ample use of the flatted seventh and raised fifth degrees of the scale to create a very bluesy modality, even though the composition ends in a major key. The structure of the song is unique for a theatre composition with an 8 bar A, another 8 bar A, a 4 bar B, and 4 bar A as a recapitulation. The song format displays a kind of nervous energy and an awkward, inarticulate quality, emphasized by the terse, colloquial lyrics, assembled in units of 10 to 12 syllables. The Prince's "Once Upon a Dream," in contrast, is built on much longer melodic and lyrical phrases, though the nine bar construction (instead of the more typical eight) creates as certain awkwardness as well, subtly connecting the Prince's personality with that of Satin. While the melodic contour of the chorus is essentially stepwise, with no skip greater than a third, the release is filled with leaps of an octave, and melody notes a full two octaves away from the lowest notes of the chorus. Again Ellington is experimenting with pictorialization, associating the concept of "castles in the air" with the higher vocal register, and the dramatic insistence of a heart trying to express itself through the octave leaps. Although the harmony of the ballad is easily accessible, the dissonant suspensions created by the melody at bars 6, 7, 15, 16, 32, and 33, create a important dramatic tension that reflects the rhyming couplets in the lyric, aching to be resolved.

"Love I'm In" is a jaunty rhythm number cued in the script by the fact that the Prince's socks do not match. The repeatable A section has 8 bars and the B section, forming a kind of coda chorus to the lyrics "It's love I'm in" repeated three times, only four. The light-hearted, consonant melody is filled with syncopation and skips, but is easily memorable since it outlines a very basic harmonic structure: tonic-dominant, tonic-subdominant, dominant-tonic. The harmonic simplicity is embellished by the use of syncopated chords in the accompaniment. A version of the melody (in the key of D♭) exists on the second page of Ellington's sketches for *Moon of Mahnomen*, and so the tune may have been composed as early as 1946.

By far, the most famous of the songs for *Satin Doll* is the title number, originally recorded as an instrumental on 6 April 1953 in Ellington's first Capitol recording session.[24] In three weeks, reaching number 27 on the *Billboard* chart, "Satin Doll" was a moderate success, becoming the last single-record hit in the Duke's career. Originally an improvised riff—one of many tossed off by Ellington in his career—the tune was elaborated and harmonized by Billy Strayhorn who added a lyric extolling his mother, and using his pet name for her as the title.[25] At some later point, Johnny Mercer added the lyrics that are known today. Written in a traditional AABA form, "Satin Doll" is exceedingly listener-friendly. It employs a repetitive two-note motif that changes pitch without changing shape, much in the same way that "Tea for Two" uses the repetition of a three note phrase on varying degrees of the scale. Beginning on ii7–V7, the harmony immediately demands resolution, but instead of resolving, it moves up a step to iii7–VI7, and after a series of harmonically altered chords, finally finds its way back to the tonic, but not by way of a traditional cadence (II♭7–I instead of V7–I). The release uses an undulating tetrachordal melody, first in the tonality of the subdominant, and next in that of the dominant, harmonically using the ii7–V7 pattern established at the beginning of the piece. The recapitulation is an exact repetition of the exposition, with no melodic change at the final note; rather than ending on the tonic, the melody ends on the fifth degree of the scale, creating a definite sense of non-resolution.

In *Satin Doll*, the number is used as a performance number by a group of ex-musicians, the "Seven Little Men," entertaining themselves with a houseguest, Satin. As a performance piece, the responsibilities of a musical number—to provide characterization or pictorialization of the dramatic moment—are somewhat relaxed, and an audience is permitted to appreciate the song as *song* and its ability to flaunt the strengths of the performers. In the earlier version of the show, a song called "Sweet Velvet O'Toole" was used in place of "Satin Doll." Dating back to Ellington's *Beggar's Holiday* period,[26] "Sweet Velvet" unsubtlely paints the picture of a grasping young adventurer, a "minor" with the "instincts of a Forty-Niner," built like a bomber, who is "nobody's fool." To create an interesting musical tension, the duple-meter "swing" melody, highly syncopated and improvisatory in structure, is accompanied in triple meter, evoking the cadence of a march. The scene introducing the song is filled with comic physical business and it is likely that Duke desired to continue the sportive atmosphere through what would otherwise be construed as a "torch song."(See Example 5.2)

Example 5.2.

Although full of interesting and memorable music and a very commercial hook, *Satin Doll* was never produced[27] and Duke Ellington continued the search for a musical theatre property even though the composition of a series of musical suites with narration and or implied plots have satisfied his dramatic yearnings. In September 1956, Ellington recorded *A Drum Is a Woman*, a concept album, narrating the story of Madame Zajj—too much like jazz backwards to be subtle—and the affect she has on a man named Joe (please note the similarities to the earlier *Cock o' the World*). The next year, Ellington premiered *Such Sweet Thunder*, an interpretation of various Shakespearean plays, and was said to be working on a forthcoming Broadway show about South Africa, titled *Saturday Laughter*, or *The Man Beneath*.

Wanting a property that would be both commercially successful and artistically satisfying, librettist Herb Martin and producer Christopher Manos first turned to Marjorie Rawlings's classic, *The Yearling*, but found that the rights were as yet unavailable. Undaunted, Martin picked up a copy of Peter Abrahams's novel, *Mine Boy*, about apartheid in South Africa from a black perspective, and realized that he had found a project that would be socially relevant, artistically stimulating, and financially rewarding. Manos acquired the rights to do a musical adaptation of the book, and Martin, in collaboration with Stephen Bates, began constructing a libretto.[28] Once an acceptable first draft had been completed, Christopher Manos commissioned Duke Ellington to compose the score. Typically, the producer and librettists had to accommodate Ellington's band engagements, and accepted the fact that either most of the work would have to be completed long-distance, or they would have to chase Ellington around the country.[29] Through the efforts of Billy Strayhorn, realizing Ellington's sketches, and the patience of the producer and librettists, 22 songs were completed for the score, and Ellington, Strayhorn and the orchestra went off on a tour of one-nighters throughout Europe.

Stuck in the United States without either composer or his right-hand man, Christopher Manos began planning for a series of readings and backers auditions for the show. Because the score Ellington and Strayhorn provided was essentially a collection of songs, only vaguely adapted to the text of the musical, Manos hired Abba Bogin as musical director to arrange the material and provide musical continuity. This was not an unusual assignment, nor does it represent a failure on Ellington or Strayhorn's part to understand the exigencies of the Broadway stage. After all, one of America's most beloved and classic musicals, *My Fair Lady*, had someone writing musical continuity (Trude Rittman), and no one ever accused Fritz Loewe of not being a "theatre composer." Not all Broadway composers create a through-composed score to accommodate the spoken text; some provide little more than a lead sheet and leave the rest to the musical director, dance arranger, and orchestrator. Suggesting that Ellington was unconcerned about the handling of his music in the show, Bogin recalls: "I met with him early on before he left with his band, and he said to me, 'I'm sure you know your business. Whatever you guys do is fine. I don't have the time to be with you. If the show gets produced, I'll try to stop in and see what you did. Until then, do whatever you want'" (Hajdu 184). The operative phrase here is "If the show gets produced." Ellington had suffered failure every time out with a Broadway show and he certainly was not going to endanger his career with his orchestra, which was in the midst of a renaissance of popularity, for a possible opening on Broadway.

A cast of African American performers was assembled to do readings and backers' auditions, including Brock Peters, Joya Sherrill, Thelma Carpenter, Diahann Carroll, and Ivan Dixon, all donating their time and energies to the production in the expectation of being hired for the Broadway production.[30] Hopes were high because, in the spring of 1958, the trade papers announced that this "tuned-up" adaptation of *Mine Boy*, produced by Christopher Manos in collaboration with Arnold Margolin, and directed by Michael Howard, was to begin rehearsals in July with a New York opening set for October.

The story of *Saturday Laughter*, so called because on Saturday, "Sorrows flee," is evocative of Nelson Mandella's life, though purely accidentally, according to Herbert Martin. Act One begins in the Malay Camp, Johannesburg, South Africa, late at night. The protagonist, Xuma, having journeyed from the north country, meets the perpetually drunk Johannes (known to his friends as J.P. Williamson) and his orphan boy helper, Leah, the matriarch of the camp who brews and sells illegal beer, and her niece, Eliza, a beautiful young teacher whose European-style clothes are very unidiomatic to the setting. Xuma is quite attracted to Eliza but she rejects his advances, arguing that they are very different people, unsuited to one another, and Xuma must be satisfied with the offer of food and shelter, and the promise of work in the nearby mines. Scene Two opens on the entrance to the mine, above ground. As the men enter to work at the mines, Johannes introduces Xuma to the white boss, Red, as his new "boss boy." After delivering a long lecture about the duties involved in leading and supervising men, Red hires Xuma on Johannes's recommendation. After experiencing the sadistic behavior of the other white foremen in the mine and the insensitivity of the Safety Engineer (who cares more about the equipment than the men), Xuma realizes that he is in a far different environment than his home, where there were no white men.

The scene changes to a street corner in the Malay Camp on a Saturday afternoon. Boys are in the middle of a soccer game and Johannes's Boy invites Xuma to join them. Various people assemble for the day's activities including: a witch doctor and his entourage, two "coon band" members, covered with gaudy body paint and feathers, a gangster of the "Lenox-Avenue type," and various individuals preparing for a picnic. Leah introduces Xuma to another of her nieces, Maisy who offers to show Xuma how the inhabitants of the camp dance to entertain themselves. Suddenly, the sound of a police whistle interrupts the festivities, and everyone runs except for Xuma, who holds his ground, claiming to have done nothing wrong. After a white policeman strikes him violently, Xuma throws the man to the ground and runs away. The scene changes to Leah's Place where Xuma is hiding. He tells Eliza what has happened, and suddenly the stage is filled with people talking about the beating and Xuma's reaction. The white police commissioner, known to the people as "The Fox," enters, trying to get someone to confess to the crime. When Xuma is questioned, he fakes a limp to hide his powerful strength, and the Fox leaves without an arrest. The Saturday celebration continues at Leah's place, during which Eliza tries to nurse Xuma's shoulder, swollen because of the policeman's attack. Clearly attracted to her, Xuma kisses Eliza but she breaks away, claiming to be no good for him because she wants what the white people have ("Inside I am not black and I don't want to be black."). Leah offers Xuma a job as bartender at her "Place," but Xuma refuses, more concerned with Eliza's rejection of him than a second job.

Scene Four occurs in the early morning, in an underground mine. Xuma enters from a tunnel carrying a mine boy who is having a serious coughing spasm. The man had refused to see a doctor, even though his condition had persisted for two months, because he was afraid of losing his income. Red offers the man full salary during his period of recovery and tells Xuma to report any miner who shows signs of illness. Encouraged by what appears to be consideration on the part of the white management, Xuma approaches the safety engineer with his concerns over structural problems in his tunnel. Unlike Red, the safety engineer is unsympathetic and Xuma remarks that everyone seems to be filled with anger here "in the city." Red forces Xuma to admit his own anger against the white men, but concludes, privately, that Xuma needs his anger to grow as a person. The scene changes to Leah's Place at dinner time, where Maisy is trying to cheer up an exhausted Xuma in song and dance. Just as she has succeeded in making him laugh, Eliza enters with another male teacher dressed in "European" clothes, and Xuma becomes angry and frustrated at the sight. Maisy ridicules the teachers' pretentious sophistication and Eliza leaves, offended. Xuma realizes that is what Eliza wants of him, "to wear those foolish clothes and talk in that funny way," and agrees to work for Leah to support his attempt at sophistication. The act comes to a close with Eliza, in love with white society, and Maisy, in love with Xuma, each lamenting their impossible dream.

Some time has passed when Act Two begins inside Leah's Place, late at night. Dressed in sharp new clothes, Xuma functions as a kind of bartender/manager/bouncer of the establishment, respected and admired by all. Leah enters with Maisy and the boy discussing the American movie that they had just seen and conclude that Americans must all be violent, rich, and fashion-conscious. Eliza enters with a suitcase, returning from a trip. Xuma explains his new employment and boasts that he now has the money to buy her whatever she desires, but Eliza, even admitting that she loves him, continues to insist that they are wrong for each other. Xuma's passionate expressions of love overcome her objections and he carries her into the bedroom to make love. The scene changes to the mine entrance where another argument between Xuma and the safety engineer is averted because of Red's intervention. Johannes teases Xuma about how much his work has improved since Eliza's return, and the boy enters with a pair of shoes Xuma sent him to buy as a gift for her. By the end of the scene, afternoon has faded into evening and stars fill the sky, creating a "beautiful night for a man in love." When Xuma appears at Leah's Place with the shoes, Eliza, unaware that they are a gift for her, calls them "gaudy" and something she "could never wear," so Xuma gives the present to Leah whose delight at the gift results in a complicated dance number in which the behavior of white society is burlesqued. Very uncomfortable with what she is seeing, Eliza screams at the crowd and runs into her room. Xuma follows her only to find her packing to go away "for good." As Eliza leaves, Maisy enters and attempts to comfort Xuma by admitting her own love for him. Xuma cannot return her love and decides to return home to the north country, even though Maisy warns him that it is impossible to return to the "country" once he has lived in the "city."

The scene changes to the underground mine where the safety engineer and Xuma continue to argue over working conditions. When Red lectures him about the hatred growing inside him against the white engineer, Xuma asks how a white man can understand how a black man feels. Red responds that he is "a *man* first" and asks Xuma to be "a *man* first, and then a *black* man."

As their discussion becomes more involved, a loud crash is heard from within the mine tunnel and Johannes is brought out, dead. Xuma refuses to go back into the tunnel when the safety engineer orders the men back to work and calls a strike. Red stands by Xuma's decision and the engineer calls for their arrest. As Xuma and Red are about to be shackled and led to prison, Xuma escapes down the mine shaft elevator. The scene changes to the exterior of Leah's Place where Xuma confesses his guilt at leaving Red to face trial alone. He decides to return to the mine and tell his story when the Commission of Enquiry is held, confident in the belief that if he *and* Red tell the truth, the truth will be believed. Accompanying him back to the mine, the boy asks Xuma if he is afraid. Xuma replies that, having experienced both hatred and love from the white man, he understands the "man beneath" the skin and has no fear, for he is a "new man" in a "new world" with happiness in his heart.[31]

Because the text was serious and operatic in scope, Ellington provided a score evoking, if not attaining, the variety and grandeur of Weill's *Lost in the Stars* and Gershwin's *Porgy and Bess*. Ellington's music ranged from the highly atmospheric "Full of Shadows," an arioso introducing Xuma, blues-like in its tonality and operatic in scope, to the more popular-sounding "J.P. Williamson," a jazz patter song, filled with syncopation and a free-wheeling, improvisatory melody, absolutely appropriate to the personality of the singer/character. Like Gershwin, Ellington knew how to combine a popular idiom with an serious one, and like Weill he was capable of creating a consistent musical texture while still maintaining a sense of musical variety. One of the centerpieces of the score, "This Man," is a bravura duet for the two principal women characters, in an operatic vocabulary that Ellington is exploring for the first time. Not only is his music capable of word-painting or characterization, now the very texture of the music—its very sound—provides a dramatic action independent of the lyrics.

"Big White Mountain" is a kind of folk worksong sung by the mine boys as they march to the mines. The simple melody is pentatonic, making use of only D♭, E♭, G♭, A♭, and B♭ in various combinations with haunting effect. The rhythmic syncopation in the accompaniment suggests mechanical movement in counterpoint to the more "natural" lyricism of the melody, evoking the dichotomy between the worker and the mine. (See Example 5.3) "The Bioscope Song," on the other hand, invokes American jazz in its use of the minor mode, "blue notes" and syncopation. With lyrics that name Jimmy Cagney, Leslie Howard, Peter Lorre, Lana Turner, Marlon Brando, and Gene Autry as typifying the American cinema, the song is a playful parody of film scenarios using an archetypical jazz sound as a kind of musical self-parody. Unlike the free-wheeling swing of "J.P. Williamson" that still sounds indigenous to the people of the Malay Camp, "The Bioscope Song" is an attempt at recreating a foreign style that reinforces the dramatic action and adds another dimension to the score. (See Example 5.4)

After several unsuccessful attempts at raising the money necessary for a Broadway production of *Saturday Laughter*, and the subsequent failure to produce the show in London in 1960, Christopher Manos left New York for Atlanta, Georgia, where he became producer of the Theatre of the Stars. While in Atlanta, Manos also developed an African American theatre company called *Just Us* that, in 1977, produced a small, abbreviated version of the musical. Brock Peters, one of the original performers involved in the

Example 5.3.

Example 5.4.

backers' auditions, attempted to secure the rights for a production in California after he had become a highly successful film and television performer, but that production—with the score completely revised by Luther Henderson—never came to pass. As recently as 1994, *Saturday Laughter* was being rewritten as *Xuma's Journey* by Henry Miller, the artistic director of the James Baldwin Theatre in New York City. Miller's text emphasizes the association between Xuma and Nelson Mandella and omits the character of Maisy. It enlarges the role of Leah, a mature woman capable of fiery and passionate love, who represses her own interest on Xuma, in favor her niece, Eliza, who gives up the man she loves because of her dreams of assimilation into a white society. Miller argues that it was the complexity of the romantic relationships in the play that rendered *Saturday Laughter* impossible to produce, suggesting that American theatre audiences have a difficult time dealing with black multidimensional love stories. The very unconventional quality of the story and its characters was what originally attracted the creative team to the project; it may also account for why, 40 years after *Saturday Laughter* was composed, it has yet to receive a first-class production.[32]

When Ellington and his orchestra returned from Europe in November 1958, he discovered that the producers had failed to raise the money for a Broadway production of *Saturday Laughter*. Believing the project now to be a dead issue, and claiming in the press to have lost interest in it because of its overly serious subject matter, the Duke looked for another high-visibility alternative to keep his name fresh and immediate in the commerce of entertainment. Instead of turning to *Satin Doll, Man with Four Sides, Be My Guest*, or *Moon of Mahnomen*, all projects yet to be produced, Ellington found himself persuaded by Sid Kuller to revive the West Coast revue *Jump for Joy (*a production discussed in an earlier chapter), for an extended run at the Copa City dinner theatre in Miami Beach, Florida. With the civil rights movement at hand, Ellington was easily persuaded that his earlier essay against "Uncle-Tom-ism" was more commercially viable than his more serious and original work for *Saturday Laughter*. But he had other properties in the trunk, at various levels of completion, equally viable, perhaps even more so. Why the Duke should prefer reviving and recomposing an older show rather than completing a new project may attest to why so much of his musical theatre oeuvre is unknown: "I'm so damned fickle. I never could stick with what I was doing—always wanted to try something new" (Hasse 335). Reviving *Jump for Joy* was a *new* challenge for the Duke, even though he put most of it in the hands of Billy Strayhorn and went off to Chicago with the orchestra to play his traditional Christmas-season date at the Blue Note from 17 December to 4 January 1959.[33]

In Duke's absence, Strayhorn and Sid Kuller produced at least three new songs for the show: a patter-gospel number called "So the Good Book Says," a schottische-style patter entitled "If We Were Any More British, We Couldn't Talk at All," and a rhythm blues number, "Walk It Off."

Although Kuller praised Strayhorn's musical contribution to the show, he noted a change in Billy's attitude toward the project: "Billy wasn't as personally excited about the show as he was when we did it in 1941. His work was fantastic.... He was a master at his craft. But I mean, he didn't seem to be overly concerned personally if the show made it or not. As soon as he was done writing, he was off. He and Paul Gonsalves [tenor saxophonist with the Ellington orchestra] went out partying" (Hajdu 186–87). Perhaps the realization that Ellington would be credited with composing *all* the songs discouraged Strayhorn from taking the project too seriously. (Strayhorn, however, did share the copyright with Ellington on the three numbers he composed in Duke's absence.) Perhaps he felt that *Jump for Joy* had run its course and was more interested in the serious jazz compositions he and Ellington had been developing (such as a *Drum Is a Woman*, or *Such Sweet Thunder*). Whatever the cause, Strayhorn made it clear that this was Duke's show, and that he was there simply to do a job and enjoy himself.[34]

Although there was much speculation in the press on whether or not the show would open (as late as 31 December, Dorothy Kilgallen announced in the *Journal American* that the show had been called off because of "money problems"), *Jump for Joy*, accompanied by Ellington and his orchestra, opened at the Copa City in Miami Beach on 20 January 1959 for what was expected to be an extended run. In the program, Sid Kuller was billed as writer, producer, and director, Nick Castle was billed as choreographer, and Duke Ellington was cited as composer. Additional lyrics and sketches were credited to Paul Webster and Hal Fimberg, while the orchestrations were said to be the work of Duke Ellington and Billy Strayhorn,[35] and vocal arrangements by Fred Weismantel. Costumes were credited to Jack's of Hollywood and Variety (New York). The cast included Barbara McNair, a popular nightclub singer and television personality; comics James (Stump) Cross, Harold (Stumpy) Cromer, and Timmie Rodgers; singers Othella Dallas, Jimmy Randolph and Lil Greenwood; Norma Miller and her dancing Jazz Men; the Miller Brothers, a vocal quintet; and Malley Torre leading a chorus of "30 Gorgeous Beige Beauties."

Some of the material presented was recycled from the original *Jump for Joy*, notably the Noel Coward parody "Resigned to Living," the orchestral bravura piece "Concerto for Clinkers," the sentimental duet "Brownskin Gal in the Calico Dress," the popular standard "I Got It Bad and That Ain't

Good," the comedy sketch "Vignette," the "zoot-suit" sketch "Made to Order," and the title song. New material included "Nerves," a patter number exploiting the goings-on backstage; "The Natives Are Restless Tonight," recalling Ellington's "jungle music" complete with nonsense lyrics ("splee dot" and "ugga-dugga-dungle") invoking the spirit of the "Broadway jungle"; "But," a comic romantic duet; "Show 'Em You Got Class," and "When I Trilly with My Filly," both evoking the classic Ellington syncopated swing style; "Three Shows Nightly," a comedy vamp number; and "Pretty and the Wolf," a hip jazz revision of the "Peter and the Wolf" tale that dates from 1955.

As in the original production of *Jump for Joy*, the creative team continued to add and subtract numbers from the running order throughout the run to stimulate audience interest but, even though tourist business was flourishing in Miami Beach, attendance was so low that the show closed prematurely on 8 February 1959, at a loss of $100,000. Unable to recover from the financial setback, Copa City remained closed for the rest of the tourist season. Although Kuller blames the show's demise on the fact that a resort crowd did not want a musical with social awareness, the reviews for the production paint a slightly different picture, suggesting once again that the show was ahead of its time. The Miami *Herald* argued that, while the cast included some stellar African American performers,

> "Jump for Joy" in the whole is not a Negro revue in the wild and abandoned sense.... It is a polite and slick presentation ... making an obvious effort to emancipate the old-time colored revue from the specialized niche it has held for decades.
>
> Here the Noel Coward and the Garrick Gaieties type of smart lyric and casual approach are integrated with the old format. It might be a commendable bit of pioneering but the public may like a bit more of the old time show religion. "Jump for Joy" has the talent to deliver it—all it needs is some readjusting [23 January 1959].

Down Beat (5 March 1959) noted that the production was to have been recorded for the Columbia label, but though such a recording was made, it was never released.

After the financial disaster of 1959, *Jump for Joy* fell into oblivion until 1988, when recordings from the original 1941 production were released in the Smithsonian Collection of Recordings accompanied by Patricia Willard's illuminating notes. A 1991 recreation of the show in Chicago by the Pegasus Players at a community-college theatre met with popular and critical acclaim but, once again, producers were uninterested in developing the property into a first-class production.

Six

"What Color Is Virtue?"

Nineteen sixty-three was an important year for Ellington. He composed music for a production of Shakespeare's *Timon of Athens* at the Stratford, Ontario, Shakespeare Festival; he led his orchestra on a long and arduous tour of the Middle East through Afghanistan, India, Pakistan, and Ceylon; and he conceived, composed, wrote, and directed a revue designed for the Century of Negro Progress Exhibition at McCormick Place, in Chicago, to celebrate the centennial of the Emancipation Proclamation. The exposition was divided into five "areas," each of which had a special focus. Area One was a greeting area displaying a replica of the state seal, a portrait of the governor, Otto Kerner, and an official document greeting visitors to the exposition. Area Two contained a manuscript of the Gettysburg Address, one of five known to be in existence, purchased by the $50,000 raised by Illinois school children and a $10,000 grant from Marshall Field, the principal department store in Chicago. Also in Area Two was a manuscript of Edward Everett's speech at Gettysburg. Everett was to have been the main speaker at Gettysburg, however his speech was eclipsed by Abraham Lincoln's. Area three displayed busts of Abraham Lincoln, showing him in the company of African Americans. In Area Three, the visitor also learns that Lincoln's barber was an African American. Area Four displayed 50 original paintings by Margaret Burroughs, and traced the history of African Americans in Illinois from the eighteenth century to the present. Area Five covered the activities of the Centennial mobile unit, containing a variety of untold facts regarding black history. And Area Six was a display of "Contemporary Negro Life" showing African Americans in government, science, sports, business, and all other walks of life (Chicago *Defender* 17–23 August: 1–2).

The principal entertainment for the exposition was Ellington's revue, titled, *My People*, performed twice daily, at 3:00 and 8:30 P.M., from 16 August to 2 September at the 5,000-seat Arie Crown Theatre, on a stage 90 feet wide and 60 feet deep. To solve the problem of the enormous playing area, where, Ellington noted, a hundred people would look like a quartet, he decided to put the band onstage, behind which would be erected a platform 12 feet high, extending all the way to the back wall, with stairs on both sides behind the band. Using this setup, with the Alvin Ailey Dance Theatre and the Tally Beatty[1] Dancers, Ellington described his vision of the beginning of the revue:

> For the opening, I would have a boy and a girl dancing at the extreme back end of the elevation—a sort of Afro dance. Then black out, fade up to green as backdrop silhouettes the dancer; fade up amber cross lights at the point where the boy is doing the head-rolling thing *á la* Geoffrey Holder; slow fade to black, and first slowly cross orchestra pit with ambers, purples, and reds, and then quickly bright up. Instead of two tiny figures in the distance, the audience was suddenly looking at forty-eight giant hands rising up out of the dark, towering over them on the orchestra pit elevator. Some were shocked by the silhouette and even cried out in fright. Thanks to Ailey and Beatty, Ellington had achieved a choreographic masterpiece on his maiden voyage [*Music Is My Mistress* 198].

In an interview with *Down Beat* Magazine (15 August 1963), Ellington revealed that *My People* was conceptualized in two parts, based on two of the songs he had written for *Black, Brown and Beige*: "Come Sunday," representing the spiritual aspect of African American life, and "The Blues," reflecting the daily trials and tribulations of work and love. Noting Ellington's desire for "entertainment, not documentation" in the presentation, *Down Beat* provided the following outline of the show:

> The production, according to the composer, will be made up of an opening statement, a work-song ballet (not the *Work Song* from *BB&B*), a five-selection spiritual-Gospel section, "rhapsodization" of the work song and

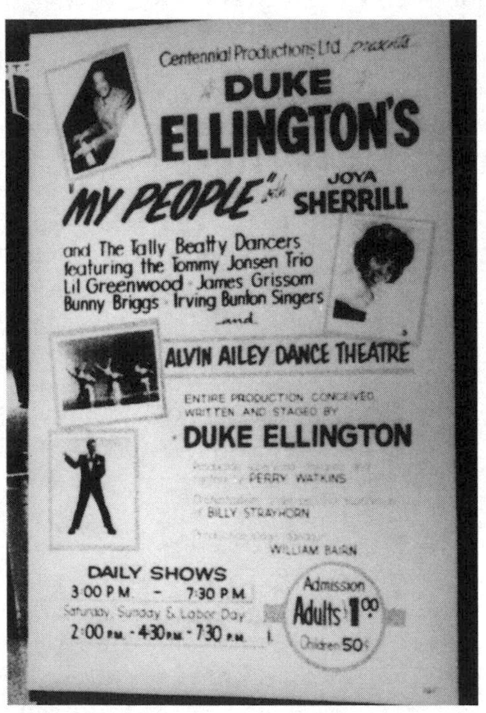

Billboard for the production of *My People* at the Arie Crown Theatre in Chicago. Courtesy of the Duke Ellington Collection, National Museum of American History Archives Center, Smithsonian Institution.

Production number from a performance of *My People*. Note the placement of the orchestra and the distribution of the singers and dancers in the cast. Courtesy of the Duke Ellington Collection, National Museum of American History Archives Center, Smithsonian Institution.

> spiritual together, the blues-and-development portion, a choir doing *King Fit the Battle of Birmingham* (an Ellington poetic comment set in a *Joshua* mold),[2] a song about mothers and fathers, a section featuring dancers Geoffrey Holder and Carmen DeLavallade, and a Bunny Briggs feature titled *What Color Is Virtue?* [11]

The cast included Ellington regulars Joya Sherrill and Lil Greenwood, as well as Milt Grayson, Jimmy Grissom, Jimmy McPhail, and the Irving Bunton Singers. Billy Strayhorn conducted the orchestra and co-wrote two of the numbers used in the show, "Strange Feeling," borrowed from the 1944 *Perfume Suite*, co-composed with Duke Ellington, and "Purple People," which became the model for "Jail Blues" and "Working Blues."[3] Perry Watkins, Ellington's former producer, was also on board as production supervisor, designing sets, costumes, and lighting for the piece.

After his experiences with *Beggar's Holiday, Moon of Mahnomen*, and *The Crystal Tree*, Watkins was used to Ellington's work habits so when cast and crew began getting nervous, days before *My People* was set to open, because musicians still did not have music to play or singers their music to sing, and Duke was an hour late for rehearsal, Watkins calmly advised, "Don't get excited. This is Duke Ellington." In an article for the New York *Post*, he confided that the Duke "changes his mind from day to day. In fact, he just called up and gave us a new lyric. That's right, he dictated it right over the phone" (12 August 1963). Typically, out of the chaos of musicians improvising and dancers marking their steps, appeared the Duke, cool and collected, acting as if he had kept no one waiting.

When *My People* opened on 16 August, Ellington's casual approach to directing did not go unnoticed. The reviews were not overwhelming in their praise, and the response was generally lukewarm. *Variety* (4 September 1963) complained that "the production didn't jell as a unified whole," even though it praised Ellington and Strayhorn's music as "first rate" and singled out Joya Sherril, Lil Greenwood, and the Tally Beatty Dancers as the major attractions of the work (62). The *Saturday Review* said that the show "dovetailed music, dance, theatre, and social criticism in a unique and stimulating fashion"—hardly a rave—and *Down Beat* (26 September 1963) complained that the staging with "30 dancers twirling at once, some gyrating downstage and others performing on a raised platform upstage, and the orchestra wailing away in center stage sometimes resembled a three-ring circus" (41).

In an interview with Dr. Marcia M. Greenlee, conducted in September 1990 for the Smithsonian Institution Ellington Oral History Project, Mercer Ellington noted that during the production of *My People*, his father not only composed and directed but painted the sets and constructed the lighting as well. So much energy went into that show because it was dedicated to "his main man, Martin Luther King." Ellington met Dr. King in Chicago during rehearsals, according to Don George, Duke's lyricist and biographer. King pulled up to the Blackstone Hotel, where Duke was staying, and sent someone inside to find him. Since it was the middle of the afternoon, Duke was fast asleep. Awakened by the news that Martin Luther King was waiting downstairs to meet him, Ellington hopped out of bed and began to dress.

> Duke was excited. "What'll I wear? What'll I wear" and eventually grabbed the same old pants and things he always wore, because he never dressed up except when he was going onstage. He just put on whatever junk was hanging around, including a white bathrobe with blue lining, and put his porkpie hat on over his stocking cap, and they came down the elevator. When they got outside the hotel, the wind was really blowing down Michigan Boulevard.
>
> King jumped out of the car, and they were introduced.... Just as they embraced, like old friends, a great gust of wind blew Duke's hat off, and Duke was standing there with his arms around King, wearing only his stocking cap, his bathrobe fluttering in the breeze, while the policemen chased his beat-up old porkpie hat down the street. (112)

Afterwards, Ellington took Dr. King to a rehearsal at McCormick Place and invited Billy Strayhorn to perform "King Fit the Battle of Alabam'" with the cast. According to Marian Logan who was with Dr. King at the time, "Martin was very moved" (Nicholson 349).

In addition to "King Fit the Battle of Alabam'," a modern version of "Joshua Fit the Battle of Jericho," with its references to sit-ins, freedom riders, and Bull Connor's oppression, for *My People*, Ellington composed "My Mother, My Father and Love," "99% Won't Do," "What Color Is Virtue?" "Walking and Singing the Blues," "Love Scene," and "Blues at Sundown." "My Mother, My Father and Love" is a lyrical jazz composition filled with chromatic harmony and a lazy, syncopated melody filled with a variety of leaps. It is another atmospheric piece, with a melody suggesting an improvisation. "99%" is essentially an exercise in repetition with a melodic statement that outlines a major triad, making it easily accessible to the ear. "What Color is Virtue?" is a Broadway-type rhythm number written in an ABA^1 structure with the middle section, twice as long as the initial statement, giving a *parlando* quality to the composition. "Walking and Singing the Blues" is exactly as its name indicates, a 12-bar blues composition in which a highly improvisatory melody spins itself out over a repeated harmonic structure: I, IV7, I, V7, I. "Love Scene" is highly reminiscent of "Don't Get Around Much Anymore" with its eight-note pickups and syncopated chordal harmony. Composed in 32 bars, the song does not fall within the traditional popular song structure but is divided into A and A^1, where the second A appears to be an embellishment or improvisation using motivic elements of the original statement.

Eddie Lambert finds the score disappointing because of Ellington's "extensive" borrowing from *Black, Brown and Beige* ("Come Sunday" and "The Blues") and the mediocre level of Duke's lyrics (rhyming "behavior" with "how brave you are") and vocal writing, which he suggests was due to Ellington's limited experience in writing for concerted voices. With such an emphasis on the chorus, Lambert complains that the orchestra is given too little opportunity to show off (250). Stanley Dance, on the other hand, applauds the show for its variety and ability to dovetail "music, dance, theatre, and social criticism in a unique and stimulating fashion," and notes that the score offers the listener a rare insight into Ellington's ability "to express his music through an orchestra other than his own" (*Saturday Review*, 28 September 1963).

Even though the performance at the Exposition failed to draw the expected crowds,[4] on 16 January 1964, *Jet* announced that plans were underway for an encore production of *My People* on both sides of the Atlantic, with one cast playing the show on Broadway and another touring Europe. Although a Broadway production never did materialize, an original cast recording made during the original Exposition was finally available as of 23 January 1964, through Contact Records, a subsidiary of ABC-Paramount. *My People* remains the only virtually complete original cast recording of any Duke Ellington musical produced during his lifetime.

Nineteen sixty-three was also the year that marked the death of Frank Tuttle, a screenwriter-turned-director with Paramount Pictures[5] and one of the founders of the Screen Directors Guild, with whom Ellington had collaborated on a Broadway-bound "Musical Mirage" entitled *Free as a Bird*, a costume jazz-operetta invoking the atmosphere of the *Arabian Nights*. Gham Al Duna, Sultan of Kapul Bash, has acquired nine dancing girls for his harem, one of whom is Lishande, the Princess of Holkar, who, singing and dancing with her slave girls, was caught up in the roundup. Suleiman, betrothed to Lishande, arrives and demands the return of Lishande, but Gham, mistrusting Suleiman's claim, refuses and Suleiman threatens to search this home. In the next scene, Hushabeide, the sultan's ex-favorite, poses as fortune teller to tell Suleiman that somebody loves him, and that Lishande is in the torture chamber. However, in the next scene, Hafiz, the black slave in charge of the harem, sets all the girls including Lishande free, and sings a song about freedom. Hafiz welcomes Reverend Hawkins, an American, who sings "Two Together," extolling the virtues of a monogamous Christian lifestyle. Lishande escapes to the United States Consul after accepting a warning from Hushabeide (hidden in a secret closet) not to marry Suleiman. Lishande assumes that the advice comes from the ghost of a previous wife, and must, therefore, be irreproachable. At the consulate, Hawkins's boy-friday, Crispus Attucks, arrogantly sings "Sweep! Sweep! Sweep up the floor" to the servants, while Hawkins explains to Lishande the concept monogamy. Suleiman enters and questions this unusual idea, ("I'm Looking for a Girl Who Will Appeal to Me"), while Lishande and Hawkins appear to be falling in love, but repressing their impulses since everything seems to be happening too fast. Exhausted from the day's adventures, Lishande falls asleep and dreams that she has a male harem ("Dream Ballet"), but suddenly awaking to find herself in strange surroundings, she screams, and the curtain falls on Act One.

Act Two begins in the harem filled with sleeping slave girls. Lishande wakes them and tries to convert them to Christianity, so that they will be free of their masters and able to move to America where they could have their own male harem. Hushabeide agrees with all Lishande says ("It's a Man's World") and begins organizing the slave girls' escape. Mustasha enters and calls the guards, but the girls fight back, and overcome the men. When the girls reach the river, they suddenly get cold feet, fearing the dangers ahead and the possibility of incarceration if they are apprehended, but Hawkins restores their courage singing, "Free as a Bird." Back at the palace, Mustasha appears to tell Gham that Lishande has escaped. Gham, who has a hangover from the night before, summons his guards but is in no condition to follow her himself.

At the river, Hawkins sings "River wash me clean" while he baptizes the girls in the Christian faith. Following the baptism, Hushabeide, wearing a veil to resemble Lishande, marries Suleiman, who storms out angrily after realizing his bride's true identity. Gham enters and threatens to "flay" Hawkins for robbing him of his harem, but Lishande offers to marry the sultan if he spares Hawkins's life. Gham accepts.

The scene changes to the street where rich Mrs. Ogdenberry watches the wedding procession, then buys a giant who is standing still, holding tent poles for his master. Sold, the giant drops the bars and follows the woman. Hawkins comes in, has a brainstorm, and picks up the poles. Using the poles as stilts, Hawkins appears at the window during the pre-wedding ceremony, which includes a dance, and Lishande jumps into his arms. Gham calls for his guards and tells them to seize her companions as hostages. In the forest, Crispus runs in to tell Hawkins that Nelson, the American consul, has landed, and Hawkins thinks that perhaps Nelson can help them. Suleiman enters, followed by Hushabeide, and sings a reprise of "I'm Looking for a Girl Who Will Appeal to Me." She begins playing hard to get, and suddenly Suleiman finds himself highly attracted to her. In the consul's room, Hawkins considers going to the United States to help the slaves, and Lishande promises to learn to cook because she wants to go with him, to be with him always.

Gham arrives with the former slave girls who pretend to have mumps—called leprosy by the sultan's doctor—so that they might be quarantined away from Gham and his soldiers. Lishande dresses all the girls up like men with beards to sneak them aboard the boat about to leave. On board the U.S.S. *Grant*, sailors are energetically singing "We're Headin' Home," while Lishande is discovered as a stowaway in a basket. Nizam Beg, her father, coincidentally aboard the ship on the advice of a soothsayer, rejoices at being reunited with his daughter and blesses her Christian marriage, noting that he plans to sue Gham for 1,000 drachmas because of the insult his family has suffered. The rest of the girls take off their disguises and the second act ends with a wild celebratory dance. With its subtle, though incisive indictment of slavery, and positive, unsanctimonious approach to Christianity, *Free as a Bird* was well in line with Ellington's own beliefs; it offered him an exotic, almost fairy-tale environment where he could preach without being preachy.

There are three distinct phases in the development of *Free as a Bird*, the first of which spans the 1940s. Initially, when Frank Tuttle and his second wife, Tatiana Zermeno, began work on the project, sharing credit as authors of the book, they had no composer in mind. After Ellington had made his mark with the Hollywood "left" with *Jump for Joy*, it was clear to the Tuttles that he was their man and Duke joined the project with great enthusiasm, producing several more or less "developed" musical sketches to Frank Tuttle's sensitive and often clever lyrics. The first is a 15-bar setting of a quatrain, sung by Mustasha, the sultan's mother, at the beginning of the play. Written in the relatively infrequent key of E♭ minor (G♭ Major), the unharmonized chant-like tune in triple meter evokes an eastern tonality. Especially interesting is the fact that the tune is introduced by a substantial amount of underscore indicating entrance cues and motifs for Mustasha and

Hafiz, the harem guard. The presence of specific instrumental cues (violin solos, harp glissandi, and a motif for horn) suggests that Ellington was seriously developing this score for presentation.

The next song composed follows immediately in the script as Hushabeide, at the behest of the sultan's mother, reminds the harem girls of their wifely duties:

> Now a Sultan's many maidens
> Will harmonize in cadence
> When he's coming home,
> Never more to roam.
> Yes, a Sultan's wives and other girls
> Must carol while his mother curls
> Their tresses.
> God bless us!
> For a dutiful wife
> Must be a beautiful wife
> When her lord and master's returning.
> Thou he's weary and lame,
> She must kindle a flame,
> Just to keep the home fires burning....
> Yes, a dutiful wife
> Must be a beautiful wife,
> As she greets her master and pets him.
> But she'll never impart
> What is locked in her heart, For her lord only knows what she lets him.[6]

Ellington complements the sensuous playfulness of the lyric with an oriental-style verse, employing melodic falling half-tones against an Eastern-sounding ostinato. (See Example 6.1) For the chorus, he reverses the direction of the melodic half-steps and accompanies them with altered jazz chords, unifying elements of two different musical cultures, in the same way that the text unites East and West. As in the earlier sketch, Ellington has

Example 6.1.

embellished the melody with several atmospheric motifs, once again implying that the work was being readied for production.

The third musical sketch introduces us to the sultan, Gham Al Duna, who like Gaston in Lerner and Loewe's Academy Award–Winning *Gigi* (1958), expresses his boredom in song:

> I'm awake,
> But I ache
> At the prospect before me.
> I'm unfurl'd
> To a world
> Whose attractions all bore me....
> There's nothing new beneath the sun,
> Nor underneath the moon.
> The jokes are few—the tales they've spun—
> I guess the point too soon.
> You find a new zip in the wine you sip. It's just the mustache on your upper lip.
> Compose a new tune—la re mi do—
> But Mozart wrote it—and years ago!

Sustaining his half-tone motif, Ellington sets the verse of this song in F-minor, emphasizing the tonic and lowered second against a standard I–V progression in the bass, creating musical and dramatic tension that is released in the chorus using an expansive melody developing out of an F-minor triad and moving, first down, then up, a half-step. The half-tones retain the exoticism that captures the atmosphere of the show while the expansive tune offers an sense of world-weary sophistication important to the development of the character. (See Example 6.2)

More traditional is "Two Together," sung by an Reverend Thomas Hawkins and written in a standard Western 32 bar, AABA form. It is important to note that the character singing the song is an American missionary and any exoticism in his musical vocabulary would appear very much out of place, and since the piece was designed to convey the initial statement of "Christian love" in the musical, it seems clear that Ellington sought to compose an easily accessible tune. The melody is an intriguing exercise in tension and release, beginning on the ninth degree of the scale and holding off the resolution to the octave until the third measure when the melodic compass expands a minor seventh. As the melody progresses to the release, we

Example 6.2.

discover that the entire tune is based on the interplay of seconds (major *and* minor) juxtaposed with some melodic skip, allowing the tune to expand. The recapitulation is also fascinating since it expands the melody to its highest point in the song, creating a fine dramatic moment with the words "Two hearts that are one" (*one* is on the highest note) in a song about physical and spiritual unity. The harmonization is heavy with chromaticism, but in altered chords that are predictable, based mostly on ii–V–I substitutions. (See Example 6.3)

The final extant musical sketch was composed for the character of Crispus Attucks III, a 16-year-old African boy-of-all-work, cleaning up the American consul's living room after dinner:

> Sweep! Sweep! Sweep up the floor!
> Brush all the dust an' the dirt out the door!
> Sweep out the cobwebs an' the spiders an' the bugs,
> Shoo away the caterpillars, inch-worms an' slugs....
> Go 'way, louse. I gotta clean up the house....
> Don't think you can
> Come back in a sheet
> Like the Ku Klux Klan....
> Yes, I'm tellin' you louse,
> We've known all yore tricks
> Since we started cleanin' house
> Back in '76.

Crispus Attucks, named after the first African American to be killed in the Revolutionary War, is an important political raisonneur in the musical. To make his sentiments accessible, however, Ellington chose to set his lyrics to a kind of jazz nursery-rhyme melody that accents the action of sweeping, rather than the volatile political content. (See Example 6.4)

Top: **Example 6.3.** *Bottom:* **Example 6.4.**

Because Richard O. Boyer refers to Ellington's having written music "commemorating Negro heroes such as Crispus Attucks" in "The Hot Bach," a three-part article he penned in 1944 for *The New Yorker*, it is likely that "Sweep!" was completed by that time. All of the sketches must have been composed prior to 1946 when Frank and Tatiana Tuttle divorced because an undated letter from Tuttle to Ellington mentioning his third wife, Carla Boehm, refers to the songs as "completed."[7] This begins the second phase of the collaboration, where Tatiana's name is omitted from the title page and replaced by George Julian Sinclair. The Tuttle-Sinclair script divides the story into three acts (instead of the original two), and reorganizes the running order of the songs. A handwritten date on a copy at the American Museum of the Moving Image places this version in 1953, two years after Tuttle appeared before the House Un-American Activities Committee and testified that he had been a member of the Communist Party. From this point, it appears that Ellington has lost interest in the project. The specter of being a Communist sympathizer had not been far from Ellington at various points in his career. Nicholson reveals that the FBI had monitored his activities as early as 1938 when he endorsed the All-Harlem Youth Conference, classified as "among the more conspicuous Communist-front groups in the Racial subclassification" (192). His association with left-wing Hollywood activists during the *Jump for Joy* period undoubtedly created even more suspicion, but it was in 1950 that Ellington's alleged Communist sympathies came to head when he was accused of signing the Stockholm Peace Petition, condemning the atom bomb. Ellington denied signing the document and threatened legal action against whoever was trying to defame his name and reputation. It is not surprising, therefore, that even after Tuttle renounced his earlier Communist sympathies, Ellington would have little to do with their collaboration.

The third phase in the development of *Free as a Bird* occurred in the late fifties and early sixties, up until Tuttle's death when Tuttle and Sinclair refashioned the libretto into two acts, jettisoned the religious motif by making the missionary a doctor, replaced Crispus with the doctor's younger brother, and added the element of Third-world oil rights, and the cold war, with references to Gromyko and the presence of Russian agents. By 1962, film composer Larry Adler had joined the team, but Tuttle's death in January 1963 cut short any further development of the project. It is unfortunate that Ellington failed the complete the score for the show because not only are Tuttle's lyrics among the finest he set in his career, but Tuttle's strong position in the entertainment industry in the 1940s could clearly have led to a production.

In 1965 Ellington was commissioned by Grace Cathedral, the new Episcopal cathedral in San Francisco, to produce a liturgical work to celebrate its year-long consecration, and Ellington complied by adapting music from *Black, Bown and Beige*, *New World a-Comin'*, and his most recent revue, *My People*, into his first *Concert of Sacred Music*. After the premiere at Grace Cathedral on 16 September 1965, the Duke began to receive a number of musical theatre offers from the Christian community. Reverend John E. Schroeder, the president of Key Productions in Indiana, responded to advance publicity about the sacred concert by writing to Ellington on 9 September 1965 inviting him to compose the score of a musical work entitled *Tiger in the Land*, a folk opera, with a rural setting teaching "the powerful message of peace in our land which begins where James Baldwin ends." In 1966, Ellington received a letter from an author's representative, Dorothea Oppenheimer, in hopes of interesting Ellington in collaborating on a Broadway show. The letter demonstrates that the writer had no sense of Ellington's unfortunate experiences with the musical stage:

> The enclosed story, A LONG DAY IN NOVEMBER by Ernest J. Gaines, will appear in an anthology of Negro stories edited by Langston Hughes that Little, Brown will publish in the fall. It was first published by the TEXAS QUARTERLY.
>
> Mr. Gaines and I believe it would make a tremendous musical and, since we both love your music, we are hoping you'll like it enough to consider doing the score. We are also looking for someone to do the book and lyrics. If you know of someone you'd like to collaborate with, so much the better.
>
> I look forward to hearing from you.

More promising was a submission from Clement ffuller [*sic*], a teacher at the Searing School, where Ellington's nephew Steve was among his students, and heavily involved with Christian liturgy. At the suggestion of Ellington's sister Ruth (Steve's mother), in October 1968, he sent Ellington a script of a musical he had written a number of years earlier, entitled *Cinque*. It had already earned a great deal of interest from Broadway producers Joe Cates and T. Hambleton because of its rather innovative production concept in which all white roles were played by African Americans, and all black roles were played by whites. Trading on the same historical information that propelled Steven Spielberg's film, *Amistad* (1997), *Cinque* begins on an island in the swamps of the Gallinas River Delta, West Africa, 1839, where Don White Man, pleased that everyone comes to him for money (since that enables him to maintain complete control of everyone and everything), is planning to marry two women of his harem. In the next scene, Don arrives at the dock to buy slaves provided by the Black Prince. Cinque is one of his products, but as the Lord of Mani's son, he wants to buy himself, with money he has back at home. The scene changes to the hold of the ship, dirty and crowded with slaves. Cinque and the rest are at sea and frightened. A slave patrol ship is sighted nearby, and all the slaves are chained with a long chain to the anchor so that if the ship is sunk, there will be no proof of anything illegal in these waters. The ship shakes off the patrol, but some of the slaves die from fright, and the rough voyage at sea.

In Havana, Cuba, an emissary comes with a letter requesting Don Viceroy not to involve his country or himself in buying West African slaves. Madden, a British member of the Mixed Commission, has come in person to warn the viceroy who replies that, since Spain has signed a treaty, Cuba, of course, will not involve themselves in the slave trade. Secretly, however, Don Viceroy meets with Slaverman who has brought the black cargo, and they pretend that all his cargo are Cuban born. To be permitted to deposit his shipment, Slaverman must pay $20 a head to get papers with Spanish names for the slaves. The cost is high, but Slaverman must accept. At the Havana Slave Market, Teme, a beautiful 16-year-old girl from Mendi, refuses to sing one of her country's songs of celebration and is threatened with harm because of her disobedience. Cinque, also there to be auctioned, is whipped when he tries to intervene, and Teme, agreeing to sing to prevent any more violence, begins to fall in love with Cinque for taking a beating for her.

The scene changes to the deck of the ship *Friendship*, in Havana Harbor, where a "semi-ballet" of 49 slaves is in progress. The beautiful Teme is then taken into the captain's quarters where she "pleases" him and returns unchained. She pretends to flirt with Ruiz, a former slave, now spy for the Spaniards, in order to get close enough to him to pick his pocket of his key. She drops the key to Cinque who unfetters the slaves, and, quickly and silently, takes over the ship, intending to sail to Africa. Actually they are headed for Long Island, a fact known by Cinque, but kept secret because his people are in desperate need of water, having virtually run out of supplies. The ship is spotted by the United States Coast Guard, and everyone is arrested, since the U.S. officials have no idea which side is right, and cannot understand the language being spoken.

Act Two begins in a tavern in New Haven with a jail in the back. The blacks are in jail and cannot answer to a list of Cuban names they are presented. Abruptly, the audience sees headlines on a screen announcing the upcoming trial and the formation of the Committee of Friends of the "Friendship" Africans by Northern sympathizers. Returning to the tavern cells, Professor Gibbs, Yale University professor of languages, begins the first attempt at communication by holding up matches in increasing numbers so that he can learn how the slaves count. This activity starts the blacks talking, and at long last, there is hope of communication. In Cinque's cell, Teme reveals to him that she is homesick, and together they sing a pretend song, fantasizing that they are married, and that everything is all right. Unlike the convention of other musicals, such as *Show Boat*, where "Make Believe" is a *fantasy* number depicting the *actuality* of the characters' emotions, "I'm Pretending You're My Wife" is *really* a fantasy, at least from Cinque's perspective, because he has a wife and children at home.

In the big cell Prof. Gibbs finally, after weeks of searching, finds a Mendi who can speak English. This man, named Convey, tells the story of how he was kidnapped in Africa, sold to a king, and intercepted by a British Slave Patrol ship, and taken to England where he learned to speak English. Headlines reveal to the audience that the Queen of Spain demands the return of all her property, which includes the blacks, warning that the United States has no jurisdiction over her possessions. At the White House, President Martin Van Burren is faced with a dilemma. He does not want to enrage the abolitionists, and he does not want a war with Spain. His only alternative is to send the cargo back to Spain. More headlines report that the president's plans have been leaked to the abolitionists who plan to take the issue to court, and at age 73, ex-president John Quincy Adams will represent the Africans. Back in the big cell, Adams arrives and meets with Cinque, but he is uncertain whether or not he can win the case if it comes to trial. If they lose, Convey has plans to get them all to the Canada by means of the Underground Railroad. The scene changes to the Supreme Court where John Quincy Adams gives a long and persuasive speech, inciting Chief Justice Yaney to hand down a verdict of freedom. The following year in the Mendi Mission it is learned that Don White Man was wiped out by a British landing force and that the Black Prince has been sold into slavery. James Steele, an American missionary who has taught Cinque how to speak English, urges Cinque to stay and build up the mission before going back home to his family, but the force drawing him homeward is too strong. Just as he is about to leave, however, an old African man enters and announces that Mani has burned to the ground. Cinque is devastated and changes irreparably. In the final scene of the play, the hold of a slave-mill, Cinque is treated as "an Emperor." He is now Don White Man, uncaring, feeling that his only alternative is to make a profit out of the slave trade. Although there is no extant music from this incisive study of slavery, many of the song titles and lyrics easily fit into Ellington's characteristic motifs: "A Man of High Degree," "Free Me!" "Now We Are People Again," "Good Is Black!" "We Cannot Pretend Anymore," "We Can't Get Out!" and "Justice!"

In December 1968, shortly after his return from the orchestra's first South American tour, Duke Ellington received a script for his perusal called *The Greatest Mother of Them All* by West-coast journalist and playwright Germaine Firth, claiming an affiliation with ACT in San Francisco, and the possible interest of Gower Champion, the celebrated director/choreographer of *Hello, Dolly!*, to direct. Labeled a "message musical" by the author, *The Greatest Mother of Them All* opens in contemporary Point Richmond, California, with Maggie, Eugenia and Earl's daughter, returning from finishing school, pleased that she will soon be rid of her mother's influence and protection now that she is about to enter "real life." Eugenia is very proud of her Victorian home and all the style and class that it implies, even though it was financed by the illegal activities of her husband, Joe Bates, a former crooked sheriff, who turned "straight" because of Maggie's dreams of being a socialite. Even though her daughter is a grown woman, Eugenia cannot help worrying about her—how she will fare in the real world—and looks to her husband for advice, "What'll we do, y'r honor, Joe?" The scene changes to the dock where Captain Billy, Eugenia's first lover, and his son Dave are the rear tug in a company of tugs, poaching near the dock. Maggie comes on inquiring why they are on her family's property. In reply, Dave hides under the dock with the nets, but falls in the water causing Captain Billy to change the subject and begin a conversation about Maggie's mother, Eugenia, whom he says he knows. In the next scene, Eugenia greets her guests for the Symphony Association and sings "Success! Success!" about how much they have all contributed. Albert, a "far-right Negro," sings "When y'r low on the list" about his rise to high society, recalling that he and his wife, Vicky, met in Eugenia's whorehouse, where Vicky was a maid, and Albert was a towel boy. All the guests are satisfied with the future they have created for themselves by illegal rum running. "It's a damn shame, Eugenia" sings Earl, an oil magnate, lamenting about taxes and diminishing profits. Joe responds to being paid off by Albert for his work, singing "That's the thanks a law man gets." More and more, Joe is beginning to think that Eugenia's desire to be legitimate was a mistake, but his thoughts are interrupted by the arrival of Captain Billy and Dave. Introduced to the party by Maggie, Billy and Dave learn about the illegal operation and want to join the conspiracy.

Act Two begins at a poker party, to benefit the Symphony Association. Joe sings "The Greatest Mother of Them All" praising Eugenia for all that she has done for the benefit and for the organization, noting that she really is the power behind them all. Albert reads a letter from his son Johnny, presently serving in the military stationed in California, requesting jobs for him and his friends when they get out of the service, and expressing the desire that the United States have a greater involvement in military action around the world, to give the soldiers something to do. Eugenia put Dave in Maggie's room during the poker party so that he would be out of the way, and after talking, Maggie and Dave decide to go to the tug boat. When the Earl, a general in the army reserve, and Johnny watch the boat on their patrol, they see oil coming out of the water. The soldiers claim the tugboat on the government's behalf, and Maggie and Dave escape over the side, running back to the house to break the news, upsetting to everyone at the party. An "Entr'acte" separates Act Two from Act Three, during which a chorus of uniformed African American men and women sing "We got moral standards," followed by a ballet illustrating standards in the United States.

Act Three begins in the house with the white characters frantically stacking furniture by the door so the African American chorus won't invade them. Albert begins singing "It ain't no use," noting that blacks cannot be bribed or bought off, even by a black man. When the blacks push their way into the house, there is talk of a revolution with Johnny singing, "Don't tote no barge," there will be change. Eugenia and Vicky begin to wonder if they can help begin the "New Freedom," and they start a square dance, after which all pick up cards to "Sing about—the New Deal?" Maggie finds out the identity of her real father and Eugenia sends everyone away happier, including Maggie because Dave wants to marry her. Eugenia and Billy reminisce about the romance of their younger days, "Talk About Richmond," and Billy concludes that, of all the woman he has known the world over, Eugenie is "The Greatest Mother of Them All."

Ellington must have found the project interesting, for two years later, Ms. Firth was still corresponding with him. Typically, Ellington was difficult to pin down. The band had returned to Europe in the autumn of 1969 following a brief summer tour of the West Indies that featured a performance of the second Sacred Concert in Jamaica. Just months after the orchestra returned from a tour of the Far East, the author virtually laid a production of the show at the composer's feet, in a letter dated 12 May 1970:

> Dears: Regarding score for THE GREATEST MOTHER OF THEM ALL:
>
> A.—I have received my insurance checks for a fire loss on my mountain land, thus am in a position to make the necessary guarantee to your organization to secure a fall date for SF opening of the musical.
>
> B.—I've contacted Bimbo's management for date when the house is available. Also had an interview with Mr. Baffrey, producer of "Jacques Brel is Alive and Well," now playing at Bimbo's. They will run this through summer and are considering another to open when this plays out. He will look at our script when music is on paper. I've seen the show at the Marine's Theatre in SF, with a stronger cast. Saw it again at Bimbo's last Saturday: the stage was too large for just a cast of four; and/or amplification was inadequate; and/or the two female voices were accurate, but *small*. But, I'm sure Mr. Baffrey can find or direct the right female voices.
>
> C.—I have forwarded a script through Carl Killibrew to Michael Butler of Los Angeles, producer of "Hair," now running at the Orpheum in SF.
>
> D.—I'm talking to Mel Goldblat, with whom I attempted to phase in a production with the cast of "BigTime Buck White" last summer at The Committee Theatre on Montgomery in SF. He is bringing out the Negro Ensemble to Zellerbach in June for 6 days plus 3 other Bay Area dates. These people and backers I've known for 4 to 6 years.
>
> E.—CASTING:
>
> Script to, and discussion with Marvin Chacere of U.C. Arts and Letters. Survey of North Richmond Theatre Workshop talent. Sitting in on rehearsal tonight with singers involved in last U.C. jazz festival. Sitting in on other auditions in SF and East Bay.
>
> Double casting is indicated, at your discretion, using Tony Watkins and Roscoe Gill plus any artists you propose for the SF opening. Whatever happens on offers from your associations or my above mentioned contacts, may determine location of opening and artists… .
>
> F.—FINANCES: With the security I have, and contacts with money men, I am capable of financing the opening without the producers and mgt.

> mentioned. I don't "have to give anything away," but would contract with a producer in order to be relieved of mgt. duties—only if a limit on their participation is agreeable.
>
> Therefore, at this time, may I have your request for the amount of guarantee required to get you out for an opening, thus getting the score rolling?
>
> When I know this, I shall additionally make contacts in the Bay Area, Sacramento, Stockton, etc., for other engagements for your regular package, and will, at your pleasure, pursue a commission for your opera (Mr. Chachere wishes to be helpful, as I do, in keeping you in the Bay Area long enough to provide you the time to complete this operatic effort). In addition I shall then make my pitch to Kaiser T-V for the documentary on Model Cities I discussed in New Orleans with you....
>
> Please contact your recording company about the completion date of the $1,300,000 studio in Berkeley, and what interest they may have in the musical.
>
> I will go back to Transamerica offices in SF (they own United Artists and the recording company that owns a good piece of "Hair" ... after you talk to your company.
>
> As a beginning, please respond immediately on the fall guarantee and the days you may have open that I can fill to keep you out here on these projects [301.4.5.4].

An attractive offer, certainly: a guaranteed commission, plus the incentive to finish *Queenie Pie*, recently commissioned by WNET in New York City, not to mention the author's contacts and her ability to finance the musical on her own. The tone of the correspondence suggests a degree of collaboration, if only epistolatory, between author and composer, and the anticipation of completing the project. Ellington had absolutely nothing to lose by scoring *The Greatest Mother of Them All* and yet, he did not.[8] Perhaps the $25,000 received in 1968 as half of the $50,000 advance promised him by Doubleday for his "autobiography" relieved the Duke of the necessity of accepting further musical theatre work. And without being able to rely on Billy Strayhorn, who had died in 1967 of esophageal cancer, composing for the theatre became a much more arduous exercise.

Seven

"Skillipoop"

In May 1950, during the Milan leg of his spring European tour with his orchestra, Ellington was approached by Orson Welles to compose the first of several "incidental" scores for the theatre. Unlike musical theatre scores requiring completed songs and developed motifs, "incidental" music tends to be fragmentary, rarely allowing the extended development of a musical idea, and while it can extend under dialogue as "underscore," incidental music for plays tends to be relegated to passage of time and scene shifts, to provide a kind of musical punctuation to the production. Irrespective of its length or development, a principal duty of incidental music is the creation of atmosphere, or mood, out of which the essence of the play can emerge. Ellington, ever adept at creating atmosphere in his compositions, was immediately interested when Welles, in the process of developing theatre projects to help finance the completion of his film *Othello*, asked him to provide music for *Time Runs*, the Faustian half of a double bill to be called *The Blessed and the Damned*, produced in conjunction with Michael MacLiammoir and Hilton Edwards of the Abbey Theatre in Dublin.

Scheduled to open in Paris at the Théâtre Edouard VII in June 1950, *The Blessed and the Damned* consisted of a satire on Hollywood's fascination with religious movies entitled *The Unthinking Lobster*,[1] and *Time Runs*, a modernization of the Faust legend demonstrating its relevance to the twentieth century and the atom bomb, with quotations from Milton, Marlowe, and Dante.[2] Both plays were to be performed in English and both were penned by the director-designer-star, Orson Welles.

Not untypically in a project involving Orson Welles, confusion reigned, and everyone involved seems to have a different memory of their participation in the event. In the December 1950 issue of *Estrad*, a Swedish magazine, Duke Ellington recalled that Orson Welles originally asked him to compose five tunes for the show which he supposedly recorded late in May 1950. While on the Stockholm leg of the tour, 3–4 June 1950, Welles was said to have contacted Duke again and asked for some 28 brief musical interludes for the show and sent Hilton Edwards to Stockholm with the script for *Time Runs* so that Duke and Billy Strayhorn could complement the text with their music. The *Estrad* article even suggests that Strayhorn and Ellington worked on the score together on a piano in a private dining room at the Grand Hotel.

Strayhorn biographer David Hajdu suggests that Ellington was too busy to get personally involved in the project and sent Billy to represent him in Paris in the weeks prior to the 19 June opening of the show.[3] According to Hajdu, Strayhorn never worked directly with Welles but met instead with Herbert Machiz, the production manager, who explained what was needed in the score. Faustus, Mephistopheles, and Helen of Troy were each to have songs to sing: "Me Is the Trouble," "Zing, Zing," "In the Dungeons of Guilt," and "Song of the Fool," but since Welles had failed to complete lyrics to any of Strayhorn's melodies as the opening night approached, only Helen of Troy's "Me Is the Trouble," completed over wine at the Café de la Paix was used in performance (112–113). Although Strayhorn reportedly scored the songs for flute, clarinet, French horn, piano, bass, and drums, the piano played by musical director Samuel Matlovsky was the only accompaniment used in the production.

The Blessed and the Damned ran for six weeks in Paris to excellent notices but thin audiences. To bolster business Welles began to tinker with the text, jettisoning *The Unthinking Lobster* and one night adding the jealousy scene from *Othello*, another night adding the Anthony-Brutus tent scene from *Julius Caesar*, and finally deciding on a 45-minute abridgment of Oscar Wilde's *The Importance of Being Earnest*, in which Orson, playing Algernon Moncrieff, appropriated many of Lady Bracknell's best lines. By 7 August 1950, when the show left Paris to tour a variety of German cities, the final scene from *Henry VI* had been added, as well as a song recital by Eartha Kitt, and a magic act by Welles, and rechristened *An Evening with Orson Welles*.

In *Music Is My Mistress*, Ellington recalled working with Welles on the project and remarked that "some good music went into that, and we recorded some of it. One number is called 'Orson'" (241). Written in a 32-bar A-A^{1}-B-A form, "Orson" as arranged by Billy Strayhorn is a lyrical arioso for solo trombone that trades on chromatically altered chords, invoking a blues-like atmosphere. The rather unpredictable harmony in counterpoint to the mainly stepwise melody creates an important dramatic tension that continually drives the piece forward, with no two statements of the theme being exactly alike. It is unknown where "Orson" was used in *Time Runs*, if at all. The melody does not correspond to the scansion of Welles's lyric to "Me Is the Trouble," so it is likely that the tune was composed as an underscore, or unused in the production. No written copy has been found of Helen of Troy's song, said to be a 12-bar blues.

Less than a year after Welles approached Ellington for an incidental score, another request came his way from Broadway producer Jack Gordun, who was scheduled to meet with Duke late in April 1951 to discuss scoring Winifred Wolfe's play, *Three Stories High*. Trading on the stories of three characters who, at different points, live in the same brownstone apartment in New York City, *Three Stories High* was of interest to Ellington because of the presence of a song writer in the script whose compositions were to provide the underscore for the entire play. Ellington would not simply be embellishing a text with his music, but would be creating a score that is integral to the action of the play. Even though the show was capitalized at a modest $60,000, Gordun was unable to raise sufficient funds to mount the show and Ellington had to wait two more years for another opportunity to create a truly integrated incidental score. Late in 1953, virtually in the middle of what Ellington biographers consider the low point of his creative career, Broadway producer Anthony Parella approached Duke about doing a background score to *Mardi Gras*, a play by Norman Rosten, beginning its pre–Broadway tour, under the direction of Peter Kass, at the Locust Theatre in Philadelphia on 13 January 1954.

Staring Lenore Ulric,[4] Steven Hill, and Lois Smith, *Mardi Gras* begins with music introducing a summer day. A married couple, Merelda and Albert, own a boarding house on the waterfront, and make extra money renting showers and towels for those going to the beach. Their tubercular daughter Cathy returns to the boarding house, having left her husband, Walter, during their honeymoon, because she felt that it was unfair to fetter him to a dying wife. Upset with Albert because he defends his daughter's decision to return home, Merelda has an affair with a spurious "Rajah," and Walter, still in love with his wife, returns near the end of the act, wanting to know what happened. Although Merelda coerced her daughter into the marriage with Walter, she keeps him away from her, explaining that her daughter needs some space. In the second act, Merelda gets Cathy made Queen of the Mardi Gras, through her connections on the city council. Cathy is forced to appear in the Mardi Gras parade in the pouring rain, and begins to run a fever. She runs into Walter who begs her to come back to him, but she is too weak to grant him his wish, and dies, deliriously happy. Albert blames Merelda for the tragedy because of her insistence on keeping a tight control over her daughter, but Merelda is certain that Cathy died happy and feels very little guilt. A girl, the same age as Cathy, appears at the boarding house after the funeral, looking for a room, and Merelda takes her in, ecstatic at having another young life to control. Reviews for the production were unanimously bad and the original production closed on 16 January, four days after it opened. It opened again with Ruth White replaced Lenore Ulric on 22 January 1954, and closed the following day, shattering any hopes of a Broadway production.

Ellington composed seven cues for the production, all of which served important atmospheric functions in the play. The first cue of the play, "introducing a summer day," was an extended composition beginning in triple meter, to evoke the amusement park adjacent to the boarding house. Ellington provides a calliope-like melody doubled in clarinet and trombone, with the flute adding a descant of undulating sixteenth notes, supported by an "um-pah-pah" motif in the cello. At the final cadence of this melody, the meter changes to 4 and the regular rhythms of the calliope motif give way to angular, irregular, syncopated riffs and harmonies, ending with a concerto-like cadenza for clarinet that fades into the scene. The change of meter suggests the sinister quality present in the play and complements the chaotic movement beginning to take form at the "jungle of houses, games, concessions, and rides" just beyond the boarding house. (See Example 7.1)

The second set of cues occur on page 1-36 of the script during a scene between Cathy and her father, reminiscing about happier days. Ellington first provides a brief flute–clarinet(?) duet, in short undulating phrases, followed by a short flute jazz solo accompanied by three unidentified instruments (clarinet, cello, bass?). Here Ellington is evoking the "memory" music convention put to good use in *The Glass Menagerie*, Tennessee Williams's 1947 hit, with his emphasis on winds. Finally, a long series of triads performed initially by cello, trombone, bass, and then by clarinet, cello, and trombone, with a bass pedal point. The top note of the triads is a variation in duple time of the opening melody of the first cue.

On page 1-39, "Party Music" is noted by hand to introduce the entrance of the Clown and Balloon Man. Ellington provides a jovial ditty for flute, clarinet, trombone, cello and bass, with the flute and clarinet in octaves on the melody (clarinet is on top). Still employing the undulating motif established earlier, the exceedingly tonal tune floats over a walking bass (cello and bass in octaves) and a syncopated counter-melody in the trombone. A two-bar vamp suggesting a I–V progression follows with the notation: "Play 4 times—change keys—tone up." Another virtuosic clarinet cadenza continues after the vamp, leading into an undulating figure for the flute (root–fifth in eight notes) and an abruptly dissonant cadence dissolving into the dialogue.

Example 7.1.

Ellington's most developed cue, extending 83 measures in length, occurs in Act Two, page 31 of the text. Merelda has just arranged for Cathy to become queen of the Mardi Gras and is convinced that the experience will cure her daughter of whatever psychological sickness is making her physically ill. After Merelda's screaming, "I'll make her want to live! She's going to live!" somewhat evoking "It's alive!" from horror movie notoriety, the music enters, first reprising the calliope theme, and then continuing through the carnival activity of Mardi Gras night. Here Ellington has composed a rhapsody based on the earlier calliope and undulating motifs, transforming them expressionistically as in the examples below. (See Examples 7.2 and 7.3)

The next cue follows almost immediately on 2-36 to mark Cathy's entrance, running and stopping at a concession stand where Walter meets her. Here Ellington makes use of the calliope tune played by woodwinds in sixths, with a syncopated accompaniment—chords on the offbeat—provided by cello and bass, double-stopped. The result is an effective arousal of dramatic tension.

A plaintive flute solo accompanies 2-43 of the script following Merelda's realization of her daughter's death. Based mostly on falling fourths, the flute melody has an improvisatory, meandering quality that renders it a successful conduit between a moment of insane grief (classical operatic literature always associated madness with flutes), and the dialogue between amusement park workers, reminding us that life continues as normal. It is significant that Ellington does not employ the calliope motif at this point in the play, but uses a neutral melody recalling all the various motifs, yet being none of them exactly.

The final cue of the play occurs on 2-47 when Merelda picks up her sewing and says "My head is full of music." Beginning as a trio for flute, clarinet, and cello, the calliope motif is reprised, with a suggestion of dissonance in the cello "um-pah-pah." As a girl enters from the street, the triple meter

Example 7.2.

Example 7.3.

of the original motif gives way to 4 (as at the beginning of the play) with a flute cadenza (instead of the clarinet cadenza), and a cadence without resolution (F minor over a G pedal point) that dissolves into the dialogue.

How much of Ellington's work was the result of the director's inclinations, or his own personal intuition, is unknown. It is unlikely that the Duke had the time to spend long hours discussing the production concept of the show with director and designers so what he wrote is probably his instinctive response to the demands of the script. It is unfortunate that the play was so poorly received by the critics because the score is the model of simplicity in Ellington's oeuvre and deserves to be heard, if only for the extended rhapsody—a work displaying much of the genius found in Ellington's "serious" work such as *Night Creature*, introduced at Carnegie Hall barely more than a year later.

Late in 1960, Ellington flew to Paris to record his score for the film *Paris Blues*, which had been composed in Hollywood in November and December 1960. While in Paris, he was commissioned by Jean Vilar of the Théâtre National Populaire to compose music for a French-language production of *Turcaret*, one of the French theatre's classic comedies, originally produced by the Comédie Française in 1709. A vigorous satire on financiers and tax collectors by Alain René Lesage, *Turcaret* dramatizes the adventures of the eponymous tax-collector and money lender, who, having bought his way into high society, deserts his wife in favor of the widow Baronne, a younger and more desirable woman. The Baronne, in turn, is bilking Turcaret of his fortune to support the affections of the Chevalier, whom she loves, but who is really a gigolo after her money. The chain of duplicity comes to a head with the arrival of Turcaret's wife, who, pretending to be a rich widow, has been courted by the Chevalier. Turcaret is revealed as a scoundrel, and the Chevalier's servant, Frontin, closely involved in his master's illicit affairs with the Baronne, runs away with his girlfriend Lisette and all the money the young widow gave him.

While the play may appear to twentieth century audiences as lightweight farce, it was considered quite volatile in its own day. At the first rehearsal of the play at the Comédie Française, the actors refused to perform in it, fearing that a riot would ensue in the theatre, leading to great destruction of life and property. It was only through the intercession of the Duc de Bourgogne, one of King Louis XIV's grandsons, who liked the author, that rehearsals of the play continued. On 14 February 1709, *Turcaret* was put before the public for the first time, and records indicate that neither the heavy snow nor the misery prevailing in the city at the time, prevented Parisians from attending the play. It was expected, of course, that the audience would be filled with the types of people the play intended to satirize, so the Dauphin sent a guard to quell any hostile demonstrations in the house. The play's adherents proved more numerous than its detractors and the evening was said to have been a resounding success, both as an entertainment and as a piece of social criticism, unveiling many of the abuses of the French tax system. In his history, *The French Stage in the Eighteenth Century*, Frederick Hawkins notes that the production of *Turcaret* "led the Duc D'Orléans to institute the Chamber of Justice for inquiring into the malversations of the loan-contractors, the revenue-farmers, and the maltôtiers. Prosecuted with due severity, this inquiry struck at the root of evils to which Lesage had drawn attention, and which never again assumed their former proportions" (1:77).

The music the Duke composed for *Turcaret* consisted mostly of brief musical punctuations used between dialogue scenes to emphasize mood and characterization, or to denote the passage of time. All the music was prerecorded by a 16-piece pick-up orchestra of French musicians on 29 December 1960 in a session that lasted until 6 A.M. the following morning. Because the music was recorded on the stage of the Palais de Chaillet—where *Turcaret* was to be performed beginning 13 January 1961—the session could begin only around midnight, after the play then in repertory had finished and the audience had left the theatre. The music thus recorded would then be edited into a production tape and played back during the performance.[5]

The score begins with "Annonce du Spectacle," or "Band Call," a jazz blues riff in A-B-A-C-A form.[6] The melody is highly syncopated and energetic while the accompaniment, beginning on V7, makes repeated use of a syncopated "Charleston" rhythm. The composition forming a kind of overture to the play, recalls the eighteenth-century practice in the French theatre to begin every play with *three* loud thumps on the floor by using rhythms and melodic figures grouped in threes.

There are a number of short cues that identify Turcaret in the play. One is called a "Heavy Strut," a short eight-bar monody full of syncopated double neighbor tones. The effect is comic in a *miles gloriosus* fashion, much in the same way that Don Knotts or Tim Conway in their characteristic comic personalities would be funny if accompanied by "cool," jazzy music. The double neighbor motif, one of Turcaret's leitmotifs, is transformed into a whirling figure for the next cue, "To Sneak Up on Baronne," that also employs harp-like glissandi resolving in chords over a much less syncopated statement of Turcaret's tune. The chords lead to a more lyrical statement of Turcaret's motif, elongating double neighbor tones that are prepared by the whirling figure. A permutation of the whirling figure is used in the third cue, "Approaches anger," in which a double-neighbor sixteenth note figure continues under a series of dissonant chords. The basic Turcaret motif is most fully developed in an expansive waltz titled "Overture" that evokes Ravel.

Another Turcaret cue, "Viv," is a syncopated jazz ditty that evokes the third-based melody of the "Band Call," over a syncopated series of block chords in the accompaniment. This motif is repeated in a cue entitled "Anger," where it is repeated antiphonally over a walking bass and chromatically altered harmonies. A cue entitled "Chevalier" makes use of a Habañera rhythm in the bass beginning on IV and resolving to I. The blues-influenced melody begins in ascending thirty-seconds notes to a IV chord then falls syncopatedly to I7. Interestingly, there is a suggestion of double neighbor tones—recalling the duplicity of Turcaret—in the melodic development.

Two of the more fully-realized motifs in the score belong to Frontin and his girlfriend Lisette. Frontin's sensual Latin theme begins as a saxophone solo and develops into a sultry wail for saxes, accompanied by a rhythmic trombone counter line. Here again Ellington evokes the duality of character by utilizing contrasting musical motifs within a single piece. Duke must have been fond of this tune because he will use it again as "Sempre Amore" and in a somewhat revised fashion in "Moon Bow," both recorded in 1963. Lisette begins with a flute cadenza that leads to a kind of recitative over chromatically altered block chords, creating the impression of a bird (flute) wanting to escape its cage (chords). The flute recitative gives way to a saxophone improvisation over brass chords, acoustically associating Lissette with the sonorities of Frontin, her boyfriend. Lisette's motif is often used in connection or in counterpoint with the "Baronne" motif that represents her mistress. Seductive, sultry, slow, and syncopated, Baronne's music is evocative of the temptress without the presence of a sinister element: she is honey to the bees that buzz around her in the play. Especially notable is the presence of Turcaret's double-neighbor motif in the development of the Baronne tune. Again, Ellington is creating dramatic association through musical association, and the way motifs fit together aurally prepares the listener—or reminds him/her after the fact—of the visual/textual relationships in the play. Of particular note is an improvisatory monody in triple meter in the key of E♭, labeled "4 end—Baronne melancholy to 5—Lisette reading."[7]

In all, Ellington spent eight happy weeks in Paris, mostly in the company of Fernanda de Castro Monte, a forty-ish blond he had met in Las Vegas where she was a featured nightclub singer. Fernanda, who spoke five languages, was to have a profound—and expensive—effect on Ellington's lifestyle, causing him to dress more casually, and change his eating habits.[8] Ruth Ellington, the Duke's sister, recalled that "She did a lot for Edward. She interpreted for him. She did research. She was very intellectual. I certainly liked her, as I liked anyone who could make Edward happy. She left New York after he died, and even when he was alive she wasn't here *all* the time. She was always going off to the Caribbean visiting with friends" (Quoted in Jewell 136).

Two years after *Turcaret*, Ellington was commissioned by Peter Coe to compose incidental music for a new modern-dress production *Timon of Athens,* one of Shakespeare's lesser-known plays, he was directing at the Stratford Festival in Ontario, Canada. The play tells the story of a man (Timon), born very rich, and approaching middle age, who decides to share his wealth by giving freely to his friends and noble causes, with no hidden motives, only a somewhat idealistic vision of friendship. Steadfast in his belief in the goodness of man, Timon spurns the advice of Apemantus, the cynic, who warns that reckless generosity can only lead to disillusion and ruin. When Timon's wealth has been drained away as a result of his compulsive generosity, Apemantus's predictions begin to come true, and all of his friends refuse to loan him the money to pay his creditors. Angry and offended, Timon invites his friends to a banquet where he tells them what he thinks of them, then leaves Athens, desiring to live a hermetic life, alone in a forest by the sea. There, digging up roots for sustenance, he discovers buried treasure, and again he becomes a wealthy man. Seeking revenge on Athens, the city that exiled him because he dared to criticize its politics, Alcibiades makes an overture of friendship to Timon who refuses the gesture, but offers Alcibiades his wealth to assist in the destruction of Athens. Apemantus visits Timon in his exile, and helps him restore a balanced perspective to his view of the world. As a result, Timon writes his epitaph and chooses a place for his grave that will always be washed by the sea. The Athenian government, frightened of Alcibiades's ever-growing army, looks to Timon to save the city, offering him the premiership if he will return home. Timon refuses and dies. News of Timon's death reaches Alcibiades just as he is about to attack the city, but hearing a description of Timon's grave, and reading his epitaph, soften the hatred in Alcibiades's heart, and he enters Athens, in the spirit of absolution.

By the time Ellington got around to composing the score, Coe had been replaced as director by Michael Langham, the artistic director of the Straftford Festival. Even though Duke had worked with Coe on the project in England, when the change of directors was announced, he held up any further progress on the score until he could find out what "Mr. Langham had in mind," or so he said to the Canadian press when he arrived in Stratford a mere two weeks before the production was set to open, without a note of the music on paper. Ellington's now celebrated habit of procrastination was again in evidence, and the production team at the Shakespeare Festival, although familiar with Duke's almost magical ability of meeting his obligations at the very last minute, were anxious to say the very least. The festival had previously commissioned *Such Sweet Thunder* (a Shakespearean suite that premiered at Town Hall in New York City on 28 April 1957 and was performed at Stratford on 5 September) but that work was not associated with a specific play in their season and could be realized independently of their production schedule. The score for *Timon of Athens* was another thing entirely.

At his first meeting with Michael Langham, with typical Ellington bravado, without a note of the score on paper, Duke managed to fulfill the director's expectations by playing musical themes off the top of his head and altering them effortlessly, according to Langham's specifications. Not only was Langham impressed with Ellington's ability to capture his concept in musical terms, Duke had an intense admiration for the director who he said, "describes his needs so beautifully in words."[9] In *Music Is My Mistress*, Ellington notes that Langham was his inspiration in directing *My People* in Chicago: "In Stratford, while the orchestra was rehearsing the music for *Timon*, I would watch Michael Langham direct the actors, and when I went to Chicago I would stand in front of my cast, extend my arm as Michael did, and make like a heavy director" (198).

Originally composed for 16 musicians in the pit and six more on stage,[10] Ellington's incidental score for *Timon of Athens* premiered on 29 July 1963. It was performed again in a revised orchestration by A. Stromberg at the Chichester Festival in England, beginning on 8 April 1964, and subsequently revived by the Shakespearean company at the Stratford Festival Theatre on 7 June 1991, when the score was substantially reworked by musical director Stanley Silverman before the play moved to the National Actors Theatre in New York City on 4 November, the same year. Composed in taxicabs, the theatre's green room, and the director's kitchen, the score to *Timon* comprises 30 cues, beginning with an "Overture" in C minor, a hot, syncopated jazz tune that establishes the musical vocabulary of the work and sets the tone of the play.

After a fragmentary horn motif entitled "Conscience," and a trumpet and percussion piece anticipating the "Revolutionary" motif heard later in the play, one of the most prominent themes in the score is introduced as "Counter Theme," where a plaintive oboe melody hangs suspended over a trombone counter-melody and a bass line suggesting a Latin beat. The atmospheric dinner music accompanies Timon's distribution of his wealth and suggests a kind of "Siren's call" to him, a spell-charged atmosphere.

"Skillipoop" follows as a bright, energetic dance interlude for stage band and dancers, clearly meant to evoke an "Eastern" modality. As in the Cotton Club period, where each revue would attempt to produce a new dance craze, Ellington told the press that "Skillipooping" would become the rage, replacing the "Twist," and the number of newspaper articles that focused on the dance suggest that Ellington was right. As choreographer Alan Lund explained in the *Northern Daily News*, 18 July 1963, "instead of twisting the legs as you would in the twist, the main movement consists of raising the hips. It's a very provocative dance." The following cue for stage band entitled "Impulsive Giving" gives the clarinet the lead in a slow, lyrical, plaintive melody filled with wide, dramatic skips.

Nervous eight-note figures in the vibraphone, brass, and woodwinds identify the "Gossip" music that follows as cue 9. "Revolutionary Music," a bright march that wanders between major and minor tonalities, includes a syncopated counter-melody for saxophones that provide forward motion in counterpoint to the regal, fanfare-like melody in the brass and woodwinds. A series of fanfares follows entitled "Regal Banquet" built on mediant chords: C–E–A♭; E♭–G; F–A–D♭; A♭–C. The mediant relationship is continued in the next cue, "Banquet Music," where a solo flute, skipping in thirds, soars over vibraphone and guitar accompaniment. A cello melody follows, recalling the earlier cue entitled "Impulsive Giving" with its dramatic skips and lyrical mood.

"Smoldering," which makes prominent use of the cello in tremolo effects and highly virtuosic passages, evokes the Eastern ambiance of "Skillipoop" and anticipates "Gold" later in the score. "Angry" recalls the "Impulsive Giving" motif with much greater dissonance and rhythmic vitality than the previous cue. The brass rhythms recall similar figures in the "Mars" movement of Holst's *The Planets* and instill a similar kind of dramatic tension. Like "Smoldering," "Gold" features the cello in its evocation of the Eastern ambiance of "Skillipoop" and adds woodwind chord clusters that shimmer like the gold they evoke, against a foreboding trombone, bass, and cello ostinato. "Ocean" capitalizes on sixteenth notes rolling up and down, creating a variety of tonal patterns over changing progressions in the bass. Both melodically and harmonically, this piece ebbs and flows with continual motion. Finally, a cue entitled "Storm," beginning with a dissonant chord held for four beats and augmented by percussive "thunder," followed by a measure filled with descending sixteenth notes, suggests the storm music composed by nineteenth-century Romantic composers.

Critics were generally positive about Ellington's contribution, identifying "Skillipoop" and the "Revolutionary Music" as the most memorable and successful of the evening. However, while *Newsweek* (12 August 1963) praised Ellington's score because it helped "banish the sense of time from the story," giving it a more universal quality (52), *Saturday Review* (17 August 1963) complained that "while we may leave the theatre humming Mr. Ellington's revolutionary march (composed with a sort of "How High the Moon?" dissonance), we have not penetrated or even clearly heard much of Shakespeare's underwritten text" (27). The New York *Times* (31 July 1963) concurred: "The modern-dress version of 'Timon of Athens' that entered the Stratford Festival's repertory last night ... is so preoccupied with effects of contemporaneity that it seems to call attention to its cleverness rather than to Shakespeare" (19).

Irrespective of the notices, Ellington's score for *Timon of Athens* has enjoyed a life beyond the theatre because of Ellington's own recordings of "The Banquet Scene," and "Skillipoop," the Boston Pops Orchestra's recording of the "Timon of Athens March," and a recording, released by Varese Sarabande in 1993, of Stanley Silverman's adaptation of the score for the 1991 revival of the play at Stratford. Because the director sought to locate the play in the Mediterranean in the 1920s and 1930s, Silverman drew upon several of Ellington's earlier works to provide an authentic musical atmosphere. Ellington's original overture was replaced by a version of "Black and Tan Fantasy," originally recorded in 1927. "The Mooch," dating from Ellington's "jungle music" period at the Cotton Club, was added to "Skillipoop" to create a more period dance, and "Creole Love Call," published in 1928, was used as music for "Compulsive Giving," as well as the second banquet scene.

In 1964, while his score was being performed in England, Ellington gave permission for it to be used for a modern dress production of *Timon of Athens*, directed by Mrs. Ethel Rich on 16–18 May at the 11th Annual Festival of the Arts at Milton College in Milton, Wisconsin.[11] Ellington had been introduced to Mrs. Rich at the University of Wisconsin, during one of his tours, and credits her with deepening his understanding and appreciation of the Episcopal Church. In *Music Is My Mistress*, he recalls:

> From the first day we met at the University of Wisconsin, where we were playing a concert or a prom, ... she has religiously sent me every issue of *Forward*, a publication of the Episcopal Church. Ever since I saw the first copy, this little book has been my daily reading. It is very clear, easy to understand, written in the language of the ordinary man, and always says things I want to know. It is extremely instructive, and it has played a great part in the adjustment of my perspective on the approach to the relationship between God and the human being. So I am profoundly indebted to Mrs. Rich and the booklet she sends regularly four times a year [282].

Mrs. Rich, professor of speech and drama at Milton College, was also instrumental in having the college award Ellington the honorary degree of doctor of humanities on 7 June 1964.[12]

In gratitude for the honor, Ellington composed a short incidental score for T.S. Eliot's *Murder in the Cathedral*, directed by Mrs. Rich for the 13th Annual Festival of the Arts at Milton College, 21–23 May 1966. Eliot's play, written in 1935, is a two-act verse drama, set in Canterbury, England, where a chorus of poor women take shelter inside Canterbury Cathedral just as Archbishop Thomas à Becket is about to return, after seven years in exile. Although he has failed to come to an understanding with King Henry II over an ecclesiastical issue, the priests of the cathedral feel certain that peace will be restored, but the old women are less optimistic. Upon his return to Canterbury, Becket faces four great temptations, personified by Four Temptors who torment him: compromise with the king, assume power as Lord Chancellor of England, lead a struggle against the realm, or consciously seek to be martyred. Leaving his fate in the hands of God, he preaches a sermon on the mysteries of birth and death. After four days, Henry II's knights arrive and accuse Becket of treason, a charge which he denies, but refuses to exile himself again from Canterbury. While the women of the chorus bewail their fears, the knights murder Becket in the rectory of the Cathedral, and then proceed to justify their actions to the audience, after which the priests and chorus praise the act of martyrdom for infusing the church with greater strength.

Ellington's score for the Milton College production exists as a suite in six parts, composed for oboe, clarinet, two alto saxes, two tenor saxes, two French horns, four trumpets, three trombones, tuba, percussion, piano, and strings. "Women'z" evokes the presence of the chorus of poor women, who provide a regular commentary on the action of the play. Ellington's composition is a twelve-bar blues in D♭ Major, with a four-bar introduction, establishing the tonality of D♭ Major. The melody is built essentially on a falling-third motif, anticipating the wail of the women later in the play. A counter-melody in eighth-note triplets gives the work a twelve-eight feel and provides momentum to the otherwise wailing melody. The three-against-one feel of the eighth-note triplet against the quarter note invokes the Catholic ecclesiastical mystery of the Holy Trinity, one God in three manifestations: Father, Son, and Holy Spirit, an especially appropriate evocation in a play about the Catholic Church. "Becket" is a lyrical melody hovering around the fifth degree of the scale, suggesting the need for resolution (note that in traditional harmony, V always resolves to I in an authentic cadence). Against the simple, reflective tune, is a restatement of the falling third motif from "Women'z," suggesting the tragic outcome of the play. Against this interplay of motifs is an accompaniment of block chords on the first and second beats of each bar, beginning in V (G^{11}), and creating dramatic tension, as well as a jazz flavor. "Exotique Bongos," an energetic tango, recalls "Skillipoop" from *Timon of Athens*. Beginning with the falling third motif, once again, the first section of this cue appears to be a jazz improvisation over an E♭ minor ostenato, suggesting a kind of temptation with the melody wanting to go off on its singular direction, but the harmony remains steadfast. The second section of the cue, marked "Swing," displays sustained jazz chords descending in whole tones, over which an improvisatory melody insistently hammers away, ending in a return to the falling third motif.

"Gold," the only cue in the score in triple meter, recalls Erik Satie's *Gymnopédies* in its flowing chordal accompaniment, though without Satie's perpetual motion melody soaring above it. Instead, Ellington employs a sixteenth-note run, outlining a G♭ Major triad, in the first four bars of the piece. The fourth and fifth bars are in 4/4 and display an improvisatory cadenza for solo instrument. The rest of the piece returns to triple meter, using only a regular, and unalterable, accompaniment figure. "Land" invokes the sixteenth-note runs in "Gold," and develops them into a melodic motif that alternates ascending and descending over block chords that recall the mediant motif, only this time, the thirds are ascending, i.e., D♭ (C#)–E, A–D♭ (C#), B–E♭ (D#). The final cue is entitled "Martyr," in which the original falling third motif is incorporated into a melody that recalls the earlier "Becket" cue. Though in 4/4 meter, the syncopation of the accompaniment reflects the accompaniment figures in "Gold," and the quarter-note triplets beginning in bar 10 recall the triplets of the opening "Women'z" cue. Bars 12 through 15 reprise the falling third figure, emphasizing the tragedy of the situation, and the final two measures of the piece, repeated (perhaps as a vamp, though none is indicated), take the melody note back to the unresolved fifth degree of the scale, with the fifth maintaining a pedal tone in the bass. Even though the final chord of the cue is tonic, the fact that it is in second inversion implies a cadential resolution to V–I. The indeterminate ending of the piece corresponds perfectly to the lack of resolution in the play. Was Becket selfish, as the knights who killed him maintained, for choosing martyrdom rather than a course more beneficial to the people of England? Did Henry II actually give the order to have Becket killed? Will the martyrdom have a pronounced effect on Henry's reign? Questions like these are unanswered in the play. The final four cues described above correspond to the Four Temptors that Becket must face during the play. Each seems to have a different kind of power over the archbishop, and Ellington's music reflects the different colors of each temptation.

The following February, during the London leg of his European tour, Ellington was introduced to British film star Barbara Waring, then Lady Conliffe, by Renee Diamond, one of Duke's oldest and dearest English friends, whom he met as a girl at his first Paladium concert on 4 June 1933, and with whom he had kept in close contact for over thirty years. Lady Conliffe, it seems, had written a modern morality play that was to be produced at Coventry Cathedral in the summer of 1967 and had hopes of interpolating an original Ellington score. Because of the author's association with Renee Diamond, and because the religious sentiment expressed in her play struck a chord with Ellington, Duke agreed to provide a musical score for *The Jaywalker*.

The play tells the simple story of a boy named Mac who wants to stop the traffic on the highway so that people on one side of the road can have the freedom to cross to the other side. After being bullied by a gestapo-like policeman, and witnessing the callousness of the crowd at the sight of a hit-and-run accident, Mac decides to take it upon himself to stop the traffic by running out into the road where he is "crucified between a lorry and a Rolls Royce" (18). Suddenly the Messianic significance of Mac's name becomes clear to all ("Mac" means "Son of") and because of the boy's sacrifice, people are permitted to travel at will. The frenetic pace that accompanies the beginning of the play gives way to an ending that is tranquil and serene.

This project was different than Ellington's previous "incidental" scores because the score was hardly incidental; rather, it permeated the action. As an early stage direction in the script indicates, "The music continues all through the play but softens when the actors speak then comes up loud when they stop"(1). In addition, the author is quite specific about the atmosphere the music is intended to create. The opening cue is designed to suggest traffic sounds at varying levels of intensity. To accomplish this, Ellington uses brass pyramids, martial drums, and passacaglia-like figures with solo brass instruments occasionally barking like automobile horns. When the traffic is at its height, a trumpet is heard screaming over the orchestra, and what began as a blues progression becomes fragmented into dissonant short motifs, creating a kind of musical chaos.

When Mac is handcuffed and explains his use of the sign of the cross, the music becomes richer, more melodic, almost heroic in its employment of a soaring melodic line. The lyrical moment does not endure, however, and soon the music becomes the rhythmic accompaniment to a kind of rap dialogue among the characters, featuring piano, bass, drums, and trombone jamming to a blues progression. This leads to a driving dance rhythm emphasizing conga drums that accompany the dance movements of the actors that is interrupted by a statement of "God Save the Queen" that signifies a government news flash. The chaotic traffic motif is reprised at full force until Mac's sacrificial death when chorale-like brass clusters are heard, evoking a liturgical motif. Like much of Ellington's "programme" music beginning with *Black, Brown and Beige*, *The Jaywalker* score creates a dramatic situation, identifies character, supplies mood, and drives the action, entirely without the necessity of text. What the text supplies in this case—as in all plays that use music extensively to tell the story—is a specific context in which the feelings evoked through the music can be directed. Waring's text in itself is incomplete without the music for it cannot provide the chaotic traffic atmosphere within the confines of Coventry Cathedral. Together, text and music provide an emotionally powerful experience that is both religiously significant and dramatically sound. It is no wonder that Ellington borrowed sections of this score for his *Second Sacred Concert* in 1968 (most notably, the "Mac" theme, retitled "T.G.T.T." or "Too Good to Title," and "The Biggest and Busiest Intersection").

On 23 March 1967, Ellington recorded the 45-minute score at RCA Studios in New York City but for some reason, by 17 July, the author had not yet received permission from Ellington to use the score in production. With Duke's touring schedule during the summer of 1967, it comes as no surprise that Lady Conliffe had difficulty in pinning him down. Ultimately the production proceeded as planned, received warm notices, and except for the echoes of the score in Ellington's *Second Sacred Concert*, disappeared forever.

As a body of work, Ellington's incidental scores compare favorably with his "programme" suites. Even though the individual sections are not usually as extensive as those in the longer suites, they are composed with the same flourishing melodic invention, the same individual approach to orchestral voicing, and the same opportunities for virtuosic display as the more acknowledged masterpieces. That Ellington was able to complement a text without overwhelming it, to transform it without obscuring it, and function dramatically without the loss of musical integrity is yet another testament to his genius as a composer of music for the stage.

Eight

Fallen Angel

In October of 1961, Guy the Marquis de la Passardiere commissioned Don Appel, the author of the book for *Milk and Honey* (with a score by Jerry Herman), Marshall Barer, librettist for *Once About a Mattress* (with music by Mary Rodgers), and Duke Ellington to transform the classic German film *The Blue Angel* into a musical comedy vehicle for his wife, Lilo, the celebrated French chanteuse who had starred in Cole Porter's *Can Can* on Broadway, eight years before. The marquis, a real French nobleman, had begun his career as a theatrical producer in Paris with "girly shows" at the Moulin Rouge and the Naturistes, and moved on to more legitimate fare such as producing the Follies Bergère in London and reviews at the Nouveau Casino in Nice. Bitten by the Broadway bug, he moved to New York City in 1962 to be closer to the money people he wished to tap for the production, and took a position heading the international department of Martin Goodman Productions. This was his first attempt at producing a Broadway show and he had a lot to learn. His first lesson: the rights to *The Blue Angel* were unavailable, and the musical had to fall back on the novel by Heinrich Mann, *Professor Unrath*, that had served as the basis for the film. Even though he had lost name recognition with which to sell the property, the marquis, because of his social position, was ultimately able to get Henry Ford II and Mrs. Barry Goldwater to invest in the show that was born late in the autumn of 1961.

Don Appel, who had previously written two plays for Broadway—*This Too Shall Pass* (1945), and *Lullabye* (1954),[1]—transformed the priggish German professor who succumbs to the charms of a night-club singer while attempting to prevent his students from doing that very thing, into Colonel Samuel Blake, the headmaster of Stonewall Military Academy, somewhere near New Orleans in 1929. The first act of *Sugar City*, the working title of the musical, begins in a boys' dormitory room where a jive number, entitled "Swivel" is heard on the radio.[2] A wealthy student, Carson, brags to the other boys that he can bribe his way to graduation without opening a textbook, and insinuates that the board of directors (on which his father sits) is thinking of replacing the present headmaster. His preparations to sneak out to a night-club called "The Parlor" are interrupted by the appearance of cadet captain Wilson, whom he bribes to keep quiet. The scene changes to the headmaster's office where cadet Wilson is reporting the incident. Colonel Blake is intent on going down to "Sugar City" where the night-club is located to catch the boys red-handed. The scene changes to the interior of the Parlor, where Lilo (throughout the draft, the female protagonist is called by the name of the star, not the character) is discovered singing "The Spider and the Fly." She moves off to her dressing room where she finds Ricki, a very handsome, beautiful though masculine, young hustler, about 27 years old. A teasing remark, implying that he might be interested in boys, sets Ricky off and Lilo realizes that she has, unwittingly, touched a nerve. While he leaves to proposition Mona, a wealthy 40-year-old housewife, singing "I'm with You," the cadets from the military school enter and start dancing with the night-club chorines. The Colonel enters the club, and the boys run up to Lilo's dressing room to hide from him.

Lilo begins to seduce Carson who blushes and runs out of the room, while Gay Baudelaire, the club's seductive manageress, prevents the Colonel from searching the premises. As he is on his way out of the club, Colonel Blake hears Lilo's voice coming from the stage, and almost mesmerized by the sound, he allows himself to be led by Gay to a table, close to the stage, where he sits. A drunken Texan ruins the number by jumping on stage with his pants down, verbally abusing the singer. Coming to the lady's honor, the Colonel tries to talk the man off the stage, but when the Texan becomes violent, the Colonel punches him, getting a sprained hand in the process. Lilo takes him up to her dressing room, where Carson and the boys appear. Blake sends them all back to school, threatening retribution in the morning, and Lilo begins a slow seduction of the Colonel, while Gay sings "Goodbye Charlie," downstairs in the night-club. Back in the dressing room, the Colonel, overcome by alcohol, reveals that he used to play the comedian in West Point shows, wearing baggy pants and a rubber nose, but when Lilo encourages him to play the clown, he tries to kiss her. Knowing where a single kiss will lead, Lilo convinces the colonel to join the festivities downstairs, but in the midst of joining the number, he passes out. The cadets, who did not leave the premises as commanded earlier, witness the scene and its aftermath, the colonel being once again deposited in Lilo's dressing room.

The following morning, over breakfast, the Colonel finds himself attracted to the self-declared courtesan, and when he sings, "Thank You Ma'am," Lilo finds herself drawn to his simple sincerity. After the Colonel returns to the school, Ricki returns and teases Lilo about her newest conquest, and brags about his 40-year-old housewife who wants to take him back to California with her after Mardi Gras. As Ricki goes off dreaming of being a movie star, Lilo notices the Colonel's belt hanging over the rail of her balcony, and realizes that Blake is the one man she knows who honestly seems to care about her. The scene changes to the boys' dormitory where the cadets are singing a cabaret number in imitation of what they had seen the night before at the Parlor, after which they file out to the Colonel's office, where he scolds them, singing, "Rules and Regulations." In reply, the boys defiantly take out cigarettes and smoke them, singing a reprise of "Goodbye Charlie" in counterpoint to the Colonel's melody. The confrontation is interrupted by the arrival of General Leggart who dismisses the boys and questions the Colonel about his being intoxicated the night before. The headmaster admits that he had been an alcoholic but had not touched a drop in 13 years, but the last few weeks, waiting for the board to decide on his future as headmaster, have been slowly taking their toll. Leggart admits that the board has voted to replace Blake as headmaster, but assures him that he will retain his position as head of the military program, so long as he does not make a habit of seeing the woman with whom he spent the previous night. After the general exits, Colonel Blake tries to work, but cannot get the tune of "Thank You Ma'am" out of his head. Unable to resist the temptation any longer, Blake unlocks a desk drawer, takes out a whiskey bottle, and pours himself a drink, as the lights fade.[3]

Almost immediately, Appel was replaced as bookwriter by novelist Jerome Weidman, who had won the Pulitzer Prize for the book of *Fiorello!*, the 1959 hit, with a score by Jerry Bock and Sheldon Harnick. In Weidman's hands, *Sugar City* kept many of the earlier version's characters and place-names, but changed the names of the protagonists, and added a great many new songs. Act One begins in a classroom at Stonewall Academy where Colonel Wise is a Latin teacher trying to convey the beauty and significance of the Latin language to students who are more interested in sex ("I'd like to exchange a dead language—for a live, live tongue"). Class is interrupted by the arrival of General Leggett, who reprimands the Colonel for being too strict with his students. When Leggett leaves, Carson slips a picture of Pepet—the new name of the Lilo role—into Scott's belt, to get him into trouble with the Colonel, who is horrified to learn that many of his students have been to the Parlor. In the second scene, Carson and other cadets sing "Sugar City," preparing themselves for a night on the town. The scene changes to Bourbon Street, where Gay Baudelaire, the manager of the Parlor—now portrayed as an ex-madam from Storyville—greets the boys as they enter the night-club. In "A Friend You Can Count On," Gay demonstrates the relationship she enjoys with three policemen on the take: Larry, Barry, and Harry. In the dressing room, Pepet's manager, Jocko, wants her to leave the club and find more lucrative employment. Though Gay tries to persuade her to stay, Pepet is determined to be true to Jocko, even though he takes her for granted ("Impossible Is Not French"). On stage, the show girls sing, "Follow Me Up the Stairs," and flirt with the cadets from the academy. The colonel enters and complains to Gay about the near-naked pictures of Pepet being sold to his students. In the midst of the discussion, Pepet comes on stage and sings "Let's," directing much of it toward Carson who, noticing the Colonel, after the number, rushes up to the dressing room to hide. When Carson gets to the dressing room, he finds four boys there, fawning on Pepet, and warns them of the Colonel's presence. When the Colonel enters, he is outraged at finding his students in the dressing room of a night-club singer, and marches them out, while Gay sings "Goodbye Charlie" onstage. Back in the dressing room, Pepet finds a reason to delay the Colonel's exit, and he finds himself helping her with her makeup, and drinking at her behest. A Texan pushes his way into the dressing room, expecting to make love to her, but the Colonel defends her honor just as Policemen enter with Jocko, who refunds the Texan his money and admits to Pepet that he has been pimping her behind her back. Colonel Wise attacks Jocko for such ungentlemanly behavior, and Pepet begins to admire his gentility. They descend to the night-club where "Goodbye Charlie" is still in progress and participate in the singing. After the number, they return to the dressing room, noticed by Carson who announces to the other cadets that they are "off the hook" and the boys leave the club. The following morning, the Colonel sings "Thank You Ma'am" to Pepet in gratitude for the previous night, but when he asks to see her again, he is told that she and Jocko are going to St. Louis in a few days. Later that day, Carson tries to blackmail the Colonel because of the previous night, but Colonel Wise makes a clean breast of it to the General, who reprimands him for setting such a bad example to the cadets. The Colonel responds by saying that he intends to marry Pepet, and in the next scene, he proposes, offering to protect her and care for her ("Someone to Care For"). The wedding follows immediately, with Pepet, Jocko, Gay, and Colonel Wise, expressing their individual points of view regarding the event in "Each One's Time Comes" and the curtain falls on the announcement of the stock market crash in 1929.

Act Two begins in Pepet's drab dressing room in San Francisco, two years later, where Jocko continues to wonder how Pepet can put up with such a "geek" and "loser" for a husband. Since she feels responsible for her husband's misfortunes, Pepet accepts the fact that she has to support him by touring, even if it means singing in dives ("C'est Comme Ça"). A year passes and the Colonel and Pepet find themselves on the streets of Chicago, singing, "These Are the Good Old Days." Another year passes and the trio find themselves in Boston where Jocko is creating a number for the Colonel involving a clown costume, inferring a total loss of self-respect by the once strict Latin teacher. The Boston engagement leads them back to New Orleans, where Pepe and Jocko are welcomed back to the Parlor. Rehearsing a new number, "The Spider and the Fly," Pepet becomes acquainted with Aldo, the new dancer at the night-club. Watching him move (the stage directions liken him to Gene Kelly), Pepet becomes extremely attracted to him, causing the Colonel to react like a jealous husband. The scene changes to graduation day at the academy ("This Year We Graduate"), and, hearing that Pepet is back in town, the cadets decide to visit her and the Colonel ("Sugar City: Reprise"). In the dressing room, Colonel Wise sings a plaintiff song to Pepet as he puts on his clown costume ("All I Have to Live For") and Jocko enters to inform him that General Leggett and many of his former students are in the audience to witness his night-club debut in New Orleans. While the Colonel is making a fool of himself onstage, Aldo is seducing Pepet in the dressing room. When the Colonel returns to the dressing room prematurely (seeing his acquaintances in the audiences caused him to cut the performance short), he catches Pepet in Aldo's arms, and decides that the marriage is over. About to perform onstage, Pepet exits with Aldo, and the enraged Colonel throws Pepet's things to the floor while she sits on stage and seductively sings, "Let's."

On 31 August 1965, the Marquis de la Passardiere wrote to Ellington who was performing at Harvey's Resort Hotel Casino in Stateline, Nevada, with a progress report:

> I was surprised when I heard from Perry Watkins that you did not receive the Script that I mailed to you at Basin Street in San Francisco. This is why I am immediately sending a copy to the above address.... This Script will give you a general idea of the construction of the Show. (Some of the songs are not in their right place and most of the dialogue has been re-written.) The boys are working daily, re-writing scene by scene and I would say that in a couple of weeks you will receive the rehearsal script. All your comments will be greatly appreciated.

The new script was called *Follow Me Up the Stairs* and displayed a significant departure from earlier versions. Stonewall Military Academy had become Jefferson Davis Academy, an exclusive boys' college, and the late 1920s setting was changed to 1922. Colonel Wise had become Professor Ritter, Pepet was now Yvette, and Gay was called "Mother Hen." Carson was now a much more sympathetic character named John Harmon who was indebted to Yvette for $700, and Professor Ritter displayed somewhat more humanity here than in his other incarnations by giving his student the money to pay off the debt. The first scene in the club, still called the Parlor, displayed a new number entitled "Vieux Carré" that set the tone and atmosphere of the club squarely in New Orleans, and the most significant alteration of the book occurred in the first dressing room scene, where John asks Yvette to run away with him and the $700. Saying she likes it where she is, Yvette tells John to return the check, and when he appears to be pressuring her, she sings, "Do Me a Favor," and tells him to get out. Professor Ritter goes to the club as in earlier versions and finds himself defending Yvette from a drunk in her dressing room (the Texan has become a sea captain in this version) as before, but does not spend the night. Instead he returns to his quarters at the school where Doctor Stewart, the headmaster, and other students are found discussing John Harmon's recent escapades in the French Quarter. Ritter discovers that he has been earmarked as Stewart's successor when the headmaster retires and, alone in his study, reaching for a handkerchief, he pulls out Yvette's silk stocking which he inadvertently took from her dressing room and sings "My Heart Is a Stranger," aware of the inexplicable attraction he feels for the woman.

Ritter goes to the dressing room to return the stocking to Yvette, who teasingly displays her bare leg for him to put it on. As he starts to pull on her stocking, the touch of her leg fills him with lust and he seizes her in his arms, but hearing her laugh at his demonstration of affection, he releases her and begins to cry. Touched by his sincerity, she offers him a drink; he takes her in his arms, and she does not resist. They spend the night together in the dressing room and, as in all the previous versions, Ritter sings "Thank You Ma'am." Back at school, John, Ralph, and Carl, singing "Men of Experience," attach a drawing of Yvette and Ritter embracing on the professor's front door, a poster Yvette finds amusing but that embarrasses Ritter. A short scene between the couple, now very much in love, is interrupted by John, bursting into the room to deliver the 2,000 lines of Virgil Ritter assigned him the previous day as punishment for his lying about the $700. Seeing Yvette, John condemns her as a tramp, using Professor Ritter's own words, but on this occasion, Ritter defends her honor, telling John that he is in the presence of the "lady who is about to become my wife." After John leaves, Ritter proposes, singing, "I Need Someone to Care For," and Yvette accepts, even though she does not love him. At the wedding reception at the Parlor ("Let's"), the newlyweds' plans for respectability and security are shattered when John enters to announce that Ritter has not been promoted to headmaster; he has been fired instead. As Ritter wonders what the future will bring, the wedding guests sing "Let's" and the curtain falls on Act One.

Act Two opens with Ritter and Yvette, looking destitute and world weary, returning to the Parlor after several unsuccessful attempts at earning a living. During rehearsals at the night-club, Yvette becomes attracted to Danny, the new choreographer, who welcomes the opportunity to make his move ("Easy to Take") whenever Ritter, now a confirmed alcoholic, is out of the room. After several scenes depicting the disintegration of the marriage ("Settle for Less") and the growth of the relationship between Danny and Yvette ("Je N'ai Rien"), the location changes to Professor Ritter's former quarters at the school, where John Harmon, looking older, more mature, has returned to thank the professor for being instrumental in his career. He is told that Ritter is an entertainer at the Parlor, and goes down to the French Quarter to see the act. At the night-club, a very drunk Professor is running the spotlight for the chorus girls' number, and selling pictures of Yvette during her rendition of "Spider and the Fly." After the song, the comedian on stage pulls Ritter out of the audience and slams a pie in his face. Intoxicated and humiliated, Ritter attacks Danny, the choreographer sitting at the bar, just as John enters the night-club in time to interrupt the altercation. John forces Ritter to see what he has become and takes him away from Yvette, promising to set him up with a teaching post at Texas Normal. As he collects his belongings, Ritter hears Yvette singing, "C'est Comme Ça" onstage, and he exits through the alley door as the scene revolves to the night-club for one last look at Yvette.

Another version, dated 1966, using the same names as the version above, but changing the name of the Parlor to the "Chicken Coop," bears the title *Pousse-Café*, with *Sugar City* crossed out. This rendering of the plot begins with the French Quarter of New Orleans with tourists, pimps, prostitutes, and students singing "Sugar City." In the next scene, Ritter's living room ("The Nachez Trace"), the mathematics professor lends John, his favorite student and son of his oldest friend, money and learns that John's grades have been falling off at school because of his association with a French woman at the Chicken Coop, a gawdy dive in the French Quarter. There, Yvette sings "Let's," followed by the Chicks' singing "Follow Me Up the Stairs." John enters and is helped by Mother Hen through the crowd to follow Yvette upstairs to her dressing room, where John pleads unsuccessfully with the singer to go away with him. Back on stage, Yvette is singing "The Spider and the Fly" just as Professor Ritter enters in time to defend her from the unwanted advances of a drunk who knocks him to the floor. Ritter is carried upstairs to the dressing room as Mother Hen and the Chicks go into a dance routine dressed as members of the Salvation Army, in a number highly evocative of *Guys and Dolls*. In the dressing room, Yvette tells Ritter that she has no interest in John and that it would benefit the professor's reputation if he stayed away from the night-club. Back in Ritter's living room, Doctor Stewart discusses John's behavior with the professor, who feels guilty about having lent the boy money to spend in such a manner. When Stewart leaves, Ritter discovers Yvette's silk stocking in his pocket and returns to the Chicken Coop to return it to her. When he arrives at the dressing room, he discovers her taking money from a schoolboy named Charlie ("Goodbye, Charlie") and scolds the two of them for their behavior. In retribution, Yvette attempts to seduce the professor and make a fool out of him, but his simple emotions so move her that she accepts his advances and goes home with him for the night. The next morning, at Ritter's apartment, the professor, in pajamas, sings "Thank You Ma'am" to a woman's coat perched on a chair. His song is interrupted by Charlie who begs Ritter not to mention to the headmaster that he saw him at the Chicken Coup the previous night. Doctor Stewart enters complaining about Ritter's severe treatment of Charlie in the classroom (completely unaware of his generosity in other arenas), and Yvette enters from the kitchen, pretending that she has been invited to lunch. Ritter introduces her to the headmaster as his fiancée ("The Good Old Days"). Preparing for the wedding, Yvette tells Mother Hen that she does not love the professor, but wants to get married for security. However, at the wedding reception (where Ritter yodels to entertain the guests), Doctor Stewart coldly congratulates the couple and tells Ritter that his career is finished at Jefferson Davis Academy. Yvette counters by telling her husband that there is more in life than teaching mathematics, and the act ends in an extended dance number.

Act Two begins exactly as the previous version with Ritter and Yvette returning to French Quarter after failing to find success elsewhere. They discover that Charlie has graduated in the interim and become a pianist at the night-club ("Swivel"), and Yvette's earlier attraction to him as a boy is rekindled, now that he has grown into a man. Having become a confirmed alcoholic, Ritter attempts to convince Charlie to leave the Chicken Coop by offering to contact a friend in New Haven, Connecticut, who might need a good jazz pianist, but Charlie can see through the proposition and warns the professor that the problem will not be solved by sending him away because there will always be a younger man in Yvette's life (a satirical "Dream Ballet of Youth Versus Age"). Outside Ritter's former lodgings, John meets Doctor Stewart, who wrote to John's father telling him of Ritter's downward spiral. Stewart, blaming John for involving Ritter with Yvette, tells him that only he can save the professor from self-destruction. At the Chicken Coup, while Yvette sings "C'est Comme Ça" onstage, Ritter is packing up her wardrobe in the dressing room. When she enters to change clothes, he begs her to go away with him but she refuses, telling him to leave her alone, that she feels nothing for him. When he shows her a cigarette lighter he found under her pillow, she does not deny that it belongs to Charlie, and starts down the stairs to perform her next number. Calling her a tramp, Ritter rushes down the stairs after her and pulls her off the stage, in the middle of a dance routine with Charlie. The two men get into a fight over Yvette just as John enters the night-club. He sees Ritter clutch at his chest and drop, senseless, to the ground. John runs to him and carries him upstairs to the dressing room, where the Professor recovers from his mild heart attack and prepares to leave with John for New Haven where his father might be able to find Ritter a job, provided he is either a bachelor or a widower. The professor admits that the marriage to Yvette has never been consummated, so, strictly speaking, he has never been anything else. As they leave the Chicken Coup, Charlie's handsome father enters the club, and Yvette begins seducing him ("The Spider and the Fly") as the curtain falls.

By the time *Pousse-Café* opened at the O'Keefe Centre in Toronto, Canada, on 25 January 1996, Jerome Weidman was joined by advertising agency executive Melvin Isaacson on the book, and Fred Tobias, in his Broadway debut, assisted Marshall Barer—who had been fired, then rehired—on the lyrics. [4] Instead of Walter Slezak, the actor originally designated for

Lilo surrounded by attendants in *Pousse-Café*. Courtesy of Photofest.

Professor Ritter, allegedly planning his Broadway comeback, the role was played by Theodore Bikel, last seen on Broadway in Rodgers and Hammerstein's *The Sound of Music*. Lilo retained her role, but not the name of the character, for now Lilo, Pepet, Yvette, was to be called Solange. Travis Hudson was cast in the role of Gay Baudelaire, rechristened Mother Hen, rechristened Havana. Costumes, originally to be designed by Freddy Wittop, were in the hands of Patricia Zipprodt, and sets and lighting were provided by Will Steven Armstrong. Orchestrations were done by Larry Wilcox, dance music was composed by Ellis Larkins, the musical direction was by Sherman Frank, the musical numbers and dances were staged by Marvin Gordon, and the entire production was under the direction of Richard Altman, who assisted Jerome Robbins on *Fiddler on the Roof*. In Toronto, the musical numbers were as follows:

Act One:
Be a Man—John, Sourball, Harry and Bill
Rules and Regulations—Professor Ritter and students
Vieux Carré—John and ensemble
Let's—Solange
Follow Me Up the Stairs—The sextet (night-club girls)
Do Me A Favor—Solange
Goodbye Charlie—Havanna and ensemble
C'est Comme Ça—Solange
Thank You Ma'am—Ritter and Solange
He Followed Her Up the Stairs—Students
Someone to Care For—Professor
An Honest Woman—The sextet
Good Old Days—Solange, and company

Act Two:
The Years Pass By—The company
Follow Me Up the Stairs (Reprise)—The sextet
Easy to Take—Danny
C'est Comme Ça (Reprise)—Ritter
Hot Foot Hop—The Hoi Pollois
I'm Back In Love—Solange and the sextet
C'est Comme Ça (Reprise)—Solange

Before the premiere, Duke Ellington, on the West Coast with his orchestra, gave a telephone interview from a hotel in Beverly Hills where he was "writing songs over the telephone" for the musical as well as the soundtrack of Frank Sinatra's newest movie, *Assault on a Queen*. Ellington described the process of long-distance collaboration to the *Toronto Daily Star* (22 January 1966):

"It should be a gas," the grand old man of jazz commented happily from the electric piano planted in the middle of the hotel room. "The lyricist was

> out the other day and we wrote four new songs. As a matter of fact, I continue writing them on the phone, probably right up to curtain time."
>
> Ellington, who wrote his first musical in 1924, said telephone composing is a three-way obstacle course. Lyrics are phoned to him as soon as they are written; he composes the music on his lightweight electric piano, dictates it to arranger Bill Benjamin in New York, who transcribes it onto sheet music and in turn phones Toronto with the new music.
>
> "It's quicker than playing it and telling them to take it off the tape. You can also give them the harmony and all that right away," the 66-year-old Duke said.... Relaxed, carefree and apparently light years away from the last-minute high pressure of studio moguls, Ellington said the Broadway-bound musical is based on Heinrich Mann's "Blue Angel," story, "although there have been so many rewrites I don't know what it is anymore" [2:21].

What it was, according to *Variety*, was "a sour mixture which doesn't live up to its name as a bright after dinner drink in which colorful liqueurs are set delicately one on top of the other. The sum of its parts is not any better than the numerous flaws in plot or the distinct lack of bouncy come-away-and-whistle tunes or snappy toe-tapping music" (2 February 1966: 58) Unfortunately, the Toronto critics were equally unimpressed by Ellington's technique of long-distance collaboration and the score was judged "one of monumental anonymity. It is not bad—it is not anything; it is, in fact, impregnable. Lots of brass, lots of woodwinds, lots of strings and cymbals and drums. But no emotion—no love, no hate, no greed, no grab" (*Toronto Daily Star* 26 January 1966: 35).

As a result of the poor notices in Toronto, the running order of the show was changed during its pre-Broadway tryout in Detroit at the Fisher Theatre 8 February through 5 March. In this incarnation, the musical numbers were as follows:

Act One:

Be a Man—John, Sourball, Harry and Bill
Rules and Regulations—Professor Ritter and students
Vieux Carré—John and ensemble
Vive La Difference—Solange
Goodbye Charlie—Havanna and ensemble
Let's—Solange
Thank You Ma'am—Ritter and Solange
Funeral—Ensemble
Someone to Care For—Professor
An Honest Woman—The sextet
Let's—Solange

Act Two:

The Years Pass By—The company
Follow Me Up the Stairs—The sextet
Easy to Take—Danny

Act Two: (continued)
C'est Comme Ça—Ritter
Hot Foot Hop—The Hoi Pollois
I'm Back In Love—Solange and the sextet
C'est Comme Ça (Reprise)—Solange

The alterations in Detroit seemed only to make matters worse, and desperate measures were in order. Director Richard Altman was replaced by José Quintero, the celebrated director of Eugene O'Neill dramas, Valerie Bettis, who had choreographed *Beggar's Holiday*, was hired to redo the choreography, though Marvin Gordon would retain credit for "staging" the musical numbers and dances, Patricia Zipprodt was forced to share costume billing with Albert Wolsky, and lighting responsibilities were taken away from set designer Will Armstrong and given to V. C. Fuqua.

Melvin Isaacson's name was dropped from the playbill and Jerome Weidman was given sole credit for the book that no longer cited Heinrich Mann's novel as a basis.

Having accepted the responsibility of directing the show, based on hearing Ellington's music, Quintero quickly realized that even a score he so strongly believed in could not salvage a show that had already undergone so much revision—Marshall Barer notes that by the time *Pousse-Café* reached Broadway, there had been 12 different versions of the script. In addition, Quintero found a significant lack a chemistry between the stars, a situation he had not anticipated, nor was prepared to fix since he could not recast the show.[5] Although he begged the Marquis to cancel the New York opening, arguing that the musical was simply not ready to face the New York critics, *Pousse-Café* opened at the Forty-Sixth Street Theatre on Friday 18 March 1966, and closed there the following day after three performances. On Broadway, the musical numbers were as follows:

Act One:
The Spider and the Fly—Havana and dance ensemble[6]
Rules and Regulations—Ritter and students
Follow Me Up the Stairs—Solange
Goodbye Charlie—Havana and ensemble
C'est Comme Ça—Solange
Thank You Ma'am—Ritter and Solange
The Eleventh Commandment—Students
Someone To Care For—Ritter
The Wedding—Ensemble

Act Two:
Entr'Acte—Orchestra
Let's (Rehearsal Scene)—Danny, Louise, and dancers
The Good Old Days—Solange and male chorus

Act Two: (continued)
Easy to Take—Danny and Solange
C'est Comme Ça—Ritter
C'est Comme Ça (Reprise)—Solange
Let's—Solange and male dancers
Old World Charm—Ritter
The Spider and the Fly (Reprise)—Solange

The reviews in New York City were even more caustic than they were in Toronto or Detroit. Only John McClain of the *Journal American* was positive about the score, calling the music "captivating," with "excellent numbers, like 'Goodbye Charlie,' 'Someone to Care For,' 'C'est Comme Ça,' and 'The Spider and the Fly,'" but even he had to admit that the show was a failure (*Theatre Critics' Reviews* 27: 329). In the New York *Times*, Stanley Kauffmann judged Ellington's work "a tuneless score," and the show "a total disaster" (*Theatre Critics' Reviews* 27: 326–327), a sentiment echoed by Normal Nadel in the New York *World Telegram*, adding that "Even the orchestrations are trite, and the music certainly is far, far from the best Duke Ellington ever composed" (*Theatre Critics' Reviews* 27: 327). Walter Kerr, writing in the *Herald Tribune*, referred to the music as "'Mood Indigo' chopped up in little pieces and flung to the winds that blew the 1920s away," and concluded that, "The show doesn't need its music, doesn't need its pretense at dances, doesn't need its busy turntables, because the story tells itself without them and tells it in just about twenty minutes" (*Theatre Critics' Reviews* 27: 328). Reiterating the judgment of Richard Watts, Jr., in the New York *Post*, who called the musical "singularly incompetent in every way" (*Theatre Critics' Reviews* 27: 329), the unidentified reviewer for *Newsweek* argued that the creative team should be "burning with shame. Especially, and most sadly, the great Duke Ellington, a genius whose score is so incomprehensibly poor as to arouse the feeling that Broadway is even more villainous a syndrome than it has been accused of being, to foul up the foremost American musical talent of the last 30 years" (28 March 1966: 88). Of the performers, only Travis Hudson, who played Havana, and Gary Krawford, cast as John Harmon, were singled out for praise. Theodore Bikel and Lilo were dismissed, not as incompetent or untalented, but as simply miscast.

Unfortunately for the Marquis de la Passardiere, his troubles did not end with the closing of *Pousse-Café*. On 7 April 1966, the New York *Times* issued a report of alleged violations committed by the Marquis against the theatre control law, noting that he was ordered by Supreme Court Justice Saypol to give a full financial counting to Attorney General Lefkowitz's office, and to the 110 investors in the show.[7] The article continued:

> Affidavits from the Lefkowitz office charge de la Passardiere, of 40 Central Park South, with having "improvidently" failed to file any of the financial

> statements required by the new laws, even though the producer raised more than $325,000 for the launching of "Pousse-Café," including $106,000 in "front money."
>
> He is further charged with having spent "several thousand dollars" of the "front money" more than two years before forming a limited partnership; with "a confusion as to the exact identification of limited partners," and with "consistent failure ... to maintain adequate records" of transactions involving "the rights and interests" of his investors.
>
> A source in the Attorney General's office noted that it was the first such action brought against the management of a quick-flop Broadway show. "In years past, they just used to thumb their nose at us," he said.
>
> The company manager of "Pousse-Café" was Monty Schaff, 57, of 530 Park Av., who in November, 1964, was fined $250 in Criminal Court after pleading guilty to the charge that he had received a $7,500 kickback from a scenery builder for the musical, "Tovarich."
>
> "Pousse-Café," after widely reported difficulties on the road ... closed "at an estimated loss of $450–$500,000." The Lefkowitz affidavits specify that its total capitalization was $400,000 plus 20 per cent overcall.
>
> In an affidavit of his own, producer de la Passa[r]diere said: "I deny the allegations ... but nevertheless consent" to Justice Saypol's ruling" [47].

As a result of the inquiry, the Marquis de la Passardiere was temporarily barred from producing other Broadway shows.[8]

Ellington's score for *Pousse-Café* was not as great a disappointment as the reviews suggest. It was filled, originally, with rags and blues and be-bop jazz tunes that were a lively celebration of the musical's New Orleans environment. By the time the show reached New York, much of the variety was stripped of the score, first by the incessant tinkering on the road, with the composer in absentia, and second by the monochromatic orchestrations that made even subtle melodies sound like big-band arrangements. The opening number in New York, "The Spider and the Fly" is a "slow blues" in C minor, written in a *scottishe* style (dotted eight–sixteenths throughout), with particular melodic emphasis on the flatted fifth that creates a sultry effect musically. A relatively short vocal solo, accompanied by an onstage pianist, gives way to an extended dance break that suggests Las Vegas more than New Orleans with its saxophones buzzing in sixteenth notes around hopscotching brass. It is unfortunate that a relatively simple melody should have to bear the weight of over-blown arrangements; it is even more unfortunate that Ellington's original setting of the lyric was unused. An earlier version of the song, copyrighted in August 1962, displays a steady quarter-note melody weaving up and down in half steps, not unlike the spider motif John Kander will employ in *Kiss of the Spider Woman* thirty years later. The earlier setting suggested perpetual motion, quarter notes incessantly weaving in and out of the C major tonality, as a fine example of word-painting. The Broadway version depicted sultry slow blues and little else.

"Rules and Regulations" underwent a similar metamorphosis on the road. The Broadway setting is an indistinctive patter song in march tempo, heralded by four trumpets with harmon mutes and a military drum cadence in the percussion. The number fades in and out of dialogue and is only a vehicle to illustrate Professor Ritter in the classroom. An earlier version, copyright 30 August 1965, is a more successful march patter with a far more interesting melody because it employs, at several key points, quarter notes ascending and descending chromatically, the same device used in "The Spider and the Fly," to suggest, subliminally in the minds of the audience, an association between Ritter and Solange, who performed the number in earlier versions of the text. It should be clear by now that Ellington was not simply a hack writer of tunes when it came to scoring theatre works. He had extraordinary theatrical instincts and could imply connections between characters and events with great subtlety in his compositions.

"Follow Me Up the Stairs" did not undergo a transformation from its inception to Broadway, but because of its *scottishe* melody and proximity of range to the Broadway setting of "The Spider and the Fly," it is not as effective as it was designed to be. It is interesting that in earlier versions of the musical, "Follow Me Up the Stairs" was designated for the chorus girls at the night-club, almost as a throw-away transitional number. It is unusual that the star's introductory number in a musical should be this kind of utility number, appearing to be a reflection of a song, already sung by a secondary character, at the beginning of the evening. "Goodbye Charlie," one of the few numbers cited as worthwhile by the critics from Toronto to New York City, is an easily assimilated ABA rhythm number beginning with a pentatonic melody that develops, offering the listener few surprises. A stop-time interlude resolves into a vocal reprise that suddenly expands into a production number, complete with cakewalk, evoking "Hello Dolly!" and anticipating "Mame," both staples of the Jerry Herman canon.

"C'est Comme Ça" is a chanteuse-like song, anticipating "Kiss Her Now," from *Dear World*, another Jerry Herman show. An exercise in neighbor tones, the melodic shape of the first four measures is repeated on different scale degrees in four bar increments until measure 17, where the melody changes to eight note phrases, falling in thirds. Parlando in nature, the composition allowed Lilo a fair amount of rhythmic and dramatic license, and because of her performance, was cited as one of the more successful numbers of the show. "Thank You Ma'am," an AABA charm song, has a Broadway-style melody reminiscent of Jule Styne or Richard Rodgers, beginning on a non-chordal tone and resolving down to the next scale degree. The accented tension and immediate resolution on the next strong beat evokes both the instinctual awkwardness of Professor Ritter in dealing with a woman like Solange, and his new-found comfort in her companionship. "Thank You Ma'am" is one of the few numbers that survived from the earliest version of the musical.

"The Eleventh Commandment" is a utility rhythm number for the cadets filled with energy, counterpoint, and modulations, teaching that the eleventh commandment is "Thou shalt not get caught." It replaces a similar number, lost in Detroit, called "Funeral," about the many ways in which people can circumvent Prohibition. "Someone to Care For" is the most "Ellingtonian" composition thus far in the score. Another survivor from earlier versions (it was copyrighted in August 1962), it makes excellent use of non-chordal melody notes and surprising chromatic accompaniment. The melody that emphasizes the seventh scale degree is both celebratory and sad, implying a kind of indecision on the part of the character, anticipating musically what Stephen Sondheim accomplishes in the lyrics of "Sorry, Grateful" in *Company* by almost a decade. One of Ellington's more evocative jazz songs, "Someone to Care For" was the only one of Professor Ritter's numbers cited as noteworthy by any of the critics.

Act One ends with "The Wedding," an extended production number recalling "Rules and Regulations," and "Thank You Ma'am," and concluding with a dixieland dance. The non-sung number covers the preparations for the wedding, the ceremony itself, and the celebration afterwards. The extended amount of dance music in the show, in which Ellington had no part in composing,[9] demonstrates the direction *Pousse-Café* was taking. Of the nine numbers indicated in the New York program, four had extended dance breaks. The propensity for instrumental music continues into the second act where the original "Overture" has become an "Entr'Acte" leading to a rehearsal of yet another dance number. After 20 bars of fanfare, the entr'acte introduces the melody of "Let's" in brass and woodwind chords, followed by a reprise of "Thank You Ma'am," emphasizing the strings, and an extended statement of "Vieux Carré," a song that had been jettisoned in Detroit. A barbershop quartet follows entitled, "The Good Old Days," displaying another tonal melody—this time outlining major/minor sixth chords—in an AABA format. An interesting modal change to the relative minor at measure 33 provides a fine complement to the change of tone in the lyrics, but otherwise, the song's melodic structure and harmonic accompaniment are regular and predictable. This is another illustration of Ellington's initial instincts being adversely affected by endless revisions. An earlier version of the song, copyrighted August 1962, displays a tonal, but upward moving melody, with a greater intervallic variety, both in direction of movement and actual skips, even though the essential shape of the song remains the same. The B section, reharmonized in the Broadway version, shows accented non-chordal melody notes providing much more musical (and dramatic) activity in the melodic line. The Broadway version concludes with another extended dance number, not composed by Ellington.

"Let's," a dirty blues number evocative of Minski's Burlesque, is another survivor from the earlier days of *Pousse-Café*. Copyrighted in October 1963,

"Let's" is a rhythm blues number, making significant use of syncopation, blue notes (flatted third and seventh especially), thick chromatic accompaniment, and a walking bass. Although "Let's" is a night-club performance number for Solange, it could have easily been sung by Havana with the male chorus, given its similarity to "The Spider and the Fly," which is a less successful composition. "Old World Charm," a performance number for Ritter at the night-club, begins with a series of false starts, followed verse that anticipates much of the Baker's Wife's patter in Sondheim and Lapine's *Into the Woods*, some thirty years later. The chorus, which vacillates between minor and major modalities, begins with an A section, in ascending half-notes, provocatively on an accented non-chordal tone (one of Ellington's favorite devices for energizing a melody), followed by a B section in parlando style, heavy with accented dissonance in the melody. Although the non-chordal tones do resolve easily and quickly, the fact that the dissonances are mostly on heavy beats allows the ear to emphasize the tension rather than the resolution of the piece. Structured in an unusual A-B-A-B-B-A format, "Old World Charm" also invokes the unbalanced mental state of Professor Ritter and the discomfort he experiences on display as a night-club performer.

Among the numbers that were disgarded from earlier versions of *Pousse-Café*, "Swivel," a rhythmic be-bop number, "My Heart Is a Stranger," a dramatic soliloquy, and "Fleugel Street Rag," a dixieland cakewalk, perhaps most deserve to be rescued from anonymity. Happily, nearly a decade before his death in 1998, Marshall Barer produced a studio recording of songs from *Pousse-Café*, performed by club-singer Barbara Lea and himself and arranged by Ellis Larkins, the show's original pianist and dance arranger, for small jazz ensemble.[10] Even though the recording does not recapture the original Broadway sound of the piece, it is notable in that it includes many musical numbers omitted from the New York production and remains the only recorded source of unused material such as "My Heart Is a Stranger," "Fleugel Street Rag," "Up Your Ante," "Be a Man," "Swivel," "Settle for Less," "If I Knew Now (What I Knew Then)," and the original version of "Spider and the Fly." Reviewing the recording for *Stereo Review* (April 1993), Roy Hemming concluded that "whatever was wrong with the show, it wasn't the songs" (89).

Why did *Pousse-Café* fail? As Walter Kerr noted in his review, "the show was really over on the day they released the film"(*Theatre Critics' Reviews* 27: 328). The transformation of a beloved classic is dangerous in the best of situations, and the conditions surrounding *Pousse-Café* were far from auspicious. The failure of the show has prompted many to suggest that Ellington turned away from the theatre after 1966. The correspondence discussed in another chapter regarding *Cinque* and *The Greatest Mother of Them All* demonstrates that Ellington was not adverse to considering new projects after *Pousse-Café*, nor was he unwilling to commit himself to the rigors of actual composition.

During the pre-Broadway tour of *Pousse-Café*, Ellington had spent about five weeks in Europe touring with his band, during which he performed the Sacred Concert at Coventry Cathedral in England, on 21 February, which was televised and broadcast in the United States on 10 April. In April, Ellington and the orchestra performed at the first World Festival of Negro Arts in Dakar, Senegal, and premiered *La Plus Belle Africaine*, a large-scale work adapted by Ellington and Strayhorn from some of the material previously written for the unproduced musical, *Saturday Laughter*. The following month, the orchestra made a second concert tour of Japan, and in July, Ellington returned to the south of France where the band performed at the Côté d'Azur. The *Pousse-Café* debacle on Broadway had in no way affected Ellington's commercial appeal or his work habits, for in 1969, in and around orchestra dates in Berlin, Paris, Prague, Barcelona, and Las Vegas, Ellington began scoring a three-act musical drama based on the legend of John Henry, entitled *Shout Up a Morning*. With a book by Peter Farrow, and lyrics by Farrow, and his partner, Diane Lampert, *Shout Up a Morning* appealed to Ellington's strong religious beliefs, while allowing him a forum to continue to speak out against racial prejudice, in a score filled with gospel hymn tunes, folk-like work songs, jazz waltzes, and musical soliloquys that verge on the operatic. [11] Unlike *Pousse-Café*, a "white" Broadway score written by an African American, *Shout Up a Morning* was to be an African American score, emphasizing the black influence on American music, by the foremost African American composer in America.

A prologue to the John Henry legend introduces the audience to a barren mountain in West Virginia in April 1868 where deeply religious—and superstitious—African Americans are tunneling through the mountain, singing "Long Way Out of Egypt," to a gospel melody, evocative of black folk music in the nineteenth century, with its ponderous, earth-bound chorus, and rhythmic solo interludes. Into this ominous environment enters John Henry, looking gigantic, tossing boulders out of his way as he walks, and asking for employment. He announces that he has been newly freed from heaven where he had been working for the Lord because God was impressed with Lincoln's Emancipation Proclamation, and heard that men were being hired to dig a tunnel through the mountain for a railroad. When the workers warn him not to profane God by working on the Sabbath, John Henry replies that he has not worked on a Sunday since the seventh day of creation, when God asked him how he liked what he saw, and John Henry suggested a few changes ("Who Bend the Rainbow?" a 20-bar gospel blues). The new man introduces himself to Bull Maree, a white foreman, who hires him for a dollar a day. A waterboy named Bright asks if John Henry really can speak to God, and the giant replies with a reprise of "Who Bend the Rainbow?"

A rooster crows, marking daybreak, and three Irishmen, asking for Bull Maree, pass Leah, the matriarch of Jack Moses's work gang, on their way through the work camp. Leah asks her brother Aaron if he knew a young man named Shadrach Taylor when he worked on the other side of the tunnel. One of the Irishmen, Jack, overhears the question and replies that Shadrach was sold off before the war. Leah, lamenting the fact that Shadrach Taylor is gone away forever, is comforted by Carolina, Jack Moses's 20-year-old granddaughter, who tells her that in all creation, every creature can find its way home. Carolina's song, "Bornin' Place," is the first truly lyrical moment in the score. Beginning with a distinctive minor seventh leap, the melody is an exquisite example of word-painting as it dips and soars with the bird imagery of the lyrics, and develops almost operatically, in a through-composed style emphasizing the scansion of the lyric rather than traditional structure of music theatre songs. (See Example 8.1)

The scene changes to the tunnel, near sunset, where the gangs are working, singing a virile worksong, "Joshua," evoking the Biblical legend of the fall of Jericho's walls. John Henry, who enjoys displaying his strength, earns the jealousy of Reuben, the "top driver" of the gang, who asks the newcomer who was in Heaven while he was working there. John Henry answers in a gospel patter song, "Who Up In Heaven?" that white men were there, along with Baptists, Methodists, and Jews, but the one thing that heaven did not have was a woman as fine as Carolina. In the short scene that follows, John Henry learns that Carolina and her brother, Bright, are bound for Mississippi, their birthplace, to escape being sold as slaves. John Henry kisses her, and though Carolina wants to give in to him, she breaks away and runs off into the dark, an action that causes John Henry to look up to Heaven and ask God if he is doing to the right thing. In reply, a shooting star crosses the sky.

Back at the camp, mid-morning some days later, children singing "Whatcha Gonna Make for Your True Love's Supper" (a folk song in a minor mode), are interrupted by the sudden appearance of Jassawa, the idiot son of Grandy the witch-woman, stealing flour out of the pantry. Carolina retrieves the stolen flour, and the children playfully chase Jassawa away with a broom, making a children's game out of the event, to the tune of "The Broomstick Song," a sing-song rhythm number, in A♭, the major key relative to the minor mode of the previous number. After the game, which ends with Jassawa at the batter bowl, Carolina asks the witch-woman how to interpret the recent

Example 8.1.

darkness of the moon, and Grandy replies that Shadrach is coming back home to carry Carolina away. Not appreciating the prediction, Carolina pulls out the peacock feather John Henry gave her a week earlier and tries to "unwitch" the witch-woman, causing Grandy to go into a kind of trance. Carolina inquires if Shadrach is gone for good and before the witch-woman can provide a clear answer, the children reenter singing "The Broomstick Song," and the scene ends.

A day later, at the river landing, Billy, a steel driver returned from the South, leads the stevedores in the expression of dreams for the future, "Forty Acres and a Mule," in which each man can support himself by the land. The score does not provide a setting for the lyric in the text, but substitutes a rhythmic folk-like tune in D minor that begins with the lyric "Living high you and I," and celebrates the possibility of money coming from trees, plows, pies, and cows, in a gospel-like development of the theme of "money coming out of the land." Carolina enters to buy material for a new "Sunday gown" because, as she expresses in a bluesy jazz waltz, she's "Gonna give lovin' a try." This catchy tune recalls one of Ellington's signature structures: an eight-bar A section, and eight-bar B section, and a four-bar recapitulation. The abbreviation of the last A energizes the structure, propelling it to the next statement, or musical interlude, and gives it an improvisatory spontaneity, suggesting that Carolina is forming the thoughts as she sings them. (See Example 8.2) So rhythmic and catchy a tune easily develops into a dance during which Carolina is given everything she came for, but the mood turns sour when the dance concludes as Carolina encounters a chain gang on her way home, humming the "Chain Gang," and supervised by a Pinkerton man.

The scene changes to the work camp, several days later, where Reuben, still jealous of being "second hammer" to John Henry, wants to move on. When Jenny, his wife, suggests that he get over his jealousy, Reuben threatens to leave without her, warning that there are a lot of available girls who would jump at the chance to go away with him. Neither threatened nor amused, Jenny throws his belongings out of their shack, singing, "Grind Your Own Coffee," and Reuben exits humiliated. John Henry enters, kisses Carolina, and tells her that he plans to build a house for them. Carolina responds

Example 8.2.

to his offer by breaking down in tears, saying that she has the blues, not only about their relationship, but about all of them, walking from place to place, without a home, just waiting for "Ol' Kingdom-Come ... so maybe we can do a little livin' when we die" (1-5-59). John Henry replies with "Stayin' Place," arguing that God did not create the earth as a roof for Hell, but as the floor of Heaven, a happy place where His chosen children can live. Ellington's setting of the lyric begins with a highly melodic, though parlando, verse followed a country-style melody that develops operatically as if through-composed. Ellington appears much less concerned with traditional song forms in this work, but rather spins out his melodies as if they were folk tunes, improvised by story tellers, changing their shape to fit the tale being told.

The scene changes to the top of a hill overlooking the camp that same night, where Jack Moses announces that the Carolina and Ohio Organization is cutting the men's back wages in half, and that a new locomotive "steam-drill" is about to replace all of the men currently digging the tunnel. Later, the same night, on the roadside below the camp, Reuben convinces the other workers that John Henry is to blame for all the trouble that has arisen since his arrival and, in a kind of African ritual, they put a hex on him. When the marked man arrives with Carolina—wearing her new "Sunday gown," an applebud dress—the crowd freezes in terror, claiming to have meant no harm by the hexing ritual. Admitting that he has been fired along with the rest of them, and claiming that he could destroy the locomotive drill as easily as a wooden spinning wheel, John Henry announces that he is taking Carolina home to Mississippi, and offers to lead the others there as well, singing "Shout Up a Morning," a bombastic, rhythmic, gospel tune, with an interesting rhythmic interlude between the first and second phrases of the melody that suggests hands clapping, or work implements clanging to a Charleston-like beat. (See Example 8.3) Leah stops Carolina from going with John Henry, who fades into the darkness as the wail of the locomotive drill pierces the night air.

Act Two follows immediately, without intermission. At the workcamp, two months later, a pregnant Carolina begins to taunt Bull Maree, who is assembling women and children for "scutting" the tunnel through the mountain. Later, Carolina, leaving the work crew to look for John Henry,

Example 8.3.

encounters the chain gang whose guard, the Pinkerton Man, tries to convince her that John Henry was hanged as a felon many years earlier, while the inmates taunt about her lover. Carolina sings a prayer to the river to "Flow him home to me," while Jassawa plinks the tune of the "John Henry Ballad" on the broomstraw and the curtain falls. None of the lyrics indicated in the script for Act Two were set by Ellington except for a fragment of Carolina's prayer that appears in the third act as counterpoint to the opening number.

Act Three begins several weeks later on a road between the levee and the railroad, with Jassawa calling out for John Henry who appears as if a ghost, replying, "Anybody Need a Big Man?" The 12-bar refrain reveals a catchy, bluesy, country song in F minor with a tonal melody mainly outlining minor seventh chords. The song, recalling lyric motifs from the first act ("Bend the Rainbow"), develops into a contrapuntal musical scene, not unlike the "Tonight" quintet in *West Side Story*, with the Rousters singing about the railroad route while they work, and Carolina singing a reprise of the prayer that ended the second act. (See Example 8.4) At the conclusion of the number, Jassawa is manacled and tossed into a linking pen where he joins John Henry among the other prisoners, but fails to recognize him because he appears to be the normal size of a man. Jassawa, recently orphaned by the death of his mother, expresses concern over being shackled to the other prisoners and is unable to swallow the rough bread that he is offered to eat. As the sheriff begins to bind the prisoners together, Jassawa recognizes John Henry and begs him to smite down the white folk, but John Henry refuses and claims that he no longer has super-human strength, singing "Nothin' But a Man."

The sheriff, discovering John Henry's identity, has him put in double irons, but to no avail, for as soon as John Henry is shackled, he rips off the irons in a show of great strength and kills the sheriff. Weeks later at the working camp, against the underscore of the "Chain Gang," Jenny advises Carolina to carry her child proudly, without any shame. Unexpectedly, looking haggard and streaked with dust, John Henry appears (followed by Jassawa, looking in even worse condition), announcing their escape and plans to move out West. At this point, the score sketch has a ditty for Jassawa "On

Example 8.4.

his bones," describing the escape from the linking pen in a patter melody, outlining C-minor triads. Carolina replies to John Henry's proposal that she will accompany him wherever and sings a reprise of "Staying Place," interrupted by the arrival of Bull Maree with a Pinkerton Man. John Henry pulls Bull Maree aside and claims his right to be "top hammer" on the crew.

In the following transitional scene, John Henry buries Bright, Carolina's brother, and in a long, revival meeting–like monologue incites the crowd and himself with the courage to take on the white man's machine, the engine driver. The scene changes to the following dawn when Maree announces a digging competition between John Henry and the engine driver. While the match is on, the crowd sings the "Ballad of John Henry" to mark the passage of time from dawn to sunset. In his attempt to keep up with the machine, John Henry falls dead at Carolina's feet, and she mourns the loss of both his life and her hopes, singing, "Jesus, Where You Now?" An epilogue follows immediately, during which the crowd hums "Long Way Out of Egypt." Jack Moses entrusts the responsibility of leading the people to Mississippi to Jassawa, even though the boy claims to have no special powers. While Carolina is sleeping, Leah complains about her "shameful behavior," by getting herself pregnant, but Jack Moses scolds her, saying that Carolina felt as proud as Mary in what she did, and sings, in counterpoint to the spiritual being hummed, a prayer for Carolina's safe delivery of her own Jesus, and the curtain falls.

It is a great loss that Ellington never completed the score because it contains at least four of his most original and interesting compositions for the stage: "Bornin' Place," "Gonna Give Lovin' a Try," "Stayin' Place," and "Shout Up a Morning." As a musical entity, *Shout Up a Morning* is one of Ellington's more unified compositions, unaffected by the demands of directors, choreographers, producers, and the idiosyncrasies of stars. Why the work was abandoned is impossible to suggest with certainty. Perhaps there was no interest in a professional production, or the money raised was insufficient. Perhaps, as the Duke reached his 70th birthday, the tours with the band had become more taxing than before, and his energies had to be directed only toward those projects with a guaranteed performance, such as the ballet commissioned by the American Ballet Theatre, *The River*.[12]

Nine

Water Music

Early in 1970, Lucia Chase, the director of the American Ballet Theatre, commissioned Duke Ellington to compose a ballet to celebrate the company's 30th anniversary, and approached African American choreographer Alvin Ailey, unaccustomed to working in the style of classical ballet, about choreographing the piece.[1] In spite of any misgivings Ailey might have felt about working in an idiom foreign to him, he welcomed the challenge and the opportunity to collaborate once again with the Duke, whom he had met for the first time in 1963, during the production of *My People*, when Ellington had asked his help in staging the show.[2] In April, Ailey was flown out to Vancouver, British Columbia, where Ellington's band was performing, to meet with the Duke to discuss the project. Since Ellington's club date ended at 1:30 in the morning, and he was scheduled to fly to Los Angeles at 7:30 the same morning, Ailey had no choice but to stay up all night listening to the Duke talk about a project that had been on his mind for at least a year, called *The River*, intended to be a suite of dances based on water, invoking the passage of life from birth to death. By 5 A.M., Ellington began to play music on the electric piano that traveled everywhere with him, and Ailey was so impressed with what he heard that *The River* was agreed to on the spot. Initially, Ailey found the collaboration with Ellington to be exhilarating, noting in an interview in *Newsweek* (6 July 1970) that "he's like Stravinskiy. There's an inner rhythm and always great feeling" (86). When he flew to Toronto in May to continue discussions about the ballet, he found that Ellington had done meticulous research on water music from various musical periods, including Handel's *Water Music*, Debussy's *La Mer*, Britten's *Peter Grimes*, and Smetana's *Moldau*. As Ailey recalled:

> I had a room right down the hall from him. He had done major research on water music and had gathered together every piece of music with a water reference you could think of. He would play something for me on an electric piano and ask if I liked it. His calls to me at four o'clock in the morning became a ritual. He would say, "Hey, Alvin, you ready to work?" He liked to work from four-thirty until seven o'clock in the morning. Then he would

> go to bed and sleep until three or four in the afternoon. He would tinker again on the piano before getting dressed up, looking for all the world like Big Daddy, and going down to orchestra rehearsal.... At eight his room would be full of sixty-year-old ladies, probably Canadian, whom he called girls.... The shows were at nine and eleven, and during the interval between shows he would party with the ladies. (Ailey 116)

According to Don George, Ellington's lyricist and biographer, Ailey considered Duke "a real genius" exemplary in his ability to balance his concert tours with his creative projects. Typically, however, Ellington's band dates made collaboration extremely difficult and Ailey's admiration soon turned to complaints about a composer in absentia, who was feeding him the score page by page rather than in completed sections.[3] He had worked out sections of the ballet previous to the three weeks allotted for rehearsals at Lincoln Center, but after those portions of the work had been staged, the choreographer was incapacitated without the rest of the music. Ironically, just as Ailey was ready to walk out on the project and Lucia Chase ready to program another ballet in its place, in walks Ellington with a big grin on his face, and hands Ailey a tape of the completed score, remarking, "If you stopped worrying about the music and started worrying about the choreography, you'd be a lot better off." That was the way the Duke worked, on his own schedule, no one else's.

Of the ballet's eleven principal sections (a twelfth was the reprise of the first), only six had been recorded before rehearsals began. In New York City, on 11 May 1970, Ellington recorded piano versions of "The Spring," "The Run," "The Lake," "The Giggling Rapids," "The Meander," and "Stud" ("The Neo-Hip-Hot-Cool Kiddies Community"). In Chicago on 25 May 1970, the Ellington Orchestra recorded "The Spring," "The Run," "The Meander," "The Giggling Rapids," and "The Lake." In New York on 3 June, four more sections were recorded by the orchestra: "The Whirlpool," "Riba," "The Neo-Hip-Hot-Cool Kiddies Communities," and "The Village of the Virgins." "The Falls" was recorded on 8 June in New York and, finally, "Her Majesty the Sea," completing the score, was recorded on 15 June in New York, barely ten days before the ballet was to open at Lincoln Center. Having too little time to choreograph the entire ballet, Alley presented only six of the sections at the premiere: "Spring," "Vortex (Whirlpool)," "Falls," "The Lake," "Riba," and "Two Cities (The Neo-Hip-Hot Kiddies Communities and The Village of the Virgins)." In "Riba," for example, solo dancer Dennis Nahat, who had begun choreographing his own work a year before, was told by Ailey to go out on stage and improvise.[4]

Whitney Balliett, a writer for *The New Yorker* in attendance at the 8 June recording of "The Falls," provides a rare insight into an Ellington recording session. Meeting Ellington around 3:30 in the afternoon at the National Recording Studios at 56th Street and Fifth Avenue, Balliett recalls that,

Duke Ellington at work. Courtesy of the Duke Ellington Collection, National Museum of American History Archives Center, Smithsonian Institution.

although Ellington did not get to bed until 10 A.M. that morning, it did not affect his desire to work:

> He went immediately into the recording booth, which, like most of the places Ellington goes, was crowded with relatives, friends, … and a couple of admiring women. Ellington examined some sheet music and went out into

> the studio. He spoke to several members of the band and got loud laughs in response, and, standing in the center of the studio, said, just before the first take, "We're going to get lucky on this one, Derum, derum, derum! One, two, three, four!" Rufus Jones started a rapid machine-gun beat on his snare drum, which was echoed on a glockenspiel and on timpani. The band came in, and the piece, called "The Falls," turned out to be unlike anything I had heard Ellington do. But then nothing new of his is quite like anything he has done before. The section passages of "The Falls," are brief but dense and booting, there are solo parts by Paul Gonsalves, and there are extraordinary dissonant full-band chords. And all this is done against the furious *rat-tat-tat-tat* of the snare, the glockenspiel, and the timpani. It is exciting, tight crescendo music, and it reminded me of some of Stravinsky's early stuff, except that it was unmistakably a jazz composition. Ellington conducted (Wild Bill Davis sat in on piano), using the traditional upside-down-T-square motions in a slow, wooden way, as if he were swimming through molasses. All the while, he chewed on something and rocked his head from side to side. [*New Yorker* 27 June 1970: 52–53]

After the premiere on 25 June 1970, nine days after the American Ballet Theatre began its summer season at Lincoln Center,[5] the critics were unanimous in their praise for the score. Hubert Saal, writing in *Newsweek* (6 July 1970), called it "a tone poem, … like a river, constantly flowing, changing speed and shape, instantly accessible melodically" (86), and Clive Barnes reviewing for the New York *Times* (26 June 1970) called the music "marvelous. It sings out—it is that rare thing among classic scores, something that is contemporary, moving and yet totally unsentimental. I was very impressed by it—Mr. Ellington writes with an authenticity and authority that regrettably few of our contemporary composers can muster" (30). An immediate popular and critical success, *The River*, a ballet in which Alvin Ailey had been able to bridge the gap between modern dance and classical ballet, became a staple of the American Ballet Theatre's repertoire. In the 1971 season, Ailey added three more sections to the ballet in an attempt to provide the Ballet Theatre with the complete work for future productions. Stanley Dance confided to Derek Jewell that Ellington was disappointed with the final product, suggesting that it failed to live up to his original conception. "He never did think anything was as good as it should have been—except for *My People*, when he did the lot. I suppose he was unreasonable, really, because he never gave people too much of a chance. He was always working up to the very last minute, so how could you expect a dance company to have had time to fit everything together with the music" (Jewell 197). Ellington's dissatisfaction must have been based on what he saw at rehearsals because, according to Alvin Ailey, the Duke never saw a performance of the ballet.[6]

In September 1971, the American Ballet Theatre became the official ballet company of the newly-opened Kennedy Center in Washington D.C., and *The River* was among the works chosen for the opening gala performance on 11 September. *Saturday Review* (25 September 1971) called it a "beautiful ballet, ... flooded with the glow of humanity, the beacon of brotherhood, carefree frolic, both reverence and irreverence, and mass moments of great architectural splendor"(65). The audience not only gave the work a standing ovation but cheered its creator Alvin Ailey and Lucia Chase, the woman who commissioned it, as well. Following the performance, on 28 September 1971, former president Lyndon Baines Johnson, having received a Christmas card from Ellington illustrated with a passage from *The River*, sent Ellington the following communication:

> Dear Mr. Ellington:
>
> "The River" makes a beautiful message for Christmas or any other season, and we are happy to be among the fortunate folk who received a copy of it.
>
> Thanks for your thoughtfulness ... and congratulations on all that talent.[7]

Ellington's original conception of *The River* is outlined in great detail in his memoir, *Music Is My Mistress*. The work begins with "The Spring," representing a newborn baby "wiggling, gurgling, squirming, squealing," in a highly improvisatory piano solo, recalling Debussy in its use of whole tone scales, ostonato, and its playful juxtaposition between major and minor modes. Suddenly, the baby falls from the cradle on to the floor and goes into "The Run," where he marches forward like a toy soldier until he is distracted by a puddle. After various adventures, including the escape from a bubble about to overwhelm him, the baby tires of marching and passes into "The Meander," where the baby rolls from one side of the floor to the next, until he sees a door leading to the outside world. Beginning with a long flute cadenza, this section evokes Gershwin in its shuffling in and out of blue notes, and chromatic harmony. The child goes through the door to the outside world ("The Giggling Rapids"), where he runs and explores to the syncopated rhythms of a jazz waltz, until, exhausted, he rolls down to "The Lake," serene, God-made beauty untouched by the hand of man. Admiring the beauty of the lake, people "begin to discover new facets of compatibility in each other, and as a romantic viewpoint develops, they indulge themselves. The whole situation compounds itself into an emotional violence that is even greater than that of the violence of the vortex to come" (202). This movement displays a sultry lyrical melody soaring over an easily accessible accompaniment suggesting a lazy Latin rhythm. "The Falls," a transitional movement, with driving percussion and dissonant brass, leads us into "The Whirlpool (Vortex)," a storm-like section, heavy on the xylophone and dark low brass runs, that suggests the hazards of life each man must face. It leads to "The River," where the child grows out of adolescence and matures to a 12-bar blues and variations section. At the river delta, there are two cities on opposite sides of the river ("The Neo-Hip-Hot-Cool-Kiddies Community" and "The Village of the

Virgins"), signifying that there is always something that can be gotten on one side of the river that cannot be attained on the opposite side. Here Ellington recalls Smetana's *Moldau* in his musical imagery. After the river passes the two cities and reaches "The Mother, Her Majesty the Sea," where "we realize the validity of the foundation of religion which is Heavenly Anticipation of Rebirth. The mother, in her beautiful romantic exchange with the sun, gives up to the sky that which is to come back as rain, snow, or fog on the mountains and plains. So the next time we see it, it is like a newborn baby" (202–203) that materializes, in the circular cycle of birth and death, as "The Spring," recalling the opening piano improvisation that fades into black.

Although *The River* remains Ellington's single work actually commissioned as a ballet,[8] his music was no stranger to the ballet stage. As early as 1936, Esther Jungen had used Ellington's "jungle music" to accompany her dance entitled *Negro Sketches*. In the fall of 1958, Talley Beatty, the other choreographer involved in staging *My People*, introduced a half-hour ballet called *The Road of the Phoebe Snow*, named for the legendary passenger train running on the Erie Lackawanna Railway between Hoboken, New Jersey, and Chicago, Illinois, and utilizing "Tymperturbably Blue" as well as excerpts from *Toot Suite*, *A Drum Is a Woman*, and *Anatomy of a Murder* by Ellington and Strayhorn. A part-symbollic, part-realistic ballet of gang warfare, mass rape, innocent love and suicide, ranking as "one of the great achievements of jazz dance" (New York *Times* 18 December 1965: 37), Talley Beatty's work became a staple of the Alvin Ailey Company's repertoire in 1964. In 1960, Beatty added another Ellington-inspired ballet to his list, *Congo Tango Palace*, and in 1968, using music from *Black, Brown and Beige*, Beatty choreographed *Black Belt*. Both ballets quickly entered the repertory of the Alvin Ailey company.

In 1962, Donald McKayle choreographed *District Storyville* for his company of dancers performing at the 92nd Street "Y" on 22 April. Dancing the story of a young brothel musician in the Storyville district of New Orleans who dreams of being crowned "King of Jazz," the ballet borrows melodies from Ellington and other jazz composers and transforms them into an integrated score, credited to dance arranger Dorothea Freitag. In the same year, the First International Jazz Festival in Washington, D.C., sponsored a Jazz Ballet Theatre performing at Howard University's Cramton Hall between 30 May and 2 June. Among the works presented was *Cottontail*, danced to Ellington's music by Alan Johnson, Eliot Feld, and Michael Bennett. Also in 1962, Alvin Ailey had premiered *Reflections in D*, a lyrical solo danced to Ellington's piano composition of the same name.

In 1963, Ellington had composed a short Stravinsky-like piece for Ailey and Minnie Marshall during the rehearsals of *My People*, and later in that year, Alvin Ailey choreographed *First Negro Centennial* to an Ellington score. In 1972, with the formation of the Alvin Ailey Repertory Ensemble, Ailey proposed a festival to celebrate the music of Duke Ellington that was realized to some extent in a television broadcast in November 1974, *Ailey Celebrates Ellington*, created for the CBS Festival of Lively Arts for Young People. Only two dances from the television show entered the repertoire, *The Mooche*, and *Night Creature*, both based on Ellington compositions. Danced through billowing smoke, against a background of mirrors and screens, with a neon sign advertising the title, *The Mooche* is a tribute to the blues heroines of an earlier day, Florence Mills, Marie Bryant, Mahalia Jackson and Bessie Smith and uses "The Mooche," "Black Beauty," "The Shepherd," and "Creole Love Call" as its score. *Night Creature* is a three-part suite of varying moods, danced on a star-flecked stage by a blithe free-spirit, the men competing for her attention, and the corps, star-like, in their silver and white costumes. The ballet takes its name from Ellington's 1955 symphonic work commissioned by conductor Don Gillis for the Symphony of the Air, and recorded in 1963 by the Stockholm Symphony (1st and 2nd movements) and the Paris Symphony (3rd movement).

In 1976, Alvin Ailey produced another Ellington festival, *Ailey Celebrates Ellington*, in August at the New York State Theatre in Lincoln Center, during which the American Ballet Theatre would dance *The River*, and Ailey's Company would perform *Night Creature*, *Blues Suite*, *The Mooche*, *Reflections in D*, Ailey's new pieces, *Black, Brown and Beige*, *Three Black Kings*, and *Pas de Duke*, a juxtaposition of classical ballet with modern dance designed for Mikhail Baryshnikov and Judith Jamison ,[9] Lester Horton's *Liberian Suite*, Talley Beatty's *The Road of the Phoebe Snow*, Milton Myers's *Echoes in Blue*, Louis Falco's *Caravan*,[10] and works using Ellington's music, commissioned especially for the festival: Cristyne Lawson's *Still Life*, Raymond Sawyer's *Afro-Eurasian Eclipse*, Dianne McIntyre's *Deep South Suite*, Gus Solomons, Jr.'s, *Forty*, and Alvin McDuffie's *New Orleans Junction*.

The president's wife, Mrs. Betty Ford, appeared on opening night to give her official blessings to the proceedings, and Coretta King appeared for the premiere of *Three Black Kings*, a choreographic tribute to Balthazar, one of the kings at the Nativity, King Solomon, and Martin Luther King, to Ellington's symphonic score.[11] To open each performance, Mercer Ellington led the Ellington orchestra in a medley of his father's more well-known tunes, assisted by singer Anita Moore, who belted out the rhythm numbers with gusto and sang the mellower ones with a lyrical simplicity that reinforced the genius of Ellington's melodies.

Although *The Mooche, Reflections in D, The River*, and *Night Creature* were well received by the critics, *Three Black Kings* was considered vulgar, betraying a "slapdash quality bordering on disrespect," and Ailey's choreography for the Martin Luther King section, "more suitable to musical comedy," because here, "Ailey emphasized the celebration and discarded the substance" (*Dance Magazine*, November 1976, 21). Louis Falco's *Caravan*, utilizing a Michael Kamen pastiche of Ellington-Strayhorn themes such as

"Caravan," "Sophisticated Lady," "Do Nothing Til You Hear from Me," "'A' Train," and "Satin Doll," was judged the runaway hit of the program, while Gus Solomons, Jr.'s, *Forty*, utilizing "Tap Dancer's Blues," "Don Juan," "Fat Mess," and "Never Stop Remembering Bill," was considered the most unrestrained, independent, and unstructured of the Ellington works. Cristyne Lawson's *Still Life*, danced to Ellington's "Diminuendo and Crescendo in Blue," was viewed as cute but insubstantial, and Sawyer's treatment of Ellington's *Afro-Eurasian Eclipse*, musically describing the day when races will become indistinguishable, was termed "screwy." *Echoes in Blue*, choreographed to "Harlem" and "Mood Indigo," by Milton Myers, and *New Orleans Junction*, choreographed by Alvin McDuffie, were both considered successful mood pieces that captured the sultry night life of both north and south.

Ellington compositions have found their way into the repertoire of a number of dance companies throughout the United States.[12] The Inner City Repertory Dance Company, in October 1972, produced Donald McKayle's *District Storyville*, a ballet that would remain part of the repertoire of the Donald McKayle Dance Company for years to come. Gary McKay designed *There Ain't No Leaves* for the Thomas Holt Dance Ensemble at the Washington Square Church in June 1974; Erin Martin choreographed and performed *Daddy's Girl* at The Yard in Chilmark, Massachusetts, in August 1974, at Marymount Manhattan College in New York City, the following May, at the American Theatre Laboratory in November 1975, and again in November 1977. Jean Sabatine's Jazz Dance Theatre produced *Nameless Hour* set to music by Duke Ellington at Pennsylvania State University in April 1975, and at the Cubiculo in New York City in 1977. The Xoregos Performing Company of San Francisco produced *The Duke on Love* in May 1975, while *Satin Doll* was choreographed by Gene Murray at the Dancing Machine in Boston, Massachusetts, during the 1975–76 season and performed by Lee Theodore's the American Dance Machine at the Century Theatre between 14 June and 26 November 1978.

Becky Arnold and the Dancing Machine premiered *Dear Duke* in Boston in 1976; Nancy Hauser choreographed *A Celebration* for her own dance company in Minneapolis during the 1976–77 season; Merrily Carter designed *Tribute to the Duke* for the Mississippi Coast Ballet the following year; and Richard Jones choreographed *Salute to Duke* for Les Ballets Jazz, performing at the Roundabout / Stage One in February 1978. Ellington and Strayhorn's suite, *Such Sweet Thunder*, was choreographed by Sophie Maslow for her dance company performing at the Theatre of the Riverside Church in 1976, and staged by William Carter for the Ballet Hispanico of New York, performing at the Henry Street Settlement Playhouse in April 1978. The Pepsi Bethel Authentic Jazz Dance Theatre produced *Tabernacle* and *The Apple*, both based on Ellington material, at the Graduate Center Mall of CUNY in July 1977.

Susan Dibble's *Day* was performed at the Riverside Dance Festival in June 1978 and the Clark Center Dance Festival on 7 July. Using excerpts from "The 'A' Train," "Flamingo," "Solitude," "Satin Doll," "Caravan," "Bakiff," "Passion Flower," and "I'm Beginning to See the Light," Joyce Trisler staged *Little Red Riding Hood* for her own company performing at the Riverside Church Theatre in March 1978. The Mitchell Rose Dance Company presented *In a Sentimental Mood* at the American Theatre Laboratory in New York City, in April 1978; Tance Johnson choreographed *Egghead and Cookie* for his company in San Francisco during the 1977–78 season; and Doris Jones staged *Three Jazz Pieces* for the Capitol Ballet Company in Washington, D.C., during the same season. Julie Maloney designed *Golden Attitude* for her own dance company performing at the Loft / Mercer Street in January 1979; Lynn Daly and her dancers performed *Duet* at the American Theatre Laboratory in August 1979.

At the Space at City Center in New York City, Joyce Trisler's company performed *Jitterbug* in the spring of 1981; the Inner City Ensemble Theatre and Dance produced *Rhythm Chase* for the Riverside Dance Festival in New York City in December 1984; Beverly Blossom performed *Inch* at the Nikolais/Louis DanceSpace, New York City, in November 1987; Frank Conversano danced *Duking* for the Danspace Project in November 1990; Cynthia Gregory, Donald Williams, Lynn Glauber, Alan Hineline, and Peter Lentz performed *Red/Ellington* at Florence Gould Hall in New York City in March 1991. *Circles*, choreographed by Ze'eva Cohen, was produced at the Intiman Theatre, Seattle, Washington, in March 1992, and the Next Wave Festival produced *The Harlem Nutcracker* to Ellington/Strayhorn's transcription of Tchaikovsky's ballet at the Brooklyn Academy of Music in December 1996.

In July 1998 the Bates Dance Festival in Lewiston Maine produced *Scene Unseen* using "Lotus Blossom," "Tonk," "Cashmere Cutie," "A Flower Is a Lovesome Thing," "Chelsea Bridge," and "Blood Count," all identified as Billy Strayhorn compositions, and the Ellington/Strayhorn collaboration, "Just A-Settin' and A-Rockin'." Finally, in June 1999, *Duke!* was performed by the New York City Ballet in conjunction with the Jazz at Lincoln Center series. *Duke!* is divided into three movements, each with a different choreographer. The first, a tribute to 1940s swing dancing, *Rockin' in Rhythm*, was choreographed by Robert La Fosse of the New York City Ballet, the third, *Blossom Got Kissed*, by Broadway choreographer Susan Stroman, featured an a-rhythmic ballerina in a pale blue tutu transformed by a kiss bestowed by the orchestra's triangle player; and the middle work, *Ellington Elation,* was designed for two couples and an ensemble of ten by Garth Fagan, whose highly original, idiosyncratic mixture of dance styles had ten years previously found the perfect expression for Ellington's last composition for the stage, *Queenie Pie*.

Ten

Gilbert and Sullivan on Hallucinogens

As a self-proclaimed composer of "Negro folk music," attempting to display the natural feelings of African Americans, Duke Ellington had, as early as 1931, cherished the desire to compose "a musical evolution of the Negro race," that would replace the "lamp-black Negroisms" present in works such as Gershwin's *Porgy and Bess* with music that would "express terror and defiance in colorful Negro musical idioms which have remained melodious despite a life of injustices" (Ulanov 241).[1] In December 1935, Ellington had criticized Gershwin's work in an interview with Edward Morrow, appearing in the *New Theatre*, and dismissed the possibility of his writing in that genre, arguing that "an opera would not express the kind of things I have in mind" (*The Ellington Reader* 116).[2] The Duke's initial aversion to so European a form as the opera is not surprising. Mercer Ellington, in a frequently quoted passage, noted his father's dislike of formal training and adherence to rules because he found inspiration not only in discarding rules, but in making them work in reverse.[3]

In July 1936, an article appeared in *Down Beat* entitled "Duke Is Living for the Day When He Can Write an Opera," implying that Ellington had discovered a way to adapt the European conventions of opera to his own musical idiom. Ulanov reports that the Duke was laboring on a musical comedy during this period tentatively titled *Air Conditioned Jungle*, intended to reverse some of the stereotypical thinking about blacks in the thirties. The work opens in the chic living room of the King and Queen of one of the ancient tribes of Africa. Dressed in a Schiaparelli gown, she relaxes with brandy and coffee as her husband, in a dinner jacket, answers the telephone. Slamming down the phone, he complains to his wife that another expedition from America is coming to Africa to search for the roots of jazz, and notes that they will have to get out their leopard-skin costumes to behave in the expected fashion for their guests. The scenario continues as an investigation into the perceptions of Negro culture in America and Africa, in an attempt to determine which are true and which are false. The outline of this musical work was never developed, and the music transformed into a composition for clarinetist Jimmy Hamilton, entitled *Air-Conditioned Jungle.*[4]

In October 1938, however, *Down Beat* reported the completion of an operatic work in an article called "Ellington Completed Negro Opera at Bedside." The article was misleading since the opera to which it referred, *Boola*, was never finished as an operatic work, but formed the basis for two important compositions, *Ko-Ko*, recorded in 1940, and *Black, Brown and Beige*, recorded in 1943. Variously described as an opera, an operetta, a suite in five parts, and a symphony, *Boola* traced the career of the eponymous character from his African beginnings through the twentieth century. A holograph manuscript at the Smithsonian Institution, identified by John Edward Hasse as the scenario for *Black, Brown and Beige*, provides the details of Boola's journey into the twentieth century. Along the way, he encounters great suffering aboard a slave ship, where he is chained to the hull, and has little respite from his pain other than his music. He is sold into slavery in America where he works the fields and creates the "Work Song," a song of burden, punctuated "by the grunt of heaving a pick or axe." He is converted to Christianity; the Bible gives him hope because he discovers that his Lord "is greater than the man with the whip," and his music fuses with the hymns he hears in church to create the Spiritual, the music through which he communicates with God. He attempts to join the Colonial Army but is refused, even though 700 free Haitian soldiers came to the aid of the colonists at the siege of Savannah.[5] Moving to the Civil War, Boola helps the Union soldiers, serving as their guide when they are lost, and their nurse when they are wounded, until the Emancipation Proclamation set him free, a mixed blessing since many older African Americans, unable to work, found themselves without a home, since they were forced to leave the plantations. Boola becomes the hero of San Juan Hill in the Spanish American War, but discovers the negative side to fame—soldiers fortunate enough to come home from the wars were not always lucky to find their women waiting for them—and he learns to sing the blues. With a short interrogation into the science of the blues, the autograph scenario ends.

Although Ellington did not use the first two sections of the scenario in *Black, Brown and Beige*,[6] there does exist a 16-bar sketch of a melody with the words, "Down beaten down to the ground tied and bound, Bulah, Bulah [Poor Bulah.] Pain sick with pain in a chain, blood-stained chain, Bulah, Bulah Poor Bulah," which corresponds to the situation and word choice in the Africa section of the autograph scenario. The melody outlines a harmonic minor scale beginning on C: C–E♭, B–E♭, Ab–E♭, G, G, F–E♭, C. It is unknown whether the fragment was intended for *Boola* as a separate work, or as part of *Black, Brown and Beige* that was subsequently discarded, but its existence demonstrates that Ellington had, at some point, begun setting the earlier sections of the scenario to music. *Ko-Ko*, the instrumental composition universally accepted as originally belonging to some version of *Boola*,[7] is also regarded as one of Ellington's masterpieces, evoking Debussy in its utilization of ostenato, whole-tone scales and bitonality (an evocation that will be repeated much later in his career in *The River*). Ken Rattenbury, noting Martin Williams and Gunther Schuller's enthusiastic views on the work, concludes that "*Ko Ko* clearly shows Ellington to have been a genuine composer rather than simply an arranger. He had the technique and depth to create large structures from small components ... to hold the attention of his audience without resorting to singable tunes.... *Ko Ko*, once a new composition, has passed into the standard repertoire owing to its energy and atmospheric quality.... The piece exemplifies Ellington's synthesis of blues and ragtime elements, and his ability to recognize and integrate the idiosyncratic talents of his musicians" (140–141).[8]

James Lincoln Collier suggests that *Queenie Pie* dates from 1936 when Ellington began a musical about Sarah McWilliam Walker (Madame C.J. Walker), a Harlem beautician who had made a fortune from a patented hair-straightener (217).[9] On 7 January 1945, the Columbus, Ohio, *Dispatch* ran the Associated Press announcement that Ellington was beginning work on an original American opera, after receiving encouragement from Metropolitan Opera tenor, Lauritz Melchior, who promised that, if the work suited his abilities, he would appear in it. Hasse gives the date of origin as the 1950s, and Jewell notes that some version was in existence as of 1963 because entrepreneur Norman Grantz claimed to have had a script of the opera, supposedly intended for Ella Fitzgerald.[10] In 1970, WNET, New York City's public television station, commissioned Ellington to complete the work, now earmarked for Lena Horne, by 1972. Between 1970 and 1972, the Ellington Orchestra toured Europe, Australasia, the Far East, Russia, South America, Mexico, with a return engagement in Japan, the Philippines, Thailand, Singapore, Indonesia, Australasia, and Fiji. It is not surprising, then, that in 1972, *Queenie Pie* was still incomplete and Ellington turned to conductor Maurice Peress to assist in the creation of a vocal score.[11] By June 1973, a presentation was made to WNET of the opera, but, because of the delays and the subsequent loss of production funds, the project never materialized.[12]

Undeterred by the cancellation, Ellington proceeded to transform his hour-long television opera into what he termed a full-length "street opera" that remained unfinished at the time of his death on 24 May 1974, even though as Derek Jewell maintains Duke was working on it to the very end of his life (227). What was virtually complete was the 44-minute television opera in seven scenes, with a cast that included:

Queenie Pie, a Lena Horne-type jazz singer-actress
Lil' Daddy, a blues singer-actor

Holt Fay, a stand-up comic, slick, handsome, ballad singer
Café Olay, a gorgeous dancer
Lady Reporter, a legit singer-actress
King, a jazz singer-actor (bass)
Crown Prince, a legit singer-actor (baritone)
Witch Doctor/ Band Leader, jazz singer-actor (baritone)
Male Quartet, barbershop or "Inskpot" type
Solo Soprano 1 and 2, bluesy but legit
Solo Mezzo, bluesy but legit;

and an orchestration for four trumpets, three trombones, two French horns, five reeds, a tuba, bass, drums, two percussionists, a harp, and eight or more strings.

A manuscript, dated 31 August 1973, and calling the piece an "Opera Buffa," shows Scene One beginning with "New York, New York," a tribute to the city's multitudinous delights, including its claim to be a "Beauty Festival." A narrator (also referred to as "Duke" in the manuscript) reveals that "Queenie Pie" is the honorary degree given annually to the beautician or cosmetologist judged to be the most successful. The reigning Queenie Pie enters amid fanfare and flowers, but her celebration is short-lived when the narrator announces the presence of a real competitor, Café Olay (spelled *Au Lait* in the text), the Queen from New Orleans who uses a dixieland band to promote herself. After her adherents attempt to discourage the opposition, Queenie Pie, believing to have won again for the eleventh straight year, welcomes her opponent with largesse, and the scene ends with a dance production number for Café Olay.

The music for the first scene begins with a short-phrase jazz tune, "New York," in E♭ major, with a repeating syncopated melodic hook beginning on the sixth scale degree, proceeding to the tonic, then the supertonic, back down to the sub-mediant, and resolving on the tonic. A significant melodic change occurs with the words "Summer festival" (in the manuscript, the words are "Beauty festival" which, given the context of the dramatic action, and the emphasis placed on the words by the melodic change, would make more sense) by holding out the second syllable of "Summer" for emphasis. Ending in an augmented eleventh chord becoming V of the following number, the be-bop style of the opening, gives way to a more legitimate Maestoso section in which Queenie Pie's followers pay her tribute. This 6/8 composition in A♭ recalls Gilbert and Sullivan's introductory choruses with its lyrical interludes for solo voices and thick choral harmonies. "Second Line" follows, borrowed from the *New Orleans Suite*, copyrighted 1971. This is a traditional AABA 32-bar song in B♭ major. Against an accompaniment of falling fifth seventh chords, the melody swings like an improvisation in a downward spiral from the leading tone to the sub-mediant an octave lower. Designed to introduce the atmosphere of New Orleans, "Second Line" provides a syncopated swing alternative to the almost European structure of Queenie's fanfare. Musically, Ellington manages to create a succinct tonal difference between the women that complements the dramatic conflict in the text. "Café Au Lait," copyrighted in 1957, follows in an A B structure, in which the A is a thickly scored choral piece against a walking bass, and the B is an improvisatory solo, structured like the opening phrase of "Concerto for Cootie" (or its pop-song equivalent, "Don't Get Around Much Anymore").

Scene Two, dated 3 September 1973 in the manuscript, begins with a celebratory party for Queenie Pie who introduces Café Olay to everyone as the guest of honor. When Holt Fay meets her he is stunned and sings, "Woman Beautiful Woman," describing the effect that the New Orleans beauty has on him. The narrator adds that, because Holt sees Olay as the most beautiful girl in the world, he must make everyone else see her in the same way.

The music for this brief scene begins with "Patty-Cake for Queenie Pie,"[13] an A B A^1 jazz-scat tune built around the tonic, sixth, and fifth degrees of the scale, with a clapping rhythmic interlude in the third bar of the four-measure melody. Café Olay enters to a restatement of her musical motif, followed by "Woman," an AABA jazz ballad copyrighted in 1968, filled with chromatic alterations of both melody and harmony that create a "cool" musical texture. Three versions of a news reporter's ariette follow, all dealing with the concept of "Peace." One version, beginning "I love peace," is an eight-bar lyrical melody in G♭ major accompanied by a very traditional tonic, dominant, and sub-dominant harmony. A second "I love peace" is marked "Menuetto" in F major, although it is in 4/4 meter. It is actually structured like a Gavotte with the melody beginning in a solo voice and a contrapuntal accompaniment entering in the second measure. In bar seven, a "Chopsticks"-like figure appears in the accompaniment, reversing the rhythm of the melody and creating a forward pulse by striking a note on every beat of the bar. The third version, "Pees," begins with the alternative lyric, "Peace is a happy face" and suggests Percy Grainger in its almost classical neatness. Again Ellington is using musical idioms to differentiate character types. The fact that he refers to the lady reporter who sings the ariette as a "bitch" suggests why he might give her music an old-fashioned, constricted format.

Scene Three consists of news reports, television commercials, and interviews, in an order "to be determined." One news flash reports the jealousy of Café Olay over any woman who even comes near her man. A commercial advertises Queenie Pie's "Beauty" lipstick. Another news bulletin reports that Holt Fay has been appointed First Vice President of Café Olay Beauty Products Inc. In an interview with Holt Fay, Queenie Pie reveals that she will wear her chinchilla trench coat and drive the Rolls station wagon to the dog-track on Friday, while Café Olay turns into a tigress when asked what she would do if someone threw their arms around Holt Fay. A news flash reports that Holt Fay has been appointed President of Olay Beauty Products, but must also approach his public relations projects with caution, lest Café Olay think he is flirting with other women.

The music for scene three is in the form of short, satirical, commercial tunes, burlesquing the various kinds of music used to sell products on television or radio. The first presented is a pseudo–Viennese waltz in A♭ major, Straussian in its use of syncopation and half-step resolving melody. Commercial "A" is an ascending be-bop tune filled with chromaticisms in both melody and harmony, selling "Queenie Pie" makeup. "B" is a Jerry Herman–like melody selling lipstick, in which the initial melodic motif is repeated isorythmically up the next scale degree every four measures. Commercial "C" is a Scottische ditty, teasingly sensual, advertising Café Olay's products. "D" combines melodic leaps and sustained harmony to create an almost operatic fragment, ending in a syncopated ii7 I7 jazz cadence. The melody of commercial "F" makes use of the harmonic minor with its flatted sixth and natural seventh to create an oriental/Egyptian atmosphere complementing the lyric "Cleopatra was a lass." The harmony is a contrapuntal ostenato alternating with a chromatic walking bass. Commercial "H" employs a C pedal against which diminished chords in first inversion rising in half steps provide the melody. A jazz ditty with a walking bass, commercial "K" is in the Lydian mode with a raised fourth scale degree. Each of the commercials has a different musical character designed to represent the different sales gimmick used.

Scene Four is set on the stage of Radio City Music Hall where Queenie Pie is seated on a great throne located center stage and the judges are elevated on a dais beside it. After a reprise of "All Hail the Queen," Holt Fay is discovered acting as master of ceremonies, telling jokes to the crowd, and presenting various girls modeling Queenie Pie fashions. Offstage, the lady reporter confirms to Café Olay that Holt had been seen at Queenie Pie's apartment. Olay goes into a rage, rushes on stage, steals a gun from a policeman's holster, and shoots Holt dead at the height of his act. She tries to get a shot at Queenie but is prevented by the security police who drag her away. The judges determine that Café Olay's behavior has disqualified her from the competition and award the crown for the eleventh straight year to Queenie Pie, lamenting the fact that her victory had to be marred by tragedy.

Scene Five takes place in Queenie Pie's apartment after the contest where Lil' Daddy is discovered scrubbing the floor and singing "The Hawk" about traveling to New York on the wings of a Hawk, discovering that the bird had died, and realizing that he can never return home. Queenie Pie enters at the end of the number and admires herself in the mirror, singing "Oh, Gee." Her image in the mirror sings the song back to her, and her escorts whisper "Narcisse," in counterpoint. Lil' Daddy gives Queenie a drugged cigarette and, singing "My Father's Island," tells Queenie about the NUCLI, a kind of fountain of youth, miracle drug, and all-purpose cleaner that grows in a certain tree on the island and that will some day be the basic ingredient for every modern product imaginable. Having convinced Queenie of the power of the NUCLI, Lil' Daddy gives her a map of the island ("hidden under the bandage he always wore up his sleeve"), and special cigarettes to help her navigate safely through the Coral Reefs, and tells her that she must approach the tree exactly at midnight, the only time the tree opens its limbs to reveal the NUCLI. Queenie announces that she is going away for a vacation on her yacht, and her friends see her off, singing "Bon Voyage."

"Hawk" employs the same kind of vacillation between major and minor modes used by the Duke in the "Revolutionary March" in *Timon of Athens*. The melody is functionally a recitative complementing the lyric with the interesting word painting of a musical fall-off or slide accompanying the word "expired." Queenie's narcissistic tune, "Oh, Gee," copyrighted in 1947, is an A A^1 song in C major 32 bars in length, with a melodic hook of a long note followed by a series of shorter notes, not unlike Jerome Kern's "Who," from *Sunny*. More interesting, perhaps, is "My Father's Island" in E♭ minor with its syncopated Latin bass line and highly atmospheric melody relying on the ninth and seventh degrees of the minor scale and a lowered fifth in the cadence. Each statement of the melody is interrupted by a recitative section, for which Ellington provides only the chord structure. The second statement of the tune is embellished by musical melismas accompanying added words in the lyric. "Bon Voyage, Queenie Pie" is an antiphonal march in "New York, New York" tempo, against a walking bass line. The simple melody and harmony of the contrapuntal section resolve in a coda characterized by thick chorus harmony, ending on a I7 chord in third inversion.

Scene Six, on board Queenie Pie's yacht, Queenie laments her decision to leave New York City, singing "Sure Do Miss New York." While the crew is in the cabin drinking, Queenie hears the soprano voice of the tree calling out to the full moon. She goes inside the cabin to inquire who was singing just then, and she is told "No one" and invited to drink and sing along with the crew ("There's a Bottle in the Bucket"). Suddenly a trio of voices emerge from the tree and the drunken party stop to listen, but as the tree voices begin to fade the drinking picks up once again as well as the crew's singing ("Long Life, Much Money"). For a third time, the drunking debauchery is interrupted by the singing tree that begins to perform a "Limb Dance" as the hour reaches midnight. Just as the tree opens its limbs to embrace the moon, Queenie Pie captures the NUCLI and returns it to her yacht, singing "Hey Now, I Don't Need Nobody Now." She asks for one of her special cigarettes to get through the Coral Reefs, but is handed the wrong one and she is unable to control the yacht in a storm that emerges from out of nowhere. The ship is destroyed and everyone is washed overboard, including Queenie Pie, who is still hanging on to the NUCLI.

"Sure Do Miss New York" is basically an improvised scat song whose basic melody consists of two descending scale phrases, the first descending from a lowered seventh to a lowered third, the second falling from the fifth to the tonic. A repeated contrapuntal syncopated figure employing the submediant, tonic, and supertonic is the only other fragment of tune written. In the recitative B section, the words are indicated over chords and a pseudo rock and roll shuffle bass (dotted quarter, eight, dotted quarter, eight). "When You Leave New York," an immediate segue from the previous number and sung by the ship's crew, begins in chorale harmony, making great use of a step-wise melody, but is interrupted by an improvised recitative section, for which only the accompaniment is provided. Most interesting is the orchestral interlude in bars five and six that anticipates the motif sung by the tree in the next number of the score. "Full Moon at Midnight" is a 12-bar G minor blues melody against a Latin bass line in the accompaniment. The melody itself makes heavy use of upper neighbor tones first beginning on the fifth scale degree, then repeating the patter from the second degree of the scale. The alternation of these two patterns forms the entire melody of the piece. The first drinking song, "Bottle in the Bucket," is an AABA ditty in a confusing tonality. The key signature indicates the key of B♭ major, but the melody and choice of harmony suggests the key of F, a more likely choice because this drinking song leads directly to "Tune In" which is in the key of B♭ major. "Tune In," sung by the captain of the yacht, is a quick 12-bar shuffle with an initial melodic statement outlining a B♭ major 6 chord. A four-bar B section repeats a melodic phrase (C, A, F, G) four times, though in slightly altered rhythms.

The second appearance of "Full Moon at Midnight," in a minor, is prefaced by an eight-bar introduction making extensive use of falling seventh leaps, but proceeds as in the initial statement of bar nine. The next drinking song, "Long Life, Much Money" as an a cappella chorus number evoking the madrigal sequence in most Gilbert and Sullivan comic operas. The third appearance of the tree song is in D minor, first introduced as a canon for soprano I and alto and leads into a concerted number of operatic complexity. The atmospheric "Full Moon" motif, with its whirling upper neighbor tone, becomes the isorhythmic model for the melodic solos given to the first and second soprano. The whirling effect, introduced as eighth and sixteenth notes, is now augmented to appear as dotted halfs and quarters. A harmonic trio follows, recalling the drinking song chorale; this, in turn, leads to a scherzo-like 2/4 section evoking the breeze of the four winds. A section using orchestra bells outlining triads in triple meter precedes a recitative blues section in 4 against sustained chords that resolves, in turn, in a passionate tribute to the man in the moon, in a soaring, operatic melody and chromatic harmony. A canon-like recapitulation of the initial "Full Moon" motif ends the number as the whirling motif slows to quarter and dotted half notes.

This, the most extensive contrapuntal writing in the entire opera, anticipates similar treatments such as "Moonfall" from Rupert Holmes's *The Mystery of Edwin Drood* in the evocation of a mysterious, sultry, romantic atmosphere using operatic devices.

Queenie's "Don't Need Nobody, Now" comes from a different tonal universe than the previous number, and the juxtaposition of Queenie's bluesy, syncopated, three-bar tune with the more classical rhythms and vocalizations of the tree reaffirms the universe of the play. Queenie's world is the world of jazz, an entirely different plane than the magical world of the tree. It is fascinating that Ellington, who disliked formal training, should house the NUCLI in the most classical-sounding environment in the opera. Since Queenie ultimately loses the object, perhaps the juxtaposition of tonalities is Ellington's way of preparing the audience for that fact, suggesting that the NUCLI and Queenie Pie are essentially incompatible. After the reiteration of the three-bar melody (followed by a single bar of bass interlude), "Don't Need Nobody, Now" becomes another recitative for which Ellington provides only the accompaniment. "Hevl" follows immediately with rising and falling half steps to suggest a storm, in the manner of Rossini (Overture to *William Tell*) or von Suppé (Overture to *Poet and Peasant*). A recapitulation of the "Full Moon" motif, at the quarter tone, and later in half steps, connects the magical atmosphere of the NUCLI with the natural disturbance of the storm. The piece ends as ascending half note chords over a D♭ pedal tone resolve to a syncopated figure in minor ninths.

Scene Seven begins on the beach where Queenie Pie, having washed up ashore, is found amid gawking natives. A crown prince, approaching the group, announces that it is good that Queenie lost the NUCLI because if she had kept it, she would have caused the destruction of the entire island, and herself as well. He welcomes her to the island in a recitative and inquires if she is some kind of a goddess. Queenie Pie replies that she is not and asks if the crown prince is the only one who speaks English. She is told that the king, his father, and the witch doctor (the band leader) also speak and understand English. Queenie decides that, given the improbability of ever leaving the island, she will contrive to marry the king and create her own social milieu on the island. She decides to give a party where she will get the king very drunk, and, since there is no alcohol on the island, she proceeds to make her own.

The scene shifts to the island party where the King, somewhat intoxicated, sings, "Let the Good Time Rock." Queenie takes advantage of the situation to lead the king into her boudoir ("Won't You Come into My Boudoir"), an event that does not go unnoticed by the Witch Doctor, who begins to sample what the king has been drinking. When the King and Queenie emerge from her bedroom, she is wearing his robe, with the King's Crest across her chest. Everyone bows to her as Queen, except for the inebriated Witch Doctor who slaps her on her backside, infuriating her majesty.

The scene shifts abruptly to the verandah of the palace where Queenie, "rocking in her air-conditioned Throne Hammock," sings a long soliloquy in which she rhapsodizes about luck, fate, and loneliness.[14] A native announces the appearance of a boat coming ashore and the King orders the air conditioning to be turned off and the natives to put on their skins and carry their spears. In traditional native dress, they go do to the shore and perform a dance for the incoming tourists ("Stick It In") who reward them with trinkets and postcards from various places, including one from 125th Street and Lennox Avenue, New York City, which Queenie identifies as her home. One of the tourists recognizes her as Queenie Pie and offers to take her back to New York, an offer Queenie immediately accepts. As she is about to leave with the tourists, the Crown Prince stops her announcing that "No Crown head must EVER leave this Island!" At this point, the manuscript ends and the opera ends with Queenie's forced expatriation.

The crown prince's opening recitative is a four-measure blues in F minor, accompanied by the natives chanting "Eenoof, Ayenoof, Angalong, Dangalong." Queenie's reply regarding her goddess status is in F major with the consistently raised fourths suggesting the Lydia mode. Throughout the recitative dialogue between Queenie and the Crown Prince, Ellington makes use of the "Full Moon" motif to recall the magical environment that brought her to the island. The section ends in short duet in which Ellington recalls the chord progression of "Brown Skin Gal in the Callico Gown" and suggests the pop hit, "The Witch Doctor" in his setting of those words. The King's solo, "Let the Good Times Rock," follows in an easy jazz four. An oddly shaped 22-bar song through-composed as an improvised chorus, "Let the Good Times Rock," is all that Ellington provides as characterization for the intoxicated King. The surprising twists and turns of the melody certainly suggest the spontaneity of someone under the influence, and the syncopation and easy leaps of the tune suggest a fun-loving free-spirit, ripe for Queenie's machinations. Her seduction piece, "Won't You Come into My Boudoir," recalls the seductive "Full Moon" motif on the word "Majesty," as if that word were magic to her. Called a "Menuetto," it is a gavotte in which the opening melodic phrase (I) is repeated a fourth higher (IV) and followed by a classically structure authentic cadence (V7). Once the king enters the boudoir, Queenie's tone changes to swing, and the ersatz classicism of the opening bars gives way to a hot jive cadence.

Queenie's "Soliloquy," after the "Full Moon" trio, the most extended piece in the opera, begins as an AABA patter, with the first A having five bars, the second A six bars, the B eight bars, and the final A six bars. The imbalance created by the different number of bars per section creates a very parlando, spontaneous quality in spite of the fact that the music is repeating as in a more traditional song formula. After the patter section, the "Soliloquy" moves to a recitative in a fast waltz where Ellington, as is his usual practice, provides only the accompaniment. A return to duple meter introduces another melodic motif, here repeated four times with slightly different melodic resolutions. A second waltz recitative interrupts the flow of the new melody briefly but the patter-like pattern returns, leading to an ascending figure creating a dramatic effect with the words, "Then fate decided I should be a real Queen," and resolving in a surprise modulation to the key of E♭ major where a passionate coda, recalling the initial accompaniment to the King's song, brings Queenie's comtemplative aria to a close. Like the famous "Soliloquy" from *Carousel*, Queenie's number is about making decisions through music that is varied in meter, style, and tonality. While Ellington's effort is less polished than Rodgers's, it is nonetheless effective as a dramatic turning point for Queenie Pie.

"Stik" is the last number contained in the vocal score. Another fast jazz tune in AABA form, it is antiphonal in nature with one group shouting "Stick it in" and the other "Jab it!" in lyrics that are quite suggestive sexually. The B section is interesting for its use of the tritone leaps in the melody to emphasize the words "wear war paint" and "though you ain't." The number is cited as a dance in the manuscript text and is designed to evoke a more jungle atmosphere than the otherwise more sophisticated aspects of the score. With this number, Ellington returns to the jungle music of his early days at the Cotton Club, complete with all the energy, pulsating bass and harmonies, and sexual innuendo of the earlier compositions.

During the last five years of Duke Ellington's life, he was assisted in his correspondence and in much of his creative writing by Betty McGettigan, a woman Duke met when she was coordinating the 9 March 1969 benefit concert for the California Youth Symphony in Palo Alto, California. After Ellington's death in 1974 there arose a bitter dispute between his son, Mercer, and McGettigan over the rights to *Queenie Pie*. Because McGettigan had written some of the lyrics and inspired the development of some of the music, she claimed a right to share in the copyright of the opera and it was impossible to produce the piece until the claimants could come to some kind of an agreement.[15]

After 12 years of often acrimonious negotiations between Ellington's son, Mercer, and Betty McGettigan,[16] *Queenie Pie* was finally produced by the American Music Theatre Festival at the Zellerbach Theatre in Philadelphia from 18 September to 5 October 1986,[17] followed by a month's run at the John F. Kennedy Center for the Performing Arts in Washington, D.C., from 18 October through 8 November.[18] For the production, a new libretto, based on Ellington's scenario, was created by George C. Wolfe, and lyrics were credited to Ellington and George David Weiss. The music was adapted by Maurice Peress and orchestrated by Barrie Lee Hall, Jr.[19] Teresa Burrell starred as Queenie Pie, Larry Marshall played Lil' Daddy, Patty Holley played Café Olay, and Wendell Pierce performed Holt Fay. The production was directed and choreographed by Garth Fagan, a Jamaican choreographer and director of the acclaimed Bucket Dance Theatre, replacing Robert Kalfin, who is credited as conceiver of the original production.[20] While the story remained basically the same, the characters on the island were played by characters Queenie knew in Harlem, so that the competition or conflict between characters was maintained throughout the performance. Café Olay, for example, reappeared as the Chief's first wife who opposes Queenie's attempts to move in with her husband. Holt Fay reappeared as the Witch Doctor, and Harlem's Mayor, a nonexistent role in Ellington's original, became the Chief or King of the island.

Variety (1 October 1986) found the dialogue in rhymed couplets to be "drearily devoid of yocks" and the cast to be unsympathetic, calling the heroine "greedy and self-centered" and the hero "innocuous" (114). Writing in the *Washington Post*, Megan Rosenfeld dismissed the plot as "preposterous," but found the "astounding array of musical and theatrical styles"—ranging from *Guys and Dolls* to "Gilbert and Sullivan on hallucinogens," to be suprisingly effective. John S. Lang, reviewing for *U.S. News and World Report* (3 November 1986), likened the rivalry between Queenie and Café Olay in the opera to Ellington's concern, toward the end of his life, that the popularity of jazz was being severely threatened by the emergence of rock and roll, and concluded that if *Queenie Pie* endures, "it may also show how opera can accommodate vernacular works" (74).

However the critics viewed the libretto, Ellington's score met with unanimous critical approval. The New York *Times* (9 October 1986) found that it "far transcends the ordinary 'Broadway musical'"(C28); the Boston *Globe* agreed that "most of the songs are newly discovered gems" (31); and the *Christian Science Monitor* (4 November 1986) concluded that "Ellington's music is the most beguiling thing about 'Queenie Pie'" (25). Writing in the *Wall Street Journal* (8 October 1986) Karen Monson went beyond the usual plaudits to Ellington's ability to write jazzy "listenable" music, and compared the variety of Ellington's score with works of the operatic masters:

> The music of Duke Ellington and the current Duke Ellington orchestra make it happen. Ellington fans and scholars will notice familiar numbers, somewhat revised, sometimes even more effective than the originals. Opera traditionalists will glimpse the Marschallin of "Der Rosenkavalier" in Queenie Pie's monologue when she sings her soliloquy at her mirrored dressing table. They'll think of Gilbert and Sullivan when Queenie Pie ends up on her tropical island ("The Belle of the ball has become the belle of the bush"), and maybe spot remnants of Wagner's Rhine Maidens (updated with some sounds of the Supremes) in Queenie's associate hairdressers [32].

Another version of *Queenie Pie* was performed in concert at the Brooklyn Academy of Music on 3 December 1993 by the Ellington Orchestra under the auspices of Mercer Ellington in conjunction with the Brooklyn Philharmonic Orchestra, conducted by Luther Henderson.[21] For this performance, Mercer Ellington claimed to have removed all of the revisions done by Maurice Peress and George C. Wolfe for the 1986 production, though the presence of "Creole Love Call," and "Jam with Sam" suggests that he did not return to his father's original score. Although the performance featured Melba Moore as Queenie Pie, Vivian Reed as Café Olay, Ken Prymus as the Chief (and Mayor of Harlem), and Brian Mitchell as Holt Fay, the critics found this version of the work less appealing, with Edward Rothstein noting in the New York *Times* (19 December 1993) that "'Queenie Pie' seemed stillborn here, its songs hyped up to compensate for wooden lyrics and the scarcity of compositional imagination" (31). Irrespective of the weaknesses of the score or scenario—and there are many, indeed, for Ellington was not an expert librettist[22]—*Queenie Pie* does succeed at invoking an African American musical spirit. As Michael Walsh wrote in his review for *Time* magazine, "*Queenie Pie* has the authentic sass and soul of black America. This is what really happened to Bess after she left Catfish Row" (29 September 1986: 70).

Eleven

"Play On!"

It is ironic that after Duke Ellington's death in 1974, his music has found greater success on the New York City stage than it ever did during his lifetime. In 1975, the Theatre at Noon series, operating out of St. Peter's Church, produced *Skrontch!,* a critically acclaimed compilation of songs from *Pousse-Café*, *Beggar's Holiday*, *Jump for Joy*, and the Cotton Club shows. The same year saw *A Musical Jubilee*, a celebration of American popular music featuring Ellington's "Sophisticated Lady," produced by the Theatre Guild and directed by Morton Da Costa at the St. James Theatre. The following year, the ANTA Theatre presented *Bubbling Brown Sugar*, a retrospective Harlem revue using great Harlem night spots such as the Savoy Theatre and Lennox Avenue as contextual environments for the songs of "Fats" Waller, Shelton Brooks, Maceo Pinkard, Eubie Blake, Billy Strayhorn, and Duke Ellington. Beginning on 2 March 1976, audiences were captivated by "Sophisticated Lady," "Solitude," "I Got It Bad and That Ain't Good," "It Don't Mean a Thing If It Ain't Got That Swing," and Strayhorn's "Take the 'A' Train," for a total of 776 performances, more than twice the total number of performances of all of Ellington's shows after the Cotton Club.

On 4 October 1979, the big-band revue *The All Night Strut*, conceived, directed, and choreographed by Fran Charnas, opened at Theatre Four with "It Don't Mean a Thing If It Ain't Got That Swing" among its hits, and in the same week, *The 1940's Radio Hour*, written and directed by Walton Jones, treated audiences at the St. James Theatre to "I Got It Bad and That Ain't Good." The next year, *Blues in the Night*, conceived and directed by Sheldon Epps and choreographed by Gregory Hines, opened at Playhouse 46 on 26 March, featuring Strayhorn's "Lush Life," the Strayhorn-Ellington "Something to Live For," and Ellington's "Sophisticated Lady." Advertised as "three women and a piano player in a cheap hotel—their lives, their memories and the music that gets them through the long lonely night," *Blues in the Night* moved to the Rialto Theatre on 2 June 1982 for a run of 66 performances. Although *Black Broadway*, billed as a "concert musical" offering a nostalgic look at show tunes from 1902 to 1940, at Town Hall beginning 4 May 1980 with "Creole Love Call," "Brownskin Gal in the Calico Gown," "Jump for Joy," and "Cotton Club Stomp," continued the stream of Ellington hits on the New York stage, it was *Sophisticated Ladies*, opening 1 March 1981 at the Lunt-Fontanne Theatre, that firmly established Duke Ellington as a music-theatre composer.

Originally conceived by choreographer Donald McKayle as a chronological review of Ellington's most celebrated tunes strung together by brief narrated continuity, the show opened in Philadelphia to terrible notices.[1] Before moving the show to Washington, D.C., the producers, described by Stephen Suskin in *More Opening Nights on Broadway* as "the fightingest bunch of producers since Cyma Rubin stripped Harry Rigby of his billing on the opening night of *No, No, Nanette*"(869), decided to replace McKayle's written continuity with monologues by playwright Samm-Art Williams whose drama *Home* had just completed a respectable New York run. Williams's version had principal dancer Gregory Hines act as a kind of raisonneur—the voice of Ellington describing the development of his creative process—to string together the musical numbers in a new running order. Such changes in the show's format required patient rehearsals and time to settle in but the producers could not afford to delay the Washington opening. As a result, the Washington critics saw a tentative, unfocused, under-rehearsed revue, and panned the show.

As a result of the Washington fiasco, Gregory Hines, the ostensible star of the production who tended to voice his opinions too loudly, was fired and his understudy Gregg Burge was called upon to replace him. Not expecting to have to perform the new version of the show immediately, Burge had only learned the Philadelphia script, and the producers had to rehire Hines so that the continuity of performance would not be seriously interrupted. Ultimately, with Hines's return, the Samm-Art Williams "improvements" were jettisoned, director Donald McKayle was replaced by Michael Smuin,[2] co-director of the San Francisco Ballet who stripped the show of its spoken narrative, and tap choreographer Henry LeTang was hired to stage the specialty numbers.

Sophisticated Ladies opened on 1 March 1981 to rave notices in New York City with Frank Rich, crowing in the New York *Times*:

> In the course of his extraordinary career, Duke Ellington did just about everything with jazz that any mortal could be expected to do. Yet, strangely enough, there was one goal that eluded this giant of American music right up to his death in 1974: he never had a hit Broadway show to call his own. Well, it sure looks as if he has one now [2 March 1981:13].

Starring Gregory Hines, Judith Jamison, and Hinton Battle who won a Tony Award as best supporting actor in a musical, and featuring Ellington's granddaughter Mercedes Ellington, the show also sported a 20-piece onstage band led by Duke's son Mercer who called the experience the realization of his father's dream of finally making it on Broadway.[3]

Of the 35 musical numbers used in the production, only a handful were originally designed for musical shows: "I've Got to Be a Rug Cutter" (*Harlem Is Heaven*), "I Let a Song Go Out of My Heart" (cut from *Cotton Club Parade of 1938*), "Satin Doll" (*Satin Doll*), and "I Got It Bad and That Ain't Good," "Bli-Blip" "Just Squeeze Me" (*Jump for Joy*). The remainder were chosen from Ellington's band compositions, designed to appeal to audience recognition. After 767 performances on Broadway, *Sophisticated Ladies* spawned a number of national companies, playing in major cities all over the United States.

On 21 August 1984, the "Cotton Club Cabaret Musical," *Shades of Harlem*, opened at the Village Gate in New York City, reprising the ubiquitous "Take the 'A' Train," "I Got It Bad and That Ain't Good," "Satin Doll," and "It Don't Mean a Thing If It Ain't Got That Swing" for 229 performances. *Ann Reinking … Music Moves Me* danced to "Hit Me with a Hot Note" at the Joyce Theatre beginning 23 December 1984, and *Uptown…It's Hot!*, conceived by Maurice Hines as a revue of American popular music from the 1930s through the 1980s, played the Lunt-Fontanne Theatre from 29 January through 16 February 1986, using "Cotton Club Stomp" and "Daybreak Express" in its "Swing Time" section. *Stardust*, a revue featuring the lyrics of Mitchell Parish, opened at the Biltmore Theatre on 19 February 1987 with Ellington's "Sophisticated Lady," and *Black and Blue*, a retrospective revue of the jazz age, conceived and directed by Claudie Segovia and Hector Grezzoli, opened at the Minskoff Theatre on 26 January 1989, playing 824 performances. Featuring Ellington's "Black and Tan Fantasy," "Come Sunday (from *Black, Brown* and *Beige*)," "East St. Louis Toodle-Oo," and "In a Sentimental Mood," the musical was nominated for ten Tony Awards, with Ruth Brown winning the award for best leading actress in a musical, and Cholly Atkins, Henry LeTang, Frankie Manning, and Fayard Nicholas winning the award for best choreography.

On 20 March 1997, *Play On!*, a musicalization of Shakespeare's *Twelfth Night* using a pastiche Ellington score, opened at the Brooks Atkinson Theatre for a disappointing two-month run.[4] Conceived and directed by Sheldon Epps, with a book by Cheryl L. West, and choreography by Mercedes Ellington, *Play On!* translates Shakespeare's Ilyria into the "Magical Kingdom of Harlem" where Vy (the bard's Viola) goes to make her mark as a songwriter. Her uncle, a womanizing sharp-dresser named Jester, disguises her as a man and introduces her to a composer by the name of Duke (Shakespeare's Orsino) who is in the process of courting an indifferent Cotton Club star, Lady Liv (Olivia). As in the original play, Lady Liv falls for Vy, thinking that she is a he, and Vy falls for the Duke. The trio is rounded out by Rev, the club's manager who is smitten with Lady Liv.

Relying on Ellington's versatility as a composer—his uncanny ability to provide music appropriate to almost every situation imaginable, the collaborators attempted to create a seamless union between the centuries-old plot and the jazz-inspired score. Unfortunately, according to critic John Simon, such a union was impossible because most of the tunes were so famous in their own right that they resisted assimilation into a score. Only the Strayhorn-Ellington "Something to Live For" was found to work in both musical and dramatic contexts. Although Simon's critique may appear harsh, his point is well taken, for only five of the songs used in *Play On!* had not been previously heard in *Sophisticated Ladies*, a revue with no pretense to dramatic context, and of these five, "Don't You Know I Care," "I Ain't Got Nothin' But the Blues," "I Didn't Know About You," "Prelude to a Kiss," and "In a Mellow Tone," each achieved a certain degree of popularity, if not classic status.

Perhaps John Simon's comment accounts, in part, for Ellington's difficulty in finding acceptance as a theatre composer during his lifetime. As the preeminent composer of jazz in the twentieth century, and one of the great bandleaders whose career spanned five decades, Ellington created music that was immediately associated with driving dance rhythms, big-band sound, and improvisation. While such elements are not necessarily inimical to music theatre—and certainly Ellington's suites have demonstrated his ability to develop a musical line dramatically—the very mention of the name Ellington conjures up, for most people, a visceral involvement with the sound, either through immediate kinetic motion in dance, or virtual kinetic motion in concert—both images far removed from the audience experience in a theatre in the days prior to rock musicals where the event is somewhat closer to concert than it is to play.[5] In fact, it would only be with the development of the rock genre that composers known primarily for their work in a "popular" genre could be taken seriously as composers of music theatre: Burt Bacharach (*Promises, Promises*, with Hal David, and Neil Simon, 1968), Roger Miller (*Big River*, with William Haupman, 1985), the Who (*Tommy*, with Des McAnuff, 1993). Previously, however, though popular songs might emerge from the musical theatre, there were composer who wrote shows (Irving Berlin, Richard Rodgers, Cole Porter, George Gershwin, Jule Styne, Fritz Loewe, Charles Strouse, et al.) and those who wrote popular songs.

Duke Ellington was among the first to challenge the division and he was well equipped for success. He had an incontrovertible gift for melody and a finely tuned theatrical instinct that enabled him to manipulate the reactions of his audience with great subtlety, in both serious and comical ways. What went wrong then? The answer perhaps lies in one of Ellington's greatest attributes: his resistance to category. In his eulogy to Ellington, at the funeral service on 27 May 1974, at the Cathedral of St. John the Divine in New York City, Stanley Dance said:

> As a musician, he hated categories. He didn't want to be restricted, and although he mistrusted the word "jazz," his definition of it was "freedom of expression." If he wished to write an opera, or music for a ballet, or for the symphony, or for a Broadway musical, or for a movie, he didn't want to feel confined to the idiom in which he was the unchallenged, acknowledged master [Tucker, *Ellington Reader* 383].

Richard Hornby once argued that plays are not written in imitation of life, but in imitation of other plays, and the same can be said of the musical theatre that continues to be governed by the dramatic and musical formulas that characterize its various genres (i.e., the book musical, the "concept" show, the revue, the operetta, etc.).[6] With the emergence of the Rodgers and Hammerstein formula of the "musical play" in the early 1940s, earlier musical comedies that hung highly diverting songs and dances upon the slenderest of plot threads were judged inferior to the more through-composed musical theatre works, carefully integrating the music with the development of character and incident throughout the play. In addition, music theatre literature demonstrates that, typically, a song begins with a verse that sets up the dramatic context, followed by a chorus of 32 bars accompanying a lyric that is more universal in its appeal.[7] Ellington knew this formula but, as his son Mercer has said, he resisted becoming "involved with anything that anybody had already set down in a pattern" (159). Instead, Ellington was able to transcend that pattern in the creation of music that was evocative of time, place, character, and action but not necessarily limited to the formulaic vocabulary of music theatre songs, relying rather on 12-bar blues progressions or elongated binary forms.

Ellington's insistence on freedom of expression exhibited itself vividly in his resistance to theatre politics. He did not compose "on spec"; he needed to know that the work would be performed before he completed it. He did not participate in long arduous backers' auditions to raise the money for production. He did not participate in the rehearsal process unless he was directing the show or his band was, in some way, involved with the production. He was satisfied with composing the melodies for the project and leaving the rest to the arrangers and orchestrators. In these things, he is no different than Irving Berlin (who could not read or write music himself), Cole Porter (who rarely attended rehearsals of his shows before *Kiss Me, Kate*), or the dozens of composers working today who provide their musical directors with lead sheets or less. What makes Duke different is the fact that he could compose the underscore, and do the orchestrations and all of the continuity himself if he wished. The underscore attributed to *Cock o' the World*, the "Arabian Nights" underscore composed for *Free as a Bird*, complete with orchestral cues, the operatic recitatives eventually cut from *Beggar's Holiday* all point to a composer who understood the craft of shaping a musical. The magnificently dramatic incidental score to *Mardi Gras* or the idiomatically quirky motifs composed for *Turcaret* are but two examples of Ellington's ability to control audience response through aural manipulation using through-composed techniques. The question, then, lies not in an understanding of the musical theatre form, or its politics, but in why Ellington resisted them.

One guess involves the economics of the theatre. Duke Ellington could not sacrifice touring with his orchestra to stay in New York during rehearsals or travel with a show during its out-of-town tryouts. He was the front man of a great band—the "personality" of the group. While the primacy of the orchestra is in evidence in all of the night club scenes and performance contexts in his musical shows, it is especially clear (from a practical view) with the production of *My People* in Chicago when Billy Strayhorn had to conduct alumni members of the Ellington Orchestra because the current band was on tour and therefore unavailable.[8] Duke would not even allow a production he wrote, directed, designed, and choreographed interrupt the completion of a tour. For Ellington, the tour must go on—not the show! In addition, why would the Duke compromise the guarantee of his concert and dance bookings for the uncertainty of a theatrical run?

Another guess concerns Ellington's musical aesthetic. Suggesting that "music, popular music of the day, is the real reflector of the nation's feelings," Duke insisted that he did not compose jazz but wrote Negro folk music that was "trying to play the natural feelings of a people" (Balliett, "Celebrating the Duke" 136). The music theatre, particularly in the Rodgers and Hammerstein model, was a European form that did not always permit Ellington the freedom to express "the natural feelings of a people." Typically, except for the produced revues *Jump for Joy* and *My People*, none of Duke's music theatre compositions that deal with the African American experience exist complete because of the lack of performance commitment (even the "completed" television version of *Queenie Pie* needs continuity). Most have finished scripts, and some like the quasi-operatic *Saturday Laughter* and gospel-blues *Shout Up a Morning* have much of the music—an indication that a production was imminent but ultimately unrealized. Although all of Ellington's shows were in some way integrated projects, shows that traded on the white experience appear to have received less attention, indicated certainly by the fact that Duke never even attended a rehearsal or performance of *Pousse-Café*.

What is certain, however, is that in spite of Ellington's failure to produce a Broadway hit, he did leave behind a body of theatre music that most successfully intoned the dichotomous life force fostered by African Americans in the twentieth century. Personified in the character of Simple in the stories, poems, and plays of Langston Hughes, this double nature is naive yet aware, foolish yet honorable, countrified yet hip, and driven by a love of language, life, and laughter. Although these qualities pervade Ellington's work in general, they are especially applicable to his work for the stage because of the natural dichotomies of lyric and music, speaking and singing, emotion and movement, and the conflict (tension) and resolution (relaxation) inherent in all of them. Like many other theatre composers, Duke Ellington's stage work is inconsistent, ranging from the facile to the extraordinary. Critics most often find fault with his lyrics though they compare favorably with many of the lyrics from rock shows like *Hair*, *The Coldest War of All*, or *Your Own Thing*. The New York *Times* obituary (25 May 1974) called Ellington the "greatest figure in jazz history" and prophesied that "posterity may decide that he is only surpassed by a very small handful of his fellow countrymen in *any* [emphasis mine] sphere of music." At the centennial of Ellington's birth, it is perhaps time to welcome him into the ranks of American theatre composers, the men and woman who have embodied the American experience in the rhythms, harmonies, and melodies of the twentieth century, a time of unrest and celebration, of jazz and swing and rock and roll, of segregation, integration, bigotry, and love. Such is the stuff of the musical stage, and in Ellington's hands, it swings.[9]

Appendix

Duke Ellington's Compositions for the Stage, 1925–1999

Chocolate Kiddies

Musical Revue. Wintergarden Theatre, Berlin, 25 May 1925. Lyrics: Jo Trent.

"Deacon Jazz"; "Jim Dandy"; "Jig Walk"; "Love Is a Wish for You"; "Skeedely-Um-Bum"; "With You"

Cotton Club Show

Musical Revue. Cotton Club Uptown, 4 Dec. 1927. Principal composer: Jimmy McHugh; principal lyricist: Dorothy Fields. Ellington's songs composed with Bubber Miley.

"Black and Tan Fantasy"; "The Blues I Love to Sing"; "Creole Love Song" (also known as "Creole Love Call") (from Rudy Jackson's adaptation of "Camp Meeting Blues" by King Oliver)

Cotton Club Show Boat

Musical Revue. Cotton Club Uptown, 1 April 1928. Principal composer: Jimmy McHugh; principal lyricist: Dorothy Fields.

"Black Beauty"; "Hot and Bothered"; "The Mooch" (also known as "The Mooche") (With Irving Mills); "Swampy River"

Hot Chocolate

Musical Revue. Cotton Club Uptown, 7 October 1928. Principal composer: Jimmy McHugh; principal lyricist: Dorothy Fields.

"The Mooche" (with Irving Mills)

Spring Birds

Musical Revue. Cotton Club Uptown, 31 March 1929. Principal composer: Jimmy McHugh; principal lyricist: Dorothy Fields.

"Cotton Club Stomp" (with Johnny Hodges and Harry Carney); "The Duke Steps Out" (with Johnny Hodges and Cootie Williams); "Goin' to Town" (with Bubber Miley); "Mississippi Moan"; "Misty Mornin'" (with Arthur Whetsol)

Show Girl

Musical Revue. Ziegfeld Theatre, 2 July 1929. Principal composer: George Gershwin; principal lyricist: Ira Gershwin, Gus Kahn.

"African Daisy"

Blackberries

Musical Revue. Cotton Club Uptown, 29 September 1929. Principal composer: Jimmy McHugh; principal lyricist: Dorothy Fields.

"Lazy Duke"; "Oklahoma Stomp"

Blackberries of 1930

Musical Revue. Cotton Club Uptown, 2 March 1930; lyrics: Irving Mills.

"Bumpty Bump"; "Cotton Club Stomp" (with Johnny Hodges and Harry Carney); "Doin' the Crazy Walk"; "Swanee River Rhapsody" (lyrics by Clarence Gaskill and Irving Mills)

Maurice Chevalier Show

Musical Revue. Fulton Theatre, 30 March 1930.

"Awful Sad"; "Black Beauty"; "East St. Louis Toodle-Oo" (with Bubber Miley); "The Mooche" (with Irving Mills); "Swampy River"

Brown Sugar: Sweet But Unrefined

Musical Revue. Cotton Club Uptown, 28 September 1930. Principal composer: Harold Arlen; principal lyricist: Ted Koehler.

"Mood Indigo" (with Irving Mills and Albany Bigard); "Old Man Blues"; "Shout 'Em Aunt Tillie" (with Irving Mills)

Sweet and Low

Musical Revue. 46th Street Theatre, 17 November 1930. Principal composers: Harry Warren and Will Irwin; principal lyricists: Billy Rose and Ira Gershwin

"East St. Louis Toodle-Oo" (with Bubber Miley)

Rhythmania

Musical Revue. Cotton Club Uptown, March 1931. Principal composer: Harold Arlen; principal lyricist: Ted Koehler.

"The Breakfast Dance"

Earl Carroll's Vanities of 1932

Musical Revue. Broadway Theatre, 27 Sept. 1932. Principal composer: Harold Arlen; principal lyricist: Ted Koehler.

"Rockin' in Rhythm" (with Irving Mills and Harry Carney)

Cotton Club Parade, Second Edition

Musical Revue. Broadway at 48th Street, 17 March 1937.

"Black and Tan Fantasy" (with Bubber Miley); "Peckin'"; "Rockin' in Rhythm" (with Irving Mills and Harry Carney)

Harlem Is Heaven

Musical Comedy. Uproduced, 1937?. Scenario: Will Strickland.

"Azure" (with lyrics by Irving Mills); "Inside Harlem" ("Harlem Is Heaven"); "I've Got to Be a Rug Cutter"

The Cotton Club Parade of 1938

Musical Revue. Downtown, 9 March 1938. Lyrics: Henry Nemo and Irving Mills.

"Braggin' in Brass"; "Carnival in Caroline"; "Dinah's in a Jam; "A Gal from Joe's"; "If You Were in My Place"; "I'm Slappin' Seventh Avenue"; "A Lesson in C"; "I Let a Song Go Out of My Heart" (with Irving Mills and John Redmond; cut prior to opening.); "Skrontch"; "Swingtime in Honolulu"; (Songs recorded but not listed as part of show.) "At Your Beck and Call"; "Birmingham Breakdown"; "Downtown Uproar" (with Cootie Williams); "Harmony in Harlem"; "Oh, Babe! Maybe Someday"; "Riding on a Blue Note" (with Irving Gordon and Irving Mills); "Rose Room"

Boola

Opera. 1939. Libretto and music by Ellington never produced. Music used to create the following:

"Black, Brown and Beige"; "Ko-Ko"

Jump for Joy

Musical Revue. Mayan Theatre, Los Angeles, 10 July 1941. Book by Richard Weil, Langston Hughes, Sid Kuller, Charles Leonard, Hal Fimberg; lyrics mainly by: Paul Francis Webster.

"Baton"; "Bli-Blip" (lyrics by Sid Kuller); "The Brown-Skin Gal in the Calico Gown"; "Chocolate Shake"; "Concerto for Klinkers"; "Flame Indigo"; "Give Me an Old Fashioned Waltz" (lyrics by Sid Kuller); "I Got It Bad and That Ain't Good"; "Jump for Joy" (with lyrics by Sid Kuller and Paul Webster); "Noel Caed"; "Nex"; "Sharp Easter" (lyrics by Sid Kuller); "Shhhh! He's on the Beat" (lyrics by Sid Kuller and Hal Fimberg); "Subtle Slough"; "Tailor Shop"; (Songs added during the run of the show) "Bessie—Whoa Babe"; "Clementine" (by Billy Strayhorn); "The Giddybug Gallop"; "Just A-Settin' and A-Rockin'" (with Billy Strayhorn);

"Nostalgia"; "Rocks in My Bed" (with Billy Strayhorn); "Take the 'A' Train" (by Billy Strayhom)

Jubilee: A Cavalcade of Negro Theatre

Musical Revue. Designated for the Negro Exposition, Chicago, 4 July–4 September 1940.

"Diamond Jubilee Song" (composed with Billy Strayhorn)

H. M. S. Times Square

Musical Comedy. Unproduced, 1943–45. Based on "This Strange Bright Land" in *Collier's Magazine,* 30 January 1943 by Harry Henderson and Sam Shaw; lyrics: Bob Russell.

(Titles listed according to the running order) "We're in There Pitchin'"; "A Woman and a Man"; "I Wanna Stop and Go"; "Where Is the Mayor?"; "One Big Good Times Square"; "It Couldn't Have Happened to a Sweeter Guy"; "What Is a Woman to Do?"; "Love Is Everything"; "I'm Afraid I'll Live"; "S-T-R-A-T-E-G-Y"; "I'm Gonna Say No"; "I Got a Steady Job"; "Something Always Needs Changing"; "A New World of Happy People"; "Now There's Love And Love"

Blue Holiday

Musical Revue. Belasco Theatre, 21 May 1945. Principal composer and lyricist: Al Moritz; Songs added by E.Y. Harburg, Earl Robinson, and Duke Ellington.

"Mood Indigo" (with Irving Mills); "Sophisticated Lady" (lyrics by Mitchell Parish and Irving Mills); "Solitude" (lyrics by Eddie de Lange and Irving Mills)

Beggar's Holiday a.k.a. Twilight Alley

Musical Comedy. Broadway Theatre, 26 December, 1946. Book and lyrics by: John Latouche.

(Titles listed according to the running order) **Act One:** "The Chase"; "When You Go Down by Miss Jenny's"; "I've Got Me"; "TNT"; "Take Love Easy"; "I Want to Be Bad"; "When I Walk with You"; "Wedding Ballet"; "The Scrimmage of Life"; "Ore from a Gold Mine"; "Tooth and Claw"; "Maybe I Should Change My Ways"; "The Wrong Side of the Railroad Tracks"; "Tomorrow Mountain".

Act Two: "Chorus of Citizens"; "Girls Want a Hero"; "Lullaby for Junior"; "Quarrel for Three"; "Fol-De-Rol-Rol"; "Brown Penny" (lyric based on a poem by W.B. Yeats); "Women, Women, Women"; "Ballet"; "The Hunted"; "Finale"

Songs cut prior to New York opening: "All Ablaze"; "All the Space"; "Bible of My Days"; "Boll Weavil"; "Bride"; "Brown Betty"; "Daddy's in the Hospital"; "Duet of Polly and Lucy"; "Employment of Life"; "The Fight"; "A Fox Will Steal Your Chickens"; "Get Out"; "Git Moving"; "Gutter Stutter"; "A Guy Name of Macheath"; "Hell Hath No Fury"; "He Makes Me Believe He's Mine"; "How Happy Could I Be with Either"; "I Am Bubbled"; "I'll Have a Drink"; "In Between"; "In My Frivolous Youth"; "It Must Be Me"; "Jelly Beans"; "The Kindly Worm" ("You Wake Up and Breakfast on a Cigarette"); "Live for the Moment"; "Loose Living" ("Life Looks Better"); "Lose Your Head"; "Macheath Will Die Today" ("We Brighten Lives"); "Nothing Is More Respectable Than a Reformed Whore"; "Peachum's Recitative"; "O, Polly, Poor Polly"; "Our Polly Is a Silly Dope"; "Polly at His Side"; "A Rooster in the Barnyard"; "Rooster Man"; "Seriously"; "She's Got My Head on Fire"; "Silky Harpy"; "Sucker for a Kiss"; "Sweet Lucy"; "They're Taking Poor Macheath Away"; "True Love Is Not an Atonement"; "Utopiaville"; "We Don't Want the Wings of an Angel"; "We Skipped an Hour"; "When You Criticize the Age"; "You Act, You Giddy Flirt"; "You're Like a Rooster in the Barnyard"

Moon of Mahnomen

Unproduced musical comedy, 1947. Libretto by Charles M. Underhill

Titles listed according to the running order. "Mahnomen"; "Live and Love"; "Plenty of Rice"; "High Above an Eagle Wheels"; "Someone's Upsetting My Apple Cart"; "In a Misty Mood"; "Everyone's Against Me"; "This Is Our World"; "Stop That Rain"; "Qui" ("Oh Gee"); "It's Just as New as Old"; "In Time We Trust"; "Freedom of the Press"; "Just a Peaceful Picket Line"; "Half a Loaf Is Better Than None"; "You Can Count on Fear"; "Look Down on Today from Tomorrow"

Cock O' the World

Musical. Unproduced, 1931–1951. Libretto: Kaj Gynt and Langston Hughes; Music composed in collaboration with Billy Strayhorn.

"L'amour Diable"; "Cake-walk"; "The Chant of the Slaves"; "Claire de Lune"; "Cock o' the World"; "Diamonds"; "Flowers in My Hair"; "Kalulu"; "The Leavin' Song"; "Miner's Song"; "My Little Black Diamond"; "The Snake Eye Blues"; "To Fling My Arms Wide"

Time Runs

Théâtre Edouard VII, Paris, 19 June 1950 (Play). Written: Orson Welles (Incidental music); Music supervised: Billy Strayhorn.

"Orson" (composed with Billy Strayhorn)

Be My Guest

Musical Comedy. Unproduced, 1953–54. Book and lyrics: Doris Julian; Music composed by collaboration with Billy Strayhorn.

(Titles listed according to the running order) "What's New, What's New?"; "Be a Girl"; "Women, Women, I'd Rather Have a Fluff!"; "Night Time" (Composed with Billy Strayhorn.); "Live a Little"; "Night into Day Ballet"; "Streetcleaner's Blues"; "It's a Sunny Day, Honey"; "Poodle Ballet"; "Heart Be Still"; "Clarion Rag"; "Like the Way I Look"; "Give Me a Man"; "Murder I Want"; "Spillaine Ballet"; "Another Woman's Man"; "Be My Guest"

Mardi Gras

Opened 13 January, Locust Theatre, Philadelphia (Incidental music; Play by Norman Rosten.

(Titles listed according to the running order) "Opening" ("Calliope Music"); "1–36" ("Miscellaneous"); "1–39" ("Party Music"); "2–31" ("Mardi Gras"); "2–36" ("Cathy Enters"); "2–43" ("Flute Solo"); "2–47" ("My Head Is Full of Music")

Man with Four Sides

Unproduced, 1955. Produced as stage reading 20 February 1997, St. Peter's Church, New York City; Play with Music; Libretto by Duke Ellington.

(Titles listed according to the running order) "Once There Was a husband"; "Who Am I?"; "Like a Train"; "She"; "Weatherman"; "Standing on the Corner"; "When I First Came from the Country"; "Got a Woman in the House and One in the Street"; "Rumor"; "You Goofed—Dad—You Goofed"; "Woman Blues"; "Twilight Time"; "I Don't Care"; "The Blues" (from *Black, Brown and Beige*); "There Comes a Time"; "Fugue Finale" ("Weatherman," "She")

Satin Doll

Musical. Unproduced, 1948–1958. Book and lyrics: T. Hee, William Cottrell, and Lowell Matson. Lyrics to "Satin Doll" by Billy Strayhorn and Johnny Mercer.

(Titles listed according to the running order) "Love Is Just a Four Letter Word"; "I Could Get a Man"; "Once Upon a Dream" (with Billy Strayhorn); "If a Body"; "A Word from Our Sponsor"; "It's Love I'm In"; "We Will Never Do That Again"; "Satin Doll"; "Adam Was a Good Man"; "Ain't It a Shame"; *(Songs omitted from earlier drafts);* "Hi de Hi–Hi de Ho"; "A Long Time Ago"; "Sweet Velvet O'Toole"; "There Is No Other Way"; "Wishy Washy Bubble Soap"

Saturday Laughter

Musical. Unproduced, 1957–1967. Produced by *Just Us* in Atlanta, Georgia,

1977. Book by Herb Martin and Stephen Bates; lyrics: Herb Martin.

(Titles listed according to the running order) "Full of Shadows"; "J. P. Williamson"; "I Get Lonely for a Plaything"; "You Are Beautiful"; "You Are Lonely"; "'Big White Mountain"; "My Home Lies Quiet"; "It's Saturday"; "He Outfoxed the Fox"; "I Am Angry"; "I Like Singing"; "This Man"; "The Bioscope Song"; "My Arms"; "They Say"; "New Shoes"; "Only Yesterday"; "You Walk in My Dreams"; "The Man Beneath"

The Road of the Phoebe Snow

Ballet. The 92nd Street "Y," New York, 4 December 1958. Written in collaboration with Billy Strayhorn; choreographed by Talley Beatty. Ellington gives the date of copyright as 1971.

"Tymperturbably Blue"; "Red Garter" from *Toot Suite;* "Congo Square" ("Matumbe") from *A Drum Is a Woman;* "Anatomy of a Murder"

Jump for Joy

Musical Revue. Revival, Copa City, Miami Beach, 20 January 1959. Lyrics: Sid Kuller.

(Titles listed according to the running order) "Nerves, Nerves, Nerves"; "The Natives Are Restless Tonight"; "Resigned to Living" ["If We were Anymore British (We Couldn't Talk at All)" (with Billy Strayhorn)]; "Concerto for Clinkers"; "Brownskin Gal in the Calico Dress"; "So the Good Book Says" (with Billy Strayhorn); "Don't Believe Everything You Hear"; "Walk It Off" (with Billy Strayhorn); "But"; "The Wailer"; "Show 'Em You Got Class"; "Three Shows Nightly"; "I Got It Bad and That Ain't Good"; "Made to Order"; "When I Trilly with My Filly"; "Pretty and the Wolf"; "Jump for Joy"; (Songs cut from the production) "Just Squeeze Me" (lyric by Lee Gaines) (Same music as "Subtle Slough"); "Strictly for Tourists" (with Billy Strayhorn); "Within Me I Know"

Turcaret

Theatre National Populaire, Paris, 13 January 1960. Incidental score for the play by René LeSage.

"Anger" ("Colère de Monsieur Turcaret"); "Annonce du Spectacle" ("Band Call"); "La Baronne"; "Le Chevalier"; "Frontin"; "Lisette"; "Madame Turcaret"; "Mathilde"; "Motif de Flamand"; "Overture"; "Turcaret" ("Viv")

Reflections in 'D'

Ballet. Brooklyn Academy of Music, April 1962. Choreographed by Alvin Ailey to Ellington's piano solo, copyrighted in 1953.

Timon of Athens

Incidental Music for Shakespeare's play. Stratford, 29 July 1963.

"Action in Alexandria"; "After Gossippippi"; "Alcibiades"; "Angry"; "Banquet" ("Counter Theme"); "Conscience"; "Desolation"; "Gold"; "Gossip"; "Gossippippi"; "Impulsive Giving"; "Ocean"; "Regal Format"; "Regal"; "Revolutionary"; "Skillipoop" ("Mc Blues"); "Smoldering"; "Storm"

My People

Musical Revue. Arie Crown Theatre, Chicago, 16 August 1963. Book and lyrics: Duke Ellington.

"After Bird Jungle"; "Ain't But the One"; "Autumnal" (from *Paris Blues*); "Bird Jungle"; "The Blues Ain't" (from *Black, Bown and Beige*); "Come, Sunday" (from *Black, Brown and Beige*); "David Danced" (from "Come, Sunday"); "Jail Blues"; "Jungle Triangle" ("Skillipoop" from *Timon of Athens*); "King Fit the Battle of Alabam'"; "Lovin' Lover"; "Montage" (from *Black, Brown and Beige*); "My Man Sends Me"; "My Mother, My Father"; "My People"; "99%"; "Purple People" (by Billy Strayhorn); "Strange Feeling" (by Billy Strayhorn); "What Color Is Virtue?"; "Will You Be There?"; "Workin' Blues"

Free as a Bird

Musical. Unproduced, 1943–1963. Book by Frank Tuttle and Tatiana Tuttle; lyrics: Frank Tuttle.

(Titles listed according to the running order) "A Dutiful Wife"; "There's Nothing New Beneath the Sun"; "Lishande's Phoenix Dance"; "I'm Much Too Young to Be Old"; "Free All Their Lives"; "Two Together"; "Gham Al Duna's Spinning Patter Song" ("Oh, the Common People"); "Sweep! Sweep! Sweep Up the Floor"; "I'm Looking for a Girl" ("It's a Case of Many Girls or None for Me"); "It's a Man's World"; "Free as a Bird"; "River Wash Me Clean"; "No Matter Where"; "Leap Year"; "We're Headin' Home"

Pousse-Cafe aka **Sugar City**

Musical Comedy. 46th Street Theatre, 18 March 1966). Book by Jerome Weidman; lyrics by Marshall Barer and Fred Tobias.

(Titles listed according to the running order) Act One; "The Spider and the Fly" (attributed to Michael Leonard and Herbert Martin); "Rules and Regulations"; "Follow Me Up the Stairs"; "Goodbye Charlie"; "C'est Comme Ca"; "Thank You Ma'am"; "The Eleventh Commandment" (attributed to Michael Leonard and Herbert Martin); "Someone to Care For"; "The Wedding"; Act Two; "Let's"; "The Good Old Days"; "Easy to Take" (adapted from "Sugar Hill Penthouse" in *Black, Brown and Beige*); "Old World Charm"

(Songs discarded before the New York opening, i.e., not listed in the New York program.) "Amazing"; "Be a Man"; "The Colonel's Lady"; "Do Me a Favor"; "Flugel Street Rag"; "Forever"; "Funeral"; "A Girl's Best Friend"; "He Followed Her Up the Stairs"; "Here You Are"; "An Honest Woman"; "Hot Foot Hop"; "Hump Ballet"; "I'm Back in Love" ("Solange"); "Je N'ai Rien"; "If I Knew Now (What I Knew Then)"; "Mother–Patter"; "My Heart Is a Stranger"; "Natchez Trace"; "Pousse-Cafe"; "Salvation"; "Sam's Sugar City"; "Sugar City"; "Settle for Less"; "Southern Comfort"; "Spacious and Gracious"; "Spider and the Fly" (original version); "Swivel"; "Up Your Ante"; "Vieux Carré"; "Vive la Difference"; "We Are Alone"; "The Years Pass By"

Murder in the Cathedral

Milton College, Milton, Wisconsin, 23 May 1966. Incidental Score composed for a college production of T.S. Eliot's play.

"Becket"; "Exotique Bongos"; "Gold"; "Land"; "Martyr"; "Women's

The Jaywalker

Coventry Cathedral, Coventry, England, July 1967. Incidental score to the religious drama by Barbara Waring, Lady Conliffe.

"Be Your Man"; "The B.O. of Traffic"; "Cross Climax"; "Letter B in Reverse"; "Mac" ("T.G.T.T."); "Polizia"; "The Queen"; "Star"; "Traffic Cop"; "Traffic Extension"; "Untitled Blues"

Shout Up a Morning

Musical drama. Unproduced, 1969–70). Book by Peter Farrow; lyrics: Farrow and Diane Lampert.

(Titles listed according to the running order) "Long Way Out of Egypt"; "Who Bend the Rainbow?"; "Bornin' Place"; "Joshua"; "Ten Mile of Mountain"; "The Six-Forty Seven"; "Who Up in Heaven?"; "Whatcha Gonna Make for Your True Love's Supper?"; "The Broomstick Song"; "Mumbletalk"; "Grass"; "Rouster Chant"; "Forty Acres and a Mule"; "Gonna Give Lovin' a Try"; "Chaingang Theme"; "Grind Your Own Coffee"; "Stayin' Place"; "Shout Up a Morning"; "When I Blow My Whistle"; "Anybody Need a Big Man?"; "Pray White"; "Nothin' But a Man"; "Little, Little Mary"; "Ten on the Enjine"; "Poundin'"; "The Ballad of John Henry"; "Jesus, Where You Now?"; "If I Was Jehovah"

The River

Ballet. Lincoln Center, 25 June 1970. Composed for American Ballet Theatre and choreographed by Alvin Ailey. Performed incomplete at the premiere, 3 sections were added in 1971.)

(Titles listed according to the running order) "The Spring"; "The Run"; "The Meander"; "The Giggling Rapids"; "The Lake"; "The Falls"; "The Whirlpool"; "The River"; "The Neo-Hip-Hot Kiddies Communities"; "The Village of the Virgins"; "Her Majesty The Sea"; "The Spring"

Forty

Ballet. City University Graduate Center Mall, 29 June 1975; American Dance Festival, New London, Connecticut, 5 July 1975. Choreographed by Gus Solomons, Jr., to Ellington works previously composed.

"Tap Dancer's Blues"; "Don Juan"; "Fat Mess"; "Never Stop Remembering Bill"

Night Creature

Ballet. City Center, 22 April 1975; New York State Theatre, August 1975. Based on the 1955 three-movement work for symphony and jazz band, and originally choreographed by Alvin Ailey for the CBS television special *Ailey Celebrates Ellington*, November 1974.

The Mooch

Ballet. New York State Theatre, August 1975. Choreographed by Alvin Ailey to "The Mooch" composed in 1928. Originally choreographed by Alvin Ailey for the CBS television special *Ailey Celebrates Ellington*, November 1974.

(Titles listed according to the running order) "The Mooche" (with Irving Mills); "Black Beauty"; "The Shepherd"; "Creole Love Call" (with Bubber Miley and Rudy Jackson)

Skrontch!

Musical Revue. Theatre at Noon, St. Peter's Church, New York City, 14 October 1975.

Songs from *Pousse-Café, Beggar's Holiday, Jump for Joy*, and the Cotton Club revues.

A Musical Jubilee

Musical Revue. St. James Theatre, New York City, 13 November 1975. Produced by the Theatre Guild; libretto by Max Wilk, directed by Morton Da Costa.

"Sophisticated Lady" (lyric by Mitchell Parish and Irving Mills)

Liberian Suite

Ballet. City Center, 28 November 1975. Adapted from the suite composed in 1947 and choreographed by Lester Horton. Restaged and adapted by James Truite.

Echoes in Blue

Ballet. City Center, 7 December 1975. Choreographed by Milton Myers.

"Mood Indigo" (with Irving Mills); "Harlem"

Bubbling Brown Sugar

Musical Revue. ANTA Theatre, New York City, 2 March 1976. Conceived by Rosetta Lenoire; book by Loften Mitchell.

"It Don't Mean a Thing" (lyrics by Irving Mills); "I Got It Bad and That Ain't Good" (lyrics by Paul Francis Webster); "Solitude" (lyrics by Eddie de Lange and Irving Mills); "Sophisticated Lady" (lyric by Mitchell Parish and Irving Mills); "Take the 'A' Train" by Billy Strayhorn

Pas De Duke

Ballet. City Center, 11 May 1976. Choreographed by Alvin Ailey.

Black, Brown and Beige

Ballet. City Center, 12 May 1976. Adapted from the original suite composed in 1945, choreographed by Alvin Ailey.

Three Black Kings

Ballet. New York State Theatre, 12 August 1976. Written in collaboration with Mercer Ellington and choreographed by Alvin Ailey.

"Balthazar"; "Solomon"; "Martin Luther King"

Deep South Suite

Ballet. New York State Theatre, 12 August 1976. Adapted from the original suite, composed with Billy Strayhorn in 1946, and choreographed by Dianne McIntyre.

Afro-Eurasian Eclipse

Ballet. New York State Theatre, 12 August 1976. Original Suite composed in 1971, choreographed by Raymond Sawyer.

Still Life

Ballet. New York State Theatre, 12 August 1976. Choreographed by Cristyne Lawson

"Diminuendo and Crescendo in Blue"

Such Sweet Thunder

Ballet. Riverside Church, 2 December 1976. Composed with Billy Strayhorn. Adapted from the 1957 Shakespearean Suite and choreographed by Sophie Maslow. Re-choreographed by William Carter for the Ballet Hispanico of New York in 1978.

Little Red Riding Hood

Ballet. Riverside Church 12 April 1978. Choreographed by Joyce Tristler for the Joyce Tristler Dancecompany.

"Bakiff" (by Juan Tizol); "Caravan" (music by Juan Tizol and Duke Ellington, lyrics by Irving Mills); "Flamingo" (by Grouya and Anderson); "I'm Beginning to See the Light" (music and lyrics by Ellington, Don George, Johnny Hodges, and Harry James); "Passion Flower" (by Billy Strayhorn); "Satin Doll" (music by Ellington and Strayhorn, lyrics by Strayhorn and Johnny Mercer); "Solitude"; "Take the 'A' Train" (by Billy Strayhorn)

Day

Ballet. Riverside Church, 15 June 1978. Choreographed by Susan Dibble.

The All Night Strut

Musical Revue. Theatre Four, New York City, 4 October 1979. Conceived, directed, and choreographed by Fran Charnas.

"It Don't Mean a Thing" (lyrics by Irving Mills)

The 1940's Radio Hour

Musical Revue. St. James Theatre, New York City, 7 October 1979. Written and directed by Walton Jones.

"I Got It Bad and That Ain't Good" (lyrics by Paul Francis Webster)

Blues in the Night

Musical Revue. Playhouse 46, New York City, 26 March 1980. Also produced at the Rialto Theatre, New York City, 2 June 1982. Conceived and directed: Sheldon Epps, choreographed by Gregory Hines.

"Lush Life" (by Billy Strayhorn);"Something to Live For" (music and lyrics by Billy Strayhorn and Duke Ellington); "Sophisticated Lady" (lyrics by Mitchell Parish and Irving Mills)

Black Broadway

Musical Revue. Town Hall, New York City, 4 May 1980. Produced: George Win, Honi Coles, Robert Kimball, and Bobby Short.

"Brownskin Gal in the Calico Gown" (lyrics by Paul Francis Webster); "Cotton Club Stomp" (composed with Johnny Hodges and Harry Carney); "Creole Love Call" (with Bubber Miley and Rudy Jackson); "Jump for Joy" (lyrics by Sid Kuller and Paul Francis Webster)

Sophisticated Ladies

Musical Revue. Lunt-Fontanne Theatre, New York City, 1 March 1981. Conceived by Donald McKayle. Choreographed by McKayle, Michael Smuin, and Henry LeTang.

(Titles listed according to the running order) "I've Got to Be a Rug Cutter"; "Music Is Woman" ("Jubilee Stomp") (lyrics by John Guare); "The Mooche" (composed with Irving Mills); "Hit Me with a Hot Note and Watch Me Bounce" (lyrics by Don George);

"Love You Madly" / "Perdido" (music by Juan Tizol); "Fat and Forty" (music and lyrics by Al Hibbler and Duke Ellington); "It Don't Mean a Thing (If It Ain't Got That Swing)" (lyrics by Irving Mills); "Bli-Blip" (lyrics by Duke Ellington and Sid Kuller); "Cotton Tail"; "Take the 'A' Train" (by Billy Strayhorn); "Solitude"; "Don't Get Around Much Anymore" (lyrics by Bob Russell); "I Let a Song Go Out of My Heart" (lyrics by Henry Nemo, Irving Mills, and John Redmond); "Caravan" (music by Juan Tizol and Duke Ellington, lyrics by Irving Mills); "Something to Live For" (music and lyrics by Billy Strayhorn and Duke Ellington); "Old Man Blues" (music and lyrics by Duke Ellington and Irving Mills); "Drop Me Off in Harlem" (lyrics by Nick Kenny); "Rockin' in Rhythm" (music by Ellington, Irving Mills, and Harry Carney); "Duke's Place" (lyrics by Bill Katz and R. Thiele); "In a Sentimental Mood" (lyrics by Danny Kurtz and Irving Mills); "I'm Beginning to See the Light" (music and lyrics by Ellington, Don George, Johnny Hodges, and Harry James); "My Love"; "Satin Doll" (music by Ellington and Strayhorn, lyrics by Billy Strayhorn and Johnny Mercer); "Just Squeeze Me" (lyrics by Lee Gaines); "Dancers in Love"; "Echoes of Harlem"; "I'm Just a Lucky So-and-So" (lyrics by Mack David); "Hey Baby"; "Imagine My Frustration" (music and lyrics by Ellington, Strayhorn, and Gerald Wilson); "Kinda Dukish"; "Ko-Ko"; "I'm Checking Out Goombye" [*sic*] (music and lyrics by Ellington and Strayhorn); "Do Nothing 'Til You Hear from Me" (lyrics by Bob Russell); "I Got It Bad and That Ain't Good" (lyrics by Paul Francis Webster); "Mood Indigo" (music by Ellington, Mills, and Albany Bigard); "Sophisticated Lady" (lyrics by Mitchell Parish and Irving Mills)

Shades of Harlem

Musical Revue. Village Gate, New York City, 21 August 1984. By Jeree Palmer.

"Cotton Club Stomp" (composed with Johnny Hodges and Harry Carney); "Daybreak Express"; "Perdido" (music by Juan Tizol); "Take the 'A' Train" (music by Billy Strayhorn)

Ann Reinking ... Music Moves Me

Dance Concert. Joyce Theatre, New York City, 23 December 1984. Produced by Lee Gross; directed by Alan Johnson.

"Hit Me with a Hot Note" (lyrics by Don George); "Satin Doll" (music by Ellington and Strayhorn, lyrics by Billy Strayhorn and Johnny Mercer)

Uptown ... It's Hot

Musical Revue. (Lunt-Fontanne Theatre, New York City, 29 January 1986). Conceived by Maurice Hines.

"Cotton Club Stomp" (composed with Johnny Hodges and Harry Carney); "Daybreak Express"

Queenie Pie

First produced at Zellerbach Theatre, Philadelphia, 12 September 1986. "Street" Opera. Conceived as a one hour television program, Ellington later developed it as a full-length work. Left unfinished at his death, it was produced posthumously under the supervision of Mercer Ellington. New libretto by George C. Wolfe; new lyrics by George David Weiss; score revised by Maurice Peress.

(Titles listed according to the running order) "Harlem Scat"; "All Hail the Queen"; "Style"; "The Hawk"; "Café Au Lait" (copyright 1957); "It's Time for Something New"; "Queenie Pie"; "Creole Love Song" (see *Cotton Club Show of* 1927); "Soliloquy"; "My Father's Island"; "Oh Gee" (copyright 1947); "Two Cat Scat Fight"; "Woman" (copyright 1968); "The Hairdo Hop"; "There"; "Discovery of Queenie Pie on the Beach"; "Stix"; "Full Moon at Midnight"; "Smile as You Go By"; "Rhumbop" (from *A Drum Is a Woman*); "A Blues for Two Women"; "Won't You Come into My Boudoir";

"Hey, I Don't Need Nobody Now"; "Island Revolt"; "Truly a Queen"

(The original television opera had the following musical numbers and running order.)

Scene One: "New York, New York"; "All Hail the Queen" ("Queenie Pie"); "Second Line" (from *New Orleans Suite*); "Café Au Lait" ("Café Olay")

Scene Two: "Patty Cake for Queenie Pie"; "Café Au Lait"; "Woman (Beautiful Woman)"; "I Love Peace" ("I Love to See Those Happy Faces"); "I Love Pees" (alternate); "Pees" (alternate)

Scene Three: "T.V. Commercials—Waltz"; "T.V. Commercials" A–K

Scene Four: "All Hail the Queen" ("Queenie Pie")

Scene Five: "Hawk"; "Oh, Gee (You Make That Hat Look Pretty)"; "My Father's Island"; "Bon Voyage, Queenie Pie"

Scene Six: "Sure Do Miss New York"; "When You Leave New York"; "Full Moon at Midnight"; "Bottle in the Bucket"; "Tune In" ("Drink Gin"); "Full Moon at Midnight"; "Long Life, Much Money" ("Drinking Song"); Trio: "Smile as You Go By" ("Tree Song"); "Don't Need Nobody, Now"; "Long Life, Much Money"; "Hevl"

Scene Seven: "Discovery of Q.P. On Beach"; "Let the Good Times Rock"; "Won't You Come Into My Boudoir"; "Soliloquy"; "Stik" *(Addenda)*; "Si, Si, Si, Si" ("Drinking Song"); "Pretty Woman"

Stardust

Muscial Revue. Biltmore Theatre, New York City, 19 February 1987. Lyrics: Mitchell Parish; directed by Albert Harris.

"Sophisticated Lady" (lyrics by Parish and Irving Mills)

Black and Blue

Musical Revue. Minskoff Theatre, New York City, 26 January 1989. Conceived and directed by Claudie Segovia and Hector Grezzoli.)

"Black and Tan Fantasy" (composed with Bubber Miley); "Come Sunday"; "East St. Louis Toodle-oo" (composed with Bubber Miley); "In a Sentimental Mood" (music and lyrics by Ellington, Irving Mills, and Manny Kurtz)

Play On!

Musical Comedy. Brooks Atkinson Theatre, New York City, 20 March 1997. Book by Cheryl L. West; conceived and directed by Sheldon Epps; choreographed by Mercedes Ellington.

(Titles listed according to the running order) "Take the 'A' Train" (by Billy Strayhorn); "Drop Me Off in Harlem" (lyrics by Nick Kenny); "I've Got to Be a Rug Cutter"; "I Let a Song Go Out of My Heart" (lyrics by Henry Nemo, Irving Mills, and John Redmond); "Mood Indigo" (music by Ellington, Mills, and Albany Bigard); "Don't Get Around Much Anymore" (lyrics by Bob Russell); "Don't You Know I Care" (lyrics by Mack David); "It Don't Mean a Thing" (lyrics by Irving Mills); "I Got It Bad and That Ain't Good" (lyrics by Paul Francis Webster); "Hit Me with a Hot Note and Watch Me Bounce" (lyrics by Don George); "I'm Just a Lucky So and So" (lyrics by Mack David); "Solitude" (music and lyrics by Ellington, Eddie de Lange and Irving Mills); "I Ain't Got Nothin' But the Blues" (lyrics by Don George); "I'm Beginning to See the Light" (music and lyrics by Ellington, Don George, Johnny Hodges, and Harry James); "I Didn't Know About You"; "Rocks in My Bed" (music and lyrics by Ellington and Billy Strayhorn); "Love You Madly"; "Prelude to a Kiss" (music and lyrics by Ellington, Irving Gordon and Irving Mills); "In a Mellow Tone" (lyrics by Milt Gabler)

Duke!

Ballet. Jazz at Lincoln Center, 3 June 1999.

(Titles listed according to the running order) *Rockin' In Rhythm* (choreographed by Robert La Fosse); "Echoes of Harlem"; "Rockin' in Rhythm" (by Duke Ellington, Irving Mills, and Harry

Carney); "Old King Dooji"; *Ellington Elation* (choreographed by Garth Fagan); "Ad Lib on Nippon" (from the *Far East Suite*); *Blossom Got Kissed* (choreographed by Susan Stroman); "It Don't Mean a Thing If It Ain't Got That Swing" (lyrics by Irving Mills); "Lotus Blossom" (by Billy Strayhorn)

Notes

Introduction—Dramatis Felidae

1. Cook insists that Dvorak did not like him as a pupil. See the excerpt from his autobiography in *Theatre Arts* 31 (September 1947): 61–65.

2. John W. Isham was Sam T. Jack's advance man with the Creole Burlesque Company. When he took to producing on his own, he altered the theatrical conventions of the minstrel show, eliminating the semicircular format, the interlocutor's formal introductions, and the farcical "wit" of the endmen redolent in bad puns. Instead, Isham's new format consisted of various specialty acts, songs, or dances, layered within a thinly plotted play, and ending with a military drill for the whole company. See Thomas L. Riis, *Just Before Jazz* chapter 2.

3. In the third installment of "The Hot Bach" in *The New Yorker* (8 July 1944), Ellington recalled that he and Cook used to ride around Central Park in a taxi and discuss music composition. "I'd sing a melody in its simplest form and he'd stop me and say, 'Reverse your figures.' He was a brief but strong influence. His language had to be pretty straight for me to know what he was talking about. Some of the things he used to tell me I never got a chance to use until years later, when I wrote the tone poem 'Black, Brown, and Beige'"(29).

4. In his unpublished dissertation, "Philosophies of African American music history," Willie Frank Strong relates that "Ellington self-deprecatingly considered his education equivalent to that of a pool-hall musician; he states that he received most of his formal training by listening to and duplicating the feats of other musicians" (197).

5. See Mercer Ellington, *Duke Ellington in Person: An Intimate Memoir* 158–159 for a discussion of Ellington's often contradictory attitude toward formal education.

6. With a book by Flournoy E. Miller and Aubrey Lyles, the authors of the book to *Shuffle Along*, *Runnin' Wild* trades on the continued misadventures of Sam Peck and Steve Jenkins who are run out of Jimtown because they are unable to pay their rent. They return in disguise as mediums and engage in a number of vaudeville-liek routines as they foretell the future and bilk the unsuspecting dupes of Jimtown.

7. Stuart Nicholson suggests that Ellington probably met Johnson after a performance of *The Twentieth Century Jazz Revue* at the Convention Hall in Washington D.C. on 25 November 1921. At this meeting, Ellington was encouraged to play Johnson's famous "Carolina Shout" which Ellington had been rehearsing to sound like the piano roll.

8. The plot of *Shuffle Along* concerns the mayoral race in Jimtown, Dixieland, between grocery-store owners Steve Jenkins and Sam Peck, and the reform candidate Harry Walton, whose campaign song is the hit, "I'm Just Wild About Harry."

African-American composer William Grant Still provided the orchestrations and Paul Robeson and Adelaide Hall were members of the chorus. Among the innovations in the production was the employment of a serious love interest, a plot device that had not been used successfully in a black musical, and a limited use of blacking up among the major characters. This aspect will have a profound effect on Ellington who will forbid the use of blackface in his musical revue *Jump for Joy* (1941).

9. The script of *Rang Tang* was written by Kaj Gynt, one of Ellington's collaborations on *Cock o' the World.*

10. Although Ellington and his orchestra performed several floor shows and revues in movie theatres prior to the screening of the film, these performances are not included in this study, nor are the various choreographed productions of his suites designed for television broadcast.

1.—Jungle Music

1. Although Bushell recalls the Berlin production opening with the plantation scene (55), accounts of the performances in Copenhagen and Stockholm cite the Harlem cafe as the opening sequence. It is not unlikely that the revue might have undergone changes in its format during its European tour. See John and Hans Larsen, "The Chocolate Kiddies in Copenhagen" (3), and Bjorn Englund, "Chocolate Kiddies: The show that brought jazz to Europe" (45) for full accounts of the Copenhagen and Stockholm tour.

2. Mark Tucker notes a quotation from Emmett's "Dixie" in the first ending of Ellington's song, and finds the harmonic vocabulary of the piece, with an emphasis on seventh chords, and a plagal turn in the final measures to be evocative of other songs of the twenties such as "Somebody Stole My Gal" or "Baby Face" (124). Here Ellington seems to be rejecting the aesthetics of both Bob Cole and Will Marion Cook, and writing, instead, in a color-blind fashion.

3. Tucker argues that Ellington was consistently bringing "fresh ideas" to the traditional popular song formulas (126).

4. Horst Bergmeier asserts that the piece was probably written earlier. See Tucker (126).

5. See Tucker for a transcription of the promotional excerpts (133).

6. The title page of each publication shows a cartoon of the revue's comedy team, the Three Eddies (Tiny Ray, Chick Horsey, Shaky Beasley) wearing tuxedos, bowler hats, white-rimmed glasses, gloves, and spats. Arms spread and feet apart, the trio appear to be in the middle of an energetic dance step. In addition to the authors' credits, Arthur S. Lyons is cited as the producer of the "Coloured Revue" and Victor Alberti is noted in connection with the "Musikalienhandlung Graphisches Kabinett" in Berlin.

7. Baker and Chase argue that German racism was the major cause of cast changeover in the *Chocolate Kiddies* (126).

8. Dan Healy, who had also appeared on the legitimate Broadway stage in Rodgers and Hart's *Betsy* and Kalmar and Ruby's *Good Boy*, was a gifted, young and energetic dancer, singer, and stand-up comic. He is generally credited with creating the Cotton Club "style." In *Harold Arlen: Happy with the Blues*, Edward Jablonski cites Healy's explanation of the formula: "The show was generally built around types: the band, an eccentric dancer, a comedian—whoever we had who was also a star. The show ran an hour and a half, sometimes two hours; we'd break it up with a good voice ... [a]nd we'd have a special singer who gave the customers the expected adult song in Harlem" (55).

9. Between *Chocalate Kiddies* and Ellington's tenure at the Cotton Club, the Washingtonians took to the stage of the Lafayette Theatre where they did double duty, playing in the pit and on stage, for Clarence Robinson's revue *Jazzmania*, beginning 10 October 1927. They followed this with a performance in *Messin' Around*, another October revue produced at the Plantation Café in the Winter Garden Building. By mid–November, the band was back at the Lafayette Theatre, performing in *Dance Mania*, another Robinson revue. In the early days of his band, Duke Ellington had first-hand experience in accompanying singers as well as providing the obligatory up-to-date dance music.

10. In an interview conducted by Stanley Crouch in January 1979 for the Smithsonian Institution Jazz Oral History Project, Sonny Greer noted that Paul Whiteman was an ardent fan of Ellington at the Cotton Club. One night George Gershwin remarked to Whiteman that what he was hearing from Ellington's band was "Jungle Music," and the sobriquet stuck.

11. See *Music Is My Mistress* 493 ff. for Ellington's personal list of compositions and collaborators.

12. With the exception of *Blackberries of 1930* and *The Cotton Club Parade, Fourth Edition* (1938), none of Ellington's compositions used in the Cotton Club revues appear to have been specifically written for the shows. Instead, Ellington interpolated various recently recorded compositions, capitalizing on their popularity.

13. Ellington credits Will Vodery, Florenz Ziegfeld's African American arranger, with getting the band the job (*Music Is My Mistress* 98).

14. For a fuller discussion of this show, see Dr. Klaus Stratemann, *Duke Ellington: Day by Day and Film by Film* 2–4.

15. Reviewer J. Brooks Atkinson was not impressed by Ellington's contribution to the evening's performance. In his *New York Times* review of 31 March, he notes that "Duke Ellington, the djinn of din, and his colored Cotton Club Orchestra, devote an hour to elaborate devices for making noise. By comparison with this blaring bobbery, Mei Lan-fang's squealing orchestra was rhapsodically melodious. Give Mr. Ellington a familiar tune and his gleaming Negro musicians can rip it apart by sticking a derby hat over the mouth of a horn or thrusting a wad down its brassy throat" (24).

16. Busby Berkeley choreographed the production. Unfortunately, because of the presence of stars of the magnitude of George Jessel and Fanny Brice, the newspaper reviews gave little notice to the efforts of anyone else, with the possible exception of the scenic designer, Jo Mielziner, because the scenery was too large to fit in the theatre. See *New York Times* 18 November 1930, 28:5.

17. The title refers to a suburb of St. Louis, across the Mississippi in Illinois. Generally denegrated as a slum by the upper-classes across the river, it was the location of many run-down tenement houses and a high incidence of crime. Leaving East St. Louis, therefore, implies an elevation of social status.

18. Jim Haskins recalls that it was not unusual for the Cotton Club performers to go to the Lenox Club on Lenox Avenue and 144th Street at 5 A.M. on Monday mornings for a weekly breakfast dance. There, "Duke and the other musicians from clubs ... that were out of the jazz mainstream could get down to real jazz and find stimulation from other experimenters in the medium" (59).

19. "Rockin in Rhythm" was recorded in January 1931. *Earl Carroll's Vanities of 1932* was composed mainly by Harold Arlen and Ted "Rockin'" Koehler and directed by Vincente Minnelli. It featured Helen Broderick and a very young Milton Berle. The *Vanities* were spectacular revues, trading on lavish scenery, scantily-clad young women, satirical comedy, and huge production numbers.

20. See Stratemann for a superlative study of Ellington's films during this period.

21. Also called the *Cotton Club Parade, Second Edition*, this was the ninth Ellington's Cotton Club opening.

22. Also known as the *Cotton Club Parade, Fourth Edition*.

23. According to Barry Ulanov, Henry Nemo was a good-natured, corpulent man who would entertain anywhere and at any time. Although he was fond of using fast-paced hip jargon in his conversation, claiming he put "the hoi in hoi polloi," and describing himself as "The Neem Is on the Beam," he was a sensitive, exceptionally musical lyricist (194).

24. The program credits Will Vodery with the orchestrations and "musical supervision" of the show. In its 26 March 1938 issue, however, *Billboard* credits the arrangement of "A Lesson in C" to Chappie Willet (12), though Stratemann suggests that this account is unverified (152).

25. A longtime friend, Claire Gordon recalls that Henry Nemo said that the title "I Let a Song Go Out of My Heart" came to him while sitting in the bathroom. Whether this is an example of Nemo's continual urge to entertain, or the way it really happened, is impossible to verify.

26. Typically the Cotton Club Girls were light-skinned African Americans; some were even light enough to marry into prominent wealthy white families. Lucille Wilson was hired in 1932 on a provisional basis because of her dark complexion. Cotton Club management was uncertain of the reaction of the white clientele to a chorus girl with such dark skin. The fact that she remained with the club for eight years indicates that there was no significant objection to her color.

27. Among the musical manuscripts at the Strayhorn Estate is an incomplete set of lyrics about "Madame La Croquinole"[*sic*] and her fame as a beautician. The lyrics that exist compare Croqinole to Frederick Douglass and Cleopatra in a style not unlike P.G.Wodehouse's lyric to "Cleopatterer" in *Leave It to Jane* (1917).

28. A national tour of another show called *Harlem Is Heaven* began in 1937 featuring African American performer Christola Williams.

29. Although Duke Ellington did not complete work on Strickland's scenario (if indeed, he wrote anything *specifically* for the show) he evidently maintained contact with the author as late as 1965 when Charlotte and Wilbur Strickland were invited to Philharmonic Hall at Lincoln Center for the premiere of "The Golden Broom and the Green Apple."

2—The Sun-Tanned Revu-sical

1. Gerald Bordman gives the Royale Theatre but Bernard L. Peterson, Jr., notes the revue opening at the Majestic Theatre. Both agree that the production ran in excess of one hundred performances. See Boardman 426; Peterson 287.

2. The typescript of *Jubilee* indicates that Ellington's composition was to be featured as the finale of the program. Unfortunately, the script does not include the lyrics and the music appears to be lost.

3. See Berry for a further discussion of Langston Hughes's troubles with the Hollywood Theatre Alliance (301).

4. The guests included John Garfield, Bonita Granville, Lana Turner, Tony Martin, Groucho and Harpo Marx, Mario Castelnuovo-Tedesco, and Skitch Henderson. Also present were white writers who would contribute music and sketches to the show, Hal Borne and Hal Fimberg, and producer Walter Jurmann, who would act as "chairman" of the producing organization, the American Revue Theatre.

5. Strayhorn had officially joined the Ellington entourage during the week of

20–27 January 1939, when the band was playing the Paramount Theatre in Newark, New Jersey. Almost immediately, Strayhorn became a member of the Ellington family and Duke's creative soulmate for the remainder of his life.

6. According to Sid Kuller, Mickey Rooney's real ambition was to be a successful songwriter. When he and Sidney Miller contributed "Cymbal Sockin' Sam" to the revue, it was accepted on the strength of Mickey Rooney's name, not on its musical values which were, according to Kuller, "pretty awful" (Willard 8).

7. In an undated page of notes to Ellington, Billy Strayhorn is cited specifically regarding "Uncle Tom's Cabin": "The center part of this would be restaged in order to bridge the lull that precedes Ivie's singing, and I would like to have Billy Strayhorn available for a conference on this." There is no awkwardness here in terms of chain of command. Clearly Strayhorn was part of the creative team.

8. This number included Ellington's "Prologue" and Paul White's pantomime, "Only Propaganda" in which the actor, pursued by a ghost, frightens the ghost to death, and tells the audience, "It's only propaganda!" Paul White was the appropriate choice for this routine since he had been white bandleader Ted Lewis's "black shadow" for many years. Ellington's "prologue" in verse discussed the unrealistic stereotyping of African Americans typical in "Black revues."

9. Jeffreys and Dandridge were reported to be the portrait of young love: he, dressed in a white suit with blue shirt, and she dressed in a pale blue calico hoop skirt and picture hat.

10. Smith had been promised writer's credit in the program. When he did not receive it, he ad-libbed an introduction to his routine, announcing his authorship of the material. Though admonished by management for ad-libbing, Smith continued to do so until proper credit was given him in the program.

11. In his biography of Billy Strayhorn, David Hajdu assigns the composition of "Cindy with the Two Left Feet," "Bugle Breaks," "Uncle Tom's Cabin Is a Drive-In Now," and "Rocks in My Bed" to Billy Strayhorn. See *Lush Life* 92.

12. Authors are not listed in the opening night program. Credit found in Henry T. Sampson, *Blacks in Blackface* (244).

13. In this sketch, Potts plays Luscious Beebe, a "fugitive from *Esquire*" in search of an Easter suit. Tailors Pan and Skillet outfit him in a "Zoot" suit to the accompaniment of Ellington's rhythm section. Barry Ulanov argues that "the first extensive treatment of the 'zoot suit with a drape shape and a reet pleat' was in this revue" (243).

14. Sid Kuller notes that "Sharp Easter" opened with the whole cast promenading in pastel costumes designed by René Hubert. "The girls were absolutely stunning. At the end of the parade came the tailors dressed in gold and purple … leading Potts … in the loudest, most outrageous checkered suit ever constructed. The pants came up to his armpits, the vest was two or three inches long, even the lining was blinding. The house fell down" (Willard 17).

15. See Willard 17–19. Hajdu argues that the Los Angeles reception was basically poor with the exception of Ed Schallert of the *Times*, and Almena Davis of the *Los Angeles Tribune*, an African American weekly (91).

16. Special notes to Ellington asked for a "hot chorus" in "Calico Gown" and a bridge into the chorus of "Bli-Blip," a dance arrangement of those two numbers for the Pot, Pan, and Skillet specialty dance, new music for the "Rent Party," a change of music for Al Guster's tap routine (the suggestion was "Chocolate Shake"); a restaging of "Jump for Joy" with a "hot chorus" for the dancers during which Rex Stewart can haul out his trumpet and "give"; the introduction of some of the choir into "Shhhh! He's on the Beat"; and, a request for the completion of "Mardi Gras" so that the dance routine can be choreographed.

17. John Garfield and Sylvia Blankfort, the manager's wife, had both suggested major revisions of the show. It is not known how many of their suggestions are represented in Blankfort's memo. See Willard 21–22.

18. Welles, who considered Ellington the only genius he ever knew (besides himself), had been highly impressed by Duke's performance of "Chocolate Shake" and "Brown-Skin Gal with the Calico Gown" on the MBS "Salute to Canada Lee" broadcast from New York City on 9 June, a month before *Jump for Joy* opened. Because Ellington was on the West Coast at the time, his selections were wired in from Hollywood. The day after *Jump for Joy* opened in Los Angeles, Welles and Ellington announced plans to collaborate on a documentary called "Saga of Jazz." Duke was hired at $1,000 a week, offered a role in the film, and subsidiary rights to the music. The project was dropped, but not until Ellington had written about 28 bars of a trumpet solo, and collected $12,500. Although this project failed to materialize, another, involving incidental music for a production of *Faust*, directed by Welles, did fall into the Duke's lap. Since Ellington was busy touring Europe with the band, his creative alter-ego, Billy Strayhorn, traveled to the Théâtre Edouard VII in Paris to complete the task. See Chapter Seven below, and David Hajdu (111 ff.) for a description of the chaos that followed in the collaboration between Strayhorn and Welles.

19. Two of the more controversial pieces in the show were Wonderful Smith's monologue and the musical number, "I've Got a Passport from Georgia." Smith's monologue—a phone conversation between the President of the United States and an African American—was viewed as "an unthinkable scenario for the day," while "Passport from Georgia" with its reference to lynching gave rise to bomb threats (Holmes 84).

20. In the early 1940s, several "fables" were submitted to Duke Ellington in which he and the band were featured characters. Perhaps the most interesting of the lot was *Aesop Wasn't Hip*, a satirical Negro musical revue, by Moxley Waldo Willis, Sr., dated 5 August 1943. Basically a moral dialogue between Ellington and a character called Hip Joe who sets out to prove that Aesop was wrong in thinking that "the memory of a good deed lives on," the revue takes place in Harlem and offers great opportunities for spectacle (the "Negro Easter Parade"), and music ("A Shipyard Symphony"). After trying for 18 scenes to change Hip Joe's perspective, Duke Ellington finally admits that Joe and Aesop will never agree on anything, and proceeds to lead his band in a series of energetic dance numbers suggesting a Broadway floorshow in a swanky Broadway night club. The moral: "Aesop wasn't hip!"

21. Taft Jordan, who was a member of the band from 1943 to 1947, and Cat Anderson, employed 1944–47, were not involved in the original production of *Jump for Joy*.

22. This idea will reach its full development as "Patty Cake for Queenie Pie" in Duke's opera *Queenie Pie*. See Chapter Ten.

3. "I'm Afraid I'll Live"

1. Among those pictured were "pleasant, nineteen, and too shy to jitterbug," Seaman Baker, Seaman Gunner Banks, Telegraphist Philpot, Lieutenant Harvey, and "sourpuss" Torpedoman Corby, who found little to like about America.

2. Wine: "No town has just one pub. Instead, they seem to be filled with them.... Americans drink very fast and, where we might spend an evening over a pint, they will have several." Women: "They use much more make-up than English women, but they seem to apply it in a less noticeable fashion. At any rate it is very difficult to judge their ages, and a girl of sixteen and a woman of thirty-six may both seem to be

about twenty-six.... They are freer, more outspoken, peppier and more aggressive than English womenfolk." Slang: "Do not worry about American slang. Most of it you are already acquainted with through the cinema" (25–26)

3. Henderson and Shaw knew they were not writing another *Oklahoma!* Their piece had to be topical because of the war. Still they maintained that both shows viewed the United States as a country being renewed at an important time in its history.

4. See *Black Musical Theatre*, Chapter 2, and *Blacks in Blackface*, Chapter 1.

5. See Hasse, *Beyond Category: The Life and Genius of Duke Ellington*, Chapter 8 and Nicholson *Reminiscing in Tempo*, Chapter 7 for an appreciation of the composer's non-theatrical activities during this period.

6. See Gerald Bordman, *American Musical Theatre: A Chronicle*, passim for an appreciation of the various *Pinafore* revivals in the United States.

7. See *American Musical Theatre: A Chronicle* 547–48 for brief summaries of these shows and *Opening Night on Broadway* passim for complete reviews.

8. The list of characters and synopsis is derived from the typewritten libretto housed in the theatre collection at the Lincoln Center Library for the Performing Arts in New York City. A cast list and one-page synopsis in the Ellington Collection at the Smithsonian (301.4B.5.9) suggests an even greater debt to *Follow the Girls*. In this version Hughie is depicted as funny, fat, and likeable, clearly capitalizing on the popularity of Jackie Gleason's character, Goofy Gale, in the earlier show. He is accompanied by a character missing in the script, the more restrained Robert Stratford-Merrie, who provides the love interest in this version of the play.

9. The name is an obvious play on Huey Long, the recently assassinated U.S. Senator whose flamboyant style made him the object of satire both in life and in death.

10. Each of Ellington's musicals allowed for a club environment and "performance numbers" by a torch singer.

11. In the one-page synopsis, Cameo is called "Monty." Sandra and Cameo were intended to be played by African American performers.

12. The celebrated tabloid columnist and broadcaster who coined the phrase "making whoopee" in his gossip column for the *Daily Mirror* (Arnold Shaw 209–10).

13. In 1939 two jazz versions of Gilbert and Sullivan's *The Mikado* appeared on Broadway during the month of March. The first to open was called *The Swing Mikado*; the later entry was titled *The Hot Mikado*.

14. In the synopsis, Monty threatens to shame England, smash the Allies and "win the war for Hitler" if Sandra and the Englishman do not cooperate. He is significantly less politically volatile in the finished script.

15. An allusion to Fiorello LaGuardia's practice of broadcasting homespun advice over the radio.

16. The structure of this scene has all the earmarks of a Kaufman and Hart farce.

17. One of the most significant of *Oklahoma!*'s legacies was the ballet which found its way into most musicals after 1943, usually as a dream sequence. This scene is also evocative of the final scene of *On the Town*, the 1944 collaboration of Betty Comden, Adolph Green and Leonard Bernstein which is set at the arcade in Coney island.

18. See *American Musical Theatre: A Chronicle* 485 and Tommy Krasker's notes to the 1987 CBS recording for a synopsis.

19. The sequence is reminiscent of Agnes deMille's choreography for Louise's ballet in Act Two of *Carousel*, the second of the Rodgers and Hammerstein collaborations.

20. In 1946 real life imitated art when LaGuardia was appointed director general of the United Nations Relief and Rehabilitation Administration, a post he held until his death in 1947.

21. Vinton Freedley, along with Alex Aarons, was among the old guard of Broadway producers having produced the early Gershwin hits *Lady, Be Good!* (1924), *Tip-Toes* (1925), *Oh, Kay!* (1926), *Funny Face* (1927), and *Girl Crazy* (1930). On his own, Freedley would also produce Cole Porter's *Anything Goes* (1934), *Red, Hot and Blue!* (1936), *Leave It to Me!* (1938), and *Let's Face It!* (1941). Freedley's involvement would certainly have legitimized the project.

22. As late as 1963 Ellington was being approached by Edward Small, a distinguished film producer, to composed the score for his version of *Frankie and Johnny*, with lyrics by Leonard Adelson who (along with Sid Kuller and Martin Charnin) had written lyrics for Vernon Duke's musical, *Zenda*, that opened in San Francisco on 5 August 1963 and closed in Pasadena the following 16 November. In the November 1963 issue of *Music Journal*, Small describes his quest for production, inviting readers to send him "Frankie and Johnny" memorabilia in an attempt to secure audience interest in the project. Although Small had produced memorable films, such as *I Cover the Waterfront, The Melody Lingers On,* and *Witness for the Prosecution*, he was unable to realize his dream of mounting the "Frankie and Johnny" legend.

23. At the Lafayette Theatre in Harlem, Watkins designed *Moon of the Caribbees, In the Zone*, *Bound East for Cardiff*, and *The Long Voyage Home*, all by Eugene O'Neill (27 October 1937); *Horse Play* by Dorothy Hailparn (27 August 1937); *Haiti*, by William DuBois (2 March 1938); and *Androcles and the Lion*, by George Bernard Shaw (16 December 1938). On Broadway, he designed *Mamba's Daughters* by Dorothy and DuBose Heyward (Empire Theatre: 3 January 1939; revival, Broadway Theatre: 23 March 1940); *Under This Roof*, by Herbert Ehrmann (Windsor Theatre: 22 February 1942); *Three Men on a Horse*, by John Cecil Holm and George Abbott (revival, Forrest Theatre: 9 October 1942); *Run, Little Chillun,* by Hall Johnson (revival, Hudson Theatre:11 August 1943); *Bright Lights of 1944,* by Norman Anthony and Charles Sherman (Forrest Theatre: 16 September 1943); *Manhattan Nocturne*, by Roy Walling (Forrest Theatre: 26 October 1943); and *Take It as It Comes*, by E.B. Morris (48th Street Theatre: 10 February 1944).

4—"Here's a Strange Mess'"

1. Daniel C. Caine argues that, because of the show's bi-racial content, it "must be viewed as a statement by and for the political left," a kind of "last hurrah" before the blacklisting of the 1950s (76).

2. This is often what is known as "option" money, a fee paid by the producer to the creative team to guarantee the producer's exclusive right to produce the show within a specified period of time. In addition, the composer, book writer, and lyricist would each earn a royalty of (typically) 2 percent of the gross receipts of the show. Ellington's share of *Beggar's Holiday* was 4 percent. Often a celebrity composer or lyricist would receive an "advance against royalties" guaranteeing a specified amount of money to be earned. While an advance against royalties is not unusual in composers' contracts, it does tend to distance the composer from an immediate concern over the fate of the work since he can never receive less than what he had been guaranteed by his advance.

3. See Hajdu 191. Rare are the individuals who actually prefer the work to the recognition.

4. He began work on *Ballet Ballads* in collaboration with Jerome Moross

during this period. Later, in 1954, Latouche and Moross will produce the celebrated *Golden Apple*, a modernization of the Greek myth, not unlike the unproduced *Swing, Helene, Swing.*

5. Niles Marsh notes, however, that African American leaders had responded poorly to the announcement of the show because they felt that "the low-lifes of 'The Beggar's Opera' would only encourage black stereotypes in this updated version. For this reason, pressure was put upon Lena Horne to reject a role in the show—which she did" (*Beggar's Holiday* liner notes).

6. Wasserman will later win fame as the author of the play adaptation of *One Flew Over the Cuckoo's Nest*, and of the musical adaptation of *Don Quixote*, *The Man of La Mancha.*

7. Ray would become a celebrity in almost a decade as the director of films such as *Johnny Guitar* and *Rebel Without a Cause.* At this point in his career, he was a handsome, complicated man. As John Houseman described him: "he was a potential homosexual with a deep, passionate and constant need for female love in his life. This made him attractive to women, for whom the chance to save him from his own self-destructive habits proved an irresistible attraction of which Nick took full advantage and for which he rarely forgave them. He left a trail of damaged lives behind him" (Bradshaw 246).

8. *Beggar's Holiday* was the New York title of the production. When it opened on tour, it was known as *Twilight Alley*, and Latouche's earlier drafts are titled *Beggar's Opera* and *Street Music.*

9. Daniel C. Caine suggests that Watkins's original designs were "lackluster" while those of Oliver Smith were "lavish and boldly original" (87–88).

10. Hajdu notes Bill Dillard's recollections of Strayhorn's delight in being among the boyish homosexuals in the cast—the so-called gypsies—and feeling at home in the company of other gay African Americans (103–104). It has been whispered in Broadway circles that Latouche and Strayhorn shared a love for drink, and that the two fueled one another's alcoholic tendencies. Rumors even existed that, because of Latouche's attraction to African American boys as sexual partners, that he and Billy Strayhorn were lovers. There is no evidence to confirm the rumor and all that can be said with certainty is that the environment surrounding the production of *Beggar's Holiday* provided Strayhorn with comfortable stimulation for creativity.

11. Houseman notes that Zero Mostel had "prodigious vitality and inexhaustible invention" and made the Peachum scenes work irregardless of the writing. Houseman also notes that Alfred Drake was charming but not enough as Macheath and that Jet MacDonald was rather pale, constently being overshadowed by a dancer named Majorie Belle (later, Marge Champion). The director's desire to switch the women in their respective roles was cut short by Drake's infatuation with his leading lady (Houseman 192–193).

12. *Billboard* offers the following pre–Broadway itinerary for *Twilight Alley*: Shubert Theatre, New Haven: 21–23 November; Newark Opera House: 25–30 November; Philadelphia: early December. A week in Hartford substituted the Newark and Philadelphia dates. The last two weeks of tryouts occurred at the Opera House in Boston starting on 3 December 1947.

13. Both Stratemann and Caine note that the real New York opening occurred the night before on Christmas, as a benefit performance for Paul Robeson's Council on American Affairs, an organization that would soon become a favorite target of the HUAC investigations. Caine also notes that the show was to have opened at the Harlem Opera House during the third week of December 1946 but never did.

14. Here and throughout the script, the lines for the chorus men and women

are noted by their real (actor) names, with their characters' names handwritten beside them.

15. One of the major problems with the show out of town was the ending. The original script ended with a collective guilt sermon, indicting all mankind with the greatest crime of all: sitting back and letting things happen. Even though a deus ex machina finish turns everything right and ends the play on a positive note, the severity of the Beggar's diatribe, unprepared for by the rest of the evening, was simply too much for the audience to accept. A similar situation will occur during the tryout of Stephen Sondheim's *Company* (1970), when the deeply disturbing "Happily Ever After" will be replaced by the more uplifting "Being Alive."

16. Houseman's complaints about Ellington's score are problematic. Perhaps during the early stages of the production when the musical was more closely alligned to the ballad opera format, a through-composed score might have been appropriate, and certainly Houseman was correct in asserting that Ellington did not provide a through-composed score. However, as the musical developed into a more familiar musical comedy format, the potpourri nature of the score is appropriately atmospheric and dramatic, offering abundant opportunities for character nuance. That Ellington borrowed musical material from his "trunk" is also no reason to condemn his work. Many classic musicals have trunk songs, one of the finest examples of which is Jule Styne's *Gypsy* (1959).

17. Although Ellington does resolve to the tonic harmony earlier in the song, the melody note above the tonic harmony is not the tonic note. As a result, there is the sense of non-resolution until the final bars of the piece.

18. Not every review, of course, was favorable toward the score. Writing in *Theatre Arts*, Cecil Smith contradicted most of the theatre critics by judging Ellington and Latouche's attempts at music drama a failure, arguing: "It is one thing to write short pieces that are entertaining in themselves because of their lilt and instrumental color. It is quite another to follow sophisticated prosody and to aid in the articulation of wry, complex lyrics; to epitomize the shifting moods of the various songs and of evanescent passages within each song; and to keep a long series of similarly patterned set pieces always fresh and inviting by maintaining a sufficient variety of rhythmic ideas, harmony and orchestral texture. Heard one at a time on the radio or phonograph many of the Ellington songs will sound charming. When they are strung together for two hours and a half they become monotonous" (31 [March 1947]: 27). The unidentified critic for the *New Yorker* refutes Smith's position, but still dislikes the show: "Whether or not you are likely to enjoy 'Beggar's Holiday' depends, I should say, on a great many matters of personal taste. The customer, that is, who is really going to have the time of his life at the Broadway should have at least a majority of the following qualifications: He should be an admirer of a kind of music that is apt to be described as interesting rather than melodious, since Duke Ellington's score is less distinguished for the qualities that get tunes on hit parades than it is as a single, sustained composition, establishing a mood—often, it seemed to this conventional ear, by the use of rather alarming and monotonous dissonances" (4 January 1947: 46). Finally, *The Commonweal*, calling the musical "a strange mess," concluded that the mixture of John Gay, Duke Ellington, and John Latouche "is not only sad, but bad" (45 [17 January 1947]: 351–52).

19. Stratemann indicates that, as one of the most expensive Broadway productions of its day, *Beggar's Holiday* would have had to earn $27,000 a week in ticket sales just to break even. Although a capacity audience at the Broadway Theatre could bring in $46,000 a week, *Beggar's Holiday* revenue was never higher than $40,000 (in its first week) and declined steadily to below $20,000 in its closing week. Why was the show

so expensive to produce? Both Ellington and Latouche received 4 percent of the gross while Houseman and Abbott each received 2 percent. Both Alfred Drake and Libby Holman were drawing at least $1,000 a week in salaries (he got $1,250; she got $1,000 plus a percentage), and Zero Mostel was earning $900 plus 5 percent over a weekly gross of $25,000. Bernice Parks, who replaced Libby Holman as Jenny, was only earning $450 as was Avon Long.

20. In October 1994, the Chicago-based Pegasus Players did a full production of the show, directed by Dennis Courtney, with scenery designed by Todd Rosenthal, and costumes by Claudia Boddy. Although the production was substantially scaled down from the original Broadway show, reactions from critics and public alike reinforced the view of the Washington critics that *Beggar's Holiday* is a musical that deserves to live.

21. On 31 July 1947, Underhill sent Ellington a copy of the libretto with the explanation that Perry Watkins expected the complete draft by 30 August. The typescript of the musical dated 28 July 1947 in the Ellington Collection at the Smithsonian bears the designation: "Music by Duke Ellington, Book and Lyrics by C. M. Underhill" (301.4.7.15). It is unlikely that Ellington would have begun sketching out the score before August 1947.

22. Although this might appear to be inequitable given Ellington's track record and Underhill's novitiate status, it is not. Normally a $5,000 advance would be divided in thirds: one third given to the author, another third to the lyricist, and the third portion to the composer. Under the usual conditions, then, Underhill should have received two-thirds of $5,000. The fact that he and Ellington shared equally demonstrates Ellington's superior status.

23. It is ironic that Ellington should copyright in 1947, at the time of his involvement with *Moon of Mahnomen*, two works called "The Beautiful Indians": "Minnehaha," and "Hiawatha," that Collier calls "short jazz pieces that Ellington grouped on very slim musical grounds" (279). Perhaps Ellington recycled some of his work on the musical into the compositions for orchestra, as he would do years later with *Saturday Laughter*, much of which was recast as *La Plus Belle Africaine*.

5—"Night Time"

1. She would go on to write a number of plays on record at the Library of Congress: *Such Stuff as Dreams Are Made* (1957), *The Winter of Our Discontent* (1958), *Spinning on the Wind* (1964), and *A Bed of Roses* (1964). In news releases, she is also credited with working with John Latouche and writing poetry and short stories for a variety of magazines.

2. Ron Fletcher had been signed to choreograph the show and Perry Watkins was on hand to design the settings. See Ken Bloom, *American Song: The Complete Musical Theatre Companion*, (79).

3. An earlier version of the text has "Night Spell," an "Old Black Magic" kind of number in its tone, but full of intricate, and often awkward, internal rhymes, unidiomatic to an easily assimilated popular song.

4. There are three pages of lyrics for this number, including "encore" verses. Undoubtedly, Doris Julian was anticipating a commercial hit.

5. Ironically, another farce entitled *Be My Guest* was copyrighted in 1953, by Tom Taggart. It also involved an exchange of identities in a New York City setting, this time between a plain young lady and a glamorous debutante.

6. See also Derek Jewell, *Duke: A Portrait of Duke Ellington*, Chapter 5.

7. The change of bass figure is a dynamic one since, for the first time in 30

measures, the ear hears a different pedal note. In bar 32, the ostenato rhythm recurs, but on pitches different than those of the first 30 bars. Bars 34–40 have an identical octave C ostenato, followed by the original ostenato figure to the end.

8. Among the musical manuscripts in the Strayhorn Collection, the songs, "Be My Guest," and "Sunny Day, Honey," have materialized. It is unknown whether Strayhorn composed these pieces on his own, or if he was simply realizing Ellington's sketches. Given Julian's emphasis on Strayhorn's cooperation in the project, it is likely that the tunes are his for no sketches have been identified in the Ellington Collection that correspond to those titles.

9. Doris Julian's previous correspondence had been written on letterhead paper that read: "Perry Watkins / Doris Julian: Perry Watkins Inc. two hundred west fifty seventh ncy 19." Her present letterhead reads, "Doris Julian 315 Central Park West—New York 25, N. Y."

10. The New York *Daily News* of 8 December 1956 cited 14 February 1957 as the starting date for rehearsals.

11. The production was directed by Billie Allen; choreographed by Walter Raines; conducted by J. Leonard Oxley; with set design by William R. Waithe, lighting by Mark Diquinzio, and costumes by Bernard Johnson. The cast featured Ira Hawkins as Jojo, Jean Du Shan as Della, André Morgan as Lasson, Grenoldo Frazier as Maxie, Marta Videl as Millie, Norman Matlock as Adam, and Val Eley as Mary.

12. In *Music Is My Mistress*, Ellington discusses the Aquacade experience: "I had very little to do except play a piano solo, after which the house conductor took over and the cats had to blow. So I could go and get some work done at home. That was when I wrote my play, *Man with Four Sides*" (191). Hasse notes, however, that Ellington had been pursuing the project since at least 1952 (317), and a copy of *Lane* in the Ellington Archive dated 1944 implies an even earlier date that Hasse suggests.

13. The text indicates a production number arising from the number with choreography and synchronized lighting effects.

14. Ellington specifically refers to Banardosky's Concerto in A♭, a bogus work.

15. Mercer Ellington notes a great deal of self-portraiture in his father's creation: "Pop never carried a watch, and he always had his fingers in so many pies that he once called himself 'Tentacles'" (117).

16. A handwritten direction at this point in the typewritten text indicates the insertion of "Rumor" at this point.

17. A stage direction was added by hand to the text: "Lane walks to table and sits down with Snooky. The boys in the room break up their party and start down the stairs—they wave goodnight to bartender" (2/1/18).

18. A hand-printed stage direction suggests that both the wife and the girl have breakaway costumes, under which they wear traditional apache costumes (2/1/23).

19. A handwritten note identifies this act as Act II scene 2.

20. In my math, this implies that the producer was attempting to raise $400,000 (100 x $4,000 = $400,000).

21. Although José Ferrer was known primarily as an actor, on Broadway and in film, in the late 1950s and 1960s, he attempted to establish himself as a director as well. By the 1980s, Ferrer had retired to Miami where he assumed the artistic directorship of the Coconut Grove Playhouse.

22. For that production I reconstructed several of the numbers from Ellington's sketches in an attempt to assemble a performance score.

23. Because the lyrics for "Satin Doll," credited to Billy Strayhorn and Johnny Mercer, are used in this version of the musical, the text must have been produced after 1958 when the lyrics to the song were copyrighted. The earliest copyrights to "Satin

Doll," in 1953 and 1954, list only Duke Ellington as composer. Only on 4 November 1958 does the copyright registration include Billy Strayhorn and Johnny Mercer.

24. Hasse notes that Ellington had severed his ties with Columbia Records in early 1953 and signed with Capitol, a company the Duke felt would more vigorously promote his music (313). See also Jewell 119.

25. See David Hajdu 140–41.

26. On the verso of the manuscript sketch is a list of songs from *Beggar's Holiday*, as well as a sketch for "Wishy Washy Bubble Soap," one of the commercial ditties in the original *Cole Black and the Seven Dwarfs*.

27. As late as 1990, *Cole Black and the Seven Dwarfs* was seeking a producer. A new version of the script by William Cottrell, T. Hee, and yet another collaborator, Doug Miller, was registered for copyright on 13 August 1990. Nothing appears to have materialized from this latest attempt to produce the show.

28. Apparently Herbert Martin began the project alone because the copyright registration dated 6 July 1956 for *Children of Heaven*, "a play in two acts with music, adapted from the novel *Mine Boy* by Peter Abrahams" is in Martin's name alone. The copyright notice for *Saturday Laughter*, dated 28 February 1958, names both Martin and Stephen Bates as authors, and lists Duke Ellington as composer.

29. Martin tells of an amusing incident in Chicago when the creative team was supposed to meet for a production meeting in Ellington's suite at the Sherman Hotel. Because of his late-night schedule, the Duke was still asleep when the others arrived, and stayed in bed throughout the conference. Much of the information concerning this show is derived from the tape recording held in the Ellington Collection at the Smithsonian (301.6.390) of the TDES Meeting on 21 September 1994, during which members of the original production met to discuss its past and future.

30. Brock Peters and Diahann Carroll had appeared in *Carmen Jones* on Broadway; Thelma Carpenter had sung with the Count Bassie Band, just as Joya Sherrill had sung with the Ellington Orchestra. Ivan Dixon will later find success on the television series *Hogan's Heroes*.

31. A number of different versions of the script exist with slight variations of the running order and specific details of the plot. The text entitled *The Man Beneath* tells the following story. Act One begins in the Malay Camp, at 3 A.M. The hovels depicted on the set demonstrate the lack of wealth among the people there. Xuma enters, telling everyone that he has come from the north, and he is introduced to everyone there by Leah, who brews illegal beer, and buries it at night to hide it from the authorities. Xuma is given food and a place to sleep.

When Xuma awakens, it is Saturday, when everyone takes to the open air. Xuma wants to work, even though the only work available is in the mines. Maisy wants to dance, and teases Xuma into dancing with her. White policemen suddenly appear to take Xuma away for disturbing the peace, but Xuma holds his ground, claiming to have done nothing wrong. The policemen delight in beating him for no apparent reason, but Xuma fights back, gouging out a policeman's eye, noting that now he cannot be identified. When the reinforcements arrive, Xuma's bravura fails him, and he runs away. That night Xuma is discovered by Johannes, also known as J.P. Williamson, and befriended by Eliza who withdraws from him when he expresses his attraction for her. A short time later, Xuma gets a job working in the mine, as a boss boy, overseeing the men's work, because he shows strength and promise. Later, a riot ensues when the street pass of Joseph, a mine worker from the village, is torn up by mistake after Johannes infuriated a black police officer who only wanted to see their passes, and the wrong one was torn. When peace is restored, Xuma enters, exhausted from work. Maisy continues to ask Xuma to dance with her, and in spite of his fatigue, he dances with Maisy again anyway because he finds her so full of life. His real attraction, however, is for Eliza who continually rejects him because she wants a white lifestyle, not what Xuma represents. In spite of this, Eliza finds herself falling in love with him and the curtain falls on act one.

Act Two begins underground in the mine. Xuma and Red, the boss, are friends, but although Xuma respects him, he does not believe in Red's point of view regarding equality: that *all* hearts are the same. Experience has proven to him that the color of a person's skin can be a significant disadvantage in certain situations. Having saved some of his earnings from the mine, Xuma has moved out of the Malay Camp to his own apartment. But often he visits the camp to see Eliza. On one of those visits, Eliza tells him she loves him. Eliza and Xuma spend the night together, but when Eliza leaves in the morning, she is grief-stricken from what she believes she has done (given her desire to exist in a white society). While Xuma tries to convince her that he is unaffected by her prejudices, Eliza knows that Xuma would be better off loving someone without this "sickness." Finally realizing the futility of her affection for Xuma, Maisy is broken-hearted. A short time later, in spite of all the guarantees from management about the safety of the mine, the tunnel collapses and kills the boy, Johannes, and a white worker. Xuma refuses to go back to work until the tunnel is repaired, and the workers stand behind him on this issue. Even Red, the boss, joins what the top man calls "a strike" and the police are summoned to arrest the agitators. Xuma escapes on the mine-shaft elevator, uncertain what to do. Xuma decides to go back and stand along with Red and the other workers, finally understanding what the boss meant about "equality." Even though he is certain to be tried and convicted, he is willing to acknowledge his responsibility for the strike. Maisy and Leah believe that he is doing the right, and honorable thing, and at long last, Xuma, galvanized by the strength of his convictions, discovers the man beneath the skin.

32. Admitting that the premise of *Saturday Laughter* was its undoing, Christopher Manos noted that trying to produce a Broadway musical about apartheid from the black perspective at the very beginning of the civil rights movement in the United States was idealistic and impractical: "We were young and idealistic. But the money people weren't" (Hajdu 185). A backers' audition recording of the score confirms the high quality of the music and lyrics and clearly accounts for the sustained interest in the project over the last third of a century. As recently as December 1999, Herbert Martin was reworking the lyrics of *Saturday Laughter* for a projected studio recording. Perhaps, early in the next millenium, Ellington's extraordinary score and Martin's sensitive libretto will finally be realized.

33. On 28 December 1958, the Chicago *American* noted that Ellington had three days off from the Blue Note before Christmas and had planned to fly to Miami to work on *Jump for Joy*. An airline strike during the holidays forced him to cancel his trip.

34. See Hajdu 185–87.

35. The Miami *News* (25 November 1958) reported that Jerry Fielding, a film and television composer, would assist Ellington in the arrangement of the score, and Stratemann adds Tom Whaley, who joined the Ellington organization as a copyist in 1941, to the list of musical adapters, although he is not credited in the playbill.

6—*What Color Is Virtue?*

1. Tally Beatty had been one of the male dancers in the Copa City production of *Jump for Joy* in 1959.

2. Jewell notes that "King Fit" was first recited by Ellington at the Newport Jazz Festival, and recast in a choral arrangement for *My People*. He adds that "The

biblical walls of Jericho, which of course fell down, were equated in the show with the white police chief, Bull Connor, and the fire hoses and police dogs he directed against blacks claiming their rights in schools and buses" (146).

3. Mercer Ellington notes that the budget for *My People* was insufficient to hire the Ellington orchestra, so the Duke had to construct a band out of alumni from the orchestra while the Ellington orchestra would continue to tour on the road (165). This is a list of the musicians that were hired for the gig: Rudy Powell, Russell Procope, Bob Freedman, Harold Ashby, Pete Clark, reeds; Bill Berry, Ray Nance, "Ziggy" Harrell, Nathan Woodard, trumpets; Britt Woodman, John Sanders, Booty Wood, trombones; Joe Benjamin, bass; Louie Bellson, drums; Jimmy Jones, piano; Billy Strayhorn, celeste and conductor. Hajdu notes that during the run, Jimmy Jones took over as conductor, while Billy Strayhorn took part in the March on Washington on 28 August 1963, as a demonstration of black pride (229).

4. *Variety* noted that the "Century of Negro Progress" exposition at McCormick Place was a box-office bust. At the end of 15 days (with only three days remaining), only 73,000 people attended, instead of the expected 800,000. Low attendance had a significant affect on revenue, and *My People*, charging $1.00 for adults and $.50 for children was in great financial trouble. A month after the exposition closed, Duke sued the American Negro Emancipation Centennial Authority for $4,726.50, claiming that he had not been paid the $102,000 as agreed to produce a revue during the exposition. The suit stated that the "defendant has paid to the plaintiff ... the sum of $97,564.63" but still owed a balance of $4,435.07 plus legal fees (*Jet*, 24 October 1963).

5. Among Tuttle's most celebrated films are *Miss Bluebeard* (1925), *Kid Boots* (1926), *Blind Alleys* (1927), *The Big Broadcast* (1932), *Roman Scandals* (1933), *The Glass Key* (1935), *College Holiday* (1936), *Waikiki Wedding* (1937), *Doctor Rhythm* (1938), *This Gun for Hire* (1942), *The Hour Before Dawn* (1944), *The Great John L.* (1945), and *Hell on Frisco Bay* (1956).

6. Lyrics quoted through the generous permission of Helen Tuttle Votichenko, Frank Tuttle's daughter.

7. In his letter, Tuttle also mentions that Ellington completed a song titled "I'm Much Too Young to Be Old," but this writer has been unable to find any existing evidence of sketches bearing that title or lyrics. If it should materialized in the Strayhorn Collection, that would be an important indication of Strayhorn's participation in the project. Because Tuttle never mentions Strayhorn in his correspondence with Ellington, and his daughter remembers her father's enthusiasm in working with Duke, it is unknown what part, if any, Ellington's musical alter-ego played in the collaboration.

8. In a final letter dated 14 December 1971, Germaine Firth, now residing in New York City, once again inquires into Ellington's interest in writing a score for her show. Although her tone is still quite amiable, there is a suggestion of impatience in her attempt to get Duke to commit himself in any way: "If it is a definite no, then I'll proceed with script only. If you wish to state a possibility of interest, then, when I approach producers, I'd simply state your possible interest.... I would appreciate an early yes, no, or maybe, as 3 producers will read after the 1st of the year, and two others should have scripts to them now." It is unknown whether Ms. Firth ever received a reply.

7—"Skillipoop"

1. In the play, a crass producer, Jake Behoovian (played by Orson Welles), gives the role of a saint to a studio typist named Miss Pratt (played by Suzanne Cloutier) who managed to perform real miracles on the set. Suddenly the film studio becomes a shrine for everyone in need of a miracle and the entire film industry is

disrupted. Both God and the Hollywood moguls become displeased with the situation, and through the efforts of an overwrought archangel, a compromise is reached: Heaven will cease the disruptive miracles if Hollywood stops making religious movies.

2. *Time Runs* begins with a trio of young women coming out of the audience, discussing who will play the part of Helen of Troy in the school play. Suddenly they come upon a statue of Faust (played by Orson Welles) that comes to life. Mephistopheles (played by Hilton Edwards) enters and discusses Helen of Troy with Faust when, suddenly, one of the three girls (played by Eartha Kitt) transforms into Helen of Troy, approaches Faust, and makes him immortal with a kiss. The scene changes to a modern setting where Helen of Troy (now called "Mary") and Faust (now called "John") are in fear of being captured by the "mob." Ultimately the mob takes John away and the play ends with Mary leaving one of John's inventions, a box that ticks, on stage in a spotlight. As the curtain descends, the ticking gets louder and louder.

3. The opening night has been cited as 15 June, 17 June, and 19 June by various sources. According to Welles biographer Frank Brady, the opening had been delayed at least four times due to technical difficulties.

4. Ulric had become a star under the tutelage of David Belasco in the 1920s. Before *Mardi Gras*, her most recent appearance on the New York City stage had been in the role of Charmion in Katharine Cornell's production of Shakespeare's *Antony and Cleopatra*, in 1947.

5. Hasse notes that *Paris Blues*, recorded in Paris, and *Turcaret* were two of the very rare cases when Ellington wrote for an orchestra other than his own (338). According to the French press, the same musicians were used for both recording sessions, and Duke Ellington and Billy Strayhorn alternated on the piano part.

6. Dr. Theodore R. Hudson notes that this was the same "band call" Ellington used to call his own musicians to the stage during their club and concert dates. The tape I have heard of *Turcaret* uses only the first four measures of the piece.

7. The score of *Turcaret* presents a series of cues that are labeled according to their placement within the five-act structure of the play. These begin with "Frontin 1–2," and continue with "Frontin 2–3," "Lisette 3–4," and "Baronne 4–5." Cues with undesignated placement are: "Annonce du Spectacle," "Overture," "Turcaret–Anger," "Turcaret–Viv," "Chevalier," "M. Turcaret," "Motif de Flammand." The recording of *Turcaret* on the ORTF broadcast presented a different placement of cues:

Frontin; Baronne (piano solo); Turcaret–Anger; Lisette (flute solo); Annonce du Spectacle (piano solo); Overture (Turcaret motif in full development); Lisette; Chevalier (only first four measures); Baronne, followed by Lisette (on piano); Unidentified motif (perhaps Ellington's version of the French folksong, "I Shall Go Back to See My Normandie"); Frontin into the Baronne motif; Turcaret–Viv (repeated twice); Annonce du Spectacle (piano solo); Overture; Motif de Flammand; Turcaret–Viv; Frontin

It is unknown how these cues were utilized in the production since the production tape does not seem to exist. The copy of *Turcaret* in the Ellington Collection at the Smithsonian offers few clues as well. The anonymous translation into colloquial American idioms was supposedly earmarked for an American stage production of the play and, although it is filled with notes in Ellington's hand, it tells us little about the French text and how Ellington's music was used in Paris in 1961.

8. Jewell records that Fernanda's influence led Ellington to drinking vodka and eating caviar. In fact, he concludes, "for Fernanda he would eat or drink almost anything" (135–136).

9. The New York *Herald Tribune*, 4 August 1963, also noted Ellington's appreciation for Langham's descriptions because Duke "had enough trouble trying to understand that old English."

10. The onstage band consisted of trumpet, clarinet, French horn, guitar, bass, and drums. The pit ensemble included flute, oboe, English horn, clarinet, three saxophones, two trumpets, two French horns, a trombone, guitar, cello, bass, and two drummers.

11. No longer in existence, Milton was a small, independent, coeducational liberal arts college, chartered in 1867, on a 30-acre campus. At the time of Ellington's association with the school, Milton had fewer than 800 students. However, its arts programs were substantial and the annual arts festivals drew a great deal of attention. For *Timon*, for example, Herbert Crouch's stagecraft class constructed a three-tiered set modeled after the one designed for the Stratford production, and Ellington's score was realized by music professor Robert Bond who conducted an onstage band of five, and an orchestra of 15 musicians in the pit.

12. According to Ellington's memoirs, this was the second such award. The first had been a doctor of music from Wilberforce College in 1949. He would go on to earn 13 more honorary doctorates from prestigious institutions such as Yale University, Brown University, Berklee College of Music, Howard University, and the Christian Theological Seminary. See *Music Is My Mistress* (476 ff.) for Ellington's list of his awards and honorary degrees. At the awards ceremony on 7 June 1964 at Milton College, Mercer Ellington accepted the honor on behalf of his father who was engaged at Tin Pan Alley in Redwood City, California, at the time. On 24 November 1964, Ellington was officially "hooded" in an afternoon ceremony at Milton College.

8—Fallen Angel

1. He will go on to produce three additional plays, *A Girl Could Get Lucky* (1963), *Hot Shot* (1977), and *Kindling* (1978), all published by Samuel French.

2. The New York *Times* of 17 May 1962 announced the title as *Red Petticoat* but an October press release indicated that the title had been changed to *Sugar City* by Duke Ellington after he began working on the score.

3. Albeit inconclusively, this is where the Appel draft ends.

4. *Pousse-Café* had been scheduled to open on 24 January 1966 but Lilo was confined to her bed with a throat infection and the opening was postponed to the following night. See *Toronto Daily Star* 25 January 1966: 20.

5. In his autobiography, Theodore Bikel tactfully explained that the leading lady "just couldn't handle the demands of this role" and suggested that, even though Quintero attempted to breathe life into the project through rewrites and the reorganization of scenes, "with Lilo's limitations that was a virtual impossibility" (314–15). Bikel also blamed the show's failure on Ellington's absence, claiming that the producers, who appeared blind to the problems inherent in the show, "did not want to pay the Duke for being around, and so he stayed away" (314).

6. In his *American Song: The Complete Musical Theatre Companion*, Ken Bloom assigns the music and lyrics of "The Spider and the Fly" and "The Eleventh Commandment" to composer Michael Leonard and lyricist Herbert Martin. The previous year, Leonard and Martin had collaborator on the musical *The Yearling* which, incidentally, was also orchestrated by Larry Wilcox. The conductor's copy of "The Spider and the Fly" shows a completely different melody than Ellington's copyrighted original with only minor alterations in the lyrics.

7. Among the investors listed by *Variety* were: Peggy (Mrs. Barry) Goldwater, of Phoenix, $1,000; Henry Ford II, of Grosse Pointe, Mich., $1,600; Kenneth Banghart, of 24 W. 55th St., $2,000; Irving Maidman, of 1501 Broadway, $8,000; C. Henry Behl III, of Geneva, Switzerland, $1,600; Lydia Morrison, of 834 Park Av., $56,000;

Arthur Levine, of 1136 Fifth Av., $26,000; Justice Saypol's ruling was obtained by Attorney General Lefkowitz under the theatre control law passed after the 1964 Broadway "ice" and kickback scandals.

8. See Ken Mandelbaum, *Not Since Carrie*, 177–78.

9. Although the dance music was generally built around Ellington's melodies, he had no control over how they would be developed or orchestrated. In fact, other than creating the tunes—the raw material of the score—Ellington had little to say about how his music would be realized in performance.

10. Recorded in New York and Los Angeles in 1989–90, the album was released in 1992 by Audiophile Records, a company coincidentally based in New Orleans.

11. Diane Lampert was a lyricist adept at variety of styles and genres. She had co-written the Oscar-nominated song from *Silent Running* as well as the libretto for *Nell Gwen, the Protestant Whore* with popular composer Peter Schieckele. With Peter Farrow, she created the score for *O'Halloran's Luck*, an NBC television special, starring Art Carney and Barbara Cook, in addition to *The Wizard of Bagdad* and *Sean O'Fey* (with composer David Saxon), and *All for Your Love* (with composer Graham Turnbull).

12. A substantially revised version of the text that credits the lyrics to Lampert and Farrow and the book to Lampert and George W. George, "from material by Paul Avila Mayer, G.W. George and Peter Farrow," was scored by Julian "Cannonball" Adderley and his brother Nat in 1974. The new work, entitled *Big Man*, was produced in concert at Carnegie Hall in New York City in July 1976, with Joe Williams in the title role. Though some of Adderley's music evokes Ellington's setting of the text in scansion and modality, the score for *Big Man* is much more "pop" oriented than Duke's version. An original cast recording of the show was issued by Fantasy Records in 1975, as a "concept album," prior to the work's premiere.

9—Water Music

1. As Alvin Ailey tells the story, Lucia Chase was adamant about having both Ellington and Ailey on the project. He recalls her exact words: "Alvin, I've got a ballet for you to make. You and Duke Ellington. We must have the two of you," and confessed that "when she put her mind to something, you had to go along because she was a force of nature." See Ailey 114–116.

2. See Don George 192–196.

3. As usual, Ellington composed *The River* whenever and wherever the inspiration struck him. Duke's friend Bob Udkoff recalled driving him to a performance at the Oakland Coliseum on 21 April 1978 during a rainstorm when, using his turn signal, the sound of the signal in conjunction with the windshield wipers inspired Ellington to jot down a musical idea on the back of a match cover. Nearly a year later, Duke played Udkoff a tape of *The River* and pointed out the sound of his windshield wipers in the score. See Nicholson 394.

4. See Jennifer Dunning, *Alvin Ailey: A Life in Dance*, 257. Although the ballet had been advertised as "Seven Dances from a Work in Progress Entitled 'The River'" the section "Two Cities" actually combined "The Neo-Hip-Hot-Cool Kiddies Community" and the "Village of the Virgins" into a duet for a man and a woman who dance apart in individual spotlights.

5. *The River* had been scheduled for the opening night of the season but had to be postponed because of the late arrival of the score, and the insufficient rehearsal time.

6. See Ailey 116; Dunning 308. Jewell notes that once *The River* had been

recorded, Ellington went back to Europe where his itinerary included a performance of his Sacred Concert in Orange, France (201).

7. Derek Jewell notes that Ellington typically sent out his Christmas cards to arrive in April and May (232). President Johnson was evidently moved by both the performance and Ellington's card.

8. In the Ellington Archive at the Smithsonian, there exist several typed or handwritten scenarios for ballets, presumably by Ellington. One entitled *Black Blonde Ballet* tells the story of a young man faced with three tasks to please the girl next door: (1) to croon like Bing Crosby; (2) to play Romeo to her Juliet; and, (3) to sing to her on his knees. After the young man humiliates himself in an attempt to satisfy the girl's three requests, she decides that she has better things to do and leaves him to conclude, "Ain't Dames Hell" (Ruth Ellington 415.5.6.10) This scenario was never provided with a musical score. Another much more developed plan for a ballet involves a Prince; his fiancée, Purity; a villainous Emperor; and a huge serpent (created by having 32 girls dancing end to end) that the prince dismembers and returns to the villain's camp. To abduct Purity the emperor's henchmen disguise themselves as friendly animals and drag her to the villain's castle, where (though the efforts of the magic dabbler) thousands of pamphlets have fallen announcing that the Prince's father has struck gold. The emperor, distracted by greed, temporarily forgets about marrying Purity and sets about attacking the Prince's kingdom for the gold. While the emperor's army is on its way to attack, the magic dabbler changes the prince into a beautiful bird that flies over the heads of the army unnoticed to the emperor's castle where he rescues Purity. This fairy-tale scenario was never realized musically.

9. Baryshnikov had pulled a muscle and was unable to perform the work as planned, and Ailey's *The Mooche* was presented in its place.

10. For *Caravan*, composer Michael Kamen adapted various Ellington/Strayhorn compositions into a through-composed piece. The works used included "Caravan" (by Juan Tizol), "Sophisticated Lady," "Do Nothing 'Til You Hear from Me," "Take the 'A' Train" (by Billy Strayhorn), and "Satin Doll" (by Ellington and Strayhorn).

11. *Three Black Kings* was unfinished at the time of Ellington's death. It was completed by his son, Mercer, following his father's instructions regarding the completion and performance of the work.

12. Although this is only a brief representation of Ellington's work adapted for the ballet stage, it is sufficient to conclude that Alvin Ailey was correct when he suggested that all of Ellington's music is danceable.

10—Gilbert and Sullivan on Hallucinogens

1. See also Dunning 300, 306; Hasse 260–263; Jewell 18–19; Jennifer Ottervik 54–59. *Variety* for 10 July 1934 announced that Duke Ellington had composed a full-length opera that traces "Negro life from the jungle to Harlem"(1) Radio City Music Hall was said to be interested in staging the work. Stratemann notes that the idea of a music theatre work about the creation of the African American culture, from its jungle roots to its Harlem maturity, had been discussed as early as 1931 between Ellington and his mentor-lyricist-publisher, Irving Mills (115).

2. Ellington also notes that since he has to make a living, he has to depend on an audience; he does not believe that a large audience exists for the opera: "I do not believe people honestly like, much less understand, things like *Porgy and Bess*. The critics and some of the people who are supposed to know have told them they should like the stuff" (*The Ellington Reader* 116).

3. See Mercer Ellington, *Duke Ellington in Person* 158–159.
4. See Ulanov 241–246.
5. Here Ellington notes that the echoes of Africa were stronger in the West Indies than they were in America because of the maintenance of authentic African religions and sexual dances. The savage passionate African music, flavored with a Latin influence will have a pronounced impact on "jazz" 150 years later.
6. Hasse suggests that the omission of the pain and suffering contained in the "Africa" and "Slave Ship" sections of the scenario indicates, perhaps, Ellington's innate patriotism and a desire, given the wartime context of the work, "to emphasize positive aspects of American pluralism" (261).
7. In several articles in *Composer*, 1974–1975, Brian Priestly and Alan Cohen argue that *Ko-Ko* was excerpted from *Boola*'s score, a position accepted by Derek Jewell, James Lincoln Collier, and Ken Rattenbury. Since Ellington was also reputed to have been at work on *Cock o' the World* during this same period, *Ko-Ko* (which bears a greater resemblance to the title of the latter) could have been derived from that unfinished score as well. *Boola* and *Cock o' the World* might have even shared musical motifs, since both scenarios dealt with similar issues.
8. See Rattenbury 104–142 for a complete analysis of this work.
9. At the time, Ellington was probably at work on *Harlem Is Heaven*. It is likely that the character of Madame Croqinole was based on Madame C.J. Walker as well. As noted previously, it was not unusual for Duke to borrow elements from the musical theatre works composed with various librettists and include them in his own.
10. Maurice Peress notes that Ellington had the opera in mind since 1962. See Jennifer Ottervik (56).
11. In a BBC Radio interview with Stanley Dance in 1971, Duke Ellington maintained that *Queenie Pie* was "at the point of realization," and all that was needed was a producer and a performance date. "You say what day you want me to present it and I'll finish it. I wouldn't finish anything if I didn't know when I was going to play it" (Nicholson 406).
12. In the Betty McGettigan Collection at the Smithsonian, a page giving timings for the various scenes in the opera bears the handwritten notation: "Preparation done June '73 for presentation to WNET to justify 'advance' to Ellington" (Box 3 folder 6). Evidently the public television station was concerned that Ellington had not earned his commission. A handwritten cast breakdown, dated 4 September 1973, offered the following schedule:

October: Clean in Chicago?
December–January: Cast and start director–choreographer work
March: Orchestrate and finish dances (et al.)
April: Rehearse and film.

In the manuscript notes, Donald McKayle was suggested as director-choreographer on the strength of his recent Broadway musical, *Raisin*, and the fact that Maurice Peress had enjoyed working with him on Bernstein's *Mass*. See the Duke Ellington Collection #301, series 5, box 3 folders 3–4. In an article in the Boston *Globe* (13 October 1986), Maurice Peress argues that it was Ellington's illness and hospitalization (from the end of March until his death in May) that caused the cancellation of the television production of *Queenie Pie* (31).
13. Note the similarity to "Patty Cake for Sweetie Pie" in *Jump for Joy*.
14. The island sequence of the scenario is highly evocative of the atmospheric details Ellington created for *Air Conditioned Jungle*.
15. Handwritten notes in the Betty McGettigan Collection at the Smithsonian reveal the woman's frustration at being considered the villain in trying to estab-

lish her creative contribution to the work. What is especially interesting is the inability to discern who actually wrote what part of the libretto. Lines definitely ascribed to Duke were actually written by McGettigan, while those in a different type were assigned to the secretary, when in fact they were written by Ellington himself. See McGettigan Collection #494, box 3, folder 6.

16. According to the *Washington Post* (22 September 1986), the relationship between the two claimants began to improve in 1984, and the final legal settlement was made on 28 March 1986 when it was decided that McGettigan would receive a percentage of profits and program credit as "special consultant" for *Queenie Pie*.

17. The musical numbers were listed as follows:

Act One—"Harlem Scat" (from "Jam with Sam"—not in the original); "All Hail the Queen"; "Style" (not in the original); "The Hawk"; "Style" (Reprise); "Café Au Lait"; "It's Time for Something New" (not in the original); "Queenie Pie"; "Creole Love Call" (not in the original); "Soliloquy"; "My Father's Island"; "Harlem Scat" (Reprise—not in the original); "Oh, Gee"; "Two Cat Scat Fight" (not in the original); "Woman"; "The Hairdo Hop" (not in the original); "Finale Act 1" (not in the original); "There" (not in the original). Act Two—"Discovery of Queenie Pie on the Beach"; "Stix"; "It's Time for Something New" (Reprise—not in the original); "Queenie Pie" (Reprise); "Full Moon at Midnight"; "Smile as You Go By"; "Rhumbop" (from *A Drum Is a Woman*—not in the original); "A Blues for Two Women" (not in the original); "Won't You Come into My Boudoir"; "Hey, I Don't Need Nobody Now"; "Island Revolt" (not in the original); "Truly a Queen" (not in the original); "Finale" (not in the original)

18. The Washington, D.C., opening had been delayed ten days from the advertised opening on 8 October. The musical numbers in Washington followed basically the same program as those in Philadelphia, except for the second-act additions of "Island Update 1" between "Stix" and the reprise of "It's Time for Something New," "Island Update 2" between "Smile as You Go By" and "Rhumbop," and "Recovery of the NUCLI" and "Earthquake," were both inserted before "Hey, I Don't Need Nobody Now." The second-act number, "Island Revolt," was omitted.

19. In the Philadelphia playbill, Maurice Peress was credited with "Musical Adaptation and Development." In the Washington program, he is also credited with supervising orchestrations, dance, and vocal arrangements. In both playbills, Barrie Lee Hall, Jr., is credited as "Principal Jazz Orchestrator."

20. In the Philadelphia playbill, both Robert Kalfin and Garth Fagan are credited as directors.

21. The production was staged by veteran Broadway choreographer George Faison.

22. For an idiosyncratic evaluation of Ellington as a lyricist see Collier 294–296, and Lambert 249–50.

11—"Play On!"

1. The problems in Philadelphia appeared more technical than conceptual. The neon lights used heavily in the design of the show were damaged in shipping and so the time usually spent in run-throughs on the stage was devoted to correcting technical problems. It seemed clear to everyone involved that the show was not ready to open when it faced the critics in Philadelphia.

2. Since much of McKayle's original choreography was retained, he was co-credited with Smuin for musical staging and choreography when the show opened in New York.

3. In both the liner notes of the cast recording of *Sophisticated Ladies* and in his book, *Duke Ellington in Person*, Mercer Ellington exhibits a special fondness for his father's work in the theatre. He recalls urging Duke to create a "Blueprint Show" by putting various songs—ostensibly from the shows that never made it to Broadway—on the floor and mixing them around to come up with a structured story. In a similar fashion, *Sophisticated Ladies* was created from Duke's greatest hits, with the various ladies in Ellington's life represented in song and imagination.

4. Shakespeare's *Twelfth Night* seems to be a particular favorite among adapters. It served as the source of *Your Own Thing* (1968), score by Hall Hester and Danny Apolinar, book by Donald Driver; *Love and Let Love* (1968), music by Stanley Jay Gelber, lyrics by John Lollos and Don Christopher, book by John Lollos; *Music Is* (1976), music by Richard Adler, lyrics by Will Holt, book by George Abbott.

5. Stuart Nicholson argues that, although Ellington had a strong desire to go beyond the category of "jazz" composer, "his accomplishments remained forever tied to his audience's received notion of what the term meant, so increasingly defining him in terms of his past accomplishments rather than his current aspirations" (248).

6. See Richard Hornby, *Drama, Metadrama, and Perception*, 17.

7. Don George notes that Ellington had a very idiomatic style of composition that is closer to that of the rock musician than that of the theatre composer. While most songwriters compose the melody first and then decide on the harmonization, typically, Ellington would begin with the chord structure, sometimes ignoring the melody entirely. See *Sweet Man* 29–30.

8. Mercer Ellington suggests that there was too little money budgeted for the orchestra in *My People* to support the Ellington Orchestra so the show had to use a pick-up band of musicians, including some ex–orchestra members. See *Duke Ellington in Person* (165).

9. As this book goes to press, the York Theatre Company has announced a production of *Beggar's Holiday* in their 1999–2000 season. Although the York company produces musicals with only a piano accompaniment, it is hoped that the richness and variety of Ellington's score will interest prospective producers in mounting fully orchestrated productions of his musical theatre compositions.

Bibliography

Published Music

Ellington, Duke. "Azure." Lyrics by Irving Mills. New York: Exclusive Publications, Inc., 1937.

_____. "The Brown Skin Gal in the Calico Gown." Lyrics by Paul Francis Webster. New York: Robbins Music Corporation, 1941.

_____. "Bumpty Bump." Lyrics by Irving Mills. New York: Mills Music, Inc., 1930.

_____. "Chocolate Shake." Lyrics by Paul Francis Webster. New York: Robbins Music Corporation, 1941.

_____. *A Collection of Songs from "Beggar's Holiday."* Lyrics by John Latouche. New York: Chappell and Co., 1947.

_____. "Doin' the Crzy Walk." Lyrics by Irving Mills. New York: Mills Music, Inc., 1930.

_____. "Don't Believe Everything You Hear." Lyrics by Sid Kuller. New York: Robbins Music Corporation, 1959.

_____. *The Great Music of Duke Ellington*. Melville, N.Y.: Belwin Mills; distribution, New York: Dover Publications, 1973.

_____. "He Makes Believe He's Mine." Lyrics by John Latouche. New York: Robbins and Sons, Inc., 1948.

_____. "I Got It Bad and That Ain't Good." Lyrics by Paul Francis Webster. New York: Robbins Music Corporation, 1941.

_____. "I'm Slappin' Seventh Avenue (With the Sole of My Shoe)." Lyrics by Irving Mills and Henry Nemo. New York: Mills Music, Inc., 1938.

_____. "I've Got to Be a Rug Cutter." New York: Exclusive Publications, Inc., 1937.

_____. "I Want to Love You." From *The Asphalt Jungle*. Lyrics by Marshall Barer. New York: Robbins Music Corporation, 1961.

_____. "Jump for Joy." Lyrics by Paul Francis Webster and Sid Kuller. New York: Robbins Music Corporation, 1941.

_____."Just Squeeze Me." From *Jump for Joy*. Lyrics by Lee Gaines. New York: Robbins Music Corporation, 1946.

_____. "A Lesson in C." Lyrics by Irving Mills and Henry Nemo. New York: Mills Music, Inc., 1938.

_____. "The Natives Are Restless Tonight." Lyrics by Sid Kuller. New York: Robbins Music Corporation, 1959.

_____. "Nerves, Nerves." Lyrics by Sid Kuller. New York: Robbins Music Corporation, 1959.

_____."On the Wrong Side of the Railroad Tracks." From *Beggar's Holiday*. Lyrics by John Latouche. New York: Mutual Music Society, Inc., 1947.

_____."Rocks in My Bed." From *Jump For Joy*. New York: Robbins Music Corporation, 1941.

_____. "Show 'Em You Got Class." Lyrics by Sid Kuller. New York: Robbins Music Corporation, 1959.

_____. "Skrontch." Lyrics by Irving Mills and Henry Nemo. New York: Mills Music, Inc., 1938.

_____. "Swingtime in Honolulu." Lyrics by Irving Mills and Henry Nemo. New York: Mills Music, Inc., 1938.

_____. "Take Love Easy." From *Beggar's Holiday*. Lyrics by John Latouche. New York: Mutual Music Society, Inc., 1947.

_____. "Three Shows Nightly." Lyrics by Sid Kuller. New York: Robbins Music Corporation, 1959.

_____."Tomorrow Mountain." From *Beggar's Holiday*. Lyrics by John Latouche. New York: Mutual Music Society, Inc., 1947.

_____."When I Walk with You." From *Beggar's Holiday*. Lyrics by John Latouche. New York: Mutual Music Society, Inc., 1947.

_____. "Within Me I Know." Lyrics by Sid Kuller. New York: Robbins Music Corporation, 1959.

Ellington, Duke, Clarence Gaskell, and Irving Mills. "Swanee River Rhapsody." New York: Mills Music, Inc., 1930.

Ellington, Duke, and Bubber Miley. "Black and Tan Fantasy." New York: Gotham Music Service, Inc., 1927.

_____."East St. Louis Toodle-Oo." New York: Gotham Music Service, Inc., 1927.

Ellington, Duke, and Irving Mills. "The Mooch." New York: Mills Music, Inc., 1929.

Ellington, Duke and Billy Strayhorn. "If We Were Any More British." Lyrics by Sid Kuller. New York: Robbins Music Corporation, 1959.

_____. "Just A-Sittin' and A-Rockin'." Lyrics by Lee Gaines. New York: Robbins Music Corporation, 1945.

_____. "So the Good Book Says." Lyrics by Sid Kuller. New York: Robbins Music Corporation, 1959.

_____. "Walk It Off." Lyrics by Sid Kuller. New York: Robbins Music Corporation, 1959.

Unpublished Music

Ellington, Duke. "Amazing." From *Pousse-Café*. Lyrics by Marshall Barer. Special Collections, Library of Congress.

_____."Be a Man." From *Pousse-Café*. Lyrics by Marshall Barer. Special Collections, Library of Congress.

_____. "Big White Mountain." Ruth Ellington Collection, Archives Center, National Museum of American History, Smithsonian Institution, 415.

_____. "Bioscope Song." Ruth Ellington Collection, Smithsonian, 415.

_____. "Boola." The Ellington Collection, Archives Center, National Museum of American History, Smithsonian Institution, 301, series 1, box 61, folder 2.

_____. "Cock o' the World." Ruth Ellington Collection, Smithsonian 415, folder 600.

_____. 'The Colonel's Lady." From *Sugar City*. Lyrics by Marshall Barer. Special Collections, Library of Congress.

_____."Do Me a Favor." From *Sugar City*. Lyrics by Marshall Barer. Special Collections, Library of Congress.

_____. "Echoes of Harlem." Ellington Collection, Smithsonian, 301.1, box 110, folders 9–13.
_____."Ever Lovin' Lover." From *My People*. Special Collections, Library of Congress.
_____."Flugel Street Rag." From *Pousse-Café*. Lyrics by Marshall Barer. Special Collections, Library of Congress.
_____."Follow Me up the Stairs." From *Sugar City*. Lyrics by Marshall Barer. Special Collections, Library of Congress.
_____."Forever." From *Sugar City*. Lyrics by Marshall Barer. Special Collections, Library of Congress.
_____. "Gham Al Duna." Ruth Ellington Collection, Smithsonian 415.
_____. *The Golden Broom and the Green Apple*. Special Collections, Library of Congress.
_____.The Good Old Days." From *Sugar City*. Lyrics by Marshall Barer. Special Collections, Library of Congress.
_____. "Here You Are." From *Sugar City*. Lyrics by Marshall Barer. Special Collections, Library of Congress.
_____. "Hushabeide." Ruth Ellington Collection, Smithsonian 415.
_____. "I Could Get a Man." Lyrics by T. Hee and Bill Cottrell. Ellington Collection, Smithsonian, 301.1, box 151, folders 24–25.
_____. "Inside Harlem." Ellington Collection, Smithsonian, 301.1, box 167, folder 3.
_____. "It's Saturday." Ruth Ellington Collection, Smithsonian, 415.
_____."Jail Blues." From *My People*. Special Collections, Library of Congress.
_____."Je N'ai Rien." From *Sugar City*. Lyrics by Marshall Barer. Special Collections, Library of Congress.
_____. *Jump for Joy*. Ellington Collection, Smithsonian, 301.1, boxes 178–187.
_____. "Let's" From *Pousse-Café*. Lyrics by Marshall Barer. Special Collections, Library of Congress.
_____. "Love I'm In." Ellington Collection, Smithsonian, 301.1, box 33. folders 16–18; box 172, folder 13.
_____. "Love Scene." Special Collections, Library of Congress.
_____. "Malay Camp." Ruth Ellington Collection, Smithsonian 415, folder 303.
_____. *Man with Four Sides*. Ellington Collection, Smithsonian, 301.1, box 215, folders 1–8.
_____. *Mardi Gras*. Ellington Collection, Smithsonian, 301.1, box 35, folder 8; box 216, folder 9.
_____. *Murder in the Cathedral*. Ellington Collection, Smithsonian, 301.1, box 232, folder 17; Ruth Ellington Collection, Smithsonian, 415.
_____. "My Arms." Ruth Ellington Collection, Smithsonian 415, folder 555.
_____. "My Heart Is a Stranger." From *Pousse-Café*. Lyrics by Marshall Barer. Special Collections, Library of Congress.
_____. "My Mother, My Father and Love." From *My People*. Special Collections, Library of Congress.
_____. *My People*. Ellington Collection, Smithsonian, 301.1, boxes 236–238.
_____."Ninety Nine Percent." From *My People*. Special Collections, Library of Congress.
_____. "Orson." Ellington Collection, Smithsonian, 301.1, box 95, folders 6–7; Ruth Ellington Collection, Smithsonian 415.
_____. *Pousse-Café*. Ellington Collection, Smithsonian, 301.1, boxes 278–295.
_____. "Pretty and the Wolf." Ellington Collection, Smithsonian, 301.1, box 296, folder 11.
_____. *Queenie Pie*. Ellington Collection, Smithsonian, 301.1, box 300, folders 1–7; box 301, folders, 1–9; Betty McGettigan Collection, Smithsonian 494, series 1.

_____. *The River*. Ellington Collection, Smithsonian, 301.1, box 308, folders 1–13; box 309, folders 1–9.
_____. "Rules and Regulations." From *Pousse-Café*. Lyrics by Marshall Barer. Special Collections, Library of Congress.
_____. "Sam's Sugar City." From *Sugar City*. Lyrics by Marshall Barer. Special Collections, Library of Congress.
_____. *Saturday Laughter*. Lyrics by Herbert Martin. Ellington Collection, Smithsonian, 301.1, box 335, folders 1–13.
_____. "Saturday Laughter." Ellington Collection, Smithsonian, 301.1, box 449, folder 3.
_____. "Settle for Less." From *Sugar City*. Lyrics by Marshall Barer. Special Collections, Library of Congress.
_____. "Someone to Care For." From *Sugar City*. Lyrics by Marshall Barer. Special Collections, Library of Congress.
_____. "Spacious and Gracious." From *Sugar City*. Lyrics by Marshall Barer. Special Collections, Library of Congress.
_____. "Spider and the Fly." From *Sugar City*. Lyrics by Marshall Barer. Special Collections, Library of Congress.
_____. "Sugar City." From *Sugar City*. Lyrics by Marshall Barer. Special Collections, Library of Congress.
_____. "Sweet Velvet O'Toole." Ellington Collection, Smithsonian, 301.1, box 34, folder 8.
_____. "Sweep." Ruth Ellington Collection, Smithsonian, 415.
_____. "Swivel." From *Sugar City*. Lyrics by Marshall Barer. Special Collections, Library of Congress.
_____. "T.G.I.T.T." Ellington Collection, Smithsonian, 301.1, box 329, folders 6–8.
_____. *Timon of Athens*. Ellington Collection, Smithsonian, 301.1, box 385, folders 8–16.
_____. *Turcaret*. Ellington Collection, Smithsonian, 301.1, box 396, folders 1–4; Ruth Ellington Collection, Smithsonian 415.
_____. "Two Together." Ellington Collection, Smithsonian, 301.1, box 397, folder 6.
_____. "Up Your Ante." From *Pousse-Café*. Lyrics by Marshall Barer. Special Collections, Library of Congress.
_____. "What Color Is Virtue?" From *My People*. Special Collections, Library of Congress.
_____. "Workin' Blues." From *My People*. Special Collections, Library of Congress.
Ellington, Duke and Billy Strayhorn. "Night Time." Lyrics by Doris Julian. Ellington Collection, Smithsonian, 301.1, box 247, folders 4–5.
_____. "Once Upon a Dream." Ellington Collection, Smithsonian, 301.1, box 255, folders 1–3.

Published Plays

Gay, John. *The Poetical. Dramatic. and Miscellaneous Works of John Gay in Six Volumes. To Which Is Prefixed Dr Johnson's Biographical and Critical Preface*. London: Edward Jeffrey, 1795; reprint, AMS Press, 1970.
Huston, John. *Frankie and Johnny*. Illustrated by Covarrubias. New York: Albert and Charles Boni, 1930.
Lesage, René. *Turcaret*. Vol. 4, *The Classic Theatre: Six French Plays*, ed. by Eric Bentley. Garden City: Doubleday. Anchor Books, 1961.
Taggert, Tom. *Be My Guest*. New York: Samuel French, 1953.

Manuscript Plays

Appell, Don, and Marshall Barer. *Sugar City*. Duke Ellington Collection, Smithsonian, 301.4, Box 9, folders 12–13.

Ellington, Duke. *Boola*. Duke Ellington Collection, Smithsonian, 301.4, Box 3, folder 10.

_____. *Lane*. Duke Ellington Collection, Smithsonian, 301.4, Box 5, folder 17.

_____. *Man with Four Sides*. Duke Ellington Collection, Smithsonian, 301.4, Box 6, folders 3–31; box 7, folders 1–7.

_____. *My People*. Duke Ellington Collection, Smithsonian, 301.4, Box 7, folder 20.

Farrow, Peter. *Shout Up a Morning*. Duke Ellington Collection, Smithsonian, 301.4, Box 9, folder 6.

Ffuller, Clement. *Cinque*. Duke Ellington Collection, Smithsonian, 301.4, Box 4, folder 1.

Firth, Germaine. *The Greatest Mother of Them All*. Duke Ellington Collection, Smithsonian, 301.4, Box 5, folders 4–7.

Grona, Van. *Swing, Helene, Swing*. Duke Ellington Collection, Smithsonian, 301.4, Box 12, folder 41.

Gynt, Kaj. *Cock of the World*. Duke Ellington Collection, Smithsonian, 301.4, Box 4, folder 3.

Hee, T., and William Cottrell. *Cole Black and the Seven Dwarfs*. Duke Ellington Collection, Smithsonian, 301.4, Box 4, folders 4–5.

_____. *Satin Doll and the Seven Little Men*. Duke Ellington Collection, Smithsonian, 301.4, Box 8, folders 9–10.

Henderson, Harry, Sandy Morrison, and Sam Shaw. *H.M.S. Times Square*. Billy Rose Theatre Collection, New York City Library.

_____. *H.M.S. Times Square*. Duke Ellington Collection, Smithsonian, 301.4, Box 5, folders 8–9.

Hughes, Langston. *Lyrics*. Duke Ellington Collection, Smithsonian, 301.4, Box 11, folder 7.

Hughes, Langston, and Arna Bontemps. *Jubilee: a calvacade of the Negro Theatre*. New York Public Library Schomberg Collection, microfilm *ZZ-24104.

Julian, Doris. *About Face*. Library of Congress, DU 41301.

_____. *Be My Guest*. Billy Rose Theatre Collection, New York City Library.

_____. *Be My Guest*. Duke Ellington Collection, Smithsonian, 301.4, Box 3 folders 4–6.

_____. *The Crystal Tree*. Duke Ellington Collection, Smithsonian, 301.4, Box 4, folder 6.

Kuller, Sid, Paul Francis Webster, and Duke Ellington. *Jump for Joy*. Duke Ellington Collection, Smithsonian, 301.4, Box 5, folder 14.

LaTouche, John. *Beggar's Holiday*. Duke Ellington Collection, Smithsonian, 301.4, Box 3, folder 7.

_____. *Beggar's Opera*. Duke Ellington Collection, Smithsonian, 301.4, Box 3, folder 8.

[Le Sage, Alain-René]. *Turcaret*. Duke Ellington Collection, Smithsonian, 301.4, Box 10, folders 9–13.

Martin, Herbert E., and Stephen Bates. *The Man Beneath*. Duke Ellington Collection, Smithsonian, 301.4, Box 6, folder 2.

_____. *Saturday Laughter*. Duke Ellington Collection, Smithsonian, 301.4, Box 9, folders 1–3.

Milton, Paul R., and H. L. Fishel. *Frankie and Johnny*. Duke Ellington Collection, Smithsonian, 301.4, Box 4, folder 12.

Rosten, Norman. *Mardi Gras*. Duke Ellington Collection, Smithsonian, 301.4, Box 7, folders 8–10.
Strickland, Will. *Harlem Is Heaven*. Duke Ellington Collection, Smithsonian, 301.4, Box 5, folder 10.
Tuttle, Frank. *Free as a Bird*. Duke Ellington Collection, Smithsonian, 301.4, Box 5, folders 1–3.
_____. *Free as a Bird*. Special Collection, American Museum of the Moving Image. 1986.24.1170–1986.24.1173.
Tuttle, Frank and George Julian Sinclair. *Free as a Bird*. Special Collection, American Museum of the Moving Image. 1986.24.1174; 1986.24.1178–1986.24.1179.
Underhill, C[harles] M. *Moon of Mahnomen*. Duke Ellington Collection, Smithsonian, 301.4, Box 7, folders 13–18.
Waring, Barbara [Lady Conliffe]. *The Jaywalker*. Earl Okin Collection of Duke Ellington Ephemera, 1933–1987, Smithsonian, 391.
Weidman, Jerome. *Follow Me Up the Stairs*. Duke Ellington Collection, Smithsonian, 301.4, Box 4, folder 11.
Weidman, Jerome, Melvin Isaacson, and Marshall Barer. *Pousse-Café*. Duke Ellington Collection, Smithsonian, 301.4, Box 8, folders 6–7.
Wolfe, Winifred. *Three Stories High*. Duke Ellington Collection, Smithsonian, 301.4, Box 10, folders 1–4.

Recordings

Ellington, Duke. *Anatomy of a Murder*. Soundtrack of the motion picture. LP CL 1360. Columbia, n.d.
_____. *Beggar's Holiday*. Piano demo with original cast singers. LP BP 1013. Blue Pear Records, 1987.
_____. *Black. Brown and Beige: Duke Ellington and his Orchestra Featuring Mahalia Iackson*. LP JCS 8015. Columbia Special Products, 1973.
_____. *Black, Brown and Beige: The 1944–1946 Band Recordings*. 4 LPs 6641–1–RB Bluebird, 1988.
_____. Duet: Pas de Duke. Ellington Collection, Smithsonian 301.6, box 153, cassettes 11–12.
_____. *Duke Ellington at the Cotton Club 1938*. Recordings made by the composer for radio broadcast. LP S.H. 2029. Sandy Hook Records, 1980.
_____. *Duke Ellington: The Blanton-Webster Band*. Recordings made by the composer between 1940-42 3 compact discs 5659-2RB. RCA, 1986.
_____. *Duke Ellington—Cotton Club Days*. Recordings made by the composer between 1927-30. LP CL 89801. RCA Jazz Edition, 1986.
_____. *Duke Ellington in the Uncommon Market*. LP 2308-247. Pablo Records, 1986.
_____. *Duke Ellington the Private Collection: Volume Five the Suites. New York. 1968 and 1970*. CD 91045-2. Saja Records, 1987.
_____. *Ellington at Newport*. Recorded at the American Jazz Festival, Newport, Rhode Island, 7 July 1956. LP CJ 40587. Columbia Jazz Masterpieces, 1987.
_____. *The Jaywalker*. Earl Okin Collection, Smithsonian, 391.
_____. *Liberian Suite*. Original recording. LP CL 6073. Columbia Records, n.d.
_____. *Man with Four Sides*. Ellington Collection, Smithsonian 301.6, box 105, cassettes 3–4.
_____. *The Mooche*. Ellington Collection, Smithsonian 301.6, box 153, cassettes 1–2.
_____. *Murder in the Cathedral*. Ellington Collection, Smithsonian 301.6, box 87, cassettes 7–8.

_____. *My People*. Original cast recording of the complete revue. LP SL 10073. Stateside, E.M.I. Records Ltd., nd.
_____. *Night Creatures*. Ellington Collection, Smithsonian 301.6, box 153, cassettes 3–4.
_____. *Phoebe Snow*. Ellington Collection, Smithsonian 301.6, box 155, cassettes 11–12.
_____. *Pousse-Café*. Ellington Collection, Smithsonian 301.6, box 106, cassettes 1–4.
_____. *The River*. Suite from the Ballet. LP L5777. First Edition Records, 1983.
_____. *Saturday Laughter*. T.D.E.S. Meeting (21 September 1994), Smithsonian Collection 390, I–F–6.
_____. *Sophisticated Ladies*. Original cast recording of revue. 2LPs CBL 2-4053. RCA Red Seal, 1981.
_____. *Turcaret*. Ellington Collection, Smithsonian 301.6, box 105, cassettes 9–12.
_____. "A Woman and a Man." *The Studio Recordings Volume Two: 1947–1949*. Meritt Record Society, U.T.D. 2003.
The Smithsonian Institution Oral History Project: Interview with Mercer Ellington (September 1990), conducted by Dr Marcia M. Greenlee, tape 5. Archives Center, NMAH.

Books

Aasland, Benny H. *The "Wax Works" of Duke Ellington*. Danderyd, Sweden: Aasland, 1954.
Abbott, George. "*Mister Abbott*" New York: Random House, 1963.
Alkire, Stephen Robert. "The development and treatment of the Negro character as Presented in American musical theatre. 1927–1968." Dissertation. Michigan State University, 1972.
Armstead-Johnson, Helen. "Themes and Values in Afro-American Librettos and Book Musicals, 1898-1930." In *Musical Theatre in America: Papers and Proceedings of the Conference on the Musical Theatre in America*, edited by Glenn Loney. Westport, Conn.: Greenwood Press, 1984, 133-141.
Arnaud, Noel. *Duke Ellington*. Paris: Messager boiteux, 1950.
Baker, Josephine, and Jo Bouillon. *Josephine*. Translated by Mariana Fitzpatrick. New York: Harper and Row, 1977.
Baral, Robert. *Revue: The Great Broadway Period*. New York and London: Fleet Press, 1962.
Baxter, John. *The Cinema of Josef von Sternberg*. London: A. Zwemmer, 1971.
Bechet, Sidney. *Treat It Gentle*. New York: Hill and Wang, 1960.
Bikel, Theodore. *Theo: The Autobiography of Theodore Bikel*. New York: HarperCollins, 1994.
Bloom, Ken. *American Song: The Complete Musical Theatre Companion*. Second edition, 1877–1995. New York: Schirmer Books, 1996.
Bogle, Donald. *Dorothy Dandridge*. New York: Boulevard Books, 1998.
Bordman, Gerald. *American Musical Theatre: A Chronicle*. New York: Oxford University Press, 1978.
Brady, Frank. *Citizen Welles*. New York: Charles Scribner's Sons, 1989.
Burton, Jack. *The Blue Book of Broadway Musicals*. Watkins Glen, N.Y.: Century House, 1951.
Bushell, Garvin, and Mark Tucker. *Jazz from the Beginning*. Introduction by Lawrence Gushee. Ann Arbor: University of Michigan Press, 1988.
Caldwell, Hansonia Laverne. "Black idioms in opera as manifested in the works of six Afro-American composers." Dissertation. University of Southern California, 1974.

Charters, Samuel B., and Leonard Kunstadt. *Jazz: A History of the New York Scene*. Garden City, N.Y.: Doubleday, 1962.
Collier, James Lincoln. *Duke Ellington*. New York: Oxford University Press, 1987.
Dance, Stanley. *The World of Duke Ellington*. New York: Charles Scribner's Sons, 1970; reprint, New York: DaCapo, 1981.
Dexter, Dave, Jr., *Jazz Cavalcade: The Inside Story of Jazz*. With a Foreword by Orson Welles. New York: Criterion, 1946; reprint, New York: DaCapo, 1977.
Dunning, Jennifer. *Alvin Ailey: A Life in Dance*. Reading, Mass., Addison-Wesley, 1996.
Eisenschitz, Bernard. *Nicholas Ray: An American Journey*. Translated by Tom Milne. London: Faber and Faber, 1993.
Ellington, Edward Kennedy. *Music Is My Mistress*. Garden City, N.Y.: Doubleday, 1973.
Ellington, Mercer. *Duke Ellington in Person*. Boston: Houghton Mifflin, 1978.
Emery, Lynne. "Black Dance and the American Musical Theatre to 1930." In *Musical Theatre in America: Papers and Proceedings of the Conference on the Musical Theatre in America*, edited by Glenn Loney. Westport, Conn.: Greenwood Press, 1984, 301–307.
_____. *Black Dance in the United States from 1619 to 1970*. With a Foreword by Katherine Dunham. Palo Alto: National Press Books, 1972.
Fletcher, Tom. *100 Years of the Negro in Show Business!* New York: Burdge, 1954.
Gammond, Peter, ed. *Duke Ellington: His Life and Music*. London: Phoenix House, 1958; reprint, New York: DaCapo, 1977.
George, Don. *Sweet Man: The Real Duke Ellington*. New York: G.P. Putnam's Sons, 1981.
Gleason, Ralph J., *Celebrating the Duke*. With a Foreword by Studs Terkel. New York: Dell, 1975.
Graziano, John. "Sentimental Songs, Rags, and Transformations: The Emergence of the Black Musical, 1895–1910." In *Musical Theatre in America: Papers and Proceedings of the Conference on the Musical Theatre in America*. edited by Glenn Loney. Westport, Conn.: Greenwood, 1984, 211–232.
Green, Abel. *The World of Musical Comedy: The Story of the American Musical Stage as Told Through the Careers of Its Foremost Composers and Lyricists*. Foreword by Deems Taylor. 3rd ed. South Brunswick, N.Y.: A.S. Barnes, 1974.
Green, Stanley. *Ring Bells! Sing Songs! Broadway Musicals of the 1930's*. New Rochelle, N.Y.: Arlington House, 1971.
Hajdu, David. *Lush Life: A Biography of Billy Strayhorn*. New York: Farrar, Straus, Giroux, 1996.
Hatch, James Vernon. *Black Image on the American Stage: A Bibliography of Plays and Musicals, 1770–1970*. New York: Drama Book Shop Publications, 1971.
Haskins, Jim. *The Cotton Club*. New York: Random House, 1977: reprint, New York: New American Library, 1984.
Havlice, Patricia Pate, *Popular Song Index*. Metuchen, N.J.: Scarecrow, 1975.
_____. *Popular Song Index: First Supplement*. Metuchen, N.J.: Scarecrow Press, 1978.
_____. *Popular Song Index: 2nd Supplement*. Metuchen, N.J.: Scarecrow Press, 1984.
Hornby, Richard. *Drama, Metadrama, and Perception*. Lewisburg: Bucknell University Press, 1986.
Houseman, John. *Front and Center*. New York: Simon and Schuster, 1979.
Hughes, Langston, and Milton Metzer. *Black Magic: A Pictorial History of the Negro in American Entertainment*. New York: Bonanza Books, 1967.
Hummel, David. *The Collector's Guide to the American Musical Theatre*. Metuchen, N.J.: Scarecrow, 1984.

Isaacs, Edith, JR. *The Negro in the American Theatre*. New York: Theatre Arts, Inc., 1947.

Jablonski, Edward. *Harold Arlen: Happy with the Blues*. New York: Doubleday, 1961; reprint, New York: DaCapo, 1985.

Jewell, Derek. *Duke: A Portrait of Duke Ellington*. New York: W.W. Norton, 1977.

Johnson, James Weldon. "Early Negro Shows." In *The Negro Caravan*, ed. Sterling A. Brown, Arthur P. Davis, and Ulysses Lee. New York: Arno Press and The New York Times, 1969, 968–974.

Jones, Max. *Talking Jazz*. New York: W.W. Norton, 1988.

Kitt, Eartha. *Alone with Me*. Chicago: Henry Regnery, 1976.

Lambert, Eddie. *Duke Ellington: A Listener's Guide*. Studies in Jazz Series, No. 26. Lanham, Md.: Scarecrow, 1999.

Lax, Roger, and Frederick Smith. *The Great Song Thesaurus*. New York: Oxford University Press, 1984.

Lewine, Richard, and Alfred Simon. *Encyclopedia of Theatre Music: A Comprehensive Listing of More Than 400 Songs from Broadway and Hollywood. 1900–1960*. New York: Random House, 1961.

_____. *Songs of the American Theatre. 1900–1971*. New York: Dood, Mead, 1972.

Long, Richard A. "Black Influences on Choreography of the American Musical Theatre since 1930." In *Musical Theatre in America: Papers and Proceedings of the Conference on the Musical Theatre in America*, edited by Glenn Loney. Westport, Conn.: Greenwood Press, 1984, 323–329.

_____. *The Black Tradtion in American Dance*. New York: Rizzoli, 1989.

Lynes, Russell. *The Lively Audience: A Social History of the Visual and Performing Arts in America. 1890–1990*. New York: Harper and Row, 1985.

Mandelbaum, Ken. *Not Since Carrie: 40 Years of Broadway Musical Flops*. New York: St. Martin's, 1991.

Massagli, Luciano. *Duke Ellington's Story on Records 1923–*. Milan: Musica Jazz, 1967.

McLaren, Joseph. "Edward Kennedy (Duke) Ellington and Langston Hughes: Perspectives on Their Contributions to American Culture, 1920–1966." Ph.D. diss., Brown University, 1980.

Mitchell, Loften. *Voices of the Black Theatre*. Clifton, N.J.: James T. White, 1975.

Nicholson, Stuart. *Reminiscing in Tempo: A Portrait of Duke Ellington*. Boston: Northern University Press, 1999.

Nichols, Charles H., ed. *Arna Bontemps–Langston Hughes: Letters 1925–1967*. New York: Paragon House, 1990.

Obituaries from the Times 1971–1975. Compiled by Frank C. Roberts. Westport, Conn.: Meckler, 1978.

Paris, Barry. *Garbo: A Biography*. New York: Alfred A. Knopf, 1995.

Peterson, Bernard L., Jr. *A Century of Musicals in Black and White*. Westport, Conn.: Greenwood, 1993.

Petterson, Perry Willis. "A critical study of jazz-vaudeville drama (1923–1934) in the United States." Ph.D. diss., University of Denver, 1965.

Rampersad, Arnold. *The Life of Langston Hughes*. Vol. 1: 1902–1941, *I, Too, Sing America*. New York: Oxford University Press, 1986.

_____. *The Life of Langston Hughes*. Vol. 2: 1941–1967, *I Dream a World*. New York: Oxford University Press, 1988.

Raymond, Jack. *Show Music on Record: From the 1890s to the 1980s*. New York: Frederick Ungar, 1982.

Riis, Thomas L. *Just Before Jazz: Black Musical Theater in New York, 1890 to 1915*. Washington: Smithsonian Institution Press, 1989.

Salem, James M. *A Guide to Critical Reviews: Part II: The Musical. 1909*–1974. 2nd ed. Metuchen, N.J.: The Scarecrow Press, Inc., 1976.

Sampson, Henry T. *Blacks In Blackface: A Source Book on Early Black Musical Shows.* Metuchen, N.J.: Scarecrow, 1980.

Shapiro, Nat, and Hat Hentoff, eds. *Hear Me Talkin' to Ya: The Story of Jazz as Told by the Men Who Made It.* New York: Rinehart, 1955: Dover, 1966.

Shaw, Arnold. *The Jazz Age: Popular Music in the 1920's.* New York: Oxford University Press, 1987.

Simas, Rick. *The Musicals No One Came to See: A Guidebook to Four Decades of Musical-Comedy Casualties on Broadway, Off-Broadway and in Out-of-Town Try-out, 1943–1983.* New York: Garland, 1987.

Simon, George T. *Simon Says: The Sights and Sounds of the Swing Era, 1935–1955.* New York: Galahad, 1971.

Stratemann, Dr. Klaus. *Duke Ellington: Day By Day and Film By Film.* Copenhagen: JazzMedia, 1992.

Strong, Willie Frank. "Philosophies of African American music history." Ph.D. diss., UCLA, 1994.

Suskin, Steven. *Opening Nights on Broadway.* Foreword by Carol Channing. New York: Schirmer Books, 1990.

_____. *More Opening Nights on Broadway.* Foreword by Larry Gelbart. New York: Schirmer, 1997.

Swenson, Karen. *Greta Garbo: A Life Apart.* New York: Scribner, 1997.

Thomson, David. *Rosebud: The Story of Orson Welles.* New York: Alfred A. Knopf, 1996.

Timner, W.E. *Ellingtonia: The Recorded Music of Duke Ellington and His Sidemen.* 4th ed. Studies in Jazz, No. 7. Lanham, Md.: Scarecrow, 1996.

Tucker, Mark. *Ellington: The Early Years.* Urbana: University of Illinois Press, 1991.

_____, ed. *The Duke Ellington Reader.* New York: Oxford University Press, 1993.

Ulanov, Barry. *Duke Ellington.* London: Farrar, Straus and Giroux, 1947; reprint, New York: DaCapo, 1972.

Weinberg, Herman G. *Josef von Sternberg.* New York: Dutton, 1967; reprint, New York: Arno, 1978.

Wilder, Alec. *American Popular Song: The Great Innovators. 1900–1950.* Edited and with an Introduction by James T. Maher. New York: Oxford University Press, 1972.

Williams, John R. *The Duke of Note: Ellington Life Story.* Los Angeles: Duke Ellington Life Story Foundation, n.d.

Williams, Martin. *Jazz Heritage.* New York: Oxford University Press, 1985; Oxford University Press, 1987.

Woll, Allen. *Black Musical Theatre: From* Coontown *to* Dreamgirls. Baton Rouge: Louisiana State University Press, 1989; reprint, New York: DaCapo, 1991.

Magazines and Journals

Allen, Zita D. "Blacks and Ballet." *Dance Magazine*, July 1976: 65–70.

Balliett, Whitney. "Celebrating the Duke." *New Yorker*, 29 November 1993: 136–7; 140–147.

_____. "A Day with the Duke." *New Yorker,* 27 June 1970: 52-55.

Boyer, Richard 0. "The Hot Bach." *New Yorker*, 24 June 1944: 30-44;1 July 1944: 26-34; 8 July 1944: 26-31.

"Bronze Medal." *New Yorker*, 14 August 1965:19–20.

Caine, Daniel C. "A Crooked Thing: A Chronicle of 'Beggar's Holiday'." *The New Renaissance* 7 (Spring 1987): 75–100.

Cook, Will Marion. "Clorindy, the Origin of the Cakewalk." *Theatre Arts*, September 1947: 61-65.
"The Duke." *Time*, 19 May 1947: 47-48.
"The Duke in Athens: Canada's Stratford Shakespearean Festival." *Newsweek*. 12 August 1963:52.
"Duke och Stockholmsappellen." *Estrad*, December 1950: 15.
"The Duke of Jazz." *Time*, 1 February 1943: 66.
Ellington, Duke. *The Duke Ellington Scrapbooks*. The Ellington Collection, Archives Center, National Museum of American History, Smithsonian Institution, 301, series 8.
_____. "What Did Duke Ellington Know, and When Did He Know It?" *Esquire*, November 1973:158–162.
"Ellington Puts Together Show for Emanicipation Celebration." *Down Beat*. 15 August 1963:11.
Englund, Björn. "Chocolate Kiddies: The Show That Brought Jazz to Europe and Russia in 1925." *Storyville* 62 (Dec.1975–Jan.1976): 44–50.
"Fallen Angel." *Newsweek*. 28 March 1966: 88.
Gibbs, Wolcott. "Deluge." *New Yorker*, 4 January 1947: 44–47.
Gilder, Rosamond. "Rainbow Over Broadway." *Theatre Arts*, March 1947: 12–18.
Goldner, N. "Dance: Eight New Productions and Six Revivals." *Nation*, 20 July 1970: 58–60.
Goodman, Saul. "Brief Biographies: Alvin Ailey." *Dance Magazine*, December 1958: 70.
Gould, Jan. "The Negro In Show Business." *The Antioch Review*, Spring 1946: 254–264.
Grant, George C. "The Negro in Dramatic Art." *Journal of Negro History* 17 (January 1932): 19–29.
Henderson, Harry, and Sam Shaw. "This Strange Bright Land." *Collier's Magazine*, 30 January 1943: 18–20.
Hering, Doris. "Broadway: Early Spring." *Dance Magazine*, May 1966: 24–25.
Hewes, Henry. "Broadway Postscript: Stratford Ontario." *Saturday Review*, 17 August 1963: 27.
Hudson, Theodore R. "Duke Ellington's Literary Sources." *American Music* 9 (Spring 1991): 20–42.
Isaacs, Edith J. R. "The Negro in the American Theatre." *Theatre Arts*, August 1942: 494–543.
Jefferson, Miles M. "The Negro on Broadway, 1945-1946." *Phylon*, 1946: 185–196.
Lang, John S., and Sarah Peterson. "A Night at the Opera, American Style." *U.S. News and World Report*, 3 November 1986: 73–74.
Larsen, John and Hans Larsen. "The Chocolate Kiddies in Copenhagen." *Record Research* 67 (April 1965): 3–5.
McCarten, John. "Going, Going, Gone." *New Yorker*, 26 March 1966: 120.
Marks, Marcia, and Jack Anderson. "American Ballet Theatre Reaches the Great Divide: Thirtieth Anniversary Season, New York State Theatre, June 16–July 12, 1970." *Dance Magazine*, September 1970: 28–34.
Review of *Beggar's Holiday* by John Latouche and Duke Ellington. *The Commonweal*, 17 January 1947: 351–352.
Review of *Beggar's Holiday* by John Latouche and Duke Ellington. *Newsweek*, 6 January 1947: 64.
Review of *Beggar's Holiday* by John Latouche and Duke Ellington. *Time*, 6 January 1947: 57.

Review of *My People* by Duke Ellington. *Down Beat,* 26 September 1963: 41.
Review of *Queenie Pie* by Duke Ellington. Zellerbach Theatre, Philadelphia. *Jet*, 20 October 1986: 61; 3 November 1986: 57.
Saal, H. "Dance Me a River." *Newsweek*, 6 July 1970: 86.
Small, Linda. "Dancing Ellington." *Dance Magazine*. November 1976: 20–21, 26–31.
Smith, Cecil. "Entry of 'The Warrior' into Valhalla." *Theatre Arts*, March 1947: 22–27.
"Stratford, Ontario." *Theatre Arts*, August 1963: 68–69.
Terry, Walter. "World of Dance: American Ballet Theatre: Part II." *Saturday Review*, 1 August 1970: 36.
"Three Musical Hits." *Life Magazine*, 24 February 1947: 75–78.
Tobias, Tobi. "Other Dancers: American Ballet Theatre, June 29–August 7, 1976." *Dance Magazine*, October 1976: 41–46.
Vacha, J.E. "Black Man on the Great White Way." *Journal of Popular Culture* 7 (Fall 1973): 288–301.
Walsh, Michael. "Sounding a Joyous Jubilee." *Time*, 29 September 1986: 70.
"Welcome to the Great Black Way." *Time*, 1 November 1976: 72, 74–75.
Williams, Martin. "And What Might a Jazz Composer Do?" *Music Educators Journal* 61 (January 1975): 24–31.
Wyatt, Euphemia Van Rensselaer. "Two Crocks of Gold." *Catholic World*, February 1947: 453–457.

Newspapers

Atkinson, Brooks. *New York Times*, 26 January 1947:1.
_____. "Review of *Beggar's Holiday*." New York *Times*, 27 December 1946: 3.
Bagar, Robert. "*Beggar's Holiday* A Brilliant Musical." New York *World Telegram*, 27 December 1946. In *New York Theatre Critics' Reviews*. New York: Critics' Theatre Reviews, Inc., 1946, 204.
Barnes, Clive. "Dance: Broadway Touch." New York *Times*, 30 January 1969: 40.
_____. "Dance: Nothing Less Than Superb." New York *Times*, 18 December 1965: 37.
_____. "Dance: Unfinished River." New York *Times*, 26 June 1970: 30.
Barnes, Howard. "Blue, but No Holiday." New York *Herald Tribune*, 22 May 1945. In *New York Theatre Critics' Reviews*. New York: Critics' Theatre Reviews, Inc., 1945, 218.
_____. "Cold Night for Beggars." New York *Herald Tribune*, 27 December 1946. In *New York Theatre Critics' Reviews*. New York: Critics' Theatre Reviews, Inc., 1946, 204.
Brown, Herrick. "*Beggar's Holiday* Proves Tuneful and Colorful but Dull in Its Book." *Sun*, 27 December 1946. In *New York Theatre Critics' Reviews*. New York: Critics' Theatre Reviews, Inc., 1946, 206.
_____. "*Blue Holiday*, Starring Ethel Waters, Has Delayed Premiere at Belasco." New York *Sun*, 22 May 1945. In *New York Theatre Critics' Reviews*. New York: Critics' Theatre Reviews, Inc., 1945, 218.
Brown, Joe. "Duke's Deluxe *Queenie Pie*." *Washington Post*, 17 October 1986: We 9.
Chapman, John. "Ellington's *Beggar's Holiday* Most Unusual Musical of Many Seasons." *Daily News*, 27 December 1946. In *New York Theatre Critics' Reviews*. New York: Critics' Theatre Reviews, Inc., 1946.
_____. "*Blue Holiday* has Ethel Waters, Josh White and Too Little Speed." New York *Daily News*, 22 May 1945. In *New York Theatre Critics' Reviews*. New York: Critics' Theatre Reviews, Inc., 1945, 216.
"Duke Ellington's *Queenie Pie*." *Variety*, 1 October 1986: 114.

Garland, Robert. "*Beggar's Holiday* at the Broadway." New York *Journal American*, 27 December 1946. In *New York Theatre Critics' Reviews*. New York: Critics' Theatre Reviews, Inc., 1946, 207.

_____. "*Blue Holiday* Bows at the Belasco." New York *Journal American*, 22 May 1945. In *New York Theatre Critics' Reviews*. New York: Critics' Theatre Reviews, Inc., 1945, 216.

Gerard, Jeremy. "*Queenie Pie* Feels Pull and Push of New York." NewYork *Times*, 1 October 1986: C19.

Holmes, Emory II. "The Duke of L.A." Los Angeles *Times*, 25 April 1999: Calendar 8–9, 84.

Kauffmann, Stanley. "*Blue Angel* Suffers in Musical Adaptation." NewYork *Times*, 19 March 1966: 19.

Kerr, Walter. "Review of *Pousse-Café*." New York *Herald Tribune*. 19 March 1966. In *New York Theatre Critics' Reviews*. New York: Critics' Theatre Reviews, Inc., 1966, 328.

Kronenberger, Louis. "A Classic Is Done Over and Partially Done In." *PM Exclusive*, 29 December 1946. In *New York Theatre Critics' Reviews*. New York: Critics' Theatre Reviews, Inc., 1946, 206.

_____. "Not Very Much Holiday Spirit." New York *PM*, 22 May I 945. In *New York Theatre Critics' Reviews*. New York: Theatre Critics' Reviews, Inc., 1945, 217.

Martin, John. "Dance: Good Job." New York *Times*, 6 December 1959, sec. 2:18.

Mcclain, John. "It's All Fine—But." New York *Journal-American*. 19 March 1966. In *New York Theatre Critics' Reviews*. New York: Critics' Theatre Reviews, Inc., 1966, 329.

Nadel, Normal. "*Pousse-Café* Is a Disaster." New York *World-Telegram*, 19 March 1966. In *New York Theatre Critics' Reviews*. New York: Critics' Theatre Reviews, Inc., 1966, 327.

The New York *Times*, 8 September 1930:17.

Nichols, Lewis. "One Meat Ball." New York *Times*, 22 May 1945:13.

Palmer, Robert. "*Queenie Pie* Offers 'New' Ellington." New York *Times*, 13 September 1986:11.

Rascoe, Burton. "*Blue Holiday* at Belasco: Vaudeville at Its Dullest." New York *World -Telegram*, 22 May 1945. In *New York Theatre Critics' Reviews*. New York: Critics' Theatre Reviews, Inc., 1945, 217.

Review of *Hot Chocolates*, by Thomas Wailer, Harry Brooks and Andy Razaf. New York *Times*, 21 June 1929: 17.

Review of *Jump for Joy*, by Duke Ellington. The Mayan Theatre, Los Angeles. *Variety*, 25 July 1941: 52, 54.

Review of *Pousse-Café*, by Jerome Weidman, Melvin Isaacson, Duke Ellington and Marshall Barer. O'Keefe Centre, Toronto. *Variety*, 2 February 1966:58.

Review of *Sweet and Low,* by David Freedman and Billy Rose. New York *Times*, 18 November 1930: 28.

Rockwell, John. "Putting Vernacular Opera in Its Proper Place, Finally." New York *Times*, 9 October 1986: C28.

Rosenfeld, Megan. "*Queenie Pie*: The Duke's Old-Fashioned Fun." *Washington Post*, 13 October 1986: B1+.

Taubman, Howard. "Athenians Given Guns and Podiatrists." New York *Times*, 31 July 1963: 19.

Waldorf, Wilella. "*Blue Holiday* Brings Ethel Waters Back to Town." New York *Post*, 22 May 1945. In *New York Theatre Critics' Reviews*. New York: Critics' Theatre Reviews, Inc., 1945, 217.

Watkins, Perry. "'Holiday' Is Bi-Racial Production." Chicago *Sun*, 6 April 1947: 29.
Watt, Douglas. "*Pousse-Café*, Musical Remake of *Blue Angel*, Bows at the 46th St." New York *Daily News*, 19 March 1966. In *New York Theatre Critics' Reviews*. New York: Critics' Theatre Reviews, Inc., 1966, 328.
Watts, Richard, Jr. "The Catastrophic Fate of a New Musical Play." New York *Post*, 19 March 1966. In *New York Theatre Critics' Reviews*. New York: Critics' Theatre Reviews, Inc., 1966, 329.
_____. "A Colorful but Confused Show Based on *Beggar's Opera*." New York *Post*, 27 December 1946. In *New York Theatre Critics' Reviews*. New York: Critics' Theatre Reviews, Inc., 1946, 205.
"York and King Give Zest to Palace Bill." New York *Times*, 26 May 1930: 25.

Index